LIFE AND TIMES OF CULTURAL STUDIES

PHILOSOPHY AND POSTCOLONIALITY

A series edited by Valentin Mudimbe and Bogumil Jewsiewicki

LIFE AND TIMES OF CULTURAL STUDIES

The Politics and Transformation of the Structures of Knowledge

RICHARD E. LEE

DUKE UNIVERSITY PRESS   Durham and London 2003

HONG KONG UNIVERSITY PRESS   Hong Kong 2003

© 2003 Duke University Press   All rights reserved
Printed in the United States of America on acid-free paper ∞
Typeset in Minion by Keystone Typesetting, Inc.
Library of Congress Cataloging-in-Publication Data appear
on the last printed page of this book.
This book is among a series of titles co-published by Duke University
Press and Hong Kong University Press, a collaboration designed to
make possible new circuits of circulation for scholarship. This title is
available in Asia, Australia and New Zealand from Hong Kong
University Press; in the Americas and Europe from Duke University Press;
and from either publisher in the rest of the world.

Duke University Press   Hong Kong University Press
Box 90660   14/F Hing Wai Centre
Durham, North Carolina   7 Tin Wan Praya Rd
27708-0660   Aberdeen, Hong Kong
www.dukepress.edu   www.hkupress.org

FOR MY PARENTS

You cannot understand an intellectual or artistic project without also understanding its formation.—RAYMOND WILLIAMS

Contents

Acknowledgments

Of those friends and colleagues who read early drafts of the manuscript that eventually became this book, I shall be forever grateful to Terence K. Hopkins who constantly urged me to think relationally. I was the beneficiary of constructive critique from Dale Tomich and the patient understanding, with the insistent reminder of the importance of space, from Anthony King. Diana Davies and Martin Bidney also read and commented on various chapters. Although they must remain unnamed, I wish to express my appreciation as well to the anonymous reviewers whose comments stimulated me either to rethink my positions or sharpen my arguments. Of course, the final responsibility for any factual errors and questionable interpretative inferences is ultimately mine. To Immanuel Wallerstein, I owe an enormous debt for his intellectual stimulation and scholarly example and, of extraordinary importance, for his constant encouragement. Finally, there is no way I can express adequate appreciation for the friendships, material support, and intellectual vitality that have accrued to me through my association with the Fernand Braudel Center for the Study of Economies, Historical Systems, and Civilizations at Binghamton University.

Introduction

What follows is a story with a purpose. It is thus also an intervention, and this aspect of the inquiry accounts for the particular form the exposition takes, the choice of temporal framework, and the definition of the parameters of the subject matter.

The story is that of an intellectual movement and political project, *cultural studies*. It emerged in Britain in the mid-1950s and eventually spread to the Anglophone, ex-settler colonies. As more and more theoretical approaches and methodologies, subject matters, and problematics were admitted to what was always, and purposely, a loose, eclectic pantheon, scholars and commentators from other national and linguistic communities chose to identify with the movement. No matter how vaguely or diversely defined, the cultural studies perspective has been progressively institutionalized over the past four decades in journals and book series, university courses, programs, departments, and dissertation projects. This is the story, and it constitutes a major success.

As an inquiry, this is an investigation of the continuities and alliances, ruptures and erasures that have characterized cultural studies as the movement developed. It opens up questions of the construction of meaning and the differing significance of the sites and forms of specific constructions the project has undergone. This entails an exploration of determinate conditions, that is, in terms of the practical implications of cognitive constraints, of the range and limits of what evidence, arguments, and explanations or interpretations were thinkable at specific times and places, and their consequences.

The institutionalization of the intellectual movement, however, was accompanied by what was often remarked to be an exhaustion of the political project. As an intervention, the present work asks what, if anything, cultural studies portends for the future. This involves speaking to the contemporary pessimism surrounding questions of the efficacy of politics by considering the limits and contradictions of social action from the perspective of the *longue durée* trends in knowledge production. Thus, the agenda of this book is a twofold product of the present conjuncture.

Introductions and critical and historical accounts of the cultural studies project are not lacking, and new collections appear with great regularity.[1] Foregrounding both the diversity and the activism that have defined the field and its constituting practices, Lawrence Grossberg and Janice Radway, in the editorial statement introducing the journal *Cultural Studies,* state, "Cultural studies is committed to the radically contextual, historically specific character not only of cultural practices but also of the production of knowledge within cultural studies itself" (1992: iii). Jennifer Slack speaks of "an ongoing process of re-articulating contexts, that is, of examining and intervening in the changing ensemble of forces (or articulations) that create and maintain identities that have real concrete effects" (1996: 126). As Martin Barker and Anne Beezer could already state a decade ago, if "the publication of histories of a discipline is a sign of its coming of age, then cultural studies has undoubtedly emerged from adolescence into maturity" (1992: 3). Nonetheless, much of the work invoking a cultural studies perspective, including many analytic reconstructions, however fine (and often heavily dependent on personal remembrances and subjective recoveries), exhibits a short-term approach. Such studies simply do not allow us to observe and describe how a knowledge movement is articulated with the long-term, large-scale processes producing and reproducing the world-scale structures of domination and exploitation that it is the objective of political action to change.

The work that follows proceeds on the premise that the modern world may be conceptualized as a historical system and that its processes—structures over time—form an experiential whole.[2] Nonetheless, these processes, recognizable since the beginning of the long sixteenth century, have generally been conceived as falling into three analytically differentiable arenas: that of production and distribution (the economic); that of coercion and decision making (the political); and that of cognition and intentionality (the cultural). Although this last is perhaps the least studied (as a long-term structure), it is no less constitutive than the other two. Over the long term, its construction and reproduction have organized the field of knowledge into a relational opposition: a value-neutral sphere of regularities at the privileged pole versus a value-laden realm of differences. The usual image is that of a face-off of the mutually exclusive super-disciplines of the sciences and the humanities. The present work shifts the perception of the field from this bilateral opposition of independent, objectiv-ated, and essentialized domains to recognition of a single socially constructed (historical), internally contradictory whole (structure) composed of hier-archically organized parts. Furthermore, it conceives the field of knowledge as one of borrowings, immigrations, and selective suppressions, articulated in struggle with other social forces, to disclose the complex cultural experience of legitimating representations operating as a series of contradictory and pre-carious presences and absences. From such a perspective, a history in the form of simple chronology will not do; time is a social reality, not a neutral, physical parameter.

To recuperate a sense of the imbricated trajectories—long-term trends, mul-tiple conjunctures—within which the cultural studies project falls in this whole, and to do justice to its political promise, the composite, socially constituted realities of time and space, what Immanuel Wallerstein has called *TimeSpace*, will be treated as structural unities endogenous to the analysis. Episodic-geopolitical TimeSpace pertains to the short term of the events of the post-1945 period. Cyclico-ideological TimeSpace provides the framework for concep-tualizing the restructuring of the structures of knowledge that had as a conse-quence the creation of the social sciences. It spans the period of the French Revolution through the late twentieth century. The duration of structural TimeSpace encompasses the whole of the past five centuries, from the Transi-tion from Feudalism to Capitalism through the late twentieth century. The "substantive objects" of structural TimeSpace are those fundamental relational constituents of human reality that can be recognized over the entire period, but not before. To these Wallerstein adds the TimeSpace of transformation, per-haps the next half-century or so, when even small-scale, value-driven human agency may have transformative consequences for a world in crisis (see Waller-stein 1988, 1993). Herein lies the political promise of cultural studies.

Part 1 outlines two narratives, recounts two intersecting histories out of which cultural studies emerged.[3] If one of the recurrent themes of chapter 1 is practice, the making of history by "men," in chapter 2 it becomes just as apparent that they do not make their history in conditions of their own choos-ing but within a structure of determinations the articulation of which was the result of previous practice that gave rise to the very category Britishness.[4]

Chapter 1 centers on the advent, the "event," of cultural studies as a politically active intellectual movement on the left in the mid-1950s and situates it in the immediate geopolitical TimeSpace of Britain in the post-1945 world of U.S. hegemony and the cold war. As a state of cyclical concentration and deconcentration of power in the modern world-system as a whole and as a position of military, commercial, and financial supremacy that fell to the United States after 1945 and that the United States fought to sustain for as long as possible, hegemony forms the ever-present geopolitical limiting condition of the events of the quarter century after 1945.[5] This includes those world events and movements that inspired the cultural studies project in the first place.

Hegemony is a particular, recurrent feature of the world-system that grows out of the defining structural property of the interstate system: its dislocation of (legitimate) decision-making and coercion in multiple centers called states. On the one hand, it is this characteristic that has thwarted the revolutionary agendas of those who would overthrow the structures of production and distribution, the axial division of labor, deemed responsible for world inequalities. On the other hand, hegemony is never complete (otherwise, the modern world-system would be transformed into a world-empire); interstate rivalry is typified by the alternation of struggle with the negotiated sharing of (world) power. Herein lies the structural invitation or condition of possibility for political action, or the constitution of a "third force," such as that attempted in Britain in the mid-1950s.[6]

It is in the shadow of the hegemonic ascendancy of the United States that chapter 1 begins, with a sketch of post-1945 Britain: affluence, *embourgeoisement,* and the politics of the welfare state, the end of empire, and the junior partnership with the United States (that was part of the implicit agreements sealed at Yalta for a status quo whereby the United States would control about two thirds of the world and the Soviet Union about one third). Out of this context emerged the first New Left in response to the events of 1956—Khrushchev's secret speech, Hungary, Suez—and in conjunction with the antinuclear movement. At this point, the category "culture," in relation to the themes of values, experience, agency, and class, offered a way forward for British intellectuals on the left as the orthodox base-superstructure model associated with Stalinism was discredited and the U.S. model of value-neutral quantification was rejected. Raymond Williams (1989) later cautioned against text-based histories of cultural studies that did not take into consideration its roots in the adult education movement. Indeed, his work and that of E. P. Thompson examined in this chapter did grow out of their experience in extramural education. Their concerns dealt as much with literature as with history and were formative for the first New Left and cultural studies alike.

The second story involves the English literary-critical tradition dating from the French Revolution through the late 1960s in the ideological TimeSpace of the rise and eventual collapse of the world liberal consensus. The lower limit of this period is specified by the characterization of the French Revolution as "a cultural watershed in the ideological history of the modern world-system in that it led to the widespread acceptance of the idea that social change rather than social stasis is normal, both in the normative and in the statistical sense of the world." The upper limit is indicated by the crisis of the strategies responding to the "problem of how to regulate, speed up, slow down, or otherwise affect this normal process of change and evolution" that was reached in the 1960s (Wallerstein 1991b: 245; 1995).

Chapter 2 addresses this problematic as a set of articulations and re-articulations of chains of equivalences, in which the contradictions, not only of class and capital, but of race and gender are paramount. First, this chapter traces the links between the depoliticization of critical discourse in the nineteenth century and the material conditions to which it was directly related: revolution in France, the inequalities produced by laissez-faire at home during the first half of the century, and then the violent realities of the rebellions in Jamaica and Ireland and the reform movement in the 1860s. Second, the chapter examines the discursive mechanisms through which critics contributed to the collapse of ideological alternatives on the left and the right and created the available subject positions that made possible the emergence of the (internally contradictory) liberal consensus. This compact, extrapolated worldwide, underwrote the expansion of the world-system itself to "global dominion" (Hopkins 1990: 411) at the end of the nineteenth century and the geopolitical settlement of the cold war period.[7] Third, the chapter demonstrates how cultural studies in its infancy recombined the elite tradition with the first New Left's concerns for history and popular culture just as the liberal consensus began to come apart.

Part 2 is expressly concerned with cultural studies as the intellectual project developed over three decades, from the foundation of the institutional base at the Centre for Contemporary Cultural Studies (cccs) at the University of Birmingham. As Stuart Hall says of institutionalization, "One needs to go through the organizational moment—the long march through the institutions —to get people together, to build some kind of collective intellectual project." However, of codification, he remarks that at Birmingham, "We never were one school . . . nor did we want to create that kind of orthodoxy" (1986: 59). Varied and voluminous, the literature exhibits both sophisticated theoretical exegesis, through critical debate and engagement, and carefully integrated empirical studies focused on concrete history and political struggle, without giving up a broadly Marxist platform. As the project/s developed and achieved wide currency it/they engendered a bandwagon effect, at least in name. This section, however, also reproduces the themes of race and gender, and the struggle against them, of part 1, as in the case of ethnocentricism, the "consistent pattern of ex-nomination" (G. Turner 1992: 642) in the Anglocentric extrapolation of the British model.

Chapter 3 examines the development of Hoggart's humanistic project, links work at CCCS to the events of 1968, and explores the engagement with theory in the debates over structuralism. This chapter also suggests how the substantive concerns of work at CCCS tended to recapitulate the long-term development of social critique in Britain.

Chapter 4 explores some of the fields of substantive research at CCCS and illustrates the move away from considerations of working-class culture in the subcultures and media studies work to questions of identity politics in the fields of race and gender. This move correlates with the decline in U.S. hegemony and the shift in the axis of geopolitical struggle from East–West to North–South and registers both the intellectual and eventual institutional transition from a humanistic to a (social) scientific perspective.

Chapter 5 suggests some of the ways the cultural studies project developed and mutated as it expanded, and how the frequent lack of site-specific reconfiguration upon importation has been criticized. As the project was exported to the Anglophone, ex-settler colonies of Australia, Canada, South Africa, and the United States, it was found that an export model does not always perfectly suit the tastes, or ends, of the local consumers.[8] In a significant shift, the major debates of the 1990s, the Culture Wars and the Science Wars, focused not on the search for adequate theories of human reality and social action but on the political consequences of particular theoretical perspectives in a ringing acknowledgment of the significance of the structures of knowledge for a world-in-transformation.

Part 3 widens the context of the study to the TimeSpace of the long term. This single trajectory encompasses the original construction of the relational organization of the disciplines of knowledge formation (unique in human history and coterminous with the modern world-system) in the long sixteenth century and its present crisis. It thus also implicates a TimeSpace of fundamental change, of transformation. Chapter 6 examines the period of U.S. hegemony in the post-1945 world-system and the ways order and conflict were reflected and negotiated in the sphere of knowledge production. Chapter 7 explores the challenges to the structured hierarchy of the disciplines (sciences-social sciences-humanities) as attacks that have thrown the whole into crisis. The concluding chapter sketches the long-term development of the "two cultures" structure of knowledge as a process separating systematic, "objective" knowledge from meaning and values and the logistical restructurings of the seventeenth century and then especially during the late nineteenth-century period of the *Methodenstreit* (see Lee 2003). The current controversies over the premises of knowledge production, epitomized broadly by cultural studies in the humanities and the social sciences and complexity studies in the sciences, signal a crisis. The thesis of this chapter, and the consequence of the analysis, is that the trends have created a situation "in which the cyclical rhythms are no longer capable of restoring long-term (relative) equilibrium." This is a unique event; it is a "real 'crisis,' meaning a turning point so decisive that the system comes to an end and is replaced by one or more alternative successor systems" (Hopkins et al. 1996: 8).

Crisis, of course, entails both chaos and possibility, and herein lies the key to the revitalization of politics as committed social action. If social transformation is in the offing, we are already living the transition. Its time is now (the medium-term future) and its space that of moral choice.

PART ONE From Category to Institution

CHAPTER 1

The Politics of Culture I: Limits of Possibilities, 1945–1968

The whale's belly is simply a womb big enough for an adult. . . . Short of being dead, it is the final, unsurpassable stage of irresponsibility . . . the essential Jonah act . . . to be swallowed, remaining passive, *accepting.*—GEORGE ORWELL, "Inside the Whale"

Events seemed to will men, not men events. For meaning can be given to history only in the quarrel between "ought" and "is"—we must thrust the "ought" of choice into the "is" of circumstance which in its turn defines the human nature with which we choose. . . . We must get outside of the whale. Both whales.—E. P. THOMPSON, "Outside the Whale"

The turn to culture as a major category of analysis by the independent left in Britain during the 1950s was immediately occasioned and furthered by the geopolitical events that figured in the East-West struggle and the multifaceted dominance of the United States that formed their context. The assertions of both the liberal, social democratic West and the Communist, Stalinist East were called into question and the theoretical perspectives associated with the blocs proved grossly inadequate in explaining the changes in social structure and practice that so clearly seemed to have taken place since 1945.

For a moment, the "dust" of the events of the mid-1950s was suspended in a fortuitous, if rapidly dissipated, cloud. The oppositional project it precipitated, an English third force catalyzed in 1956 by Suez, Hungary, and Khrushchev's "secret speech" to the Twentieth Party Congress, was contained within the post-1945 conjuncture of a worldwide economic expansion and the cold war logic of U.S. hegemony. These were reflected at home in the rising affluence, debated on the left and touted by the right, and the subordination to the United States euphemistically known as the "special relationship." Coupled with the new consumerism was a whirlwind of change in lifestyles and the arts. If one believes in origins (as Stuart Hall has commented), it is from this immediate matrix that cultural studies was constructed by its early protagonists and eventually emerged in its majuscule, institutional garb with the foundation of the Centre for Contemporary Cultural Studies at the University of Birmingham in 1964.

A Decade of Consensus

In the British general election of July 1945, Labour came to power in an unexpected landslide, winning 393 seats to the Conservatives' 210. The Labour Party election manifesto *Let Us Face the Future* argued that permanent social reform and security could not " 'be built on rotten economic foundations' and that for Labour to provide the extensive social reforms to which they would be pledged it was necessary and essential that industry should be socialized" (Saville 1993: xxvii). The new government embarked on a transition from wartime mobilization to a peacetime economy with moderate nationalization—the Bank of England, mines, rail and road transport, civil aviation, gas and electricity—as the logical, and relatively uncontroversial, outcome of wartime planning.[1]

The dire financial straits that characterized the aftermath of the war were only partially alleviated by a loan of $3.75 billion from the United States and the Marshall Plan of 1948. Nonetheless, improvement in the living conditions of ordinary workers and the enactment of the package of measures originally put forward in the Beveridge Report of 1942, which formed the basis of Labour's "Welfare State" legislation, fostered an air of prosperity and universality.[2] Even after the return of a Conservative government in 1951, a consensus around these basic social programs remained.

Postwar enthusiasm was tempered in 1947 by the fuel and convertibility crises and overseas withdrawals. A period of consolidation followed, during which further moves toward planning and socialism were curtailed. But by 1953 confidence was on the upswing as the previous year's rise in unemployment reversed. Achievements such as the four-minute mile and the scaling of Everest created contemporary heroes, and national pride and unity were focused on the Coronation of Elizabeth II in June. As Stuart Laing has pointed out, the event symbolized both the tradition, the Constitutional Monarchy, "unity through hierarchy," and the rejuvenation, freedom, and well-being that were possible under the Conservatives (1986: 10).

Undeniably, class distinctions did not disappear, but maintaining separate styles of existence became increasingly difficult for the middle classes. As Eric Hobsbawm writes, "An entire mode of life became obsolete," and although not particularly to their taste, "a marked emphasis on 'culture' was probably the most important innovation in the newspapers which appealed to the middle class in the post-war period" ([1968] 1969: 280). As old symbols faded or became financially inaccessible, intellectual, cultural, and leisure activities increasingly served to define class position: drama and opera versus the holiday camp and the new BBC "Third Program" versus the "Light Program" (see Morgan 1990: 62). As the purchasing power of the working class grew to fuel mass consumption, commercial interests scurried to satisfy the demand. For the first time "it was *their* demand which dominated commercially, even their taste and style which pressed upward into the culture of the non–working classes" (Hobsbawm [1968] 1969: 283–84).

In the election of 1951, although Labour led in the popular vote, Conservatives won a majority of the seats. In 1955, voter apathy was perceived as a major factor, especially on the left, in the drop in total turnout. The unequal split in the decline ensured a Conservative victory. The 1959 election repeated the story. For Conservatives, in the wake of the Suez debacle and the Eden resignation of 1957, the social theme of domestic prosperity eclipsed geopolitical dominance in the constitution of their essential message. Television sets and cars at home replaced showing the flag in foreign ports as vital indicators of a successful politics.

All the same, contemporary themes of affluence (full employment with increased wages and shorter hours supposedly leading to private satisfaction of both basic needs and ephemeral wants) and embourgeoisement (incorporation of segments of the working class into the middle class) far from described a blanket prosperity in the 1950s.[3] Although the overriding social-economic reality for a quarter century following 1945 was the end of war and a worldwide economic expansion, the immediate experience was reconstruction. Indeed, some rationing continued until 1954, and it was decidedly unfashionable at the time to flaunt one's wealth, whether old money or new expense account spending. Wage levels rose, but increase in well-being was uneven and the gap between unskilled workers and the rest of society tended to widen. Moreover, desire for material possessions and some lifestyle modifications did not automatically catapult workers—the majority of the population—into the middle class.

So domestically, during the so-called decade of consensus beginning in 1945, the social program of the Labour Party was enacted and perpetuated under the Conservatives; unemployment remained low and incomes were generally well above prewar levels; health improved; and culturally, the concentration on "things British" in the arts, which had been a part of the war effort, continued.

In the international arena, Britain was forced back on itself geopolitically and commercially. Drained by war, it had lost its place in the sun to the United States, to which it was now economically dependent. Furthermore, Britain was obliged to assume the role of junior partner in the binary logic of the cold war when it became a member of the North Atlantic Treaty Organization in 1949.[4] This was also the beginning of the end of the empire, giving the lie to the heavy veneer of pomp and circumstance and televised theatricality of the Coronation in 1953. The incongruity of the first communiqué of the new reign, announcing that Britain would explode her own atomic bomb, with the larger reality is telling. Already in 1947 Britain had referred the Palestine question to the UN and the Jewel in the Crown was carved up into two new countries, India and Pakistan. Having long ceased to be the "workshop of the world," holdings in the Americas too were divested to satisfy obligations incurred during the war.

The significance of shifting class and status relations became particularly apparent as the young, with money in their pockets between the last years of school and marriage, and intellectuals, who could no longer be recruited exclusively from the upper and middle classes, emerged as significant social groupings. Here we find the scholarship boys, a little older now and tempered in battle, whom Richard Hoggart portrayed so forcefully in *The Uses of Literacy*. When he discussed the uprootedness and the nostalgia they felt, along with their idealism and their redemptive emphasis on culture, he was looking back on his own situation.[5] They were the "aliens" with "a curiosity about their best self" that Matthew Arnold had described in the 1860s: this "bent always tends to take them out of their class, and to make their distinguishing characteristic . . . their *humanity*" (quoted in Hoggart [1957] 1967: 255). These were the "aliens" who, in their zeal to act, had joined leftist organizations in the 1930s. The impulse did not disappear in the "endless relativity" of the 1950s. Despite their cynicism, they had not cashed in: "These few, because they are asking important questions, have a special value" (258). Here Hoggart, in company with Raymond Williams and E. P. Thompson, was solidly on the terrain of the first New Left.

Consensus Contested: The First New Left in Britain

Social legislation and the very real increase in well-being tended to blunt the traditional domestic concerns of British activists on the left in the post-1945 period. This was the Great Apathy, a function of individual impotence both East and West, as E. P. Thompson (1959b) would have it. In 1956, the conservative Charles Curran noted that "nothing fails like success. . . . Full employment in a Welfare State, with universal social services financed by taxation, means the end of mass-movement politics" (19). The only question, seemingly, was how to implement such a program without inflation, a question that called for a politics of administration or, very simply, good management.

The events of 1956 foreclosed on such arguments. Already jolted by the experience of East Germany in 1953, the entire left, including the Communist Party of Great Britain (CPGB), which had preached unity and reconstruction in the immediate postwar period, was traumatized by the revelations of Khrushchev's "secret speech" and the events of Hungary and Suez. Three years after the death of Stalin, Khrushchev revealed the atrocities of the regime and denounced the "cult of personality," breaking ground for home-front "rehabilitation" and "peaceful coexistence" worldwide. In Poland and Hungary, intellectuals had a vision of a humane socialism; but while in Warsaw compromise prevailed, in Budapest students called for Soviet withdrawal and multiparty elections—a revolution that was put down in three days with ten thousand casualties. In the words of Mervyn Jones (1976) borrowing from Marx, the tragedy of Hungary was played out as farce in the Middle East. When Nasser nationalized the Suez Canal, the British and the French conspired in a secret deal with the Israelis to get it back.[6] However, Eisenhower refused to support the pound sterling, under pressure from the expense of such a deployment, and the invasion collapsed. It was from this turmoil, "power without value . . . no comfort for any honest man or woman looking for a home to put politics in, nor East nor West" (Inglis 1991: 148), whence sprang the first New Left.[7]

As developments in the Soviet East drove members out of the CPGB, so Labour's support of intervention in Egypt revealed the imperialist implications of the social-democratic consensus.[8] " 'Hungary' and 'Suez' were thus 'liminal,' boundary-marking experiences. They symbolized the break-up of the political Ice Age" (S. Hall 1989: 13). In international politics, the New Left repudiated the cold war and embraced the ideals of the Bandung Conference of 1955 by advocating an "*active* neutrality" (E. Thompson 1958: 50). In the face of Stalinism and social democracy, neither of which seemed to offer people a capacity for controlling their own lives, the New Left reaffirmed humanist values with an emphasis on experience and agency. However, to differentiate the New Left by citing its concern for cultural questions over the bread-and-butter issues of the Old Left was possible only if, as Thompson argued, "it is understood that these 'cultural' questions are questions about life. For the New Left wants political and economic changes *for* something, so that people can themselves do something with their lives as a whole" (1959b: 11). In such a campaign, or more properly, political project, intellectuals had a leading role in constructing a theory and practice to which the creativity of individuals in the production of society, politics, and history was central.[9] The corollary to this was a rapprochement among politics, art, and daily life under the star of *community*: the "socialist end has been the creation—not of equality of opportunity within an acquisitive society—but of a society of equals, a co-operative community" (E. Thompson 1960: 3).

The movement found its voice in two journals: *The New Reasoner* (summer 1957), with roots in communist politics, and *Universities and Left Review* (spring 1957), which reflected the independent socialist traditions of the left student generation of the 1950s.[10] "NR held that our political problems were constant; it asked how the transition to a new socialist morality was possible. ULR had a moral criticism of our society, but asked what a socialist politics would be like" (Birnbaum 1960: ix–x). The two merged in late 1959, forming the first *New Left Review* under the general editorship of Stuart Hall. It was "more than a journal, but not quite a movement" ("Letter" 1959: 128); "a review of the New Left not a new Left Review" (R. Williams 1960: 343). David Widgery characterized the editorial platform as "stout enough to hold together the cultural journalism of the university New Lefties with the anti-colonialist and unilateralist commitments the Reasoners had inherited from their Communist past (this blend of concerns was interpreted by bourgeois observers as humanistic undergraduates being taken for an intellectual ride by wily Bolsheviks, although in fact exactly the reverse was to happen)" (1976: 510–11).

The editors of *Universities and Left Review* spelled out clearly to the new journal their idea of what New Left represented: "a new current of feeling which has entered politics in Britain since the thaw in 1956. This current is, if you like, socialist and humanist." They were also trenchant on its motivations to action: "If any event has transformed the course, tempo and tone of politics since the crucial dates of Suez and Hungary, it is the formation of CND [Campaign for Nuclear Disarmament], and the development of a body of people drawn into politics (many for the first time in their lives) around the fight against nuclear stupidity" (Editorial 1959: 1–2).

The trajectory followed by CND was both fundamental to the development of the first New Left and symptomatic of the contradictions of political action in Britain in the late 1950s and early 1960s. The Campaign took off in 1958 from

Labour and Anglican roots after a long gestation period.[11] Masses of followers (with contending moral centers) allied themselves with CND as the facts of nuclear armament were unveiled by the movement, making it much more than the originally projected lobby or elite pressure group. Ideas from CND soon inundated the Labour left and refocused the forces of opposition. In the wake of Labour losses in 1959, unilateralist agitation came to a head, but in fact, "the Right won back much support by being clearly more willing than CND itself to spell out the implications of unilateralism." Banning the bomb meant the end of NATO, and the end of the military alliance with the United States would entail correspondingly dire consequences for the domestic economy. Nuclear armaments raised not only human and moral questions but also class and political issues. The bomb "was not just the supreme symbol of an immoral society, it was part of the logic of a social system in which vast technical power was placed in the political control of competitive, aggressive and uncontrolled ruling classes" (Widgery 1976: 107). This connection effectively crippled the movement (and the drive of the unilateralists in the Labour Party), but not before direct action led by the splinter group the Committee of 100 (including Bertrand Russell) experimented with the confrontational tactics that would be reinvented in 1968. However, at this time, even the sit-down, which gave the impression of mass power, turned into a ritualized formality of simply waiting to be arrested.

The Campaign focused the amorphous concepts of participatory democracy and radical criticism (of "the system") in political protest against nuclear weapons and absorbed tremendous amounts of activist energy, whether on the march or in print. To CND, the New Left provided the political backbone (and some key personnel) of "what was basically a moral crusade" (Duff 1971: 128). Nonetheless, the inaugural issue of *New Left Review* was specific in identifying the centrality of ideas—and the cultural realm—to the development of socialism and resistance to capitalism:

> The humanist strengths of socialism—which are the foundations for a genuinely popular socialist movement—must be developed in cultural and social terms, as well as in economic and political [terms]. . . . The purpose of discussing the cinema or teen-age culture in *NLR* is not to show that, in some modish way, we are keeping up with the times. These are directly relevant to the imaginative resistances of people who have to live within capitalism. . . . the most urgent task for socialism today remains the clarification of ideas. (Editorial 1960: 1–2)

Cultural studies was to take seriously this injunction. Ideas as a political project were exemplary in the seminal writings of Raymond Williams and E. P. Thompson. Their efforts, taken as an interrelated and cumulative series of debates and interrogations, rejoinders and influences, plot the prides and prejudices of the particularly English theorizing of class and culture on the left that nurtured cultural studies at its inception.

Work in adult education inspired both Williams and Thompson (and Hoggart, as we shall see in chapter 2) well before the break of 1956 to seriously consider culture on a relatively undifferentiated terrain occupied by both literature and history. In retrospect, Williams contended that "even in the thirties, Cultural Studies was active in adult education." Working in support of the class-conscious Workers Education Association in extramural departments was "a *choice*: it was distinctly a vocation rather than a profession" and a renewal of an attempt at a majority democratic education unattainable through the "constitution of a Leavisite 'minority' alone" (R. Williams 1989: 154).

Thompson published his biography of William Morris, the Victorian poet, painter, and designer who inspired the Arts and Crafts movement and founded the Socialist League, in 1955. As he said, it was "of interest that I and Raymond Williams, whose important *Culture and Society* appeared three years after my book, should have been, unknown to each other, working upon different aspects of the Romantic critique of utilitarianism" (1976: 84). "I was teaching as much literature as history. I thought, how do I, first of all, raise with an adult class, many of them in the labor movement—discuss with them the significance of literature to their lives? And I started reading Morris" ([1976] 1984: 13). Taking sustenance from the Communist Party Historians' Group (CPHG), he wrote *William Morris* "in an embattled mood, from a position of strong political commitment, addressing an audience in the adult education movement and in the political movements of the Left rather than a more academic public" (1977: 817).[12] To address the "significance of literature," Thompson wrote a literary biography in which text and textual analysis play a central role in establishing the turning point of Morris's life as his conversion to socialism: "the trajectory from the profoundly-subjective Romanticism of Keats . . . through the sublimated rebellion of *The Defence of Guenevere,* to the crisis of despair of *The Earthly Paradise,* in which all the values of subjective individualism were poisoned by the taint of mortality; and thence, through the recuperative societal myths of Icelandic saga, to the socialist resolution" (1976: 108).

Furthermore, in answer to "one or two books *so* dreadful and so ideological about Morris," Thompson emphasized Morris's revolutionary convictions and political activism to argue that Morris himself in turn transformed the Romantic tradition. "Although in a muffled way, because I was then still prisoner of some Stalinist pieties," Thompson is already preoccupied with "a real silence in Marx, which lies in the area that anthropologists would call value systems" ([1976] 1984: 13, 20). The role of values and culture in Thompson's project is well illustrated in the "Hope and Courage" section:

> Morris's greatness is to be found . . . in his discovery that there existed within the corrupt society of the present the forces which could revolutionize the future, and in the moral courage which enabled him to identify his cause with these revolutionary forces. . . . There can be few more striking examples in history of the revolutionary power of culture than this renewal of courage and of faith in humanity which was blown from Iceland to William Morris, across the waters of the North Sea and eight hundred years of time. (1955: 214–15)

It was the encounter with Morris ("Morris seized me"), a fascination with archives, the "comradely help" of several people (especially historian Dona Torr), and participation in the CPHG that made Thompson into a historian. But appearing when it did, with its stridency of tone and Marxist foundation, the 1955 *Morris* was more annunciatory than influential. It was anathema in all but communist scholarly circles, and it is not surprising that it dropped into a well of academic silence (E. Thompson [1976] 1984: 13; 1977: 817).

During the same period that Thompson was writing culture and values into history in a politically inspired rehabilitation of a major figure of the socialist tradition, Williams was working on an equally politically inspired history of the conservative cultural tradition. His rehabilitation of its radical components would prove far more immediately influential than Thompson's work on Morris. Like Thompson, he "first started to look at the idea of culture in an adult education class," yet they "were not in contact with each other—so . . . crucial conjunctions were never made" (R. Williams [1979] 1981: 97, 108).

Williams's *Culture and Society* was a direct response to T. S. Eliot's *Notes towards the Definition of Culture,* which had appeared in 1948. It was aimed at countering "the appropriation of a long line of thinking about culture to what were by now decisively reactionary positions" (R. Williams [1979] 1981: 97). Is culture the elitist, high ideal of the "best that is known and felt" or the anthropological "whole way of life"? Although Maurice Cranston wrote that Williams was providing a "*socialist* theory of culture" (1959: 62), Williams does not answer the question directly but approaches it "democratically," bringing to light the diversity of strands woven together in the concept with the purpose of reappropriating the "tradition" to the struggle for an egalitarian future. Williams sets as his task to describe the

> emergence of *culture* as an abstraction and an absolute; an emergence which, in a very complex way, merges two general responses—first, the recognition of the practical separation of certain moral and intellectual activities from the driven impetus of a new kind of society; second, the emphasis of these activities, as a court of human appeal, to be set over the processes of practical social judgment and yet to offer itself as a mitigating and rallying alternative. ([1958] 1983: xviii)

Initially, his analysis turns on the historical changes in the meaning of five key terms: *industry, democracy, class, art,* and *culture*—words that either came into common use or acquired significant new meanings in the late eighteenth and early nineteenth century. For Williams, the questions raised in the meaning of his first four words are concentrated in the meanings of culture. His method amounts to an examination of "a series of statements by individuals . . . trying to give meaning to their experience," and the tradition he reconstructs owes as much to its progressive as to its conservative protagonists ([1958] 1983: xix).

Williams begins with an "essay in contrasts between lastingly influential men and ideas" ([1958] 1983: 3). Edmund Burke, the prototypical conservative, attacked individualist democracy in the name of the People. William Cobbett opposed state oppression and the new class system in which he recognized a fundamental connection between rich and poor. Both, however, spoke from their experience with the old England. In a second pairing, Robert Owen, the social engineer, "in his main bearings, led to socialism and the cooperatives"; Robert Southey, "with Burke and Coleridge, to the new conservatism." In common they are both "against the political economists, in discerning the 'cause of all our difficulties,' not in human nature, but in the 'constitution of society'" (22, 26).

At the same time that political, economic, and social change is taking place, there are changes in ideas about art, artists, and their place in society. Wordsworth drew on Burke's idea of the People and insisted on its knowledge as superior. This too, Williams contends, was a primary source of the idea of Culture, as the embodied spirit of the People. Here literary theory and social criticism parallel one another. In terms similar to Burke's criticism of the new politics, the early Romantic, Edward Young, had set the *original*—a superior reality accessing the general perfection of humanity, which grows, rather than being made—over the manufactured imitation. Carlyle balanced his linkage of changes in production processes to social change (later to be appreciated by Marx) with an appeal for "the imperishable dignity of man" ([1958] 1983: 75). Although this harmony of insight and determination is lost in his later work, *culture as a whole way of life* grounds his assault on industrialism. Williams situates this aspect of Carlyle's work as a significant step in the construction of the modern idea of the artist. "It is here," with the Romantic idea of the "genius" or the "hero as man of letters," one of the main lines of criticism of the new industrial society, "that the idea of culture as the body of arts and learning, and the idea of culture as a body of values superior to the ordinary progress of society, meet and combine" (84).

Williams places Matthew Arnold in the tradition of Burke; of Coleridge, who distinguished between "the 'hectic of disease' of one kind of civilization, and the 'bloom of health' of a civilization 'grounded in cultivation' "; and of J. H. Newman, whose standard for the body was health and for the mind *perfection.* This perfection Arnold was to name Culture, as an alternative to Anarchy and "in opposition to the powerful Utilitarian tendency that conceived education as the training of men to carry out particular tasks in a particular kind of civilization." The prescription for overcoming the opposition between culture and anarchy Arnold couches in the state, which he sees, like Burke, as "the agent of general perfection" (R. Williams [1958] 1983: 111, 119).

Experience is the operative category in Williams's chapter on art and society. William Morris found in the arts the quality of life that political change was to make possible. But a reduction of his program to the simple equation "Get rid of the machines" blunted his real aim of overthrowing capitalism. John Ruskin, like Arnold, fell victim to abstraction: the first, because "he was committed to an idea of 'inherent design' "; the second, because he "shirked extending his criticism of ideas to criticism of the social and economic system from which they proceeded" (R. Williams [1958] 1983: 146). Here Williams discerns a situation in which one kind of socialist thinker and one kind of conservative thinker (Ruskin and Carlyle) use "the same terms, not only for criticizing a *laissez-faire* society, but also for expressing the idea of a superior society" in which the common enemy is Liberalism. And the situation persisted, the "organic" mode grounding both Marxist and conservative thinking (140). Continuing this "tradition" in the twentieth century, D. H. Lawrence condemns the industrial system as a frustration of "community," but the important point for Williams is that Lawrence spoke, like Burke and Cobbett, from direct experience. The working-class family, for Lawrence, represented the unit in which both material processes and personal relationships were maintained in a hitherto unrecognized richness of experience.

Williams observes that Eliot, his principal interlocutor, objected to Karl Mannheim's theory of the substitution of elites based on achievement for classes because " 'it posits an *atomic* view of society.' " However, argues Williams, the phrase belongs to the tradition: "The opposite to *atomic* is *organic,* a word on which (without more definition than is common) Eliot largely depends. His instinct, in this, is right: the theory of élites is, essentially, only a refinement of social *laissez-faire*" ([1958] 1983: 240). But Eliot sees the need for elites and, to ensure continuity, classes; indeed, "what he recommends is substantially what now exists, socially." Williams does not disagree with Eliot's critique of liberalism, but although "considering culture as a 'whole way of life,' " Eliot does not combine his objection to an atomized individualist society with the observation that the economic system is based on just this view; "if it is, as Eliot insists it must be, 'a whole way of life,' then the whole system must be considered and judged as a whole. The insistence, in principle, is on wholeness; the practice, in effect, is fragmentary" (241, 242).

Beginning in 1930, F. R. Leavis developed the idea that culture is a particular use of language. Williams notes that this goes back to Arnold, as Leavis acknowledged, and Coleridge. The effect (as with I. A. Richards) reduces a class to a minority of individuals, a literary minority in Leavis's case, instead of Coleridge's clerisy or Arnold's remnant: " ' "Civilization" and "culture" are coming to be antithetical terms,' Leavis writes. . . . This is the famous distinction made by Coleridge, and the whole development of this idea of culture rests on it. Culture was made into an entity, a positive body of achievements and habits, precisely to express a mode of living superior to that being brought about by the 'progress of civilization' " ([1958] 1983: 254). This is the line that harks back to Burke and affirms that "a society is poor indeed if it has nothing to live by but its own immediate and contemporary experience" (255). Thus Williams ties the knot!

The capstone to the tradition, in all its ambiguity or "paradox," Williams situates in George Orwell and the alienation of the exile. Orwell's attacks on the denial of liberty are "admirable," but "when the exile speaks of liberty, he is in a curiously ambiguous position, for while the rights in question may be called individual, the condition of their guarantee is inevitably social. The exile, because of his own personal position, cannot finally believe in any social guarantee" ([1958] 1983: 291). In Orwell's many analyses of the working class, he mistook his observations of particular working-class behavior for all working-class behavior and came to think "working people were really helpless." The result, then, was that the only possible dissent comes from the rebel intellectual. For Orwell the people are but an "undifferentiated mass," and so we encounter again the paradox that "the only class in which you can put any hope is written off, in present terms, as hopeless" (292–94).

At the beginning of his conclusion, Williams states that the "history of the idea of culture is a record of our reactions, in thought and feeling, to the changed conditions of our common life" ([1958] 1983: 295). This chapter is programmatic with suggestions for the present, for culture to be what it should be for Williams: the basis of community. The solidarity of working-class culture, "potentially the real basis of a society," might be made to blend with the middle-class ideals of individualism and service, which are, however, ultimately "no substitute for the idea of active mutual responsibility" (332, 320)—an optimistic assessment of the healing that recognition of a "common culture" could facilitate.

To extend the arguments of *Culture and Society* as well as respond to a changing political horizon, Williams had tentatively titled *The Long Revolution* (1961) *Essays and Principles in the Theory of Culture*. The principles had to do with the idea of cultural production or sense of cultural process that had informed *Culture and Society* and became part 1 of *The Long Revolution*. The essays were to be built around subjects Williams had taught. They had to do with cultural institutions from education to the press, and eventually made up part 2 of *The Long Revolution*. Part 3, "Britain in the 1960s," however, was written "in response to the quite new situation of '57–9, including to some extent the discussion of *Culture and Society* itself." The new book was greeted with outright hostility in the establishment press. Unlike *Culture and Society*, which had been well regarded practically from its appearance, *The Long Revolution* was judged much more dangerous by the right. It was said that Williams had been "corrupted by sociology," that he "had got into theory" (R. Williams [1979] 1981: 133, 134).

In *Culture and Society*, Williams had asserted that the revolutions in the forces of industry and democracy were at the heart of the changes, and contradictions, that he called "this long revolution" ([1958] 1983: 335). But there was a third, cultural revolution: "the aspiration to extend the active process of learning, with the skills of literacy and other advanced communication, to all people rather than to limited groups" (1961: xi). All three had to be seen as a single process, a gradual one, the protracted interplay of all three revolutions—democratic, industrial, and cultural—not separate processes of change. It is "our revolution . . . that we began in the later eighteenth century and are still committed to" ("Man in the News" 1961: 3).

In the first section, treating culture and politics and emphasizing process and relationship, Williams deploys a historical argument to oppose the way the concepts of creative mind, culture, and individual and society had been constructed. He begins with a reexamination of the idea of the creative, identifying the critical moment in the sixteenth century when creation passed from God to man, specifically, to one kind of man: the poet. By the end of the eighteenth century creation had become less associated with the soul and more with the human mind as such through the key concept of the imagination. Creation, expressing a higher reality, embodies elements of thinking that are both religious (the existence of a reality beyond human perception) and humanistic (man as supremely creative).

The artist is not only the "lonely explorer" forging new descriptions, creating new meanings; he is also the "voice of his community" reiterating common descriptions, recreating a sense of common experience (1961: 30). For both, art must function as communication. In studying the social process of communication as rendering unique experience common, the "fatally wrong approach," Williams writes, "is from the assumption of separate orders, as when we ordinarily assume that political institutions and conventions are of a different and separate order from artistic institutions and conventions" (39). Williams would have us begin with the whole texture rather than proceeding from the categories themselves. In any case, the distinction between creating new meanings and reinforcing common experience is the key to reconciling culture as "creative activity" and culture as "a whole way of life." This reconciliation extends our ability to understand ourselves and our societies.

The relationship of the individual to society is crucial to Williams's understanding of culture as "the essential relation, the true interaction, between patterns learned and created in the mind and patterns communicated and made active in relationships, conventions, and institutions" (1961: 72). During the late sixteenth to the early seventeenth century, the medieval understanding of individual as inseparable from a group or class was transformed into an absolute: the individual in his own right. Much the same thing happened to society, formerly a relationship (as of fellows), which came to stand for a thing in itself: "If man is essentially a learning, creating and communicating being . . . the long conflict between 'the individual' and 'society' resolves itself . . . into the difficulty of stating this interlocking process of organism and organization, which are not new terms for individual and society but ways of describing a continuous process within which both are contained" (100). In his chapter on the "Images of Society," Williams puts into practice the idea that we see the actual relationships in society by learning to describe them and that the abstract ideas we use are actually interpretations (both persistent and subject to change). He follows this with empirical studies of education, the reading public, the popular press, standard English, the social history of English writers and dramatic forms, and realism and the contemporary novel.

In thinking about contemporary Britain, Williams suggests analysis based on contradictions and a fresh look at categories such as *customer, consumer, user.* Is class defined by birth or work, or, as Williams suggests, is "the growing feeling that class is out of date and doesn't matter . . . being used to ratify a social system which in other terms than those now visibly breaking down is still essentially based on economic classes" (1961: 335)? The contradictions of the democratic process and economic policymaking of the post-1945 period left a legacy of confusion, and on the left, of disappointments and disarray: "The deep revulsion against general planning, which makes sense again and again in many details of our economic activity, may be really disabling in this long run. And this revulsion is itself in part a consequence of one aspect of the democratic revolution—the determination not to be regimented. Here is a substantial contradiction" (295).

Movements, such as the labour movement, were creators of alternatives, but Williams reads the Old Left and the New Right in the Labour Party as unconsciously allied in delaying new analyses that could challenge ruling interpretations.[13] Indeed, the institutions of the labor movement—the unions, cooperatives, and the Labour Party, hailed as achievements in *Culture and Society*—had found places in society, but at the cost of limiting their aims and accepting their subordination; "the wide challenge has been drained out, and what is left can be absorbed within existing terms. For many reasons this has sapped the morale of the institutions, but also, fortunately, led to crisis and argument within them" (1961: 303).

In the long shadow of the British tradition he had taken such pains in describing, Williams found that the absence of a realistic sense of community continued to distort perceptions of the social and cultural, as well as the economic standard of living. Furthermore, he considered the active, participatory democracy he favored to be limited by the actual historical development of democratic institutions. But in the end, all he can propose, besides such practical adjustments as two-year election cycles, for keeping the "unusual revolutionary activity" going, as process, is "open discussion, extending relationships, [and] the practical shaping of institutions" (1961: 355).

The hesitancy notwithstanding, Williams's ideas were profoundly disturbing to orthodoxies on the right. He exploded the debates about art versus reality: both depended on the interaction between social structure and creative interpretation. As Alan O'Connor has said, "To defend 'culture' as a symbol of individual freedom is a false argument since what is really at stake is how culture changes with changing structures of human relationships." Williams "challenges the naturalized assumption that it is simply the *best* art and writing that survives"; insisting on historical studies, he illuminates the "false grammar in sentences such as: 'Western society is good because it allows freedom of the individual'; and 'Literature is a sign of a cultivated individual.'" Williams will not allow individual and society to be used in these absolute ways (O'Connor 1989: 105). However, the absence of the dimensions of power and conflict and the dearth of "historical facts" formed the basis of contemporary criticism from colleagues on the left, especially E. P. Thompson.

In 1961, Stuart Hall invited Thompson to review *The Long Revolution* for *New Left Review*. After reading the book, Thompson (1981) recounts that he saw such a gulf between their two positions that he asked to be relieved of the task, in the fear that he would be endangering the political relations of the New Left. But Hall encouraged Thompson to write an explicit critique, which of course he did.

Thompson places Williams's production within the social reality of the cold war, the "enfeeblement of the energies which had brought Labour to power in 1945" and the "rapid dispersal of the Leftist intellectual climate of the war years." From this perspective, Williams "contained the intellectual counter-revolution at crucial points, confronted the force of obscurantism and social pessimism and in doing so re-asserted the values of the democratic tradition" (1961: 27–28). But as history, Thompson finds Williams's account truncated and as political intervention, disembodied. "His 1840s are not mine . . . with the Chartist press and the teeming political theory of the time he deals scarcely at all." Closely associated with this lack of historical facts is the absence of red-blooded actors. Williams collapses author and readers into a collective "we" of an established culture, which, at the same time, has been challenged for over a hundred years. Invisible are the "fiery, self-conceited men," Marx's "real living *man* who does everything, who possesses and fights" (28, 29, 33). Williams's analysis does not lead people toward "active confrontation, because he has given a record of impersonal forces at work and not a record of struggle" (28). He "evaded the point that what Marx offered was not a theory of art and a theory of politics and another theory of economics but *a theory of history,* of the processes of historical change as (in Williams's own notion of 'culture') 'the study of relationships between elements in a whole way of life'" (30). In essence, admonishes Thompson, Williams has depersonalized social forces and written off a good part of the socialist tradition.

By defining culture as "a whole way of life," Williams suggests that the discipline of the critic is a necessity. But the ghost of Eliot haunts Williams in another way, Thompson continues, for neither in Eliot *nor* in Williams are to be found the problems of power and conflict; "way of life" easily slides into "style of life," or else, lacking any principle of selection, culture simply equals society. For his part, Thompson insists on two propositions "not to be found in the amateur tradition" of simply naming elements: the function of culture, "what culture *does* (or fails to do)" and

> culture as experience which has been "handled" in specifically human ways, and so avoids the life equals way-of-life tautology. Any theory of culture must include the concept of the dialectical interaction between culture and something that is *not* culture. . . . It is the active *process*—which is at the same time *the process through which men make their history* . . . if we were to alter one word in Mr. Williams' definition, from "way of life" to "*growth,*" we move from a definition whose associations are passive and impersonal to one which raises questions of activity and agency. And if we change the word again, to delete the associations of "progress" which are implied in "growth," we might get: "the study of relationships between elements in a whole way of *conflict.*" And a way of conflict is a way of *struggle.* And we are back with Marx. (E. Thompson 1961: 33)

Integral to the relations of men to one another is the problem of power, and Williams's definition of man as "essentially a learning, creating and communicating being" is closely associated with the fact that "Williams has never come to terms with . . . the problem of *ideology.*" The insistence on communication as the central fact of social process results in a new reductionism. "If this is left here, then the central problem of society today is not one of power but of communication" (E. Thompson 1961: 35).

Thompson detects a rupture in the last chapter of *The Long Revolution,* where Williams seems to disregard his own conceptual scheme and draw more on the "dialectics of social process—of the *logic* of change—which is loosely derived from the Marxist tradition." The result is "splendidly constructive" writing, but in the end, Thompson must hold "back from final assent," placing the obstacle in the title of the book. He reiterates his vision of history as a way of conflict, basing it on the contention that the two poles, culture and not-culture, equate with Marx's conception of social consciousness and social being. These exist in a dialectical relationship, even though "*in a class society* 'social being determines social consciousness.'" Not "the 'pattern of culture' but class relationships have been the final determinant of [Williams's] 'distinct organization,'" writes Thompson. Although "the gap between the two notions of 'revolution' is narrow" (Thompson's too "apocalyptic" and Williams's too "bland"), "can a junction be effected between the two? Or will it continue to be a dialogue along the way?" Thompson asks. Whatever the answer, and reproducing the logic and tensions of the marriage of *Universities and Left Review* and *The New Reasoner,* he situates both Williams and himself, "all of us" in the New Left, in the search for "common good" (1961: 39).

Marxism Humanized: Agency on the Left

The aggressive intellectual presence of the New Left, spawned of the traumatic events of 1956 and following on the "real failure of nerve which deadened social and intellectual argument in Britain between 1945 and 1955" (R. Williams 1960: 346), evidenced a focus on values and moral commitment, that "common good," and a serious effort to humanize politics.[14] The question of agency was paramount. The first New Left challenged the orthodox Marxist base-superstructure model in favor of a fine-tuned cultural analysis converging on the relationship of politics and economics to art and everyday life, out of which human beings actively created their own individual identities and social organization. Here was a new kind of political entity whose intellectual focus would be articulated through cultural studies. This was a movement of ideas in which the intellectual had a leading role; however, it was not *just* a movement of ideas, but a social movement (Rustin 1989), consciously political, as well. The stress on direct human agency was manifested in vigorous resistance to the cold war—in "positive neutralism" and CND activism (although CND was not a creation of the New Left).

The foundational texts kept close touch with the real, concrete world. As Stuart Hall reminds us, "Whether historical or contemporary in focus, they were, themselves, focused *by,* organized through and constituted responses to, the immediate pressures of the time and society in which they were written"

(1980b: 58). Raymond Williams's *Culture and Society* both constituted and contributed to the tradition he presented and precluded its extension. But the new direction (culture as a whole-way-of-life abolishing the conjunction "and") was not easily charted, as the unevenness of *The Long Revolution* attests. The exploration of diverse interpretative frameworks would become an overriding theme in cultural studies and set the stage for the centrality that ideology would eventually assume. Indeed, the absence in Williams of just such a focus on ideology had been deplored by Thompson. Whether in the form of Stalinism or Natopolitanism, Thompson considered ideology the "*active* component of apathy" ([1960] 1978a: 3) and it informed his vision of a bipolar world: "both whales."[15]

Debates on the left came together under the rubric "socialist humanism." In his introduction to the proceedings of the international symposium "Socialist Humanism" held in 1965, Erich Fromm registered the movement since 1955 as international and anti–cold war, in which "the questions of the meaning of life and man's goal in living have emerged again as questions of primary importance" ([1965] 1966: viii). For Thompson, socialist humanism, the revolt "against the ideology, the false consciousness of the élite-into-bureaucracy . . . [the] revolt against *inhumanity* . . . represents a *return to man*" in two senses:

> It is *humanist* because it places once again real men and women at the centre of socialist theory and aspiration, instead of the resounding abstractions—the Party, Marxism-Leninism-Stalinism, the Two Camps, the Vanguard of the Working-Class—so dear to Stalinism. It is *socialist* because it re-affirms the revolutionary perspectives of Communism, faith in the revolutionary potentialities not only of the Human Race or of the Dictatorship of the Proletariat but of real men and women. (1957: 109)

Thompson argued that Stalinism was both anti-intellectual and nihilistic. It denied "the creative agency of human labour, and thus of the value of the individual as an agent in society." These are all in opposition to Marx's basic humanism and stem from a misappropriation, "mechanical expression," of the "superstructure-base" relationship from which "the arts as the supreme expression of man's imaginative and moral consciousness, as media, through which men struggle to apprehend reality, order their responses, change their own attitudes and therefore change themselves," escaped (1957: 132, 122).

Williams too, at the end of *The Long Revolution*, raised the standard of agency: "The human energy of the long revolution springs from the conviction that men can direct their own lives, by breaking through the pressures and restrictions of older forms of society, and by discovering new common institutions" (1961: 347). He too was unhappy with any simplistic interpretation of the base-superstructure model and his position converged with that of Thompson in critiques of reductionism and economism. Specifically, Williams felt that a Marxist theory of culture had to recognize complexity as a "first control" and speculated that Marx was offering no more than "an analogy." The model "does less than justice to the factors of movement which it is the essence of Marxism to realize" ([1958] 1983: 268).

Thompson, who had written that William Morris had not "emphasized sufficiently the *ideological* rôle of art, its active agency in *changing* human beings and society as a whole, its agency in man's class-divided history," was taken to task by Williams, who considered "Marxist" writing in the 1930s as part of the Romantic tradition coming down through Arnold and Morris: "Morris's 'master-process,' which Thompson criticizes, is surely Marx's 'real foundation,' which 'determines consciousness.' "

> Either the arts are passively dependent on social reality, a proposition which I take to be that of mechanical materialism, or a vulgar misinterpretation of Marx. Or the arts, as the creators of consciousness, determine social reality, the proposition which the Romantic poets sometimes advanced. Or finally, the arts, while ultimately dependent, with everything else, on the real economic structure, operate in part to reflect this structure and its consequent reality, and in part, by affecting attitudes towards reality, to help *or hinder* the constant business of changing it. (1958: 273, 274)

Thompson responded that in later life, Morris was "possessed of an insight into the *moral* logic of capitalism," that he "took over and *transformed* a part of the tradition when he became a revolutionary. . . . I think that in fact 'the tradition,' as something which could be contained within the conventions of bourgeois self-criticism, was breaking down: a critical point was reached in 1870 with Ruskin's *Fors Clavigera* addressed to working men. The final transformation, in Morris's life, entailed a crisis of values . . . conversion" (1961: correg.). The orthodox model was simply too mechanical to concede such centrality to culture (Williams) or experience (Thompson), agency, and the moral element of values.

In Williams's case, it was clear that "basic economic organization could not be separated and excluded from its moral and intellectual concerns" ([1958] 1983: 280); however, no simple conception of agency would do because of the longer-term concerns within which experience is embedded. To Thompson's criticism that Williams slighted class struggle, ways of conflict, Williams later replied that

> to define culture as a whole way of life excluding struggle—that would clearly have to be met with the sharpest opposition and correction. On the other hand, it seemed to me that there was a blurring between two kinds of formulation which were in fact used almost interchangeably on the left—"class conflict" and "class struggle." There is no question that class conflict is inevitable within the capitalist social order: there is an absolute and impassable conflict of interests around which the whole social order is built and which it necessarily in one form or another reproduces. The term "class struggle" properly refers to the moment at which that structural conflict becomes a conscious and mutual contention, an overt engagement of forces. ([1979] 1981: 135)

Here, it should be kept in mind the degree to which, during the 1950s, real-world social change generated honest confusion and debate around the question of class. But if there was disagreement over class and classlessness, the significance of the issue was not in doubt. As Stuart Hall remembers, it was one place where the debate about *culture* first originated: "The New Left therefore took the first faltering steps of putting questions of cultural analysis and cultural politics at the centre of its politics" (1989: 25–26).[16]

Williams sought an interpretation of social change by examining a part of the "whole social order" as structured by the interplay and cross-fertilization of contrasting positions over the relatively long and theoretically relevant period since the French Revolution. He is talking about cultural forms and social structures ("of feeling," or, in his reply to Thompson, distinguishing between overt "class struggle" and structural "class conflict"). His tradition is the continuity, the conflicted order, within which change takes place.

Agency was at the heart of Thompson's article, "Socialist Humanism" (1957), as his interlocutors realized. He is interested in people and action, the motors of change. In *The Making of the English Working Class* ([1963] 1966), his focus is on a period of active struggle, whereas Williams was interested in the periods and ways, in which struggle was contained. Thompson does, however, recognize a structural dimension: his subject matter is not class itself, which he says is not a "thing," but "a study in an active process, which owes as much to agency as to conditioning" ([1963] 1966: 9). Although he suggests that any analysis of a structure must be exclusively synchronic (but "I do not see class as a 'structure,' nor even as a 'category' ''), he asserts that class, as a historical relationship, "is a fluency which evades analysis if we attempt to stop it dead at any given moment and anatomise its structure. The finest-meshed sociological net cannot give us a pure specimen of class. . . . But if we watch these men over an adequate period of social change, we observe patterns in their relationships, their ideas, and their institutions" (9, 11). Thompson himself was to say that "no Marxist can*not* be a structuralist" ([1976] 1984: 17); he nevertheless begins not with the structure itself—always ever present historical outcome—but with "experience" as the intersection of conditions, the determinacy of capitalist social relations, and consciousness, the creative agency of individuals.[17]

Williams, as Thompson noted, allowed "way of life" to collapse into "style of life," liquidating the distinction between culture and not-culture. However, Williams accepted tradition as a structure, analyzed its "making" and the contradictions informing its remaking. His revolution is really a long-term process "transforming men and institutions; continually extended and deepened by actions of millions, continually and variously opposed by explicit reaction and by the pressure of habitual forms and ideas" (R. Williams 1961: x). This goes far to illuminate Thompson's remark that Williams's revolution was bland ("Can one revolution go on—and for how long—without either giving way to counter-revolution or coming to a point of crisis between the human system of socialism and capitalist state power?"), while terming his own too apocalyptic (E. Thompson 1961: 39). But Williams and Thompson remain confident, each in his own way. Williams "fashions his idea of working-class life in the image of Arnold's high culture, so that it stands for the best and most informed experiences the working classes have to offer rather than for working-class experience as a whole" (Gorak 1988: 56). Thompson's affirmation of the positive impact of creative human agency is both the source of his optimism and the root of his "systematic overestimation of the human potential" (Bess 1993: 38).

As Julia Swindells and Lisa Jardine have so cogently argued, Thompson and Williams fill crucial absences in one another's work, developing and mutually sustaining the English debates around culture, history, and Marxism: "Williams had been explicit about what he needed from Thompson—the historical knowledge. . . . What Thompson needs from Williams . . . is a particularly *literary* narrative, which can give agency to the characters of history, a narrative which is not the conventional one of the liberal historian, but one which can activate the categories of class and socialism" (1990: 35). Thompson's Morris is the "popular hero, individualist agent of change." Williams's "Morris is 'diluted' by regressive elements from Ruskin, to the extent that the 'larger part of his

literary work bears witness only to the disorder which he felt so acutely.'"
Whereas "the 'literary' generates Morris's ethically definitive Marxism for
Thompson," for Williams, Morris's dependence on medievalism makes the
literary element an "impediment to a unified politically aware Morris."[18] The
very multidimensionality of culture—creative change, agency (struggle), received tradition, structure (whole-way-of-life)—had provided the way forward
out of the debates of the 1950s. Culture is the link-term, which by 1980 had
"synthesized" Williams and Thompson "to provide a peculiarly English Left
historical methodology" (55, 56, 43).

The political and intellectual constituencies of those debates had always been
heterogeneous, and by the early 1960s the first New Left had clearly failed to
coalesce into an effective power bloc. At home, although men like Williams and
Thompson were intimately concerned with the working class, the contacts that
the first New Left as a whole had with rank-and-file worker militants was
limited, a fact lamented by Williams (1960: 347). Abroad, despite the constant
theme of imperialism, an unquestioning, uncritical attitude was evinced regarding the "neutral" regimes of the third world: "The language of Positive
Neutralism, New Powers, and Emergent Peoples was about as illuminating as
the rival rhetorics of Free World, Camp of Peace, Western Values and Pro-
letarian Internationalism" (Sedgwick 1964: 144). By 1963 what had always been a
rickety coalition had fallen apart.[19]

Already in 1961, Stuart Hall had left the editorship of *New Left Review*. The
new team effected a radical reorganization of the journal in the "context of a
general caution and dependence. . . . The forms of struggle which are picked
out for attention and commendation are [no longer] those of an industrial
working-class movement" (Sedgwick 1964: 146–47, 148). This "second" generation abandoned the political project for a more rigorous theoretical enterprise
that did not constitute the *question of agency* "as in any way problematic, either
theoretically or strategically" (S. Hall 1989: 31). The political objectives of the
first New Left, except for nuclear disarmament (whether expressed as workers'
control, unilateralism, nonalignment, or active neutrality), found little lasting
endorsement. In contrast, its cultural analyses continued to have wide resonance, especially in the context of the ongoing rethinking and reworking of
English Marxism occasioned by the perceived failure (and political taint) of
the base-superstructure model to explain contemporary social change and in
which the questions of class and ideology, agency and determinism were intimately involved.

As the movement faded, an institution emerged. Cultural studies, identified with New Left analyses of social change during the 1950s, waned as an activist project, while Cultural Studies, ensconced in academia, was launched as an institutionalized intellectual enterprise. By the time *The Making of the English Working Class* appeared in 1963,[20] in its own way legitimating the work of the New Left, Richard Hoggart was already in the process of setting up the Centre for Contemporary Cultural Studies at the University of Birmingham, where Stuart Hall would join him in 1964. For his part, Williams returned to Cambridge. The limits of the conjuncture had been reached and the political project atrophied until 1968.

CHAPTER 2

The Politics of Culture II: Tensions of Continuity, 1790–1968

The precept given by a wise man, as well as a great critic, for the construction of poems, is equally true as to states. *Non satis est pulchra esse poemata, dulcia sunto.* . . . Happy if they had all continued to know their indissoluble union, and their proper place! Happy if learning, not debauched by ambition, had been satisfied to continue the instructor, and not aspired to be the master! Along with its natural protectors and guardians, learning will be cast into the mire, and trodden down under the hoofs of a swinish multitude.—EDMUND BURKE, *Reflections on the Revolution in France*

When, in countries that are called civilized, we see age going to the workhouse and youth to the gallows, something must be wrong in the system of government.
—TOM PAINE, *The Rights of Man*

Don't think; try and be patient.
—MATTHEW ARNOLD, quoting John Hunter, "A Liverpool Address"

It is on literary tradition that the office of maintaining continuity must rest.
—F. R. LEAVIS AND DENYS THOMPSON, *Culture and Environment*

If the particular conjuncture of British life and place in the world in the 1950s defines the synchronic topography of the first flowering of cultural studies, we must not miss the diachronic trajectory of a tradition of English social criticism in which the role of the intellectual as social agent was inscribed. The turn to culture as a significant category of analysis by the independent left in Britain during the late 1950s was just as surely a return to culture, at least in name. *Culture* was the code word around which the notions of Authenticity, Tradition, and the Organic Community had coalesced over a century and a half, in opposition first to revolution, then to laissez-faire liberalism, and finally to the reformist progress of social engineering.

Just as surely, there was an underside to what developed as a nationalistic, ethnocentric, and textual model. Indeed, the "high-cultural" tradition of order evolved as response and corrective to the pressures generated through the practical interactions on a world scale among working people. These pressures were manifested in vocal and violent resistance to exploitation both at home and abroad, to colonial domination and to slavery.

As the legacy of the French Revolution dismantled any possibility of a static world, in England the literary intellectual in the role of social critic became a central figure interpreting that world in which change now had to be accepted as normal. Class and inequality and popular culture and education, treated as national issues, formed the terrain of the Revolution Controversy and the Condition-of-England Question during the first half of the nineteenth century. Both the rhetorical construction of ideological structures and the legitimation of, or opposition to, the institutions in which they found their material expression were developed discursively in the debates. This work was engaged and overtly political in that period when protest and insurgency were cruelly repressed.

During the second half of the century the conspicuously political role of the critic was subtly undermined from within. Social criticism was carried forward and solidified in pursuit of order (culture) and in opposition to radicalism (anarchy). Laissez-faire liberalism was transformed as it absorbed the conservative critique and, served by the new social sciences, responded to the forces of radicalism in an increasingly circumscribed nationalistic mode. An uneasy consensus colonized both the left and the right and real political alternatives withered. As the century closed, art lost its social referent and criticism slipped into aestheticism. With popular politics increasingly out of its purview, English studies did service in the war effort, underwent technical development, and was effectively institutionalized as an anchor to national identity.

From the mid-1950s through the 1970s, what self-consciously constituted itself institutionally as cultural studies in England was overwhelmingly national and contemporary in subject matter. Even as politics was reintroduced to criticism, the trend of intellectual intervention and commentary focused "internally" was extended. This registered the historical amnesia surrounding the "external" tensions associated with maintaining the long-distance exploitative relationships that had contributed mightily to the shaping of Englishness in the first place. And these tensions, which show up as erasures in the record, had profound impact on developments in knowledge structures and cultural forms bequeathed to the early practitioners of cultural studies.

Raymond Williams, from a specifically left oppositional position, which he shared with E. P. Thompson (independent left for Williams, Marxist for Thompson), took the long-term literary-critical tradition as his explicit subject matter while maintaining its nationalistic and imminently textual character.[1] Matthew Arnold emerges as the pivotal nineteenth-century figure in the line culminating with F. R. Leavis: the "process Arnold began, when he virtually equated 'culture' with 'criticism,' is completed by Leavis" (R. Williams [1958] 1983: 254). The critical issues of race and empire (as, for instance, focused through Carlyle) are eclipsed in *Culture and Society,* and Arnold's position, and the broader social reality of which *Culture and Anarchy* was a symptom, go largely unexamined. Richard Hoggart, like Williams, acknowledged his debt to Leavis, but he too ignored the relationships between culture and the material legacies of historical struggles. Some explanation may lie in Hoggart's own politics. Although he has characterized his political affiliation as simply left (Moritz [1963] 1964: 188) or "centre socialist" (Hoggart 1992: 90), Thompson described Hoggart's attitude toward Marxism in the 1950s as "one of explicit hostility" (1981: 397). As for Thompson, who asserted that "class is a cultural as much as an economic formation" ([1963] 1966: 13), he regarded the English experience as distinct and ignored inspirations with roots in the economics and politics of empire.

Notwithstanding the differences these three exhibited in practical politics or analytical emphasis, the national perspective and common concerns for education, popular cultural forms, and the "lived" experience of class, which they shared, represent a continuity in English cultural criticism that survived in the immediate directions cultural studies would take.

From Political Repression to the Suppression of Politics

Williams contributed to the recuperation on the left of marginalized or co-opted voices of dissent; Thompson rehabilitated an array of forgotten English working-class activists; and Hoggart revalorized contemporary working-class life. However, Hoggart, like Williams, can also be read as continuing a form of critical analysis estranged from the material agency of real political actors.

Indeed, in *Culture and Society,* where "subject" is "text," Williams views John Stuart Mill as trying to reconcile Bentham and Coleridge (F. R. Leavis had recently brought out Mill's two essays), but he misses the relationship with

Arnold. Williams's censure of Mill for losing contact with any experience or lived reality overlooks the immediate and strictly political factor of working-class struggle in Arnold and in Mill. In 1979, the editors of *New Left Review* noted that the discussion in *Culture and Society* of two key terms, democracy and class, appeared to exclude politics. Williams answered that a

> moment of intense illumination and regret for me occurred when I found that Matthew Arnold's *Culture and Anarchy* was written in direct response to the Hyde Park riots in the suffrage campaign of 1866, in which John Stuart Mill was centrally involved on the other side. When I saw that this was the context which politically defined what "anarchy" and what "culture" were for Arnold, I thought my God, if I had known that I could have begun the book with the political forces and issues of 1867. ([1979] 1981: 109)

This is just one instance, albeit an instructive one, of a process. We must turn to a longer-term and wider world context to grasp the mechanisms and consequences of the shift from an engaged criticism in a period of violently repressive politics to the suppression of politics in criticism itself, to which, despite themselves, Williams and his fellow innovators were heir. The issues were long in the making, products not only of the transformations at home, but also of the struggles in a supranational community in which the circulation and intermixture of ideas and action affirmed their ultimate hybridity.

Careful observers such as E. P. Thompson have argued that the roots of English radicalism were deeply embedded in contentions over the "customary rights" of the "freeborn Englishman." More recently, Peter Linebaugh (1992) has extended the argument by illustrating how the criminalization of such rights claimed by the urban working poor was a key element in the establishment of private property rights and hence class relations based on the wage-labor nexus. Authors such as Peter Fryer, Marcus Rediker, Paul Gilroy, and Linebaugh himself have added new dimensions to this view by maintaining that the black experience was crucial to the activism of the period. " 'Lesser breeds' and 'lower orders,' " Fryer writes, "had much in common, not least in the threat they presented to law and order" (1984: 169–70).

British ascendancy from the mid-seventeenth century was built on a mercantile system of colonies and shipping. The Caribbean sugar economy, especially, depended on and produced an international, multiethnic labor force. In myriad eighteenth-century popular struggles, the construction of the meaning of *freedom* was informed by the opposition to confinement and coerced exploitation on the part of an interconnected, communicating, Atlantic working class. The aspirations and struggles of this "motley crew," write Linebaugh and Rediker, "circulated *to the eastward,* from American slave plantations, Irish commons, and Atlantic vessels, back to the streets of the metropolis, London," and was "transformed into the revolutionary discussion of human rights." This interchange was predominantly urban and "took place over, around, beneath, and frequently against the artisans and craftsmen who are generally credited with creating the early working-class movement" (1990: 244). It was slaves and ex-slaves rebelling and arguing powerfully for abolition joined by an Atlantic maritime proletariat resisting prison and impressment who fueled the insurgency of the "dangerous classes" as working men began to dominate radical organizations in the 1790s.

In his 1790 *Reflections on the Revolution in France,* Edmund Burke vigorously opposed both radical and reformist change and argued for the use of force against the revolutionary movement. In an effort to fuse Whig freedom and Tory order, Burke defended continuity, and thus private property and the aristocracy (inheritance, accumulation, and limits on sovereignty), and attacked individualism. He rejected natural rights but accepted the idea of a social contract linked to divine sanction. He advocated the known, the tried and true, tradition validated in experience, over the abstract and unfamiliar. Thomas Paine replied with the voice of the radical Atlantic community in his *Rights of Man* in 1791–92. Paine was a consummate "Atlantican": sailor, journalist, revolutionary, government functionary, and citizen, variously, of England, France, and the United States. As such, he defended a universal vision of natural rights and revolution to secure or reinstate them. He characterized Burke's account of the past as fraudulent and espoused the redistribution of national income to the poor through taxation. He asked of what use were aristocracies, against which he promoted representative democracy. This was the direct parry and thrust that marked the beginning of the Revolution controversy in England. In 1792, at least, the questions surrounding revolution were practical: "Should Britain continue to be governed by owners of land? Why do so few own land? Even, why need individuals own land at all?" (Butler 1984: 2).[2]

Both revolutionaries and counterrevolutionaries were conscious that the linguistic, ideological war extended the military war; "they sensed that language and ideology are intimately intertwined and that whoever controls language controls not only the terms of 'war' but the terms of 'reality' itself" (Blakemore 1988: 2). Burke denounced the idea of social criticism, with its language of ideas, of corruption and subversion, which he connected to revolutionary violence. But his tradition, if it ever existed, was irretrievable.

Even so, several factors led to an ebbing of the Painite tide by 1795. "Pitt's reign of terror," 1792–94, targeted radical societies and proceeded vigorously against the radical press while the call to arms with the outbreak of war with France favored a turn to patriotic conservatism. Furthermore, the progress of the controversy itself led reformist intellectuals to see themselves increasingly as advocates of individual expression rather than as group spokesmen. Significantly, the "unpredictable spark" that ignited a new wave of working-class political activity in 1814 was the question of slavery. At the Congress of Vienna "a proposal was made to renew the rights of French slave-merchants. . . . Within four weeks some 806 petitions, bearing the signatures of 1,500,000 protesters, were sent to Parliament" (Fryer 1984: 212–13). During the hard times following the war, oppressive state policies embodied in the Coercion Acts of 1817 and the Six Acts of 1819 answered the unrest of Spa Fields (1816) and Peterloo (1819). This was all part of a politics of repression that included the use of informers, agents provocateurs, and the harshest of punishments.

The names of two Jamaican "revolutionary socialists," Robert Wedderburn and William Davidson, figured in a secret government document of 1819 listing "leadeing [sic] Reformers." Both had slave mothers and both were "members of the farthest left of all the radical organizations of the time." Wedderburn's revolutionary tracts were the first to be sent to the West Indies from Britain. He suggested one-hour strikes by the slaves, advised against petitions, and, with an eye to the European experience, warned slaves to keep control of the land in a "vision of a simultaneous revolution of the white poor of Europe and the black slaves" (Fryer 1984: 213–17, 225). His Hopkins Street chapel "was unsurpassed in the world for the kind of questions that were proposed and argued there" (McCalman 1988: 140). When the Peterloo massacre brought ultraradicalism to a head in 1820 and the Yeomen of Peterloo were branded murderers, Wedderburn spoke out for revolution, not reform. Working men were arming themselves all over England and a group of twenty, including Davidson, planned to assassinate the entire Cabinet and then establish a provisional government: the Cato Street conspiracy. Manipulated and betrayed, Davidson was hanged along with the influential radical Arthur Thistlewood and three companions.

The revolutionary tendencies of Wedderburn and Davidson were no accident. Rebellion had been endemic in the West Indies slave colonies since their establishment; Michael Craton (1982) counts at least seventy-five between 1638 and 1837. When the governor of Dominica put a price on the head of one of the leaders of the continuous fighting from 1809 to 1814, Quashie, the maroon leader, replied by offering "$2000 for the governor's head" (Fryer 1988: 90–91).

From the 1823 insurrection on the east coast of Demerara, disorders escalated in number and intensity to climax with the uprising in eastern Jamaica of 1831–32. This so-called Baptist War eventually led to abolition in 1833.

During the same period as the crucial uprising in Jamaica, falling wages and high food prices in England led to official pauperization of nearly 10 percent of the population. Abominable conditions brought large numbers to the brink of revolution, culminating in political crisis and violence between 1830 and 1832. The Reform Bill of 1832, through limited reallocation of seats in the House of Commons to the growing middle class, narrowly averted actual revolt but was of little consequence for the poor. On the contrary, the passage of the New Poor Law in 1834 terminating the Speenhamland system of outdoor relief probably failed to establish a more flexible labor supply but certainly did create crushing misery. That same year the Grand National Consolidated Trades Union was formed to agitate, through the mechanism of the general strike, for Robert Owen's program and an eight-hour day. Its strikes were ineffectual and the movement collapsed, but demands for fair wages had been deemed seditious and alarming enough for the government to result again in drastic repression.

The founding of the London Working Men's Association in 1836, originally to advocate for a cheap press, marked the beginning of the Chartist movement.[3] By 1838, eighty-one Working Men's Associations and thirty radical or other associations were in friendly correspondence with the London Association (Howell 1972: 89). The "People's Charter" of 1839 (universal manhood suffrage, vote by ballot, abolition of the property qualification for candidates, payment of members of Parliament, equal electoral districts, and annual Parliaments) garnered massive popular approval but failed to move Parliament.

The dislocations on the eve of the "hungry forties" were addressed by Thomas Carlyle in *Chartism*. He railed against politicians who failed to address the Condition-of-England Question. Like other middle-class observers, he feared widespread violence, but to the rhetorical question of the "meaning" of popular struggles, he answered:

> Bellowings, *in*articulate cries as of a dumb creature in rage and pain; to the ear of wisdom they are inarticulate prayers: "Guide me, Govern me! I am mad and miserable, and cannot guide myself!" Surely of all "rights of man," this right of the ignorant man to be guided by the wiser, to be, gently or forcibly, held in the true course by him, is the indisputablest. Nature ordains it from the first, society struggles towards perfection by enforcing and accomplishing it more and more. ([1839] 1904a: 157–58)

Chartism reflects what Simon Heffer calls "Carlyle's loathing of democracy" and the beginning of his "creeping authoritarianism," marking the change "from the vague desire to improve the conditions of the lower orders to a more specific desire to improve their conditions without allowing them the scope to upset the natural order" (1995: 195).

The black experience and the legacy of the golden age of sugar formed the backdrop of race-based arguments, including those of Carlyle, that became more generalized as the century progressed. The reactionism and racism of the powerful lobby of repatriated planters rested on "slave-based wealth and . . . an obsessive hatred for the West Indian black person" (Lewis 1978: 26). Witness that when the *Times* wrote of the London Chartists as "the Black man and his Party" they were referring to the black tailor, William Cuffay, one of the "most prominent leaders of the Chartist movement in London" (Fryer 1984: 238–39).

The idea that there existed a social hierarchy including a hierarchy of races, suggested by the empirical record of winners and losers in a world of Hobbesian struggle, was hardly new. But over the course of the nineteenth century, race theorizing hardened into racism. By the 1820s phrenology was already in vogue. It "justified empire-building. It told the British that they were ruling over races which, unlike themselves, lacked force of character" (Fryer 1984: 171). By mid-century, racism was functioning, writes Peter Gay, as an "alibi for aggression." In 1850 Herbert Spencer dubbed evolution a "purifying process" and laid the foundations for what would come to be called Social Darwinism. An "indifference to deprivations and resistance to any attempts at alleviating them" were codified in Spencer's expression "survival of the fittest" in 1862 (Gay 1993: 41).

"Scientific" rationales lent newfound confidence to racist arguments and the institutions of British science were conspicuous in debates over the "natural order." The Ethnological Society of London (ESL) was launched in 1842 (along the lines of the Paris model of 1838, in which racism and phrenology had played a part) as an offshoot of the Aborigines Protection Society (1837) to privilege scientific over humanitarian principles. The ESL was monogenist, espousing the essential unity of the human race, and the "model of explanation was diffusionary and historical emphasizing the environmental influences modifying human physical characteristics." Although monogeny and polygeny did not necessarily correlate with antislavery and pro-slavery positions, differences over the "Negro question" moved James Hunt, a polygenist who championed the cause of the American Confederacy, to establish the Anthropological Society of London (ASL) in 1863. For the ASL, "anthropology would be empirical, rejecting unproven hypotheses, and busying itself with the collection of facts. But it would also be practical, uncovering the 'laws [that] are secretly working for the development of some nations and the destruction of others'" (Stocking 1971: 372, 377).[4] The marginal "anthropologicals" argued that Negroes were a different species, incapable of civilization and better off as slaves, while mainstream British science, an intellectual aristocracy including Huxley and Galton, was embracing the "ape theory" of the origin of man. All the same, as Frank M. Turner documents, Carlyle's insistence on a leadership class, a new aristocracy, practical and active, whose authority would be based on talent, truth, and factual knowledge, greatly influenced the nineteenth-century scientific naturalists (including Huxley, Spencer, and Tyndall). "A direct line of intellectual descent connects Carlyle's demand for heroes," whose qualities were inborn, "with Galton's eugenics and Karl Pearson's eulogy of the superiority of the British race" (F. Turner 1975: 332).

Certainly, one man's racism might be another's Anglo-Saxonism or, for Carlyle writing in 1848, antiliberalism: "The message of the discontents across Europe . . . was the 'bankruptcy of imposture.' . . . [Carlyle] wanted to assault the priggishness and smugness of the liberal and philanthropic consensus that believed the lower orders could be reformed and improved and entrusted with greater responsibility" (Heffer 1995: 269, 274). He settled on the postemancipation West Indies as an ideal site to make his case. With the publication of "The Negro Question" (to appear, for even greater emphasis, as "Occasional Discourse on the Nigger Question") in 1849, the economics and politics of race in midcentury England could not have been made clearer.

Carlyle shared Spencer's dismissal of philanthropists who were allowing "the relation of master to servant, and of superior to inferior" to fall "sadly out of joint": "declaring that Negro and White are *un*related . . . contradicts the palpablest facts . . . [and] is leading us towards *dis*solution instead of solution!" In Jamaica, "beautiful Blacks" were "up to the ears in pumpkins" and would not work (Carlyle [1849] 1904b: 362, 380, 351). Arguably, Carlyle may be read as criticizing what he regarded as a general condition of humankind at midcentury: "The slavery of Wisdom to Folly. When Folly all 'emancipated,' and become supreme, armed with ballot-boxes, universal suffrages, and appealing to what Dismal Sciences, Statistics, Constitutional Philosophies, and other Fool Gospels it has got devised for itself, can say to Wisdom: 'Be silent, or thou shalt repent it'" (360). However, even if one were to grant that Carlyle's intervention is metaphorical (the seat of his life-long interest is the Condition-of-England Question), in the language and spirit of the particular, this is an unequivocal expression of racial legitimation of exploitation:

If Quashee will not honestly aid in bringing-out those sugars, cinnamons and nobler products of the West-Indian Islands, for the benefit of all mankind, then I say neither will the Powers permit Quashee to continue growing pumpkins there for his own lazy benefit. . . . decidedly you have to be servants to those that are born *wiser* than you, that are born lords of you; servants to the Whites, if they *are* (as what mortal can doubt they are?) born wiser than you. That, you may depend on it, my obscure Black friends, is and was always the Law of the World, for you and for all men: To *be* servants, the more foolish of us to the more wise. . . . Heaven's laws are not repealable by Earth, however Earth may try. (375, 379)

This portrayal overlaps with Carlyle's sensibility to the Irish situation and is made explicit in the phrase "Black Ireland." He had traveled in Ireland during the famine and seen firsthand the effects of the imposition of anarchic laissez-faire, which he pronounced analogous to emancipation in Jamaica: "Our own white or sallow Ireland, sluttishly starving from age to age on its ace-of-parliament 'freedom,' was hitherto the flower of mismanagement among the nations; but what will this be to a Negro Ireland, with pumpkins themselves fallen scarce like potatoes" ([1849] 1904b: 353).

What Carlyle saw in Jamaica and Ireland he had long been observing at home. Ten years earlier, in *Chartism,* he had written that laissez-faire "must either cease or a worse thing straightway begin,—a thing of tinderboxes, vitriol-bottles, secondhand pistols, a visibly insupportable thing in the eyes of all" ([1839] 1904a: 170). At that time, he had advocated education for the masses and emigration for excess population. Education was for Carlyle an antidote to radicalism in the sense that educated men "will no longer be so stupid as to cry for the panacea of universal suffrage" (Heffer 1995: 198). But if the working classes could no "longer go on without government" they were not so ready to return to the "most perfect Feudal time" (Carlyle [1839] 1904a: 155, 162). In fact, two years before Carlyle wrote of "inarticulate cries" and the "right of the ignorant man to be guided by the wiser," the London Association had advanced a program for a locally administered, state-supported system on the premise that education for all classes was a basic right.

Contrary to received wisdom, the original expansion of the public schools in the 1840s owed little to Thomas Arnold of Rugby and his ideas; indeed, it was the spread of railways that made the expansion materially possible![5] However, from midcentury, the Arnold legend "helped to popularize public school education, to increase demand, and to promote expansion" (Honey 1977: 46). Dr.

Arnold's emphasis was on action. He proposed right doing, rather than right thinking. His reforms, by which "boys from the commercial middle class [were guided] into a sanitized version of the values of the territorial aristocracy" (Harvie 1988: 503), were in keeping with the essentially conservative political settlement of 1832 and institutionalized the class values personified in the cadres of the Empire "on which the sun never set."

While the year of the Great Exhibition, 1851, marked the beginning of an upward price swing, Ireland reeled from the effects of the great famine (1845–49) in which a million died and two million had emigrated by 1855. At the same time in England, a sense of prosperity dominated as wage levels outpaced inflation. London became the center of both national and global commercial traffic in communications (rail, post, telegraph, and cable) as well as finance and trade, and British industry led the world. However, in the same year, 1851, when Thomas Arnold's son, Matthew, the "brilliant elegiac poet" (Honan 1981: vii), was appointed inspector of schools—a post he would retain for thirty-five years—England "still qualified for Thomas Wyse's description of 1837 as 'the one great exception to the entire civilized world' in that she lacked a national system of education. Education was neither free, compulsory, nor universal" (D. Jones 1977: ix). Arnold's meticulous reports from foreign fact-finding missions never failed to call attention to the deficiencies of English schooling in contrast with continental systems.

Arnold had a vision of the school as a civilizing agent, and as such he felt that examination should be from the point of view of how much the children of the laboring classes had been "humanized" and elevated toward general perfection. In 1862 a new system did away with the centralized post-1846 grant structure and instituted a decentralized system of "payment by results" that, in the laissez-faire spirit, cut education expenditures by 40 percent. This Revised Code reflected two opposed conceptions of the state: Arnold's, which "saw it as the embodiment of the collective wisdom of the nation which should use its influence to raise its people's standards even higher and higher," and the advocates' of the Revised Code, which "still held a view of the function of the State as little removed from that of a policeman" (Connell [1950] 1971: 214). According to Donald Jones, the overall effect was a perpetuation and sharpening of class divisions (1977: 44). The self-education initiatives of the Chartist movement provide clear evidence against those who argued that the working classes had no interest in anything but the rudiments of literacy and support the significance of the elementary schools under the Revised Code as tools of labor force reproduction and control. Indeed, Arnold would write that beyond the humanizing and civilizing role, in schools "the State had another interest besides the encouragement of reading, writing, and arithmetic—*the protection of society*" ([1862] 1962c: 228).[6]

Arnold the poet continued to publish throughout the 1850s and was elected to the Oxford Poetry Chair in 1857; but, recognizing a decline in inspiration, he redirected his attention to criticism after 1858.[7] Always distrustful of utopian, revolutionary solutions to the problems of society and placing his confidence only in some ill-defined long(er)-term change, he criticized Cobbett, Carlyle, and Ruskin as distracted by action for its own sake. Arnold "conceives of the critic as prophet" (Raleigh 1961: 261–62); "disinterestedness," political detachment without commitment to any specific program of action, is his fundamental rule.[8] The subject matter of criticism "is determined for it by the idea which is the law of its being; the idea of a disinterested endeavour to learn and propagate the best that is known and thought in the world, and thus to establish a current of fresh and true ideas" (Arnold [1864] 1962a: 282). Arnold ties individual action to the social condition by enlarging on the idea of the creative act to extend it to all, particularly the critic. It is by this creative act, more empirical than philosophical and more objective than partisan—this primary activity of the critic, the "disinterested endeavour to learn and propagate" but never "abstract"—that the critic/intellectual impacts society. The critic serves as an intermediary between "the best that is known and thought in the world" and a wider public, with the goal to "establish a current of fresh and true ideas." Most of all, the critic is the defender of a "central standard" that serves as the font of both social—national—and individual progress (282–84). But his is also a supranational arena, rooted as it is in a wider European or Western tradition.

Arnold, this champion of sweetness and light, had been a faithful and detailed observer of English society as inspector of schools, but his quest for objectivity tended to keep him above the fray, advocating the best that had been thought and said. But fray indeed there was during the 1860s, when a series of agitations, linked with those of the post-Napoleonic period and then the 1830s and 1840s, challenged the very foundations of order and the state. The establishment and its intellectuals, Arnold included, were shocked by the violence of events in Jamaica and Ireland and stunned by the "anarchy" of the demonstrations in favor of franchise reform. Segments of public opinion were outraged too by the degree to which the state's own legal institutions, the guarantors of order, were deployed to legitimate terror in Jamaica. Others bridled at how those same institutions were used to question the methods by which order was to be maintained. This all contributed to a general atmosphere of violence, confusion, and panic.

In Jamaica, the political, social, and economic domination of the whites had not ended with emancipation, and rebellion was precipitated by a court case at Morant Bay. The vestry, the symbol of oppression, was attacked on October 11, 1865 by a well-organized crowd of several hundred blacks. Officials and militia counted eighteen dead and thirty-one wounded; the crowd lost seven dead. In the drive for "full freedom" the revolt spread. Estates were pillaged and some whites killed, and the white and brown minority "became convinced that they were dealing with a massive conspiracy. In their view, blacks were intent on killing whites and coloureds and taking over the island. For whites it was therefore essential that the outbreak be suppressed as quickly as possible" (Heuman 1994: 97). The British governor, Edward John Eyre, declared martial law and sent troops. "Commanders were quite explicit about the objective of official violence: they intended to instill terror" (Holt 1992: 302). In the reprisals meant to reestablish order, 439 blacks were killed, 600 were flogged, over a thousand houses burned. One of those hanged, after a legally questionable trial, was George Gordon, a brown man and member of the vestry.

Eyre was largely exonerated in the Royal Commission investigation that followed. The Commission did, however, discover a number of irregularities and criticized the brutality of the repression. Eyre himself was recalled and replaced. A group of prominent "radicals and members of the scientific establishment," including John Stuart Mill, Charles Darwin, and Herbert Spencer, formed the Jamaica Committee in an attempt to bring Eyre to justice. Conservatives, members of the "literary establishment and also from landed society, the army and the Church" (Heuman 1994: 172), formed the Eyre Defence Committee; Charles Dickens and Lord Tennyson were members and Carlyle acted as chair for a while. Racist beliefs and fears dominated the defense. As Joseph Hooker declared: " 'We do not hold an Englishman and a Jamaican negro to be convertible terms, nor do we think that the cause of human liberty will be promoted by any attempt to make them so.' Black insurrection could not be treated in the same way as a white one, because 'the negro in Jamaica . . . is pestilential, . . . a dangerous savage at best' " (Holt 1992: 306). It is instructive to note that, if the currency of Eyre's defense was racial, the attack, ultimately unsuccessful, was directed primarily at Eyre's illegal action against George Gordon. In effect, it was the "order" of the rule of law that the Jamaica Committee was defending by seeking Eyre's indictment.

As a direct challenge to the British Empire, in 1858 the Irish Revolutionary Brotherhood was established in Dublin and the Fenian Brotherhood was founded in New York (where so many had emigrated during the mass starvation and mass evictions of the potato famine years and the failed revolutionary attempts of 1848 and 1849). The Irish Brotherhood was to supply the men and the American Fenians were to collect funds for the overthrow of British rule of Ireland. By 1865, the movement counted perhaps as many as eighty thousand working-class adherents plus another fifteen thousand in the British army. This was the moment of peak strength, but revolt was preempted by the British and deferred in consideration of the unreliability of support from the United States, where, in fact, resources were squandered in an unsuccessful invasion of Canada in 1866. Finally, on March 5, 1867, the general uprising in Ireland fizzled, but not before an explicit call had been made to the British working class to take up arms in a fraternal alliance. Indeed, declared the Proclamation of the Irish Republic, "Republicans of the entire world, our cause is your cause." A guerrilla strategy was rejected "in favour of a full-blown rising . . . only to be dispersed by police and troops in the most demoralising circumstances." There was to be "no Bloody Assizes, however, no hanging of captured rebels—mainly because of the furor aroused in Britain by the brutal suppression of the Jamaican rebellion in 1865" (Newsinger 1994: 55, 59).

A year after Morant Bay, one member of the Eyre Defence Committee, Charles Kingsley, explained, "The differences of race are so great, that certain races, e.g. the Irish Celts, seem quite unfit for self-government, and almost for the self-administration of justice involved in trial by jury." Allusion to the Irish instead of blacks is indicative of the way attacks on, and defense of, order overlapped and intermingled in the 1860s and underlines the degree to which the British middle class "connected the need to repel class challenges from below with support for racism and empire" (Holt 1992: 308, 307). The working classes, in contrast, demonstrated against the defense of Eyre and showed sympathy for the Irish cause. As for the Irish, the revolutionary movement had cultivated relations with English radicals and even hoped for a revival of the Chartists.

English radicals had maintained an international perspective that included secret involvements with revolutionaries on the continent and support for the North in the American Civil War, for Polish independence, and for Italian nationalism (Garibaldi was greeted by fifty thousand working men on his 1864 visit to London). Condemnation of the repression of the Morant Bay uprising had mass appeal. Nonetheless, it was the extension of the franchise that galvanized radicals during the 1860s, and lines drawn in the Governor Eyre controversy paralleled those that developed around the Reform Bill. Events climaxed with the demonstration in Hyde Park on July 23, 1866. The Liberal reform proposal would have resulted in the enfranchisement of some four-hundred-thousand town artisans. Despite Reform League and Reform Union support, this bill was defeated. When a protest rally was convened at Hyde Park, the Home Secretary ordered the gates locked. Railings were promptly pulled down and the crowd fought with police.

Increasingly illiberal, Carlyle was vehemently opposed to the reform itself. In "Shooting Niagara, and After?" ([1867] 1904c), he linked the "hypocrisy of 'nigger philanthropists'" with the "phony regard for the ballot-box." Arnold had taken care not to become directly involved in the Governor Eyre controversy, but however much he disliked Carlyle, Carlyle exerted great political influence over him. "The authoritarian tone of much of the social philosophy of *Culture and Anarchy* may owe much, ostensibly, to Arnold's father, but it owes as much to the doctrines propounded over the preceding thirty years by Carlyle" (Heffer 1995: 359, 274–75). Arnold the critic—the intellectual in society with a particular creative project engendering progress toward universal light—was appalled by the agitation, and conceived *Culture and Anarchy* ([1867] 1965) in reaction to the Hyde Park events. He observed the rioters from his balcony and came away furious from the discussion of the events in the House of Commons that followed. This was anarchy, "the Do Nothing, Think Nothing, laissez faire attitude to politics and economics, religion and morals [that] could be discerned throughout the nation" (Honan 1981: 341, 339), and had to be opposed. Although not everyone was as troubled by the riots, Arnold's response was symptomatic of the depth of anxiety about the masses harbored by cultivated society.

Arnold recommends "culture as the great help out of our present difficulties" in the same language he had formerly used for the function of criticism. The activity, criticism, and the object, culture, are directly identified one with the other. Culture, "*a study of perfection* . . . moves by the force, not merely or primarily of the scientific passion for pure knowledge, but also of the moral and social passion for doing good." And there is yet another, and equally important, aspect to this idea of culture: it is not only in the struggle to see and learn things as they are, to approach a knowledge of the universal order, but also "to make it *prevail*, [that] the moral, social, and beneficent character of culture becomes manifest." The state is the embodiment of culture and opposed to anarchy. It is "sacred" (Arnold [1867] 1965: 90–91, 93, 223). "As the corporate and collective 'best self,' " it "would have the power to restrain the excesses of each class and the intelligence to direct the strength of each class toward the proper modes of 'expansion,' that is, liberty" (McCarthy 1964: vii). Note, however, that Arnold's idea of equality rested not in an economic condition but in a common culture.

Still, Arnold faced a contradiction. Culture "places human perfection in an *internal* condition"; however, the "idea of perfection as a *general* expansion of the human family is at variance with our strong individualism, our hatred of all limits to the unrestrained swing of the individual's personality, our maxim of 'every man for himself' " ([1867] 1965: 94). What Arnold sought to do was to connect, or in any case, positively correlate the development of the individual to progress in the greater society as an extension of the idea of perfection grounding the constitution of a common culture. "Culture is not satisfied till we *all* come to a perfect man. . . . It seeks to do away with classes. . . . This is the *social idea;* and the men of culture are the true apostles of equality" (112–13). But in the end, despite Arnold's "disinterestedness," his is, in Chris Baldick's apt description, but a "gesture of postponement" (1983: 20). It emerges as a corollary to his conception of alternating critical and creative periods and his disassociation of the sphere of ideas from the realm of politics. Arnold places the highest value on ideas, but

> to transport them abruptly into the world of politics and practice, violently to revolutionise this world to their bidding,—that is quite another thing. . . . *Force till right is ready;* and till right is ready, force, the existing order of things, is justified, is the legitimate ruler. But right is something moral, and implies inward recognition, free assent of the will; we are not ready for right,—*right,* so far as we are concerned, *is not ready,*—until we have attained this sense of seeing it and willing it. ([1864] 1962a: 265–66)

Deprecating "practical criticism," that is, direct engagement, as he does, has the consequence of upholding "the existing order." Challenges to the conduct of practical affairs are ruled out—"*force till right is ready*"—and ideas are walled off from practice. The tide had turned. The activity of criticism itself had been redirected.

When Arnold's advocacy of French and Hellenist virtues was subdued by the Paris Commune and the defeat of France by Prussia, the championship of Hellenism fell to Walter Pater. Arnold's ideal criticism, the identity of the Arnoldian subject, was objectified in Pater's Renaissance man, conceived of as completeness, multiple self-completion. Arnold's general and harmonious perfection entailed a culture that was both a social phenomenon and an inward condition. In the conclusion to *The Renaissance: Studies in Art and Poetry,* Pater privileges the latter: "The whole scope of observation is dwarfed into the narrow chamber of the individual mind. . . . Not the fruit of experience, but experience itself, is the end. . . . To burn always with this hard, gemlike flame, to maintain this ecstasy, is success in life. . . . we shall hardly have time to make theories" ([1873] 1980: 187–89). Like Arnold, Pater eventually gives over the other side of the personality to established authority and an orthodoxy of religious observance. An exponent of the Aesthetic movement and "Art for art's sake," Pater advocated treating life itself in the spirit of art (contemplation rather than action). This cult of sensibility and the individual ego was both a reaction to Victorian "philistinism" and the long-term result of the Romantic idea of the poet as superior to ordinary mortals.

Institutionally, the status of English studies had been under construction since midcentury. University College first offered English as a subject in 1828 and then appointed the first professor of English in 1829. This was language study, however; the study of English literature began at King's College in 1831. Peter Barry underlines the relationship between the establishment of a national identity through English studies, and as a substitute for religion, and the Chartist agitation beginning in the 1830s. For F. D. Maurice, appointed at King's in 1840, the middle class

> represents the essence of Englishness . . . so middle-class education should be peculiarly English, and therefore should centre on English literature. . . . People so educated would feel that they belonged to England, that they had a country. "Political agitators" may ask what this can mean "when his neighbour rides in a carriage and he walks on foot," but "he will feel his nationality to be a reality, in spite of what they say." In short, learning English will give people a stake in maintaining the political *status quo* without any redistribution of wealth. (Barry 1995: 13)

In 1855, the India Civil Service opened posts to competitive examinations with English studies as one of the subject matters, and in 1861 the Newcastle Commission suggested the study of English for popular, elementary education analogous to the public school boys' study of the classics.

In the mechanics institutes and working-men's colleges and in extension lectures, the study of English literature developed alongside technical courses. English studies had also fallen to women, who were not admitted to the sciences or the professions, and such courses were instrumental in the establishment of schools of English at Oxford and Cambridge. A Board of Medieval and Modern

Languages with an English subsection was set up at Cambridge in 1878; a literary chair followed in 1911. H. M. Chadwick was appointed professor of Anglo-Saxon in 1912 and moved his department to the School of Archeology and Anthropology, leaving an English School with a literary focus to be established in its own right in 1917. At Oxford, the Merton Professorship of English Language and Literature was founded in 1884. There was intense opposition between the (Germanic) philologists and the (English) classicists, and the debates were not settled with the plans of the Congregation for a new School of English Language and Literature in 1893. Examination criteria remained an open question, but whether at Cambridge in the person of Sir Arthur Quiller-Couch or at Oxford with Walter Raleigh, the dynamics of teaching remained Arnoldian and writing and fighting were identified as "the virile alternatives to mere scientific study" (Baldick 1983: 82).[9]

The engagement of literary luminaries in the propaganda campaigns of the 1914–18 war illustrated the link between writing and fighting and enhanced the opposition to (Teutonic) philology within English studies. This latter facilitated the adoption of the new Tripos program in March 1917, but at the same time it pointed to the shaky foundations of the discipline itself. In fact, the material circumstances of wartime, especially the anticipation of more numerous, more mature students, made possible the reform at Cambridge that instituted English Tripos separate from Modern Languages.[10] As the Communist Party of Great Britain was organizing and blacks who had served in the military during the war were being excluded from victory celebrations, violently attacked, cheated, maligned, and repatriated (Fryer 1984: 298–316), the Newbold Report of 1921 on *The Teaching of English in England* (which singled out the system of schools as a key to Prussian strength) proposed rebuilding education around English as the basis of national unity. A resurgence of national pride and a recognition of the importance of education were yoked behind the rallying cry "Culture unites classes"—a distortion of Arnold. Distinct from the erstwhile genteel connoisseurism and subjectivism, Francis Mulhern concludes, "In the unstructured, indefinitely bounded space opened up by the Tripos reform, the contradictory social and cultural forces of the twenties met and mingled freely, giving rise to a debate of unprecedented breadth and vigor" (1979: 22). If, in the early 1920s, Terry Eagleton notes, "it was desperately unclear why English was worth studying at all," during the following decade, it became "a question of why it was worth wasting your time on anything else" (1983: 31).

I. A. Richards was appalled with the capacity for and the effects of the propaganda turned out by the literary establishment during the 1914–18 war:

"In war-time words become a normal part of the mechanism of deceit" (Ogden and Richards [1923] 1989: 17). He proposed a theory of value with the critic at its center to counter the "ravelling" of civilization by commercialism—dangerous attacks, "because they appeal to a natural instinct, hatred of 'superior persons' " (Richards [1924] 1925: 36). This proved formative for Cambridge English. Poetry could come to the rescue of order and psychological coherence in a world where knowledge was defined by science: "We shall . . . be thrown back, as Matthew Arnold foresaw, upon poetry. It is capable of saving us; it is a perfectly possible means of overcoming chaos" (Richards [1926] 1974: 82–83)—but only if taste could be educated. It was not the merit of works that counted, but the adequacy of the minds of the readers that was to be gauged and manipulated (Richards [1924] 1925: 285).

Fascinated by laboratory methods and behavioral psychology, Richards presented poems anonymously, purposefully shorn of any historical context, for free comment and analysis. In a manner reminiscent of Arnold's segregation of questions of attitude from questions of fact, Richards argued that emotive beliefs inspire attitudes that may be resolved through internal self-adjustment, unlike scientific beliefs that call for purposive, external action. Keeping the two separate had the effect of insulating the first from disproof and of keeping feelings from resulting in overt action, thus promoting quiescence and preserving traditional values. Richards's legacy, where the Arnoldian themes of the social function of poetry and the "disinterested" intellectual (now rigorous and professional) coalesced, was twofold: a defense of the study of literature as an agent of social order, and a teaching and examining method, "practical criticism," that could provide the necessary support for institutional success.

The new discipline was not without its detractors: the Cambridge classicist F. L. Lucas was of the opinion that, "left in the keeping of the self-appointed 'elect,' " the academic study of literature "was in danger of lapsing into 'organized orgies of opinion.' " Forced into an oppositional role, the circle that formed around F. R. and Q. D. Leavis at the beginning of the 1930s, and out of which grew the journal *Scrutiny*, was committed "to the 'vindication' of the English Tripos and yet powerless to influence the institution that housed it" (Mulhern 1979: 30, 32). The Archimedean pivot of their moral crusade in favor of a spiritual renewal (a return to the organic or traditional culture of seventeenth-century England, where high and popular culture seemed to be united) was education reform, "education *against* the environment." In the mold of Arnold, it appeared "plain why it is of so great importance to keep the literary tradition alive. For if language tends to be debased . . . then it is to literature alone, where its subtlest and finest use is preserved, that we can look with any hope of keeping in touch with our spiritual tradition—with the 'picked experience of ages' " (Leavis and Thompson 1933: 106, 82).

The Scrutineers consciously avoided political partisanship in favor of experience, the concrete, and an "organic community" rooted in the past. They saw their age as one of cultural decline and from that perspective produced a broad array of "mass" culture critiques. By casting bourgeois and Marxist alike as sharing in a machine-dependent society, the Leavisite perspective obscured relations of power and eradicated politics, leaving only economics and culture (Baldick 1983: 171). The role of the clerisy or "minority" that was Leavis's goal was specifically "ante-political, logically and, it appeared, in time"; in Mulhern's reading, "the basic and constant discursive organization of [*Scrutiny*] . . . was one defined by a dialectic of 'culture' and 'civilization' whose *main* and *logically necessary effect* was a *depreciation,* a *repression* and, at the limit, a *categorial dissolution* of *politics as such*" (1979: 79, 330).[11]

Thus, we are transported by intellectual legerdemain from a literary activism in which the relationship of order to revolution and exploitation was actually debated during a period of a very real repression of politics in the early nineteenth century to a twentieth-century suppression of politics in criticism itself. Although this was the tradition in which Williams and Hoggart were nurtured, both took a critical stance. Williams was explicit about the less attractive side of Leavisism: "The concept of a cultivated minority, set over against a 'decreated' mass, tends, in its assertion, to a damaging arrogance and skepticism. The concept of a wholly organic and satisfying past, to be set against a disintegrated and dissatisfying present, tends in its neglect of history to a denial of real social experience" ([1958] 1983: 263). On the plus side, Williams registers "Leavis's great stress on education" and the excitement of practical criticism, even though it tended "to become too dominant a mode, precisely because it evades both structural problems and in the end all questions of belief and ideology" ([1979] 1981: 66). For Hoggart, F. R. Leavis was a "looming and intransigent figure . . . one from whom many of us had learned more than from any other living critic, even if we had reservations about some of his views" (1992: 10, 62). Hoggart "became increasingly uneasy, especially with Mrs. Leavis's work," and addressed his reservations about her "separation from the material she was writing about" in *The Uses of Literacy: Aspects of Working-class Life, with Special References to Publications and Entertainments* (Hoggart, quoted in Corner 1991: 139).[12]

The Uses of Literacy cleaves neatly into two parts, both physically and intellectually. It was "written back to front—first a Leavisite kind of analysis, then the description of working-class life with which it opens" (Hoggart 1992: 5). Reminiscent of one aspect of the *Scrutiny* "Manifesto" of 1932, Part 1 is recuperative, a positive recovery of working-class culture in the anthropological (not the artistic or Arnoldian) sense as Hoggart remembers the urban North of his 1920s and 1930s childhood. This notion of working-class culture as intrinsically valuable and worthy of study presents us with one of the initial and lasting concerns of cultural studies. Part 2 is condemnatory, an indictment of "invitations to self-indulgence" (Hoggart [1957] 1967: 142), which further links it to the concerns of Leavis and *Scrutiny* as well as reflecting a long and nagging anti-Americanism associated with the debasement of popular culture. Particularly its efforts to come to grips with mass culture and resistance to it represent a second continuing concern of cultural studies.

Hoggart valued the novelist for bringing the reader close to working-class life, but the "complex and claustrophobic impression" that is left by certain novels, such as Lawrence's *Sons and Lovers,* and sociological surveys whose images are built up from additive models informs his central, and vastly influential, programmatic statement: "We have to try to see beyond the habits to what the habits stand for, to see through the statements to what the statements really mean (which may be the opposite of the statements themselves), to detect the differing pressures of emotion behind idiomatic phrases and ritualistic observances" ([1957] 1967: 18). The two major techniques he employs, which were to be thoroughly exploited by cultural studies, are literary analysis and ethnography. Certainly, one of his achievements was to extend literary critical methods to popular fields such as music, news media, and fiction. Ethnography, in this case, is a personal ethnography of his own working-class background.

Hoggart does not postulate an urban culture "of the people" that in the space of a generation gave way to a new mass culture, but rather that

> the appeals made by the mass publicists are for a great number of reasons made more insistently, effectively and in a more comprehensive and centralised form today than they were earlier; that we are moving towards the creation of a mass culture; that the remnants of what was at least in parts an urban culture "of the people" are being destroyed; and that the new mass culture is in some important way less healthy than the often crude culture it is replacing. ([1957] 1967: 23–24)

However, the "old" attitudes are resilient, neither dead nor simply confined to the older generation; they still form a highly present background to the lives of younger people.

The value judgments that punctuate the text and the absence of class as social relation and struggle situate it in the *Scrutiny* tradition and tend to set it apart from the lines of inquiry it inspired. Leavis's solution to Hoggart's "regrettable aspects of change" ([1957] 1967: 41) had been education, reminiscent of Richards and even Carlyle—a sort of downward imperialism: "We cannot, as we might in a healthy state of culture, leave the citizen to be formed unconsciously by his environment; if anything like a worthy idea of satisfactory living is to be saved, he must be trained to discriminate and to resist" (Leavis and Thompson 1933: 5). In contrast, Hoggart's work—rooted in the family, which, in turn, is inserted in a greater, dichotomous world of Them and Us—valorizes working-class culture itself with respect to massification and commercialization:

> The popular Press, for all its purported "progressiveness" and "independence," is one of the greatest conserving forces in public life today: its nature requires it to promote both conservatism and conformity. That these things have not so far had a more obviously harmful effect on the quality of people's lives is due to that capacity—one of the chief refrains of this essay—to live easily in compartments, to separate the life of home from the life outside, "real" life from the life of entertainment. ([1957] 1967: 196)

The popular arts are for use, and that use is pleasure. But this is also "a commercial racket, a money-making game at bottom." In a nutshell, "Liberty equals license to provide what will best increase sales; tolerance is equated with the lack of any standards other than those which are so trite and vague as to be almost wholly incantatory and of little practical use; any defence of any value is an instance of authoritarianism and hypocrisy" (197, 198–99). But the same mentality that keeps the Fleet Street wolves at bay turns back on working-class people in an insidious double-cross. They have turned into objects of competitive commerce, resulting in a "constant pressure not to look outwards and upwards . . . a new and stronger form of subjection . . . cultural subordination" (201).

Although evocative of popular cultural analyses to come, the contradiction between his "conflicting social and theoretical allegiances . . . from an affectionate account of the social function of popular culture to an evaluative critique of its textual forms" shows an "ambivalence about the class he has left and the limitations of the theoretical tradition he has joined" (G. Turner 1990: 49). Both his personal stake and theoretical limitations are observable in his refrain on the world of the "juke-box boys" ("perhaps . . . less intelligent than the average

... ground between the millstones of technocracy and democracy"), milk bars (which is, compared with "the pub around the corner, . . . a peculiarly thin and pallid form of dissipation, a sort of spiritual dry-rot amid the odour of boiled milk"), and his insistence that one does not need to be a reader of the *Times* to lead a good life ("There are other ways of being in the truth") (Hoggart [1957] 1967: 204, 276).

Certainly, the general issues surrounding analyses of popular culture using literary methods were to remain central to cultural studies. However, the implications of the approach as employed by Hoggart could not escape E. P. Thompson's insistent critique: the tendency to view working people as subjects, recipients, victims, data and the attendant inclination to regard cultural phenomena as autonomous of class power. "What is at issue is the mind of the working-class: its consciousness of itself, its knowledge of its own potential strength." Notwithstanding Hoggart's contention that the working-class world is resistant to change in a positive way, Thompson cited this presentation as precisely emphasizing the "passivity of the present-day working-class reader," thus inducing "a sense of hopelessness." Thompson points out the ahistorical foundation of the class and classlessness debate ("When has the working class *not* been 'built into the market'?") and identifies the same shortcomings in *The Uses of Literacy,* that is, "the misleading and anti-historical framework of the book" (1959a: 54, 52).

From a theoretical and methodological critique, Thompson quite characteristically passes directly to a call for political action to activate "positive forces which can only come from a vigorous socialist movement in which the political minority and the intellectuals make common cause." He specifies the goal to be attained as not "the jealous neighbourhood community which erects barriers" but the "socialist community which includes all" (1959a: 54). Reflecting the theoretical and methodological approaches associated with the differing political perspectives existing between Hoggart on the one side and Thompson (and Williams) on the other, this is obviously not the Them and Us that, despite the conservatism Hoggart recognizes, has for him positive, preservative, connotations.

Establishment Defied: Coming Together

In Hoggart, Williams, and Thompson, the elite, literary-critical tradition, drained of politics, intersected and melded with the theoretical and practical commitment to both politics and history at the popular level on the left. A renewed and refocused interest in the working class appeared as a common theme in the literature associated with the first New Left and claimed as formative by cultural studies: *Universities and Left Review* greeted Richard Hoggart's *Uses of Literacy* with four articles in a special section of its second issue in 1957. In the tradition of Leavis and *Scrutiny* and in reference to the "culture debate"—a continuity with a century and a half of humanistic (and conservative) social critique—Hoggart's recuperation of values and meanings contingent on the rejection, or upending, of the high/low culture distinction by reading working-class, popular, culture as a "text" was decisively innovative and informed New Left discussions of both the base-superstructure and class and classlessness questions in the 1950s. Also, *The Uses of Literacy* addressed the idea that cultural domination was replacing older forms of economic class power: "This subjugation promises to be stronger than the old because the chains of cultural subordination are both easier to wear and harder to strike away than those of economic subordination" ([1957] 1967: 201). Moreover, "old forms of class culture are in danger of being replaced by a poorer kind of classless, or . . . 'faceless,' culture . . . the emerging classless class" (280). Hoggart noted in another venue that "in some respects television would be the best instance of the emerging class culture" (1958: 122–23).

From "below," Hoggart was recuperating an urban working-class experience that was being undermined by commercialism and validating it in the face of elite cultural expressions. From "above," Williams was exposing the usurpation of texts of resistance and combating their appropriation by the forces of reaction. Both, however, were limited by the gradual exclusion of the politics of struggle from the tradition of criticism informing their work.

Thompson hailed from history and could never be accused of being anything but self-consciously a historian vis-à-vis the academy. Williams and Thompson shared a dedication to historical analysis inherent in Marxism, but neither Williams nor Hoggart seemed to be writing just history, or sociology, or literary criticism for that matter. Williams and Hoggart approached their subject matter from the humanities, but their work rejected disciplinary boundaries, and the rejection was reciprocal; they defied the disciplines, and the disciplines disavowed them. Well received for its distinction, conviction, and intellectual honesty, Hoggart's work did not fit into preestablished categories. His reviewers characterized his work as that of a "gifted amateur in a field where modern sociological techniques of inquiry seem inadequate for the task at hand" (Tropp 1958: 221), and "it must be said that this is not a report of professional social research. . . . [It] is primarily a product of sensibility" (Freidson 1958: 98). Hoggart was criticized as well for his "woman-centered" depictions (Corner

1991: 142). Arthur Calder-Marshall wrote, "Like Mr. Hoggart's *The Uses of Literacy*, Mr. Williams's *Culture and Society 1780–1950* and *The Long Revolution* are not works of scholarship but autobiographies of cultural displacement, disguised as objective studies" (1961: 217). But then *The Long Revolution* appeared "during the peak of the extremely violent press campaign against CND in the Labour party, while Gaitskell was vowing an all-out struggle against it. There was a sudden fear of the left which had not existed a few years earlier" (editors of *New Left Review*, quoted in R. Williams [1979] 1981: 134).

At the end of *The Long Revolution* Raymond Williams was notably less confident than he had been in the conclusion to *Culture and Society*. This lack of optimism is close to Hoggart: "Instead of the ritual indignation and despair at the cultural condition of 'the masses' . . . it is necessary to break through to the central fact that most of our cultural institutions are in the hands of speculators, interested not in the health and growth of the society, but in the quick profits that can be made by exploiting inexperience" (1961: 338). So what would a socialist society look like? State control? If so, then "we seem reduced to a choice between speculator and bureaucrat" (339). This allies Williams with Hoggart's view of the new commercialism.

The wider contemporary debate among British educators about popular culture, further stimulated by the expansion of television, was fleshed out at the National Union of Teachers Conference in 1960. Although Williams characterized the conference, "Popular Culture and Personal Responsibility,"[13] as "the most remarkable event of its kind ever held in this country" (1966: 7), women's issues went unexplored and race unmentioned, and to a great extent what Hoggart had called the "wider life," what audiences bring to their entertainments, was also largely ignored. The issues were the relations between schools and the mass media in actual practice. *Discrimination and Popular Culture*, edited by Denys Thompson (1964; a close collaborator of F. R. Leavis), reflected the dominant line of thinking at the conference. According to Stuart Laing, Thompson's argument "severed any links of determinacy between work and leisure and replaced a qualitative relationship with a quantitative one (if we spend more time in leisure than at work then leisure must be more important). . . . It was not so much media content as the very act of passive reception (rather than social interaction) that constituted the central danger" (1986: 212–13).

In *The Popular Arts*, published in 1964, Stuart Hall and Paddy Whannel advanced a minority position. It had roots in the authors' experiences in secondary education, and their line of argument, exploding the high/low culture divide, grew out of discussions of cinema and jazz (which they treated as serious endeavors) and how they articulated with students' cultural concerns and leisure activities. They are concerned with "actual quality" rather than "effects"; "the struggle between what is good and worth while and what is shoddy and debased is not a struggle *against* the modern forms of communication, but a conflict *within* these media. Our concern is with the difficulty which most of us experience in distinguishing the one from the other" (15). Increased spending power both fuels the youth culture and couples it to the media, and "at a deeper level, the use of the media to provide imaginative experiences through various forms of art and entertainment has a modifying impact upon young people's attitudes and values" (20).

But the process is not so simple or linear. Rejecting the assumed distinction between serious and popular arts—the educational and the entertaining, those deserving of study and those unworthy of critical discrimination—Hall and Whannel do not put all the blame on the providers for the debasement of standards. Drawing on Raymond Williams, they do not accept the "divorce between art and life," that is, between "work" subjects as preparation for making a living and "recreative" subjects emphasizing "creativity" and "appreciation." They also reject the "sharp distinction between ethical and aesthetic qualities. . . . In television and the cinema, as in literature, style carries the meaning; it is not the neutral dressing-up of subject matter" (S. Hall and Whannel 1964: 28, 30, 32). But because the authors do not see a uniform mass culture in opposition to traditional values, they argue that teaching should emphasize discrimination.

Although the similarities of *The Popular Arts* to the perspective of *Discrimination and Popular Culture* in devaluing television and rock music is indicative of the difficulties of striking out in new directions (already visible in *The Uses of Literacy*), by focusing on the issue of quality in the media, Hall and Whannel diverged radically from the majority position at the conference. At this point, we do not yet have a crisis in English studies: *Scrutiny* is still much the methodological touchstone, and the possibility of a canon, even if a changing or expanding one governed by a new set of exclusionary principles, remains intact. Nonetheless, the evaluation of Leavisism is double-edged, indicating a coming together of the long-term establishment tradition and the first New Left debates: Leavisism "contrasts the organic culture of pre-industrial England with the mass-produced culture of today. This is a perspective that has produced a penetrating critique of industrial society but as a guide to action it is restrictive" (S. Hall and Whannel 1964: 38–39). This was also a tradition based on the written word studied to fathom the author's intentions (Leavisism cast a far broader net than just "the words on the page"), but the new media cannot be taught so narrowly or defensively, and the purveyors of mass media products are not the only actors. The new media bring people together, according to Hall and Whannel, "in a new relationship as audiences, new kinds of language and expression are developed, independent art forms and conventions arise. The media are not the end-products of a simple technological revolution. They come at the end of a complex historical and social process, they are active agents in a new phase in the life-history of industrial society" (45). Responding to this assertion calls for a critical and evaluative approach: "We have to attend to the forms within which the new experiences are being presented, to discriminate between values, and to analyse our responses to them carefully" (46). Citing Leavis, and in a line that goes back to Matthew Arnold, Hall and Whannel consider criticism "a creative activity in the true sense," but again one that does not need to be defensive (47).

Well enough, the heady climate of the 1950s had produced an intellectual amalgam, but the kinds of questions addressed by *The Popular Arts* and the analytical perspective it exhibited proved inadequate to accommodate the changing cultural firmament of the 1960s. The unexamined ground on which that firmament was situated was the legacy of an exclusive, ethnocentric liberalism that had colonized both the left and the right, and it was on the verge of coming apart.

Liberalism Universalized: Order on the Right

The world-liberal compact constructed during the period of depression and declining global hegemony of Britain in the late nineteenth century maintained a precarious balance between free trade and empire, capital accumulation and human needs, with the emerging social sciences guaranteeing the empirical and ideological foundations of policy determination. This new commonsense consensus uniting left and right relied on strengthened state structures and piecemeal reform to guarantee order, that is, keep democratic tendencies in check. Its unstable equilibrium, based on the pledge of progress, prevailed for upwards of a century, until the 1960s, when its hollow promises right, left, and center were finally unmasked by those very groups on whose marginalization it had depended.

The problem of order in the social sphere, or perhaps more properly, the political question of control, had been an object of public intellectual contention in England at least since Thomas Hobbes had tried to come to grips with the civil disorders and regime reversals of the seventeenth century. The French

Revolution shattered all prospects of fulfilling Hobbes's dream of "perpetual order." The ideologies that arose "were the political agendas to be pursued *in the light of the normality of political change* and the correlative belief in popular sovereignty" (Wallerstein 1995: 94). Logically, conservatism was the first response. Burke's critique included the characterization of the French Revolution as a revolution in language and turned on an analysis of the meaning of terms (e.g., constitution). The very nature of the debate ensured the impossibility, Paine wrote, of "so much as the means of effecting a counterrevolution . . . it has never yet been discovered how to make a man *unknow* his knowledge, or *unthink* his thoughts" (quoted in Blakemore 1988: 69). The debate was pivotal, as revolutionary as the revolution, in establishing the credentials of literary activism in the form of social criticism and analysis in the struggles among competing groups as anti-laissez-faire conservatism was mirrored by radical ("liberal": all those who embraced the ideals of the French Revolution, progress, and popular sovereignty) demands for change.

In Britain, competing interests had converged in the great debates over free trade from the 1830s (both manufacturers and workers wanted cheaper bread). The Anti–Corn Law League was founded in 1838 and the defection of a contingent of Tories to the emerging Liberal coalition permitted the repeal of import duties on grain in 1846.[14] Two years later, the doctrine of mid-Victorian liberalism, that the state should refrain from intervening in the affairs of the individual, was codified in John Stuart Mill's *Principles of Political Economy,* and free trade and laissez-faire were consolidated during the midcentury economic expansion. By the time the events of the 1860s unfolded and played out through the great depression (rebellion in Jamaica and Ireland, agitation for franchise reform at home, and then the long crisis of capital accumulation), conservatives had already accepted as orthodoxy that protection was dead and that they would be unable to stem the tide of "negative" free trade measures in areas such as religious obligations and privileges, land transfers, and patronage.

Radicals wanted more democracy, an invocation of the sovereignty of the people that went back to the French Revolution and before. Conservatives despaired of ever winning another election if the electoral system were not changed to incorporate the upper strata of the commercial class and to revise the 1832 settlement that they believed, with justification, left them at a disadvantage. The Derby-Disraeli Reform Act from the Conservative side passed in 1867.[15] En route to passage, and in a series of interpretations that widened its application after it became law, it took on a life of its own. The electorate was almost doubled. This extension of the franchise—household suffrage—which included the secret ballot, was far from universal suffrage, even for males (women did not get the vote). It had, nonetheless, profound impact on both Conservative and Liberal politics.

To garner the new votes, Conservatives had to preach, and to some extent practice, social reform. To expand their appeal to the middle and lower middle classes during the 1870s, Tories advanced policies promoting progress in such areas as "artisans' dwellings, public health, Friendly Societies, river pollution, the sale of food and drugs, merchant shipping, trade unions, factories, drink licensing, and education" (Matthew 1988: 553). In their call for increased attention to social welfare, Liberals were pushed toward a stronger, more centralized and interventionist state apparatus. Even those such as Robert Lowe, who had vehemently opposed the Reform Bill (pairing "inequality" with the "order of providence"), accepted the inevitable and, as their ideal was the educated and experienced voter, concentrated on schooling for the newly enfranchised. The first step came with the Elementary Education Act of 1870, introduced by the advanced Liberal William Foster, Arnold's brother-in-law. The prevailing wisdom, all the same, viewed state intervention with extreme skepticism. Even in the area of public health, which touched rich and poor, lord and commoner alike, "in 1870 State intervention was accepted grudgingly and only after the accumulation of masses of evidence that continued inactivity did more damage to the free market than did action" (E. Evans 2001: 365).

Conservatives had called for order over the anarchy of laissez-faire and the disturbances it generated. Liberals responded with a conception of order involving a tense political and philosophical repositioning that encompassed the Conservative critique, the radical agitation, and the needs of capital. The "anarchy" of the black and the Irish experiences, both dosed with Victorian representations of the feminine as irrational, sentimental, childish, unrestrained, and overly sexualized, contributed to the long-term redefinition of freedom for all as freedom from confinement (conceived from the position of slavery and impressment) to freedom as liberty, political liberty sustained in rights and entailing responsibilities. The understanding was that this applied to the rational, disciplined, and self-sufficient subject who could be expected to preserve and uphold those rights and responsibilities—read middle-class male, individual, not Irish, not black, not female. An "ethic of improvement," as Eric Evans writes, made it "seductively easy . . . to espouse reform in the Gladstonian image, as a privilege which the respectable working man claimed by virtue of his superior skills and responsibility rather than as a right to be demanded"—a line taken even by the Reform Union (2001: 434).

Lines were clearly drawn. "*Sentiment,*" writes Arnold in 1866, is "the word which marks where the Celtic races really touch and are one . . . balance, measure, and patience are just what the Celt has never had," and again, "so eager for emotion that he has not patience for science." Arnold accentuates the femininity of the traits: "The sensibility of the Celtic nature, its nervous exaltation, have something feminine in them, and the Celt is thus peculiarly disposed to feel the spell of the feminine idiosyncrasy. . . . The Celt [is] undisciplinable, anarchical, and turbulent by nature" ([1866] 1962b: 343, 344, 347).[16] The language is very close to Carlyle's of 1849, in which he describes Quashee as "a pretty kind of man"; these blacks were "supple," "grinning," "dancing," "singing," "affectionate" (357–58). The antislavery campaign was "philanthropic," an arena associated with women, rather than political, the realm of male strength, independence, and action. Carlyle's hatred of philanthropy was "associated with the ways in which it weakened men and made them depend on others" (C. Hall 1989: 175). For Carlyle, the most important role in modern society was to be played by the hero, and in the antireform tract of 1867, "Shooting Niagara: and After?," his "Practical Hero" is in "life-battle with Practical Chaos"; "with every new Disciplined man . . . the arena of *Anti*-Anarchy, of God-appointed *Order* in this world and Nation" is widened ([1867] 1904c: 44, 45). Carlyle directly links pulling "down the railings of Her Majesty's Park, when her Majesty refuses admittance," with the Jamaica Committee and the sacrifice of Eyre by the government for Reform Bill votes (11).

The ardent supporter of reform and the most vocal advocate of prosecuting Eyre, John Stuart Mill retained a vision of an enlightened clerisy. Like Carlyle, he was an intellectual who valued disciplined intellectual work as a field on which distinction was to be won. His endorsement of universal suffrage, women included, came with property and other restrictions and a weighted voting system favoring the educated and the successful. Despite the fact that Mill had argued for a vision of a more egalitarian society, he accepted, writes Catherine Hall, "the particular form of individuality associated with masculinity, which was the common view of mid-nineteenth-century middle-class men, as being the norm to which all should aspire" (1989: 187).

Matthew Arnold's thought was flexible and ambiguous enough to forge a common bridge to the future for a wide spectrum of opinion, from those who wished to preserve past virtues to those convinced of the coming of a classless (but not necessarily egalitarian) society. He conceived of criticism as a special kind of social action. As a "Liberal of the future rather than a Liberal of the present" (Arnold [1880] 1973: 138), in his typical fashion, Arnold elides the contradictions among liberty, free trade, and inequality in favor of the civilizing influences of a particularly elite conception of conduct, beauty and manners, and growth in intellect and knowledge—order.

Bryan Cheyette exposes the potential and continuing importance of *Culture and Anarchy* for understanding the historical development of the contradictions of Liberal politics, the consequences for liberal philosophy, and the eventual transformation of the political language, by placing race at the very center of Arnold's project: the organizing opposition, "Hebraism and Hellenism," "exposes the competing needs of a universalist State, built on the foundations of an exclusivist national community."

> By emphasizing both the "essential unity of man" and, at the same time, the "scientific" or ethnographic basis of "semitic" racial difference—in opposition to "we English, a nation of Indo-European stock"—Arnold unwittingly exposes the central ambivalences at the heart of the liberal accommodation with its Jewish "other." It is precisely by foregrounding racial particularity that liberalism can lay claims to "civilize" or "universalize" the racial "others" that it "emancipates." (1993: 23, 19)

The advocate of sweetness and light was in fact much more in tune with the antidemocratic Carlyle than he would have admitted, and his organizing principle was carried forward in English prose and poetry well through the first half of the twentieth century.

In the wake of the events of the 1860s, emphasis in Liberal thought shifted from individualism and the "Nightwatchman State" to a concern for social welfare promoted by state intervention—both strands expressed in the Latin root *liber*. If, as Ian Bradley argues, a transformation from laissez-faire to a "socialist-style collectivism" is "fallacious," from at least the late 1880s Liberals did place "a much greater emphasis on the whole subject of social welfare" and the state itself began to take a "voluntaryist view" of its role (1985: 45, 50, 510). T. H. Green, the influential theorist of the "new liberalism" (the beginnings of which he situated in the Parliament of 1868, the first elected after the franchise reform of 1867), argued that "modern legislation" "with reference to labour, and education, and health, involving as it does manifold interference with freedom of contract, is justified on the ground that it is the business of the state, not indeed directly to promote moral goodness, for that, from the very nature of moral goodness, it cannot do, but to maintain the conditions without which a free exercise of the human faculties is impossible" ([1881] 1964: 56). Green was convinced that to save itself, the Liberal state had to transform itself. His theory of "positive freedom" linking the "various types of 'liberal legislation' as so many complementary ways of removing obstacles to the active power of men for self-development" grounded what would indeed develop into the philosophy of the "Welfare State" (Rodman 1964: 10, 8–9, 14).

Conservatives preached patriotism, property, and reform in appealing to the middle and working classes but held on as well to free trade. For Liberals, reform and the expansion of government control and intervention was at odds with laissez-faire, and the outcome of the anarchy and equality debates, heavily coded in terms of race and gender, placed Liberals, who nominally favored freedom and self-determination, in a difficult position when confronted with the practical questions of empire. Liberals split over home rule for Ireland in 1886. The defection of ninety-three MPs to the Tories and the rise of unionism and the Independent Labour Party in the 1890s announced the passing of real political alternatives.

During the first half of the twentieth century, the consensus, in the establishment of which the transformation of criticism had played a key role, was extrapolated worldwide in the form of Wilsonian "self-determination of nations" and Rooseveltian "economic development," the structural equivalents "of universal suffrage and the welfare state at the national level within the core zone." This was complemented by the Leninist program: "not world revolution but anti-imperialism plus socialist construction, which on inspection turned out to be mere rhetorical variants on the Wilsonian/Rooseveltian concepts" (Wallerstein 1995: 137–38). The heyday of this world-liberal compact lasted from 1945 until the upheavals of the late 1960s and coincided with the period of U.S. hegemony, tacitly sustained by the cold war and bolstered by the world economic expansion, which fueled expectations of progress through development.

In place of appeals to values, which had underpinned the politics of both the right and the left, the empirical, managerial social sciences increasingly ordered collective decision making, implementing Mill's suggestion that from the "science of society" comes "guidance" ([1843] 1988: 64). T. H. Huxley invoked the objective, value-neutral, problem-solving spirit of science to realize progress without moralism. The practical question was the replacement of the binary opposition of the Authority of Tradition to the Chaos of Radicalism with the benign synthesis of Ordered Change through Scientific Control. On the occasion of the opening of Sir Josiah Mason's Science College, Birmingham, in 1880, Huxley delivered a lecture that was an explicit challenge to Arnold. He believed that a scientific education was just as effective as a literary education in the acquisition of real culture, reminding his audience that humanism was not only a revival of letters but of science also. Nature, for Huxley, "is the expression of definite order with which nothing interferes . . . the chief business of mankind is to learn that order and govern themselves accordingly" ([1881] 1968: 150). Thus, "if the evils which are inseparable from the good of political liberty are to be checked, if the perpetual oscillation of nations between anarchy and despotism is to be replaced by the steady march of self-restraining freedom; it will be because men will gradually bring themselves to deal with political, as they now deal with scientific questions" (158–59). This certainly smacks of the "good management" invoked by Charles Curran in 1956.

Arnold responded to Huxley in the Rede Lecture at Cambridge in 1882. He agreed with the importance of knowing the "results of the modern scientific study of nature." It is part of "the best that has been thought and said in the world"; however, the physical sciences offer "*knowledge* only . . . knowledge not put for us into relation with our sense for conduct, our sense for beauty, and touched with emotion by being so put." Humane letters as the bearer of values can establish order, that is, "a relation between the new conceptions, and our instinct for beauty, our instinct for conduct." Letters, Arnold suggests, allow for drawing proper conclusions from scientific research and are a necessary aspect of progress toward his conception of order as "the need in man for conduct . . . the need in him for beauty" ([1882] 1974: 61, 65, 66, 73). As Park Honan points out, Arnold's "quarrel with Huxley had been smaller than critics and biographers later noticed: Arnold wanted *both* science and the arts studied widely" (1981: 416). Although Arnold defends poetry against religion, philosophy, *and* science, *Culture and Anarchy* evidences strong correlations with the ideals of nineteenth-century natural science. "He comes to believe in the existence of objective, universally valid moral and aesthetic laws, and to believe that these laws have been progressively revealing and developing themselves throughout the history of Western culture" (Carroll 1982: xiv). The conservatism of the project is grounded in an underlying empiricism in which he would have the critic stand apart as a neutral observer. Arnold also reduces science to an arid accumulation of facts and, in his quest for wholeness and completeness, calls on the poet as synthesizer: "Criticism thus stands in a position within culture similar to that of Arnold's ideal state in society: it rises above a multitude of petty particular interests in order to guard against any disturbances to the system as a whole" (Baldick 1983: 48).

In sum, social criticism was carried forward and solidified in pursuit of order, explicitly identified with culture by Matthew Arnold, and in opposition to the radicalism of the Reform movement and the revolts in Jamaica and

Ireland, identified with anarchy. As the century closed and the politics of social action were squeezed out of criticism, the social sciences took over the collective component of Arnold's project.[17] The activist criticism of the early nineteenth century was transformed via Arnold's espousal of order, "force till right is ready," in which he interpellated the state; Walter Pater's "internal flame" of disciplined contemplation focused in and on the individual; I. A. Richards's methodology of decontextualized close reading; and the elitism and neglect of history of Cambridge English and the *Scrutiny* circle grouped around F. R. and Q. D. Leavis. Nonetheless, although practical politics may have been expunged, values remained a primary consideration.

Hoggart found that a lack of sense either of past or future nourished a particular conception of progress in a meaninglessly changing present: "Like the clicking-over of lantern slides with no informing pattern . . . any change is a change for the better so long as it is in chronological succession" ([1957] 1967: 159)—hence the glorification of youth. It is not clear that "progressivism" has been a success, and science seems suspicious in the light of its power to harm. "If that is good which is the latest in the endless line and which meets the wishes of the greatest number, then quantity becomes quality and we arrive at a world of monstrous and swirling undifferentiation . . . to a world in which every kind of activity is finally made meaningless by being reduced to a counting of heads" (161). This harks back to Matthew Arnold's problematic of undifferentiation leading to "indifferentism," meaninglessness. All the same, *The Uses of Literacy* legitimated a return to class politics, albeit one based on the solidarities of backstreet life. If the cultural struggle and the political were indivisible, it was because the hierarchical division between Us and Them seemed an organizing principle of British social life (Samuel 1989: 56).

While Hoggart defends the values of the "order" of backstreet life, Williams bases his conclusion that "manufacture of an artificial 'working-class culture,' in opposition to . . . [a common language and intellectual and literary tradition], is merely foolish" ([1958] 1983: 321), on the implicit premise that working-class culture is an alternative to bourgeois culture. He associates this last with individualism and the concept of service that is no substitute for mutual responsibility, and links working-class culture to collective, social, and democratic initiatives and the concept of solidarity, potentially the real basis of a society. "In our culture as a whole, there is both a constant interaction between these ways of life and an area which can properly be described as common to or underlying both," and, Burke et al. aside, this has not been trampled down by any "swinish multitude" (327).

Although Williams recognizes clear lines of demarcation between bourgeois and working-class cultures, he specifies a "common culture" (beyond, above, the Them/Us divide). This common interest as true self-interest, in which individual verification lies in the community, puts a positive twist on a century and a half of social criticism, quite in line with his original project of reappropriation. Williams's working-class "solidarity" and middle-class "service" represent two corresponding interpretations of community, in practice opposed to one another but both likewise "opposed to bourgeois liberalism" ([1958] 1983: 328). But community quite belongs to the "tradition"; so, in the end, order was served, if backhandedly.

Even so, if order was served its foundational elements were severely beleaguered. As the tradition(s) out of which cultural studies emerged floundered, the institutional base at Birmingham, to which we now turn, flowered; but no new theoretical perspective had yet come forward to secure future work. The deployment of a new critical effervescence, like the rejuvenation of the political project, would have to await the wide-ranging challenges to the epistemological foundations and institutional structures of knowledge production that accompanied the world-scale assault on the liberal consensus by women, colonial subjects, and people of color at the core of the events of 1968.

PART TWO From Alliance to Bandwagon

CHAPTER 3

Centre for Contemporary Cultural Studies I

An increased respect for the life of language, and for the unpremeditated textures of experience—how are these qualities, which a training in English ought to encourage, valued in contemporary society? In what ways might a literary person concern himself with them today?

—RICHARD HOGGART, "Schools of English and Contemporary Society"

Put crudely, Althusser enabled one to take institutions and ideas seriously while still genuinely retaining a belief in the reality of class struggle and revolution.

—COLIN MACCABE, "Class of '68: Elements of an Intellectual Autobiography, 1967–81"

Mimesis, for some reason, can copy but cannot originate or create. The "adoption" of other traditions—that is, adoption which has not been fully worked through, interrogated, and translated into the terms of our own traditions—can very often mean no more than the evacuation of the real places of conflict within our own intellectual culture, as well as the loss of real political relations with our own people.

—E. P. THOMPSON, foreword to *The Poverty of Theory*

During the mid-1960s, with the political project of the first New Left at an impasse and the quest for theory foraging beyond the national setting, it was in the academic context that the alliance developed between the conservative tradition of social critique and literary-critical methods and the New Left concern for a positive, and political, reevaluation of popular culture and individual agency. In different ways, both were humanist; both emphasized values. The early years of the institutionalization of cultural studies, coinciding with the establishment of the Centre for Contemporary Cultural Studies at the University of Birmingham in 1964 by Richard Hoggart and his tenure as director, extended the program begun in *The Uses of Literacy.* That is, popular culture, or working-class culture assailed by mass culture, was distinguished from elite or middle-class culture(s) and read through the methodological lenses of the literary-critical tradition.

And then there was 1968. Although the student movement in Britain may have been a "puny specimen" (Widgery 1976: 305), in the view of Laurence Harris, an economist who participated, "it was a time 'of great rationality and consideration' leading to important theoretical developments in social science departments during the 1970s" (Caute 1988: 367). Just as the impact of the theoretical importations of continental Marxism, structuralism, and semiotics were beginning to be felt and new concerns, those of women and racial minorities, began to be explored, in 1969 CCCS lost its founding director and Stuart Hall was named acting director. These were the fuels that propelled the political activism of the late 1960s into the 1970s as the voices of repressed groups intruded on the masculinist, white discourses of working class and state in conjunction with serious reflection on the ideological sphere.

In 1979, CCCS again got a new director and for the first time found itself without either of its original animators. If, however, there was an increased emphasis on history and history writing (certainly, in part, as autocritique), as during the 1970s there had been on explorations of theory (away from humanism and toward science), the salient features of the work issuing from the Centre through the 1980s preserved the initial commitment to collective, interdisciplinary inquiry. This work would be based on a heterogeneity of theoretical and methodological tools and dedicated to cultural analyses of relationships of domination and subordination, anchored in concrete, empirical studies devoted especially to contemporary Britain.

For three decades, British cultural studies would manifest a characteristic disciplinary openness informing its analyses of cultural change and reflect a dominant national orientation characteristic of two centuries of concern for the Condition-of-England Question.

The Founding Moment

In British universities in the early 1960s, the culture and civilization/society debate was largely missing in English departments, and in the social sciences most of the work done on literature and art was "external to the nature and the experience of literature itself, for the writer or the reader" (Hoggart 1992: 93). Raymond Williams mused that his enterprise went beyond the "limits of any kind of academic prudence, for what seems to me the good reason that there is no academic subject within which the questions I am interested in can be followed through" (1961: ix). The opportunity to address the "pressure for these questions [that] was not only personal but general" (x) came in 1961, when Richard Hoggart was approached to occupy a second chair in English at the University of Birmingham.

On the postgraduate side, Hoggart wanted to set up a center of what he described as contemporary cultural studies—"contemporary," writes Colin MacCabe, "because of objections of classicists who claimed they were already engaged in the study of culture" (1992b: 1). The establishment of the center was central in Hoggart's move to Birmingham "because not to use a professor's position to try to advance the interests which had emerged in the writing of *The Uses of Literacy* would have been to throw away for the sake of a title what now seemed professionally most important" (1992: 77–78). Money for the cccs project came from Allen Lane of Penguin, plus a little from Chatto and the *Observer*.[1] Hoggart hired Stuart Hall to fill the research post, and the opening of the Centre for Contemporary Cultural Studies was announced for the spring of 1964.[2]

During the early years at cccs, literature was experienced "in and for itself" by "reading for tone" and "reading for value" as mechanisms for the extraction of the aesthetic, psychological, and cultural elements (produced in a certain kind of society at a certain period) to find "what field of values is embodied, reflected or resisted." Works of art are bearers of meaning; there "is no such thing as 'a work of art in itself.' " Thus the major assumptions are:

> that a society bears values, cannot help bearing values and deciding their relative significance; that it makes what seems like a significant or ordered whole out of experience, a total and apparently meaningful view of life; that it embodies these structures of values in systems, rituals, forms; that it lives out these values expressively, in its actions and its arts; that this living out of values is a dialectical process, never complete, always subject to innovation and change; and that no one individual ever makes a perfect "fit" with the dominant order of values of his culture. (Hoggart [1969] 1970a: 160–63)

Of course, the elite tradition did not simply evaporate: in 1966 Hoggart contended that "without appreciating good literature no one will really understand the nature of society," even though "literary critical analysis can be applied to certain social phenomena other than 'academically respectable' literature." Hoggart also remained captivated by the scientific mode: "Literary critical analysis of the mass arts is not a substitute for social scientific analysis but a useful—an essential—adjunct." But he continues to distinguish between high and mass arts: "Great art tells us infinitely more" (1966: 225, 242, 247). Such were the frontiers within which the early work at cccs developed and an impressive academic track record was soon established. Of course, with institutionalization came trade-offs. Stuart Laing assesses the mid-1960s turning point: pressed by the theoretical challenge of the new generation of the New Left, Hoggart and Williams proceeded to revise their positions just as cultural studies was "creating more sophisticated analyses of media content. . . . Crucially that sense of the immediate pressure to connect cultural analysis to the whole life experience and situation of working-class people, which the perspective from adult education had enforced, had been lost" (1986: 217).

The work of this early period is exemplified in the textual analysis that both confidently manifests the best of the theoretical and methodological past and tentatively announces the future. *Paper Voices,* by A. C. H. Smith, written with Elizabeth Immirzi and Trevor Blackwell (1975) and including an introduction by Stuart Hall, extends the engagement of the 1950s New Left with contemporary social change and deploys a full panoply of literary-critical methods.[3] As Hall tells us, there were "two main purposes: to examine how the popular press interprets social change to its readers; and to explore and develop methods of close analysis as a contribution to the general field of cultural studies" (11). *Paper Voices* covers the period of the depression and the war through the affluent and then the permissive society. Including in-depth studies of the elections of 1945, 1955, and 1964, it analyzes the rhetoric of two British newspapers, the *Daily Express* and the *Daily Mirror,* by looking at patterns of daily content, of overt appeals, opinions, and biases as a "shaping force" and treats underlying meaning-structures as the residues of long habitual practice. The hypothesis is that

> alongside any day's "news," there is a continuous and evolving *definition of what constitutes news* at any significant historical moment. . . . Against the main weight of sociological practice, we approached the newspaper as a structure of meanings, rather than as a channel for the transmission and reception of news. Our study, therefore, treated newspapers as *texts:* literary and visual constructs, employing symbolic means, shaped by rules, conventions and traditions intrinsic to the use of language in its widest sense. (16–17)

Indeed, a reading of *Paper Voices* validates Hall's statement that cultural studies "requires us to *work back* to the social and historical process *through* the necessary mediations of form and appearance, format, rhetoric and style" (21). Catherine Ann Cline concluded that the book "added a new dimension to the study of the press." But she qualified that assertion by noting that the "premise that the personality of a newspaper is a product of unconscious assumptions rather than of deliberate policy can only be established in conjunction with more traditional studies based on the papers of editors" (1976: 865).

Owed to Hoggart are the allusions to "reading for tone" and the language of the Us/Them divide employed as an organizing theme in the description of the *Mirror*: "Us/Them consciousness, with deep roots in working-class mistrust of shadowy authority" (A. Smith 1975: 67), recalls *The Uses of Literacy*. Raymond Williams's work, which had also been concerned with the press, is cited as foundational; however, *Paper Voices* is situated a step advanced from the aspects of communications developed by Williams, which, as method, belonged to the humanist literary-critical tradition (*Culture and Society* and *The Long Revolution*) or were based on historical and content analysis (*Communications*). If, as Phillip Whitehead observed, *Paper Voices* bears "the indelible influence of Stuart Hall" (1975: 683), it must be due to a move beyond Williams's position (in which determinism either dissolved in ubiquity or ended up in ad hoc formulations) with the introduction of such concepts as "codes of signification" and "a structure of complex *codes* for giving 'the news' significance" (A. Smith 1975: 19, 21). Thus, *Paper Voices* exhibits links with the past and announces the beginning of a shift toward the theoretical and methodological dispositions that would characterize the work at CCCS during the decade of the 1970s.

1968 and After: Britain and Birmingham

In 1964, Perry Anderson identified a "profound, pervasive but cryptic crisis" in Britain of which a series of books on the "condition of England question" catalogued the symptoms without offering any analysis (26). Given the corporate ideology of the English working class, even in the event of a Labour government no "challenge of an immediate socialist transformation of English society" was in the offing, Anderson wrote, for "there can be no socialism without an authentic socialist movement" (53).[4] By 1968, Anderson was still saying that a "revolutionary culture is not for tomorrow. But a revolutionary practice within culture is possible and necessary today. The student struggle is its initial form" (57). The priorities were "the fight against the authoritarianism of universities and colleges, alliance with the working-class and struggle against imperialism. . . . There is, however, another front which will have eventually to be opened. This is a direct attack on the reactionary and mystifying culture inculcated in universities and colleges, and which it is one of the fundamental purposes of British higher education to instil in students" (3).

In contrast with the United States, where there was a civil rights movement to draw on, the movement in Britain both emerged later and withered sooner. But like the movement in the United States and on the continent, questions of radical politics were reopened by events in the international sphere, and the university became a central arena of political activity.

Galvanized by Vietnam, 1968 in Britain was part of a broad, and worldwide, student movement that, however, as in Germany and unlike the movements in Italy, France, and Northern Ireland, failed to "catalyse other social constituencies to action that seriously challenged the existing social order" (Fraser: 1988, 231).[5] The late 1960s were punctuated by the appearance, and rapid disappearance, of single-issue campaigns (squatting, community affairs, immigration, workers' control). The Vietnam Solidarity Committee (VSC) campaign was also short-lived, but did manage in 1968 to attract a mass base, much as CND had on the issue of the bomb. Despite the dubious, and originally misinterpreted, outcome of the Tet offensive, it symbolized, as an Olivier Todd interview (1968) in *New Left Review* would be titled, that "the Americans are not invincible"; in fact, "they are fighting not merely to maintain a puppet régime in Saigon, but to show that attempts to wrest from imperialism one of its possessions cannot pay" ("Themes" 1968: 1). "Vietnam dominates the whole international political situation," Göran Therborn intoned, and he quoted the secretary-general of the North Vietnamese Communist Party to the effect "that: 'The Vietnamese Revolution is part of the world revolution and its success cannot be dissociated from that of the world revolution' " (1968: 3).

In March 1968, twenty-five thousand marchers converged on the U.S. Embassy in Grosvenor Square to protest the war. As Nina Fishman recalls, the point was "that it was unexpected on both sides. This is where CND is left in the past, because as opposed to making token or symbolic protest in Grosvenor Square you were really having a go." One hundred thousand demonstrated in October, but it was "very much more a set piece" (quoted in J. Green 1988: 241). Sustaining momentum and defining short-term strategy proved to be insurmountable problems, even though a profile of the demonstrators did show that the movement "had mobilized support in new social groupings" (Fraser 1988: 280).[6] The failure to place demands on Labour effectively stymied the movement at a time, as Tariq Ali recounts, when the establishment unleashed a black propaganda campaign "to isolate the march from the bulk of the population by raising the fear of violence—an old trick. . . . France shook the ruling classes throughout Europe, and the British decided to take no chances that the disease would spread. Hence the ferocious attacks on vsc—*The Times* put its crime reporters onto covering it—and on me personally. I was the foreigner, the black, the evil in our midst" (quoted in Fraser 1988: 279). Julian Nagel made a parallel assessment:

> The attack is not mainly against the contents of lectures and seminars but also against the organisation of institutions of higher learning and the mass media in general. The extent to which the latter are manipulated by small groups of people heavily committed to preserve the established order became apparent . . . in the distorted reports about incidents of student unrest . . . reasons why students criticise the established society and the ways in which they have become increasingly self-critical are seldom made the object of analysis. (1969: n.p.)

Tom Fawthrop's contention that "bureaucrats fear nothing more than spontaneity—people acting for themselves" (1968: 59) (apropos of the student demonstrations at Hull) is easily extrapolated to the whole of establishment reaction to the movement.

Student uprisings began at the London School of Economics in 1966. Unlike the violent eruptions that were paraded by the press, the demonstrations usually followed peaceful pressure and petitions ignored by university administrations. From late 1967 through 1968, sit-ins were staged at Regent Street Polytechnic, the Holborn College of Law and Commerce, and at Leicester. There was also a demonstration at Aston University, Birmingham. At Oxford, turmoil erupted over regulations and reforms, and at Cambridge, the union overwhelmingly rejected violence. More serious confrontations occurred at Hull, Hornsey College of Art, and Essex. In each case, it was the structure of the university itself that was contested. David Triesman, a leading activist at Essex, where "occupation was sparked off by an American-style factor: war-related recruitment on campus by a scientist from the government's germ warfare establishment" (Fraser 1988: 273), spelled out the strategy: "Universities are linked to a set of productivity norms which, in order to be met, need a system as authoritarian as any other factory. Expose that, by linking it with outside repressive forces, police, demands for action from the University Grants Committee and so on, and the first cracks will appear in the façade" (Triesman 1968: 71). Even though the sit-in was finally ended by ballot at Hull, 635 students, reflecting the euphoria of the times, voted to continue it. Serious confrontations persisted through 1969 at the London School of Economics, where the new chairman of the governors "issued a strong statement warning academic staff that they risked dismissal if they encouraged or took part in disorderly conduct." Members of the academic staff in turn called Robins's attention to "Article 28 of the school's Articles of Association: No member was to be punished for expressing *opinions* on any subject" (Caute 1988: 364).

Birmingham was not immune to the fever of 1968. The vice-chancellor was imprisoned in his office during an eight-day occupation and, eventually, even the Federation of Conservative Students supported the sit-in (Caute 1988: 365). The negotiated resolution gave students representation, but not the vote, on most committees. Hoggart recalls "some of the Top Brass simply assumed that the centre's graduates were the main group behind the disturbances, and probably their initiators. Our people did play a big part once the troubles began." The students "wished to see the university as a moral community"; nothing, however, "bore comparison with . . . the events of 1968 in Paris, which almost brought down the government"; nor would the troubles have anything "like the violent edge of continental or American uprisings." At Birmingham, the disturbance "focussed, rightly, on the enclosed way the university was run, on its failure to respond to questions about other ways of running a university or about its links with government, industry and commerce" (1992: 92, 137–38).

The year 1968 was also that of Hoggart's departure for UNESCO. Initially he was to stay for three years, but when the invitation was extended for a full five years, he resigned his post at Birmingham in favor of Stuart Hall. Profiting from the occasion, the vice-chancellor, "perhaps influenced by a peculiar letter in a weekly journal which claimed the centre was promoting left-wing propaganda," called for an external review before confirming either the Centre's continued existence or the appointment of a new director (Hoggart 1992: 99). Essentially, the report was very favorable. The value of the CCCS project was endorsed and Hall was confirmed as the new director.

Eventually, Hall too left Birmingham, for a chair in sociology at the Open University (assumed in 1979). He was replaced by historian Richard Johnson just at "the start of the series of increasingly severe cuts in university funding." Some in English would have been glad to see CCCS disappear, either because they were uncomfortable with cultural studies or because they resented its popularity, and CCCS migrated to the "more hospitable" faculty of social sciences in January 1988 (Hoggart 1992: 100).

The concern for theory in the 1970s was intense at CCCS. In 1969, Hoggart mentioned history, psychology, social psychology, and sociology as disciplines with which cultural studies needed to forge links. Referring to the work of Lévi-Strauss, he suggested that "the way in which an anthropologist reads the meanings of myths in primitive societies and relates them to beliefs and tensions within those societies can help with the reading of television soap-operas as much as of earlier folk-literature." Hoggart's next statement would have far-reaching consequences for work at CCCS: "The case for more interest in structuralism follows naturally. . . . Even more urgent is the case for semiology, since we do not have languages or codes to discuss many of the expressive phenomena of mass society" ([1969] 1970a: 16). Structuralism challenged the dominant epistemologies of both history and the social sciences and even, according to a 1978 editorial in *History Workshop,* represented a "mainly left-wing response to the collapse, or questioning, of evolutionary and humanist notions of progress" (Editorial 1978: 2). As such, it formed both the substance for the reexamination of conceptual bases of inquiry, the "humanist" bent of abstracting texts from social practices and institutional sites (Hall: 1980a), and one pole in a furious debate.

The major 1978 publication *On Ideology* is testimony to work that went far beyond Hoggart's "more interest."[7] Its importance lies not only in the detailed dissections of the most advanced theoretical positions informing cultural studies at the time, but in the risks taken in advancing new positions. Strikingly, the authors admit that "as part of a marxist problematic, a theory of ideology is both a centrally important area of study within the more general category of 'cultural studies,' yet has a theoretical coherence which the latter manifestly lacks." However, no accounts are given of racism, sexism, nationalism, or political ideologies as such. Nonetheless, there is a recognition of the importance of a theoretical self-consciousness, given the heterogeneity of approaches in cultural studies work and the notion that culture includes elements that "cross different theoretical terrains only one of which is that of a theory of ideology" (Centre for Contemporary Cultural Studies 1978: 6).

Stuart Hall opens the volume with a historical profile, "The Hinterland of Science: Ideology and the 'Sociology of Knowledge,'" which leads up to and introduces imports of continental theory. Hall contrasts the absence of interest in ideology in the Anglo-American tradition, related to the absence of any confrontation with Marxist concepts, with the active concern in European thought. Examples from Destutt de Tracy and Comte suggest that "from its modern inception, the concept of 'ideology' has been shadowed by its 'Other'— Truth, Reason, Science . . . [and] something central about ideas will be revealed if we can discover the nature of the determinacy which *non*-ideas exert over ideas" (CCCS 1978: 10).

Hall reviews idealist, historicist, and vitalist traditions. Then, looking at phenomenology, he writes that although Sartre's language is different, the arguments are rooted in the same problematic as the sociology of Alfred Schutz: "the Subject-Object dialectic [that] always testifies to the unexorcised 'ghost of Hegel.' . . . We are no longer concerned with the relation *between* social knowledge and social relations. Social relations are conceived *as,* essentially, structures of knowledge." This is the form in which the "sociology of knowledge" has been most influential in American sociology. Treatment in terms of historical roots, classes, and specific conjunctures and the relationships with other instances of the social formation have been lost, as has the function of ideology (CCCS 1978: 20–21).

For Marx, the historical development of society could not be reconstructed from thoughts and ideas, and accounting for why these arise remains a problem for Marxism. Schutz's concern for "how thought gained an objective facticity in the world, and thus, by shaping human actions, affected how reality was constructed" pointed to "another—and quite unexpected—convergence: a *rendezvous* of phenomenology with the tradition of positive social science as represented by Durkheim and his 'school' . . . which rejected the Germanic nonsense about ideas" (CCCS 1978: 21–22). This leads Hall into an overview of the development of structuralism: when Claude Lévi-Strauss "declared that the centrepiece of Social Anthropology would be the study of 'the life of signs at the heart of social life,' he was able to defend this enterprise as nothing more nor less than the resumption of the 'forgotten part of the Durkheim-Mauss programme' " (23).

Linguistics endowed structuralism with the promise of generating a truly scientific study of culture. The classical "structural" themes in social anthropology had considered observable structures, institutional order. Lévi-Strauss transformed this into a pursuit of deep structures, systems of relations among terms on the model of language. Both the primitive bricoleur and the modern engineer engaged in the universal activity, with synchronic and transhistorical rules, of making things mean—signification. The question (speaking of totemism) was no longer *What is* totemism? but *How* are totemic phenomena *arranged?* "This represents what some would define as the principal transformation which structuralism as a method effects. . . . It is the internal arrangement of the field of classification which has been made to 'ressemble' the internal classification of the field of natural objects and men. 'The resemblance is between these two systems of differences.' It is not the 'resemblances but the differences which resemble one another'" (CCCS 1978: 25). No longer was analysis to be directed at the contents of symbolic forms or their relationship to who conceived them; the aim of structuralism was "to *crack the code.*" This is "the moment of the formation, within the sphere of the study of culture and ideology, of a quite distinctive problematic, based on an altogether different notion of causal relationship between social and mental categories . . . 'structuralist causality'" (26).

Hall again traces the intellectual pedigrees since the 1950s. The first is Marxist structuralism, especially in the work of Louis Althusser, treated later in the book. The second is semiotics, the science of systems of signs. Roland Barthes, inverting Saussure's notion of all sign systems belonging to a general science of linguistics, declared that linguistic systems were just one of a wide field of sign systems. "Unlike Lévi-Strauss, Barthes retained the concept of 'ideology' as distinct from the general concept of *culture,* but it was the latter which constituted the proper object of 'the science of signs.' Ideologies were only the particular 'uses' of particular signification systems in a culture, which the dominant classes appropriated for the perpetuation of their dominance" (CCCS 1978: 27). This first phase of semiotics reached a high point with Barthes's "Myth Today" (in *Mythologies* [1957] 1972) "one of the few seminal treatments of the relationship between signification and ideology" (27). Jacques Lacan's rereading of Freud, Freud of the language of dreams, along with the work of Julia Kristeva, marks a break with this first phase by concentrating on the "'positioning of the subject' *in* ideology" rather than on the "terrain of ideologies arising from specific historical structures and objectivated in social representations and in public languages." Semiotics, Hall asserts, had contributed to an understanding of how systems of signification work but stopped short of analyses articulating this closed field (amenable to positivist inquiry) to social practices and historical structures. On the other hand, the materialist theory of ideology that addresses "socio-historic determinations *on* ideas" lacks a theory of representation, "without which the specificity of the ideological region cannot be constituted" (28).

Hall also addresses the work of Pierre Bourdieu, for whom Lévi-Strauss had effected a Kantian synthesis in taking the internal relations of classifications as the object of analysis. Marxism, in its emphasis on the political functions of symbolic systems treating "logical relations as relations of power and domination," represented another synthesis. Bourdieu considers both inadequate. He "wants to treat the problem in terms of the mutual articulation of two discontinuous fields" (cccs 1978: 29). Not the elements, but positions, relations, produce meaning, not only within fields (social, ideological) but among fields as well, each reproducing other fields in reproducing itself.

At this juncture, the difficulty in developing an adequate Marxist theory of ideology is that of Marxist theory as such; that is, according to Hall,

> of holding on to "both ends of the chain" at once: the relative autonomy of a region (e.g. ideology) and its "determination in the last instance" (i.e. the determinacy of ideology by other instances, and, in the last instance, by the economic). It is the necessity to hold fast to the latter protocol which has, from time to time, sanctioned a tendency to *collapse* the levels of a special formation—especially, to collapse "ideas" or ideology *into* "the base" (narrowly defined as "the economic"). On the other hand, it is the requirement to explore the difficult terrain of "relative autonomy" (of ideology) which has given the field of ideology its awkward openness. It is through this gap—to borrow a recent metaphor of Althusser's—that the "pup" of semiology continues to "slip between the legs" of a Marxist theory of ideology. (cccs 1978: 29–30)

With this overview, Hall has positioned the reader for the reception given continental theoreticians at cccs.

No matter how much the development of Marxist theory at cccs in the 1970s may have been favored by the departure of Richard Hoggart, "an avowed opponent of Marxism," as Colin Sparks says, "the popularity of Louis Althusser in Britain was, one might say, overdetermined" (1977: 23, 22). Sparks's analysis of the relationship of 1968 and the in-depth encounter at Birmingham with theoretical Marxism, of which Althusser's was only one in a constellation, turns on two points: the exhaustion of Fabian reformism and the impotence of both the liberal-conservative intellectual tradition *and* the "narrow 'technocratic' protagonists of expansion" in higher education in providing "any serious critical perspective on British society." Both were in agreement that something was awry, but the analyses they undertook formed a closed binary opposition. Any alternative had to come from outside the academy. Of those that were tried, Marxism, unlike the others, "provided an activist perspective which, over time, was bound to win out against the fundamental tendencies towards quietistic individualism which lay at the root of the competitors" (20).

The role of the industrial proletariat, workers movement, and Labour Party were widely questioned by 1968. Solutions seemed to lie either in Marcuse's mixture of practical activity with a highly abstract critical enterprise or a rejection of original analysis entirely, Sparks explains. This second was hardly attractive, but such forms of political action as student and black unrest were outside, "and to a considerable extent in opposition to, the concerns and organisations which had long characterised Marxist politics." Given their instability and ineffectiveness, there was, hence, "an inbuilt tendency in the vision of Marxism adopted by this current to theoreticism, which was once again reinforced by the very real pressures of earning one's living. The ground was well-prepared for a Marxism which systematically evaded the squalid concerns of political parties, trade unions, and all the rest of the baggage of marxist orthodoxy, and which elevated debates on culture, epistemology, etc to the centre of theoretical concern" (Sparks 1977: 22). More broadly, structuralism responded to a situation in which any revolutionary optimism and voluntarism of European Marxists was undermined by the "relative stability of capitalism in the advanced industrial nations, the peculiarities of the Chinese revolution, [and] the growing disarray in the world Communist movement" (Editorial 1978: 4).

It should be of little surprise that E. P. Thompson had a different take on the situation. "Voluntarism," he wrote in critique, "crashed against the wall of the cold war. . . . In the West our heads were thrown against the windscreen of capitalist society; and that screen felt like—*a structure.*"

> The vocabulary of structuralism was given by the seeming "common sense," the manifest appearances, of three decades of Cold War stasis. And in its most pervasive accents, this has been a *bourgeois* vocabulary, an apologia for the *status quo* and an invective against "utopian" and "maladjusted" heretics. By the 1950s structuralisms—sometimes the product of lonely minds working in prior contexts—were flowing *with* the stream, and replicating themselves on every side as ideology: psychology was preoccupied with "adjustment" to "normality," sociology with "adjustment" to a self-regulating social system, or with defining heretics as "deviants" from "the value-system" of the consensus, political theory with the circuits of psephology. (1978c: 266)

Without question, however, Gramsci and Althusser were central to the development of work at the Centre. Their importance is apparent in the chapters devoted to them in *On Ideology* and in the concrete studies they informed. Overall, the assimilation of imported theory, from Lukács to Gramsci, Althusser, and Poulantzas in *On Ideology* and semiotics and psychoanalysis in *On Ideology* and *Culture, Media, Language,* to established traditions, would produce and reproduce the eclectic mix typical of work at cccs.

Stuart Hall, Bob Lumley, and Gregor McLennan (cccs 1978: 45–76) explore Gramsci's problematic, which was "geared primarily towards political perspectives and analyses rather than general epistemological principles" (45). Breaking with the economism of the Second International and the cultural/idealist tradition of Croce, Gramsci deployed a number of concepts articulating the base-superstructure model. Civil society, between the economic structure and the state, "is the terrain in which classes contest for power (economic, political and ideological)." Here hegemony, including but not reducible to ideology, is exercised, and "the terms of the relations of the structure and superstructure are fought out" (47). Politics occupies its own level in the superstructure, and it is with an analysis of the political that Gramsci conceives of ideology. Not a question of truth or falsehood, ideology "serves to 'cement and unify' the social bloc" (48).

Gramsci "is perhaps the first marxist to seriously examine ideology at its 'lower levels' as the accumulation of popular 'knowledges' and the means of dealing with everyday life—what he calls 'common sense'" (cccs 1978: 49). Because it is unsystematic, common sense can combine contradictory knowledges; it is based on the "'naturalization' process, which for Marx was central to bourgeois Political Economy" (50). From Gramsci's "complex historicism," argue the authors, arises a need to reexamine the idea of "a theoretical equivalence between *reducing* theories and ideologies to their historical conditions of existence, and *relating* theories and ideologies to such conditions. The latter, it seems to us, is a proposition of marxism; the former is not" (72). They see Gramsci as playing a "*generative* role," but detect an uneven appropriation of his ideas by Althusser and Poulantzas, the "structuralist marxists," who proceed by dismantling historicist conceptions (57).

Althusser's work is characterized by Gregor McLennan, Victor Molina, and Roy Peters (cccs 1978: 77–105) as "the most significant contribution to marxist theory in many years" (77). Arguing for theoretically grounded critiques of Stalinism, economism, and overly humanist interpretations of Marx, Althusser focuses on the "social formation." In this structured complex whole, a unity of levels or instances rather than an expressive totality, "the superstructures exist as the essential conditions" of its existence and "historical materialism is the science of the history of social formations" (79). Political and ideological levels impinge directly on the reproduction of the mode of production and have an overdetermining capacity enjoying a relative autonomy from the economic level.

Throughout Althusser's work, "the notion that a science has to break with its ideological preconditions is fundamental" (CCCS 1978: 98–99). But as critics hold, the "idea that science is ideology-free is simply nonsense. . . . Althusser, therefore, is to be rejected on the basis that his positions are a retreat from marxism itself: conceived not as pure knowledge, but as critical science, a revolutionary weapon asserting the primacy of class *practice*" (100). In his self-criticism, Althusser repudiates the position of philosophy as the guarantor of science as untenable but retains the position of science and ideology. Yet the tension between "ideology conceived as the epistemological antithesis to science-in-general and conceived as an intrinsic element of the structure or fabric of social formations" may be irresolvable (103). Nonetheless, the "seemingly mythical ground of 'relative autonomy'—whatever its problems—remains an inhabitable position with respect to Althusser's intervention, and, indeed, to marxism itself conceived as a scientific analysis of social formations" (104).

The persistence of the two faces of analysis, ideology in general and ideologies in specific social formations, in Althusser's work is due to the necessity of structural features common to all ideology, identified as "placing a constitutive and constituted Subject at the centre of history, theory, ethics, individuality" (CCCS 1978: 99). But Marx's theoretical account is of social relations, not the development of the individual, according to Victor Molina (230–58): "Marx's conceptualization is one about *relations* and not about the *subjects* which stand in these relations . . . because . . . in general, relations can be established as existing only by being *thought*, as distinct from the subjects which are in these relations with each other." Thus, his analysis is not "*of* individuals but it is a reality within which they *stand*" (235, 237). The problem of individuals as such is not present in Marx, but they do appear as personifications, bearers of economic categories. For Molina, the real status of the category in Marx is that of Luporini's "*naked* individuals" or, as formulated by Althusser, as "*supports* of social relations." "At the center of this polemic is a heavily criticised thesis: that of Althusser about Marxism being, theoretically, *an anti-humanism*. . . . Paradoxically, there is nothing in Althusser's work which can be interpreted as a *closing* of a problematic of 'individuality'" (241, 243).

"Socialist humanism" involves a negation of the specificity of Marx's theory; it defends the "protocols of an idealist interpretation of history and class struggle" (CCCS 1978: 247). The "*methodological axis* of Socialist Humanism involves the formulation of *theoretical* equilibrium in opposition to a *real* (existing in reality) disequilibrium. This equilibrium exists in the 'Utopia,' or in the idea of a society organised according to 'human nature' (the communist society). That is why history is the self-realisation of man. The historical movement as an antagonistic process of class struggle disappears" (247). From this angle, the social relations of a future communist society are presented as natural and eternal, in accord with the laws of human nature, in much the same manner as political economy presents those of capitalism. There are true rejections of Marx's theory and "the 'humanist' position expresses theoretically the conceptual limits within which the petit-bourgeoisie, as such, can *live* both Marxist theory and revolutionary practice" (251). Finally, humanism cannot accede to "scientific" status through a "*correspondence* between the concepts of historical materialism and the categories about 'human' instances," instead of a "*reduction* of the materialist concepts into 'humanist' categories" (252). Social relations are not produced by individuals but reproduced in a process from which individuals are theoretically absent. The "search for a theoretical *coherence* for Marxist theory . . . curiously unifies this new form of scientific 'humanism' with another contemporary amalgam: that implicit in the problematic concerning 'subjectivity' . . . resolved by the amalgam of Marxism and psychoanalysis" (253–54). The moment of man has passed from the category of the individual to the unconscious. With the humanist sphere thus outside of Marxism, what is "conceived from many Marxist positions (but dominated by the 'humanist' argument) as an intervention of Marxism in psychology is here its reverse: an intervention of psychology in Marxism." However, the question of a lack of psychology in Marxism obscures a more important and decisive question of "*a lack of (Marxist) politics in psychology itself*" (254). For Molina, the implication is theoretical disorder (the theoretical absence of a "subjectivity" problematic accounted for in Marxist principles) and a loss for Marx and the revolutionary movement.

According to Nicos Poulantzas, as formulated in *Political Power and Social Classes* and filtered through the analysis of John Clarke, Ian Connell, and Roisín McDonough (CCCS 1978: 106–22), classes are produced by a combination of all the levels or instances. A "firm distinction [is] made between the *structures* and *social relations* which are the effects of the structures: classes do not appear as structures but as social relations (of production, of politics, of ideology)" (107). Hall, Lumley, and McLennan observe that Poulantzas shares with Gramsci a full deployment of the concept of hegemony and the identification of the central "cementing" function of ideology and, like Althusser but unlike Gramsci, calls for the "full advance to the theory of 'structuralist causality' " (66). Whereas for

Gramsci, hegemony is never devoid of struggle or contestation and is always a matter of a particular conjuncture, for Poulantzas hegemony "appears as a more or less guaranteed feature of the domination of the capitalist state by a ruling class alliance" (68). But in collapsing control and consent, the reason "the capitalist State, based on universal suffrage, is *par excellence* the necessary site for the generalization of class domination" is no longer clear (69). In fact, regarding ideology, Poulantzas's formulations exhibit theoretical confusion, seen particularly in "the tension between the theoretical weight attached to the notion of structural causality and the important role that class struggle is accorded," and the impossibility of distinguishing the specificity of his references to "ideology" (113–15). For the authors, the connection of the economic and the ideological is vital but "not resolved by its definition as an *imaginary* relation." These relations must "be grasped as class relations, and as a process of class struggle, at each level, both at the economic and in the 'ideological forms in which men become conscious of the struggle and fight it out'" (122). The theoretical issue takes on wide political significance, and herein lies the authors' answer to Poulantzas's difficulty in explaining the nature of the "isolation effect" of bourgeois juridicopolitical ideology: "Individualization of agents *really* occurs in the process of the exchange of commodities" (116).

Although it was in the context of media studies that questions of language and signification were first addressed at cccs, a separate Language and Ideology Group was organized in 1975 specifically to study theories of language since Saussure. Barthes's development of Saussure posed two problems: "the question of the way in which meaning is fixed within language . . . [and] the role of the speaking subject within language and by extension, within ideology and politics, including sexual politics" (cccs 1980: 183). V. N. Vološinov, in opposition to Saussure, insisted on the openness of the sign to "different meanings when seen from different, class-based, subjective positions" (183). Counterposed to this position was the neosemiology of the Tel Quel group in Paris, which rejected

> both a conception of subjectivity as rational consciousness and a denotation/connotation model of language, which relies on a rationalist theory of representation (the *a priori* fixing of meaning within the language system). Drawing heavily on Lacan's work, they retheorize language as unconscious chains of signifiers, in which the ideological effect of meaning is achieved retrospectively through the closing of the chain of signifiers by means of the *positioning of subjects* within language. (184)

The debate over theories of language and subjectivity was also heavily influenced by feminism, especially "Julia Kristeva's work on different forms of discursive practice, particularly artistic and literary discourses . . . [and] attempts to look at women's language as a function of their positioning within discourse and the symbolic order of socio-cultural relations" (185).

Steve Burniston and Chris Weedon attribute the shortcomings of Marxist approaches to art (Macherey, Lukács, Goldmann, Adorno, Brecht, Benjamin) to inadequacies of Marxist theories of subjectivity (CCCS 1978: 199–229): "Signifying practice, which is founded on the subject/object divide, must include scientific discourse within it. It is by attempting to make the veiled subject of scientific discourse self-conscious, that one might begin to retheorize the science/ideology divide and call into question, from the perspective of signifying practice, the nature of the subject and its constitution in language" (211–12). This leads them into an exploration of Lacanian theory and Kristeva's theoretical project. Kristeva begins with the Western tradition of the unified, transcendental, self-present subject (fixed in, and a base of, the subject/object relation—a prerequisite for the use of language), which achieves its clearest expression in Husserl. The phenomenological horizon pertains to the fixed meaning of the symbolic realm and the semiotic order to that which falls outside this horizon, threatens it, and is repressed—foremost here are poetic language, art, religion, and magic. These two modalities of *signifiance*, symbolic and semiotic, always coexist in varying degrees.

> It is in the speaking subject that the two realms . . . come together, and that the socio-economic mode of production meets the mode of production of the subject in signifying practice. Hence there are two levels of contradiction, articulated together; that between the forces and relations of production and the contradiction of the process of *signifiance*, which finds its expression in "the unsociable elements in the relations of reproduction (experience of sexual difference, incest, death drive, pleasure process)." . . . It is this contradiction, inherent in *signifiance* . . . "between Symbolic and semiotic inherent in any speaking being from the moment it speaks to another by means of signs" . . . which . . . makes every agent of structure an element of potential mutation. (CCCS 1978: 222)

This analysis, according to Burniston and Weedon, leads Kristeva to speculate on politics, confrontation, and social movements, which could potentially base the unifying role of the social formation on the pleasure process, rather than its repression, and leads to a "relativization of the function of the State and family and a new position for women within the Symbolic Order" (223). Such a conception would focus on dynamic (as opposed to stabilizing) elements—art and literature—"since they are constrained to a greater degree by the semiotic than other discourses, and are thus in a position to challenge the unity of the subject and its support in language and the socio-economic formation." They are thereby situated to "undermine the structures which give support to ideology itself" (223). In sum, the authors' new conceptualization "would assign a basic determinacy to the psychic, as well as the economic, as historical materialism does not" (227).

The neosemiological work is also developed by John Ellis (cccs 1980: 186–94) and by Chris Weedon, Andrew Tolson, and Frank Mort (cccs 1980: 195–216). The latter conclude that "transparent readings of language" are inadequate and stress the need to examine both "language *structure* and *usage* in historically specific locations, thereby opening up the area of the language of continually repositioned, speaking subjects within the symbolic order, thought historically to be a particular formation of social practices and discourses"(216).[8]

Writing History: Culturalism versus Structuralism

Explorations in theory presented in *On Ideology* and *Culture, Media, Language* and the deployment of new strategies in concrete studies attest to the energy and urgency committed to moving forward from the positions of the 1960s. The culturalism versus structuralism debate was very much a reality at cccs, to the extent that Stuart Hall (1980b) titled an influential article "Cultural Studies: Two Paradigms" and based his analysis of the development of work at the Centre on these two isms. But this replicated a larger intellectual predicament. By 1978, in "Thompson, Genovese, and Socialist-Humanist History," Richard Johnson was writing quite polemically about a "culturalist" break and structuralist critique. He proposed that the work of Edward Thompson and Eugene Genovese constituted a "peculiarly tough-minded and consistent project, hugely influential on both sides of the Atlantic and in parts of Europe, and fully 'culturalist' in its presuppositions" (1978: 82). Johnson situates the break into "culture" of the mid-1950s and early 1960s as a move away from "Dobb's theoretical development and complex economism to an overriding concern with 'culture' and 'experience' and a wholly 'hidden' and ambiguous relation to 'theory' or 'abstraction' " (81).

Johnson's aim was to show how existing historical practices were vulnerable to a structuralist critique in the areas of abstraction, reduction, and determination. Both culturalism and structuralism emerge in the 1950s in opposition to economism; however, in structuralism there is a double movement, away from humanism as well. Thompson, in thinking of theory as critique, as polemic, casts it as "a moment in the historian's method" leading to a "tendency to prefer 'experience' to 'theory.' " In practice, Johnson argued, this results in a concern for close study of specific cases: a "*pathological* divorce develops between those who analyse particular situations . . . and those concerned to develop 'theory.' " But even as such, Johnson continued,

> the "facts" are commonly those *about* conceptions of the world; what are in fact interrogated here are people's conceptions of their lives. But since culturalism makes "subjective experience" the final court of appeal in matters of human science—it is against this that theories must be tested— yet supplies us with no protocols of what we do when faced with radically *different* experiences or meanings, it dooms us, if consistently followed, to a relativism. If not consistently followed, we may suspect hidden and therefore arbitrary sets of criteria are in play, linked to an ascription of moral or cognitive superiority to the culture of populace or working class over that of the bourgeoisie. (1978: 89)

In both Thompson and Genovese, what "is properly an *objective* is made into a *tool of analysis*": sympathy for oppressed peoples. Although "both historians have a superb sense of the *relational* character of class . . . they have no developed conception that these relations are *over* or *in* some thing," Marx's "social relations of production." They "*do* collapse economic structure and political and cultural superstructure. . . . It follows that they are bound also to reduce the full complexity of Gramsci's conception. If Gramsci is *not* a historicist, Thompson and Genovese *are*" (90–92). While adhering to the premises that men and women make history and that history is the history of class struggle, what is missing are the "*determinant conditions* . . . which set limits to what it is possible for any group of men or women to do, *which constitute them indeed as social beings.*" Humanism makes it difficult to deploy economic categories and, in the end, explanations of "*why* things (or relations) appear as they do" fail to emerge (92, 98).

Thompson was not one to remain quiet for long. In the first place, he did not accept the term "culturalism" and he was not about to allow what he considered the errors of structuralism, particularly in the form of Althusserian Marxism, to go unchallenged. "The Poverty of Theory: or An Orrery of Errors" is a caustic refutation of Althusserianism. The crux of Johnson's point was in his reference to the actual practice of Thompson and Genovese. Thompson defends his position, theoretically: "The critical concept (unexamined by Althusser) is that of 'determination' itself; hence the importance—as Williams and I and others have been insisting for years (and to the deaf) of defining 'determine' in its senses of 'setting limits' and 'exerting pressures' and of defining 'law of motion' as 'logic of process' " (1978c: 351). The "main enemy" of communist orthodoxy since 1956, Thompson chides, had been socialist humanism— Thompson considers Althusser to be writing against Thompson himself! Because socialist humanism was explicitly anti-Stalinist, "we can see the emergence of Althusserianism as a manifestation of a general police action within ideology, as the attempt to reconstruct Stalinism at the level of theory" (323).

> In the old days, vulgar Political Economy saw men's economic behavior as being *lawed* (although workers were obtuse and refractory in obeying these laws), but allowed to the autonomous individual an area of freedom, in his intellectual, aesthetic or moral choices. Today, structuralisms engross this area from every side; we are *structured* by social relations, *spoken* by pre-given linguistic structures, *thought* by ideologies, *dreamed* by myths, *gendered* by patriarchal sexual norms, *bonded* by affective obligations, *cultured* by *mentalités*, and *acted* by history's script. . . . all arrive at a common terminus of unfreedom. (345)

This structuralism is just a new *elitism* in the same line as the literary-critical tradition, Benthamism, and Fabianism; "theoretical practice," according to Thompson, "has been a diversion, a retreat into the privacy of a complacent internal discourse, a *dis*engagement from the actual political and intellectual contests of our time" (377, 373).

Between 1960 and 1965, Althusser had sought to assert the autonomy of theory (hence his antihistoricism) as a basis for the restoration of the French Communist Party. The effect of his attacks on historicism was to bolster the party leadership against challenges from the left, and his denunciation of humanism shielded against forays from the right (see Rancière 1974). The "tragedy of Althusserianism is that the conception of society in question . . . [in his] attempt to establish the autonomy of theory . . . is that which dominates both stalinist dogmatism and bourgeois sociology" (S. Clarke 1980: 16). By the time Thompson staked out his position with "The Poverty of Theory," Althusserian theoreticism was already under attack. In 1966 Henri Lefebvre confronted what he called "the 'New Éléaticism' (Althusser's structuralist version of marxism) which values immobility above Heraclitean movement." For Lefebvre, as John Hoyles explains, structuralism and its neo-marxist variants are trapped within the ideology of neo-capitalist consumerist society; official marxism disguises its political failures and retreats into scientism and epistemology; with pedantic asceticism it eschews sensibility, sensuality, emotion and experience; space is fetishised at the expense of time; science and ideology are hypostasised into "theoretical practice" while the actual ideological situation and the actual conditions of scientific knowledge are bracketed off. (1982: 53–54)

From the early 1970s, John Fekete charged that structuralism suppresses the categories of alienation and praxis and recapitulates "the Comtean obsession with invariances and stabilities in the context of the worst excesses of dogmatic rationalism" (1977: 195–96). Lacan "eternalizes the elimination of the subject from the centre"; this, argued Fekete, is a "historical not a categorical problem, and becomes categorically decisive only for an epistemological fetishism" (197). In 1972, assessments of Althusser appeared in *New Left Review:* Norman Geras focused on the idealism of Althusser's conception of science and André Glucksmann drew attention to the metaphysical transcendentalism of Althusser's work. That *New Left Review* was a bastion of theoreticism explains Simon Clarke's remark some years later that "a renewed critique of Althusserianism is necessary, a critique which focuses on the point which [these] earlier critiques deliberately and specifically omitted, the question of the adequacy of Althusser's interpretation of Marx" (1980: 12).

In 1979, Tony Bennett joined elements of the libertarian critique of Althusser with his reworking of the Bakhtin school's formulation, to conclude that there "neither is nor can be a science of value. Value is something that must be produced. . . . To neglect this is to reify the text as the source of its own value. . . . The text is not the issuing source of meaning. It is a site on which the production of meaning—of variable meanings—takes place. The social process of culture takes place not within texts but between texts, and between texts and readers" (quoted in Hoyles 1982: 57). In his 1980 article in *One-Dimensional Marxism,* Simon Clarke blasted Althusser for an "intellectual terrorism" that drafts historicism, empiricism, and humanism to "sweep away all possible opposition. . . . Althusser cannot see that the revolutionary concept of humanity emerges as the expression of a political struggle not against the *word* of bourgeois humanism, but against its *practice,* against the practical tyranny of domination in every institution of bourgeois society of which the bourgeois concept of man is but the ideological expression" (73, 76). Kevin McDonnell and Kevin Robins, in the same venue, argued that second-generation semiotics and Lacanian psychoanalysis (*Tel Quel/ Screen*) "developed out of 1968 . . . to give intellectuals an active, revolutionary role through their association with the supposedly subversive practice of avant-garde texts" in "neat compatibility with Althusserian theory—and by implication, with marxism." The "empty formalism, which sees language as the decentred play of signifiers—no longer having any referential relation to the real world . . . has led to its easy absorption as a radical bourgeois theory" (1980: 185, 189).

On the other side, in aesthetic and cultural analysis, the body of work with both structuralist and Marxist origins emanating from CCCS deserved "special mention," according to Ted Benton; however, commenting on Clarke (1980) and Thompson (1978), he found the "pervasive judgement that Althusser's work simply re-enacts Stalinism in modern dress . . . outrageous" (1984: x, xi). Stuart Hall defended CCCS as a site where "critical engagement" was espoused from the outset and pointed out "real *convergences* between Thompson and Althusser," who were both concerned about tendencies toward reductionism and economism: "Both refute the mechanical subordination of 'superstructure' to 'base.' . . . Both recognise the importance of Engels in posing this question to orthodox Marxism: both agree he failed to resolve it. . . . [Thompson's] 'History' does acquire the same absolutist status as Althusser's 'Theory' " (1980d: 818).

Inquiries into the relationships between Marxist theory and history writing were contained in the CCCS publication of 1982, *Making Histories: Studies in History-Writing and Politics,* edited by Richard Johnson, Gregor McLennan, Bill Schwarz, and David Sutton. Not surprisingly, it was inspired by the pressure of accumulating theoretical work focusing on historical practice, particularly structuralist Marxism, and written under the general theme of the relationship among theory, politics, and research in historiography with the construction of Britishness as a subtext. Specifically, the authors contend that historiography cannot be adequately understood from one pole of the history/theory debate, nor is it concerned simply with the past, but with the past-present relation. Indeed, "the dimension supplied by popular conceptions of history illustrates how cultural studies converge with historiography. In fact, a larger 'Gramscian' task emerges here: to link the politics of history-writing to the sense of history active within contemporary cultural and political movements" (R. Johnson et al. 1982: 11).

Bill Schwarz argues that the historiography that developed from the work of the Communist Party Historians' Group (CPHG) "decisively reworked our notion of the past (so much so that for many today it now appears conventionally mainstream)," and that integral to it "was a securely founded conception of the politics of intellectual work" (R. Johnson et al. 1982: 44). Rather than developing a logical theory of historiography, the thrust of the group's work was more "to reactivate a national-popular consciousness and in this the Group cultivated a profound sense of *Englishness*. . . . In part, to generate a new popular sense of history *was* the theory" (ibid.: 54). The stress on humanism and a distancing from scientism, as initiated in the work of Dona Torr, however, risked "inverting scientism into moralism," as Anderson argues of E. P. Thompson after 1956 (69). Schwarz does not believe that conceptual "*incompatibilities* were resolved by the Communist historians, either by the 'addition' of utopia to science (or desire to necessity, or romanticism to marxism) or by interpreting a science of history as poetic. Similarly the political issue of the relation between party and people was caught in, and limited by, precisely these theoretical ambiguities" (78). Schwarz's positive assessment of the contribution of the Historians' Group hinges rather on their introduction and development in cultural theory of what Gramsci called the "national-popular" as a historical concept, "determining a peculiarly historical route through the field of cultural studies, referring to an element—or rather, a complex of elements—*within a conjuncture*, which always needs to be specified, located and historicized. . . . Predicated on the recognition of the struggles by antagonistic forces for conflicting definitions of 'nation' and 'people,' it indicates the unstable and impermanent combination of elements in any one conjunctural moment" (79).

Even as more attention was devoted to popular mentalities toward the end of the 1950s, the problem of "high" and "low" culture persisted. Two negotiations of the dichotomy were advanced: "The national culture was national *because* it was popular" neglected "those dominant literary forms which in no way could be thought as progressive"; "cultural dispossession, in which the dominant culture fleeces 'the people' of its clear-voiced heroes," could be unhistorical, presenting a single or linear tradition (R. Johnson et al. 1982: 80). Simple recovery of tradition does not penetrate the multilevel struggles of the past that produce the present, and it is in such a context that the Historians' Group's failure to carry historical analysis into the twentieth century must be understood. This is the aim of *Making Histories*, and the context of Gregor McLennan's article on E. P. Thompson (96–130) and David Sutton's piece (15–43) introducing "our general interest in 'social-democratic' politics and history through an account of the Hammonds" (12).

Although the issues of Marxism and philosophy remain obscured by the persistence of the opposition between theoretical and empirical modes, philosophy and history, Johnson agrees with McLennan that "both marxism and history-writing are clarified by being brought into relation to realist philosophy" (R. Johnson et al. 1982: 153). Johnson reformulates problems of inquiry as the nature of abstractions and problems of presentation as dealing with levels of abstraction. Marx's critiques are never simply critical but cast to produce new knowledge. They rest on clear premises: the rationalist premise as critique of empiricism; the materialist premise as critique of idealism; the historical premise as critique of eternalizing/naturalizing; the structural premise as critique of reductions. Marx enjoins those who think not only also to act, but to act practically. Thus, presentation "is the production of really useful knowledge based on really historical thinking. This knowledge, its usefulness, is to be tested in relation to transforming the world in the interests of the oppressed and exploited majorities" (ibid.: 185). But Marx is not always at his best: even as he gives hope to progressive forces in retreat in *The Eighteenth Brumaire,* " 'The Revolution' becomes a (familiar) idealist category" (ibid.: 200). Neither is *Capital* immune from breaches of one of his central premises: "The worst Marx *is* reductive, does tend to functionalist or determinist explanations, does simplify 'real history.' Abstraction emerges not as a resource, but definitely, as a problem" (200), due to the immensity of his project.

A return to the "best" Marx, argues Johnson, is helpful in the Althusser-Thompson debate, which "involves some ridiculous oppositions": "the 'rationalist,' Althusserian camp is right to stress the systematic development of categories or concepts [but] . . . Marx's old antagonists—Hegel, Proudhon and the idealist historians—*are* recognizable in much 'post-Althusserian' thinking" (R. Johnson et al. 1982: 201). As for the choice between theory and history:

> The problem of theory in inquiry is better formulated as the problem of the character of abstractions. All systematic thinking abstracts: the question is how? Are the abstractions "chaotic"? Do they present historically specific relations as everlasting shackles on human development? Do they reduce complexities to a few simple elements or principles? Do they exaggerate (in an understandable pride of the intellectual) the power of thinking and of the categories themselves? Are the abstractions made self-consciously or are there huge half-conscious absences? (201)

Presentation, contends Johnson, must work on different levels of abstraction, and handling those levels depends on requirements of intelligibility.

The collective work of the Popular Memory Group at cccs investigated the "present" pole of the past–present relation and rounds off the *Making Histories* collection. The group defines "popular memory first as an *object of study,* but, second, as a *dimension of political practice*" (R. Johnson et al. 1982: 205). History matters politically and "memory" taps directly the past-present relation. The group follows Schwarz in the notion of history as "lessons" from the past, but positively as a resource for struggles in the present. This includes Raymond Williams's *Culture and Society* tradition, E. P. Thompson's libertarian socialism or communism (Marxism plus Romanticism), the socialist feminist succession, and the Communist Historians' construction of a long line of popular democratic struggles. The past-present relation may also be conceived through strategic analysis: contemporary conditions and their genesis—scientific evaluation of the past, present today, or the more agitational mode (closer to the first category and risking triumphalism) of Marx in both *Capital* and the French and English political essays. In any case, history, particularly as popular memory, "is a stake in the constant struggle for hegemony. The relation between history and politics, like the relation between past and present, is, therefore, an *internal* one: it is about the politics of history and the historical dimensions of politics" (212–13).

After 1968, the opening up of academic forms has mostly been in the shape of popular autobiographies and oral and community histories. Read in a nonempiricist way, these are significant "for a larger account . . . because they are the product of *social individuals*"; they represent a (Marxist) meeting point in debates on theory and practice. The Popular Memory Group faults Gramsci for a neglect of social relations other than class, particularly gender, citing the contributions of modern feminism "centrally concerned [with] the relation between individual and social relations" and exhort "socialists and feminists . . . to develop a politics of later life" (R. Johnson et al. 1982: 234, 237, 244).

The Condition-of-England Question Revisited

There were two themes in the work at cccs that tended to reproduce concerns dating back to the beginning of the nineteenth century. One was the nationalist mode of social critique. A second was education as a locus of articulations between political power and class interests.

Not surprisingly, from the nostalgic and semiautobiographic mode of *The Uses of Literacy,* Richard Hoggart took it quite for granted that he would be talking about England, from its neighborhoods, writers and their products, books, newspapers and magazines (even directly compared with American counterparts), and music halls to speech and clothes. In *Culture and Society,*

Raymond Williams attempted to account for and interpret responses to changes in English society since the late eighteenth century; he asserted that though "it is true that comparable changes happened in other societies, and new forms of thought and art were created to respond to them, often in equally or more penetrating and interesting ways than in these English writers, it is nevertheless of some permanent general importance to see what happened where it happened first" ([1958] 1983: x–xi). "Where it happened first" is, of course, both an empirical and a methodological question that depends for its answer on the spatiotemporal definition of the "it" and, especially, the specification of the units from which a "where" is to be selected. In designating the problem as that of "finding a language to express . . . fundamentally new social and cultural relationships" (x), the "where" is answered in a very naturalized adjective: the *English* tradition, in English writers. Williams wrote *The Long Revolution* as a continuation of *Culture and Society* to think through what he termed the democratic, industrial, and cultural revolutions as related rather than separate processes. But again (although the scope has widened), Williams confines himself to "Britain . . . British society," because "the kind of evidence I am interested in is only really available where one lives" (1961: xiv). And too, in *The Making of the English Working Class* it was explicitly the making of the *English* working class that E. P. Thompson considered. Through the 1970s, one is hard put, in fact, to find any work, empirical work at least, from the Birmingham Centre that has anything other than a predominantly national and ethnocentric perspective. Certainly, the unexamined supposition of the Industrial Revolution as having taken place in a single nation-state, and thus theoretically reproducible in other national contexts, accounts to a large extent for the predominance of this perspective—obviously not limited to cultural studies or to this period (i.e., studies of comparative modernization that, not inconsequentially, treated cultural factors as independent variables).

It was with studies of race that this perspective began to change. In 1982 a subgroup at CCCS, which had begun studying race and race relations in England, published a collection responding to the marginalization of racist ideologies and conflicts in left analyses of the national-popular, *The Empire Strikes Back: Race and Racism in 70s Britain*. To be sure, antecedents can be found in Dick Hebdige's *Subculture: The Meaning of Style* (1979), which ties black culture to its immigrant bases; *Policing the Crisis: Mugging, the State, and Law and Order*, by Stuart Hall, Chas Critcher, Tony Jefferson, John Clarke, and Brian Roberts (1978), with its concern for the black diaspora; and among the essays in *The Empire Strikes Back*. But in *There Ain't No Black in the Union Jack* (1987)

Paul Gilroy finally explodes the dominant national mode to explore the relationship among race, class, and nation in contemporary Britain. He contends that race crosscuts the political spectrum, aspects of black culture representing responses to the prevailing racism. The sociological approach he finds wanting, and the cultural studies work ethnocentric. His preference is for an analysis in terms of urban social movements and a new emphasis on history, particularly a longer-term history embracing the marginalized and their roots *outside* Britain.

The very title of the collection *Crisis in the British State, 1880–1930,* edited by Mary Langan and Bill Schwarz (1985), acknowledges what the scope of its subject matter will be. Not readily evident from the title is the agreement on the part of the authors that the British state faces a major *contemporary* crisis involving attacks on collectivism and interventionist and welfare policies by those in favor of free market theories. "State and Society, 1880–1930" by Stuart Hall and Bill Schwarz (Langan and Schwarz 1985: 7–32) examines the fifty-year crisis that marked the transition from laissez-faire to monopoly capitalism, individualism to collectivism. It was also during this period that the typically "modern" form of state and political representation appeared, of which the inherent contradictions had become especially apparent in the 1970s and 1980s. Hall and Schwarz consider the period to have "epochal character . . . a time of organic crisis when the society as a whole was structurally re-formed" in a manner similar to the "1640s–60s (revolutionary constitutional regime)" and the "1770s to the 1840s (the formation of industrial capitalism)." The crisis beginning around 1880 is not short term but a "*succession* of crises of the state . . . a crisis of the social order itself . . . a crisis of liberalism" (9).

The capitalist class was recomposed, erasing distinctions between agricultural capital, embodied politically in the Conservative Party, and manufacturing capital, with allegiance to the Liberal Party. As the spectacularly wealthy gravitated to the Conservative Party following the split in the Liberal Party, the working class was undergoing restructuring as well, as Mary Langan shows (Langan and Schwarz 1985: 104–25). The breaking down of skills by capital "fractur[ed] and disorganiz[ed] the cultural and political ties which had held skilled labourers to Liberalism," and a revival of socialism combined "with forces pressing from below for a system of *mass* democracy, coincided with the political splits in the dominant bloc and gave a strategic leverage to those political movements emerging outside the state" (14). These issues are also addressed by Bill Schwarz and Martin Durham (Langan and Schwarz 1985: 126–50). The organization of a feminist movement, first around the repeal of the

Contagious Diseases Acts then explicitly concentrated on suffrage, are probed by Lucy Bland (192–208), Frank Mort (209–25), and Martin Durham (179–91).

During this period, liberalism was beset by an "expanded conception of politics"; although not allied, feminist and socialist movements counterposed *social* rights to the freedoms to sell one's labor in the market and choose a parliamentary representative. Victorian constitutionalism, incompatible with mass democracy, broke apart. Collectivism, "the process by which state policy became organized around class or corporate rather than individual interests," and theorized from positions ranging from Lenin to A. V. Dicey, was a common thread in many of the solutions that arose as reconstitutions of the social fabric (Langan and Schwarz 1985: 15, 16). The analysis presented here modifies the definition of the key contrasting term to collectivism: "*Laissez-faire* describes not an absence of controls, but a specific means by which market forces are politically regulated" (18). The transformation in regulative practices was from one of clearing away inhibitions to ensuring the survival of the market. It was not "merely quantitative but effectively produced a new idea of the 'social' (as in the term 'social reform'), a new discourse of social regulation, in which there arose new objects and targets for intervention" (19). This process resulted in breaking down "social problems" into their component parts and the establishment of a host of state and voluntary agencies to deal with them. Whether the impetus came from below or from above, only the state really had the power to intervene. However, the very fact that both tendencies were at work established the contradictions and antagonisms revisited in the situation of the 1970s and 1980s.

Hall and Schwarz examine three dominant collectivist currents: imperialist, new liberal, and Fabian. The social imperialism of the "collectivists of the right" recast citizenship "in a populist and activist idiom: the new citizen was to be a *participant* absorbed into the larger organic unities of race, empire and nation" (Langan and Schwarz 1985: 21). This dirigisme did not set well with the new liberals, who "evolved a conception of collectivism which was constitutional and communitarian, ethical rather than utilitarian, and which aimed to preserve individual liberties *through greater state intervention*" (22). Utilitarianism, inegalitarianism, and fear of socialism were not totally absent; however, there was a dedication to *universal* social rights even though "this was tempered and qualified by their identification of those whom they deemed were unfit for the purposes of citizenship . . . and given a negative inflection—the right, in other words, *not* to be impoverished, or ill-educated, and so on" (22). To deal with the threats of socialism and mass democracy, the new liberals internalized the rhetoric of universalism and made it their own. Fabianism was a contradictory thrust within socialism itself. At odds with other currents of socialism, it was utilitarian: reformist, bureaucratic, antidemocratic, and illiberal. "If the new liberals played a key role in defining the character of the welfare state, it was Fabianism which fashioned the ideology of rational efficiency and administrative neutrality which characterized welfarism in practice" (23).

Each of these collectivist projects is striking in its authoritarianism and clearly *statist* nature. Calling on Gramsci, Hall and Schwarz characterize the transformation in terms of a "passive revolution" in which a threat from below is met by the dominant groups' "maximizing the *exclusion* of the masses from determining political affairs and the reconstruction of the state" (Langan and Schwarz 1985: 25). Nonetheless, the restructuring at the end of the nineteenth century was significant: old political formations regrouped, the syndicalist challenge was repelled, and labor internationalism was broken by the war. State intervention hastened the transition to monopoly capitalism, and labor relations featuring the state as "neutral" mediator became fully institutionalized. This universalist ordering of institutions was accompanied by the rise of the Labour Party as the political representative of the working class and the beginning of the process of reforming the imperial state. The settlement was a victory for constitutionalism but much more ambivalent for democracy. *Neo*liberalism (with a trajectory parallel to, and contesting, new liberalism) continues to challenge the premises of collectivism (in the post-1945 period in the form of the "consensus" politics of Social Democracy), most recently quite successfully. In fact, according to Hall and Schwarz, "Social Democracy was formed out of the crisis of liberalism between the 1880s and the 1920s. We are now living through its successor—the crisis of Social Democracy" (32).

The long English tradition, dating back to the beginning of the nineteenth century and explicit in the work of the Arnolds and the Chartists as well as middle-class/liberal reformers, of relating education to wider social issues (What is entailed in expanding literacy? Does education represent a road to power?) was a second theme carried forward at CCCS. *Unpopular Education: Schooling and Social Democracy in England Since 1944*, collectively authored by the Education Group at CCCS (1981), is concerned in the largest sense with national politics in Great Britain from the perspective of education and more specifically through the lens of the major thesis "that the repertoire of Labour Party policies is largely exhausted in the forms in which it is currently conceived and presented" (7). The authors situate their work in the "gap" between *educa-*

tion, as all kinds of learning, and *schooling,* "that specific historical form which involves specialized institutions and professional practitioners" (14). They contend that critically inhabiting the world of policymakers (as, for example, Foucault does—not to extract truth value but to explore the power relations that their regimes of truth create) does not clarify agencies of change and determination of collapse or innovation. Hence the focus on the perspective of the governed. This attitude also reflects an attempt at a corrective to Marxist accounts tending to rest on relatively abstract and unhistorical external appraisals of the structures of domination.

A key theme takes the form of an examination of naturalized separations such as the school–family–production complex, where a renewed emphasis on the family is deemed crucial. Exploration of the relationships embedded in these sites leads to questions about the construction of adult/parent–child, work–leisure, female/mother/housewife–male/worker, young–old relations. Structurally, struggles are centered at two levels: both around children and teachers *within* schools and among parents and professionals *over* schooling. The authors recognize that the imperatives of capitalist enterprise strongly influence the education system. However, public representation and popular opinion do not necessarily agree; notwithstanding the asymmetry of power, the subordinated population does not accept passively the imposition but makes it an object of struggle—the process the authors identify, following Gramsci, with hegemony.

The realization of the contradiction between the limited mental requirements of most working-class jobs and what is generally thought of as the aims of education—involving *"the transformation of capitalist and patriarchal forms of social organization"* (Education Group 1981: 162)—points to the more general dilemma of the Labour Party. Labour, in fact, found it impossible to serve both popular interests and those of capital. The situation was accurately identified by the New Right from the 1960s. The power of their arguments "lies in the collision between the two elements. . . . This drama pivots on the opposition between individual freedom and state interference" (250). The consequence for education policy is parental choice, which may result in the dismantling of public schooling at the same time as the more authoritarian state is "masked by populist politics . . . as ideology declares its withdrawal in favour of entrepreneurial initiatives" (253). Furthermore, in class terms, expansion and equality are not necessarily linked in the sense that education reform cannot achieve equality within an unchanged structure of capitalist and sexual division of labor in which schooling is actually more determined than determining.

And so what of the future of a "politics of schooling" that lies well outside the boundaries of a schooling that is only intermittently educative? First, challenging "the attempt at an ever tighter functioning for capital" is one alternative; second, the "process of bidding for consent" must be denaturalized. Socialist and feminist perspectives suggest an education that "would try to redefine knowledge in terms of its ability to enable the subordinate to understand the social processes to which they are presently subjected. . . . A unitary notion of 'citizens' with their 'common culture' is no longer tenable" (Education Group 1981: 259, 260). The authors expected the 1980s to show rich development of local activities with no return to a harmony based on economic expansion. Here the larger question of political education as political activity, *learning*, becomes explicit, for "the contest between social democracy's unpopular education and Conservatism's capitalist schooling has been lost. The contest between capitalism and discipline, and socialism and education, has not even been attempted" (265).

Ten years later, *Education Limited: Schooling, Training and the New Right in England Since 1979*, published in 1991 on the heels of the Thatcherite 1988 Act and the National Curriculum, continued the interest in education at cccs manifested in *Unpopular Education*. However, whereas the latter focused on the limits of Labour or social democratic educational traditions, *Education Limited* is concerned with the New Right. Despite the problems and impediments associated with this new regime of class-based unfairness by training and vocationalism, anti-antisexism, and anti-antiracism, there are hidden or misrecognized stories, "especially the genesis of critical and reconstructive educational theories and practices" (Education Group II 1991: ix). Although the themes are generally optimistic, the authors concede that the New Right has been successful, particularly in its insistence on the cultural dimensions of the struggle.

According to Andy Green (Education Group II 1991: 6–30), the English education debate has not paid enough attention to the historically specific problems that resulted in a system based on and reproducing deep class differentiation. Like Green, Richard Johnson (31–86) dialogues with *Unpopular Education*. His account, combining analyses of political and ideological struggles and conditions with a history of policy, argues that "unpopular education . . . was the product of unpopular politics." Labour failed to be a "really educative movement, creating the knowledges to sustain its politics," and the New Right (Conservative parents and business interests) were able to capitalize on the weakness of the reform coalition, mostly educational professionals themselves (31–32). In critique, *Unpopular Education* underestimated the "generative role of the new social movements, not least for the New Right itself," and overemphasized the limits of Labour. But criticism along these lines (structural, legitimating inequalities and defensive resistances) fed into the New Right agenda and *Unpopular Education* "failed to consider alternative educational arrangements more consistent with our analysis. Disorganized in this way, we lost an historical initiative" (33). Neoliberal privatization (market, voucher system) remained the New Right goal—unrealizable in one fell swoop and thus to be pursued incrementally and surreptitiously—even though it had to take second place to neoconservative attacks on educational disorder (standards, centralization).

As a "*balance* of possibilities," the measures of the 1988 Act were neoliberal ("a free market by stealth"), creating an alternative network of schools; restructured the public system "to adapt it to market pressures and a possible future of vouchers"; and promised to "recruit parents to the theory and practice of 'choice'" (Education Group II 1991: 64–65). However, the Act is "flawed" in two directions: "as a centralizing measure because it offers complication, diversity and inequality rather than standardization, intelligibility and fairness . . . [and] as a 'devolutionary' measure because it enhances rather than checks central control" (69). The major contradiction of the 1988 Act is that between the free market and strong state; however, how far they are contradictory or even complementary lies in the "historical perspective we take." In the short term, there are strong tensions between the state and market options, but in the midterm, as a strategy, they may be complementary. For "the market is a system of social relationships, not a technical mechanism. It involves the attempt to return to more coercive relationships between labour and capital, and to conventional gender and age relationships" and "requires the strong state as an initial condition" (81). But structurally, in the long term, by increasing social divisions the New Right may also "reduce the possibility of solving them in productive ways" and even generate opposition movements (84).

Johnson (Education Group II 1991: 87–113) believes that to reform the public education system—achieving Education Unlimited—it is essential to relativize, revalue, and eventually dissolve the "deeply naturalized curriculum divisions . . . those between the manual and the mental, between the practical and the theoretical, between schooling and training, between the technical and the academic, between the academic and vocational, between the arts and the sciences, between the 'arty' and the 'bookish.'" For the "biggest failing of public education"—Education Limited—has been the installation of "socially relative points of view as neutral, natural, or absolutely valid" along with "the infantilizing features of schooling in its later phases" (270). Johnson is looking to the everyday experience of real people and putting stock in their actions, their capacity for active agency to override a uniform Britishness that never existed, the selective, invented tradition of "monoculture" that the right reinvents to prevail over diversity and change.

Interdisciplinary and Collective Work

In his inaugural lecture of 1963, "Schools of English and Contemporary Society," Hoggart indicated "many ancestors" for "contemporary cultural studies," "but Dr. Leavis in his culture and environment work and Mrs. Leavis in her studies in popular fiction are more important than most." The particularistic approach to which this alluded meshed with the departmental niche, albeit tenuous, it had found in English. All the same, Hoggart's project did not respect disciplinary lines. He divided the new field into three parts, drawing on both the humanities and the social sciences. One part "is, roughly, historical and philosophical"; this was a necessity if there was to be a serious commitment to the analysis of cultural *change*. Change implies history. But a concern for history is a concern for time and the temporal dimension had been banished from literary studies. Another part "is, again roughly, sociological"; here, Hoggart singles out biographies of artists and studies of audiences along with the production relations of culture and their *interrelations* as fundamental to the work as he conceived it. The third part, the most important, "is the literary critical"; however, the high/middle/low terminology is "useless," and "discussion of conformity, status, class, 'Americanization,' mass art, folk art, urban art and the rest is simply too thin" ([1963] 1970b: 254–55).

For Stuart Hall too cultural studies was a "conjunctural practice . . . developed from a different matrix of interdisciplinary studies and disciplines" and "emerged precisely from a *crisis* in the humanities," the extension of Leavis's project of taking questions of culture seriously, by Hoggart and Williams (S. Hall 1990: 11). Colin Sparks notes the explicitly political dimension of the crisis: the "dominant tradition was openly, unashamedly and profoundly undemocratic; cultural studies, from its inception, was a champion of democracy" (1977: 17). Because of hostility from the mainstream humanities (Arnoldian English) and social science (sociology) establishment, cultural studies "was not conceptualized as an academic discipline at all" in Britain, even though, at rock bottom, with Leavis, cultural studies shared the premise that language was the key to serious scholarly understanding of national culture. Interdisciplinarity at cccs did not mean "a kind of coalition of colleagues from different departments," but rather a decentering or destabilization of "a series of interdisciplinary fields" (S. Hall 1990: 12, 16).

Richard Johnson considered that Marx's project had been left unfinished and thus he would have regarded his own work *impractical.* His point is the limitations imposed on work done in isolation (R. Johnson et al. 1982: 186). From the beginning, research at cccs was conducted collectively. This was certainly not without its problems, as Hall remembers: "rows, debates, arguments . . . people walking out of rooms" (1990: 11). The introduction to the first issue of *Working Papers in Cultural Studies* in 1971 stated that, from its inception,

> the Centre has grouped . . . projects in such a way as to make them part of a common intellectual enterprise. This collaborative style of work has been expressed, over the years, in seminar work on common problems and issues in the field; in collective projects to which all Centre members have contributed; and, more generally, in a degree of self-government and self-direction appropriate, we believe, both to the requirements of critical research, and to the real educational needs of the field. (S. Hall 1971: 6)

As Patrizia Lombardo writes, "It would be impossible to conceive the political dimension of the New Left and the whole creation of the Birmingham Centre" apart from the "idea of people working, discussing and interacting . . . in genuine team work" (1992: 9). The number of collectively authored works and the ubiquity of collective authorship over time attest to the continuity of the vision.

CHAPTER 4

Centre for Contemporary Cultural Studies II

Macro determinants need to pass through the cultural milieu to reproduce themselves at all.—PAUL WILLIS, *Learning to Labour*

Less inhibited by prevailing orthodoxies or by vested interests, recent debates in film and television studies have proved remarkably open to new influences with the result that those working in these areas have often pioneered theoretical developments that have been only belatedly registered within more traditional disciplines.—Preface to *Popular Television and Film*, edited by Tony Bennett et al.

The structuralist intervention in cultural studies during the 1970s marked a decisive break, much as had the work of Hoggart, Williams, and Thompson during the late 1950s. It was a break, however, that did not prohibit the extension of the project. To the contrary.

The "structuralisms" of Lévi-Strauss and early semiotics and then the structural Marxists held out the possibility of rigor and scientificity, of creating a human "science," but the price (to be rendered to the linguistic model) was an atemporality at odds with the historical foundation of "culturalism," and the reliance on internal arrangements short-circuited causal logic. On the positive side, the concept of "determinate conditions" allowed a recuperation of Marx's mode of thinking about relations within a structure as not simply reducible to relations among individuals. Structuralism also brought with it an emphasis on abstraction and a strong sense of "the whole." Rethinking experience renewed interest in ideology.

The authenticating power and reference of "experience" imposes a barrier between culturalism and a proper conception of "ideology." Yet, without it, the effectivity of "culture" for the reproduction of a particular mode of production cannot be grasped. . . . culturalism *properly* restores the dialectic between the unconsciousness of cultural categories and the moment of conscious organization: even if, in its characteristic movement, it has tended to match structuralism's over-emphasis on "conditions" with an altogether too-inclusive emphasis on "consciousness." (S. Hall 1980b: 69)

In the well-known "two paradigms" analysis of the development of cultural studies, from which the above is cited, Stuart Hall acknowledged that neither culturalism nor structuralism alone presented the best hope of meeting the requirements of the field, but theirs were the names of the game in which the tensions prefigured in the partial overlap of the categorical pair culture/ ideology shaped concrete analysis.

The theorization of *articulation* as a process of making connections was developed through the 1970s and 1980s in the quest for a nonreductionist and nonessentialist solution to the problem of determination. By the term, Hall meant "a connection or link which is not necessarily given in all cases, as a law or a fact of life, but which requires particular conditions of existence to appear at all, which has to be positively sustained by specific processes, which is not 'eternal' but has constantly to be renewed, which can under some circumstances disappear or be overthrown, leading to the old linkages being dissolved and new connections—re-articulations—being forged" (1985b: 113).

One of the "most generative concepts in contemporary cultural studies," Jennifer Daryl Slack notes, articulation works not only as theory or methodology but epistemologically in thinking structures, politically in bringing out relations of dominance and subordination, and strategically "for shaping intervention within a particular social formation, conjuncture or context" (1996: 112).[1] The concept played a central role in the field of media studies, inquiry into the lived relations accessible to ethnographic investigation, work on the politics of the British state, and the emerging concerns of oppressed groups, manifest especially in issues of race and gender.

Media Studies

Questions surrounding the print media had been embedded in the literacy debate since the nineteenth century, and at Birmingham, cccs was involved in media studies from its very inception. Interest was initiated with mass communication research. This was originally concerned with the relationship between media and violence and made use of audience surveys to gauge the debasement of cultural standards. The work that followed constituted a broadening of the directions first undertaken by Hoggart and carried forward the work Williams had done on newspapers (and the novel) and the preoccupation of the early New Left with cinema. By the late 1960s, the behaviorist mode and traditional content analysis were giving way to a concern for the (linguistic) structure of the forms (which became the basis for further work, incipient in, for instance, *Paper Voices*) and an ideological conception of the mass media, especially news and the coverage of politics. There followed a "rediscovery of ideology" in the 1970s (see S. Hall 1982), and by the late 1970s, interest had shifted to media products other than hard news.

Concurrently, sociological perspectives found favor over the aesthetic-moral emphasis in analyses based on literary methods. These accounts focused increasingly on how categories of deviance and social problems were constructed and propagated through media representations and the vision of society they implied. On the very first page of the introduction to their collection *The Manufacture of News*, Stanley Cohen and Jock Young (1973) contrasted slogans of 1968 with contemporary news headlines. In a new edition (1981), the overall sociological perspective remained, but some mainstream studies were eliminated to make room for cccs work utilizing structuralist methods of textual analysis and Althusserian theories of ideology.

Roland Barthes's work was fundamental to the framework of early models of semiotic analysis deployed in England.[2] His *Elements of Semiology* was published in English in 1968, the same year Umberto Eco's "Towards a Structural Inquiry into the Television Message" appeared. In contrast with the "mass culture" models, "the question of the media and ideologies returned to the agenda a concern for the role which the media play in the circulation and securing of *dominant* ideological definitions and representations" (cccs 1980: 118). Ads do not initiate or foreclose trends but establish parameters of approved behavior; advertising "acts as a social regulator, to preserve the *status quo*," wrote Trevor Millum (1975: 179) in *Images of Women*, one of the first analyses of representations of women in visual advertising (six women's magazines of 1969) to be undertaken in England.

The concepts of *reading* and *audience* were rethought as active moments connecting culture to class and privileging a "popular" over a "mass" cultural categorization of commercial representations, especially television. Stuart Hall's "Encoding/Decoding" (cccs 1980: 128–38), which appeared in 1973,[3] associated semiological advances with Gramscian theory and communication studies. Hall recognized that the discursive form of a message has a privileged position in communication. He criticizes the positivistic treatment of a communications model through its isolated, individual elements, emphasizing that "the codes of encoding and decoding may not be perfectly symmetrical" and that the articulation of a sign and the concept of a referent are "the product not of nature but of convention" (131, 132). He identifies three hypothetical positions of decoding. In the dominant-hegemonic position, in which the viewer "takes the connoted meaning . . . and decodes the message in terms of the reference code in which it has been encoded, we might say that the viewer *is operating inside the dominant code.*" In the negotiated position there is a "mixture of adaptive and oppositional elements: it acknowledges the legitimacy of the hegemonic definitions . . . while, at a more restricted, situational (situated) level, it makes its own ground rules." Finally, operating from an oppositional position, the audience "detotalizes the message in the preferred code in order to retotalize the message within some alternative framework of reference. . . . Here the 'politics of signification'—the struggle in discourse—is joined" (136–38). Both the moment of encoding and the moment of decoding are determinate, but there remains a range of possible outcomes, produced through the pressures of other social forces. The "model defined media texts as moments when the larger social and political structures within the culture are exposed for analysis" (G. Turner 1990: 94).

The new medium of television provided the terrain on which these theoretical developments could be applied and tested. It is not surprising, however, that television was a relative latecomer as a field of interest. Although the experience of adult education (going back to the 1930s) shaped the concerns of cultural studies early on, in England it was only by the 1960s that television was widely available in working-class homes. Even then there remained the difficulty that some live programs went unrecorded.

From 1975 to 1977, the Media Studies Group at CCCS focused on the BBC popular magazine program *Nationwide.* The published analysis by Charlotte Brunsdon and David Morley, *Everyday Television: "Nationwide,"* showed how "everything in *Nationwide* works so as to support [the] mirror-structure of reflections and recognitions . . . television as a transparent medium—simply showing us 'what is happening' " (1978: 9). This work, based on a semiotic approach to the text, the encoding or production end, made apparent the need for an analysis of the consumption side, how audiences decoded the text. Morley took this up in *The "Nationwide" Audience* (1980). The result was a substantial critique of previous audience research and belonged to the general line of inquiry of the CCCS Media Group that attempted to model the communication process as a whole.

The dominant paradigm at the time was that elaborated by American researchers, a quantitative and positivist methodology developed in the sociology of mass persuasion. This in turn had been a response to the pessimism of the Frankfurt School model, a qualitative and philosophical analysis that "stressed the conservative and reconciliatory role of 'mass culture' for the audience . . . a 'hypodermic' model of the media which were seen as having the power to 'inject' a repressive ideology directly into the consciousness of the masses." Both, however, conceptualized "dimensions of power and 'influence' through which the powerful . . . were connected to the powerless" (Morley 1980: 1, 2). In contrast to the mechanistic "effects" tradition and the individualist "uses and gratifications" perspective that challenged it (but then tended to minimize relations of domination and control), Morley treats the TV message

> as a complex sign, in which a preferred reading has been inscribed, but which retains the potential, if decoded in a manner different from the way in which it has been encoded, of communicating a different meaning. The message is thus a structured polysemy. It is central to the argument that all meanings do not exist "equally" in the message: it has been structured in dominance, although its meaning can never be totally fixed or "closed." Further, the "preferred reading" is itself part of the message, and can be identified within its linguistic and communicative structure. (10)

Morley combines program analysis and audience interviews to construct and analyze a "typology of the range of decodings made" and to relate them to other cultural factors such as class, socioeconomic, or educational position and cultural or interpretative competencies/discourses/codes (23).

On one side of an important debate, both Morley and Stuart Hall had engaged the extreme textual determinacy of the British journal *Screen,* published by the Society for Education in Film and Television.[4] According to Hall, "screen theory" (developed in *Screen*) argued the inadequacy of the break with empiricist theories of language. The " 'politics' of ideological struggle . . . [had become] exclusively a problem of and around 'subjectivity' in the Lacanian sense. 'Screen theory' is therefore a very ambitious theoretical construct indeed —for it aims to account for how biological individuals become social subjects, *and* for how those subjects are fixed in positions of knowledge in relation to language and representation, *and* for how they are interpellated in specific ideological discourses." The text is central, not in the expression of meaning but to the production of a representation of " 'the real' which the viewer is positioned to take as a mirror reflection of the real world" (cccs 1980: 158–59). Taking patriarchal ideologies as his example, Hall shows that from this conceptualization it is not possible to construct an adequate idea of struggle in ideology, and dealing with this difficulty through a strategy of deconstruction does not address the problem of the production of alternative languages and discourses. For Morley, not only do subjects have histories but " 'screen theory' constantly elides the concrete individual, his/her constitution as a 'subject-for-discourse,' and the discursive subject positions constituted by specific discursive practices and operations" (cccs 1980: 169). What is required is "to work through more fully the consequences of the argument that the discourses mobilized by 'readers' in relation to any 'text' cannot be treated as the effect of a direct relation between 'discourses' and 'the real.' It must be analysed, instead, in terms of the effects of social relations and structures (the extra-discursive) on the structuring of *the discursive space*—that is, of the 'interdiscourse' " (173). In *The "Nationwide" Audience,* Morley attempts just this: to go beyond the *Screen* perspective of the abstract, decontextualized, text-subject relationship with a critique that introduces sociological/demographic factors—age, sex, race, class position—that contribute to the determination of subject responses.

First, Morley observed empirically, in the work on *Nationwide,* that with respect to the encoding/decoding perspective, social position did not correlate with decodings. Second, rejecting *Screen*'s "unjustifiable conflation of the reader of the text with the social subject," Morley argues for an "articulation between the formal qualities of the text and the field of representations in and on which it works, and [for posing] the ideological field as the space in which signification operates" (1980: 159, 155). Thus, the analysis should expose the structural factors in the struggle over the sign (and therefore meaning), where the crucial point is the recognition of the sociohistorical conditions on which the relative power of different discursive formations depends.

Morley examined two different forms of determination: textual organization of signs and traditional positional variables of age, sex, race, and class. In autocritique, he confesses that only class is "dealt with in anything resembling a systematic way" and that there is a tendency of the research to "slide back to a perspective where the question of form becomes of only marginal, or occasional interest and the principal focus is on the degree of fit or dissonance between the ideological problematics in play in the text and those articulated by the different sections of the audience" (1981: 8).

Morley's 1986 *Family Television* concentrates on the gendered domestic context in which television is watched to the detriment of the decodings made. Thus, the impact of the media on family structure tends to remain unexplored despite the positive contribution of avoiding a reification of audience or reader. In a 1992 retrospective, Morley defends his position, which had been criticized as a " 'retreat' into the private realm of the 'sitting-room' and away from the important 'public' issues of power, politics and policy." He counters that the sitting room "is the site of some very important political conflicts—it is among other things, one of the principal sites of the politics of gender and age"; it is where we need to start "to understand the constitutive dynamics of abstractions such as 'the community' or 'the nation.' " A "double focus" is needed to "understand viewing as, *simultaneously,* a ritual whose function is to structure domestic life and provide a symbolic mode of participation in the national community *and* an active mode of consumption and production, *and* as a process operating within the realm of ideology" (1992: 283, 276).

Much of the subcultural work of the 1970s had been strongly involved with media representation and the media studies of the 1980s employed ethnographic methods. By the late 1980s, it was ethnographic studies of media audiences that pointed a way back to interest in less text-based analyses of popular culture and the practices of everyday life. It nonetheless remains that media studies using ethnographic techniques were narrowly focused instead of broadly based accounts of an entire "culture." Also, media studies were primarily attentive to the structuring of dominance even as the existence of mass society was put into question by the blurring of the distinction between production and consumption and, paradoxically, "high" cultural texts were ignored as sites of resistance and struggle, reproducing a distinction that theory abjured. Subcultural analysis, to which we now turn, was much more attuned to the articulation of resistance, beginning with the group itself rather than the text.

Subcultures, Ethnography, and the Working Class

The very magnitude of subcultural research at CCCS certifies the abiding interest in working-class culture evident from the earliest kindling of the cultural studies project in the mid-1950s, and the ethnography section of *Culture, Media, Language: Working Papers in Cultural Studies, 1972–79* (CCCS 1980)[5] attests to the importance of this method in concrete studies of the cultural level. Here it is argued that at CCCS, ethnographic studies did not result in simple description or theoretical Weberianism but worked to "analyze and gauge the complex relations between representations/ideological forms and the density or 'creativity' of 'lived' cultural forms" (74). This is evident in Phil Cohen's paper of 1972, "Subcultural Conflict and Working-Class Community" (cccs 1980: 78–87), which was seminal for *Resistance through Rituals: Youth Subcultures in Post-War Britain,* edited by Stuart Hall and Tony Jefferson (1976).[6] In a world where the high-rise had destroyed the community interaction of the street, production and consumption were increasingly separated and the nucleated family further isolated, "the latent function of subculture is this," wrote Cohen: "to express and resolve, albeit 'magically,' the contradictions which remain hidden or unresolved in the parent culture" (cccs 1980:82). *Resistance through Rituals* deploys class, based largely on Gramsci's concept of hegemony—a "hegemonic cultural order tries to *frame* all competing definitions of the world within *its* range" (S. Hall and Jefferson 1976: 39)—to explain the emergence of such subcultural groups as Skinheads, Teds, Mods, and Rockers.

Right in the middle of its work on youth subcultures, the Sub-Cultures Group involved itself with the mugging project. It became the "biggest single organic influence on the development of our subsequent work and on the shaping of the theoretical and methodological position" (S. Hall and Jefferson 1976: 6). It returned transactionalism to the theoretical agenda and resulted in direct political engagement because it originated with a particular, local case. "Our aim became . . . to explain *both* social action *and* social reaction, structurally and historically in a way which attempts to do justice to all the levels of analysis" (6). In the book-length *Policing the Crisis* by Stuart Hall, Chas Critcher, Tony Jefferson, John Clarke, and Brian Roberts (1978), mugging is placed in relation to public reactions, "moral panic *about* mugging" showing that "you cannot resolve a social contradiction by abolishing the label that has been attached to it" (vii). The book, then, is "about a society which is slipping into a certain kind of *crisis*": "why and how the themes of *race, crime* and *youth*—condensed into the image of 'mugging'—come to serve as the articulator of the crisis, as its ideological conductor. It is also about how these themes have functioned as a mechanism for the construction of an authoritarian consensus, a conservative backlash" (viii).

The book draws our attention as well through the number of ways that it is exemplary of the work of cccs. It is collaborative and collective and of long gestation—not surprising, given the attention to detail that seems to produce a vast synthesis of past work at cccs as a springboard to the future. Even after four years in the making, the authors regard its arguments and positions as unfinished, thus an ongoing work, and perceive that their analysis will please no one, convinced as they are that there is nothing to be done either from a conservative (control) or liberal (reform) point of view. "The problem is that the 'present conditions,' which make the poor poor (or the criminal take to crime) are precisely the *same* conditions which make the rich rich. . . . So the 'practical remedy' involves taking sides—struggling with the contradictions" (S. Hall et al. 1978: x). The only "answer" would be in changing "present conditions."

No group starts with a clean slate, but makes something of its starting conditions; in this way culture is reproduced and transmitted. The authors of *Resistance through Rituals* are clearly talking about cultures in the plural and, moreover, as ranked, in opposition to one another, in power relations with the dominant culture representing itself as *the* culture, and "relative to these cultural-class configurations, *sub*-cultures are sub-sets—smaller, more localized and differentiated structures, within one or other of the larger cultural networks." Fundamental to the analysis is the "*double articulation* of youth subcultures—first, to their 'parent' culture (e.g. working class culture), second, to the dominant culture" (S. Hall and Jefferson 1976: 13, 15). Despite the prevalence of terms such as affluence, consensus, and embourgeoisement, *class* refuses to disappear as a major category of social structure. Youth inherit a cultural orientation from their parent class and, following Phil Cohen ([1972] 1980), "attempt to resolve by means of an 'imaginary relation'—i.e. ideologically—the 'real relations' they cannot otherwise transcend" (S. Hall and Jefferson 1976: 33).

Youth subcultural groups adopt and reinvent styles—clothes, music—as forms of group identification in ways that the market never intended. The market then appropriates and capitalizes on the trends. But the construction of style as the organization of objects with activities both expresses and consolidates groups' internal unity and implies an opposition to those groups against which they define themselves. These youth cultures differ structurally according to class: "Middle-class culture affords the space and opportunity for sections of it to 'drop out' of circulation. Working-class youth is persistently and consistently structured by the dominating alternative rhythm of Saturday Night and Monday Morning." The youth subcultures of both may be seen as a crisis of authority, as "*symptom* and *scapegoat*" (S. Hall and Jefferson 1976: 60–61, 72). For working-class youth they represent a breakdown of control, whereas for middle-class youth they embody a crisis within the dominant class, though misrecognized as an attack from without by the class itself. Speaking to the near conspiracy of the mugging scare and the intensified policing of ghetto areas and especially black youth, the authors link the move to a "Law 'n' Order" society to a conception of youth as the enemy within, responsible for the whole collapse of hegemonic domination over the period from the 1950s to the 1970s.

Notwithstanding the "finish" *Resistance through Rituals* exhibits, it appeared to be a transitional text at cccs. Gary Schwartz charged that the book showed "almost no systematic integration between theoretical categories and empirical analysis" and was "singularly free of the kind of rich ethnographic description that one ordinarily associates with studies of subcultures" (1978: 790–91). The conceptual framework that emphasizes community (a defensive, "corporate" site) over production relations is also problematic and, according to Colin Sparks, situates the work between "a mode of thought which selected sub-cultures for their oppositional content to one which saw them as incapable of expressing more than a confused and marginal response to the fact of domination" (1977: 25). Nonetheless, although underdeveloped here, the Gramscian emphasis on hegemony as a negotiated version of ruling class ideology allowed cultural studies to rejoin the issues of class and state.

In his sophisticated and sensitive study *Learning to Labour: How Working Class Kids Get Working Class Jobs* (1977), Paul Willis attempted to follow his own advice offered in "Notes on Method" (cccs 1980: 88–95) and recognize "the reflexive relationship of researchers to their subjects" (95). His data (which reproduced the dialectical inflections of the first person) corrected a criticism of *Resistance through Rituals:* "Only rarely are youth allowed to speak for themselves" (Schwartz 1978: 791). In the best ethnographic tradition, Willis attended classes and worked beside a group of working-class boys (the "lads") in their last two years of school and early months on the job—just before the English industrial economy began to decline and ceased to offer stable, well-paid employment to school-leavers. The techniques used included case studies, group discussions, and participant observation. He interviewed parents, teachers, career officers, foremen, managers, and shop stewards and made comparisons with control groups.

Willis's argument is that the "failure" to master the curriculum destines the lads for working-class jobs. But this failure is not due to any inability. The lads are genuine rebels and the school is a battleground. Their rejection of school knowledge is a form of resistance to losing their class identity and a rejection too of the middle-class values of upward mobility. At a time when cccs media studies were more influenced by Althusser, *Learning to Labour* relied on Gramscian theories of hegemony and announced the development in the mid-1980s of complex analyses of ideological formations in popular culture. Willis's work argues against any reductive materialist notion of the reproduction of industrial workers. However, neither regional or class location nor education automatically determines cultural forms. The system functions through struggles and uncertainty, and capitalism turns to its advantage the educational machine of the welfare state rather than setting it up as a form of domination.

Labor power is "the main mode of *active* connection with the world: the way *par excellence* of articulating the innermost self with external reality." It is working-class culture that prepares the lads for their destiny as manual laborers, even though their "self-damnation . . . is experienced, paradoxically, as true learning, affirmation, appropriation, and as a form of resistance . . . expressed mainly as style" (Willis [1977] 1981: 2–3, 11–12). Opposition is expressed, made concrete, through the "stylistic/symbolic discourses centering on the three great consumer goods supplied by capitalism and seized upon in different ways by the working class for its own purposes: clothes, cigarettes and alcohol." But conscious superiority over other students at school is felt by the lads in the "sexual realm" above all: they are more experienced, in all of life's pleasures and tribulations (17, 15). And it is specifically the adult world, the adult male world that supplies the privileged behavioral models, with the informal group constituting the basic cultural unit. The lads bring class experience, male dominance, and the valorization of physical labor into the school, which usually tends to exclude it, unlike the middle-class boy who finds much the same values in the home as in the classroom.

Willis remains somewhat skeptical of the powers of interview and survey techniques alone to capture the depth and breadth of (class) consciousness. All the same, he maintains that it is the lack of political organization that disorganizes the cultural level from within. The divisions of mental/manual labor, gender, and racism contribute to how the counter-school culture finally accommodates itself to the status quo without, however, losing a "conviction of movement, insight and subjective validation in individuals even as they accept this subordination" ([1977] 1981: 145). A degree of effectivity and of noncorrespondence to structures in the cultural level suggest "*some* room for action. . . . At least the illusions of official and other ideologies can be exposed" (186).

Philip Corrigan correctly noted that missing in Willis's project is a historical grounding: "The ways that working class children experienced education was and is *intended,*" that is, working-class schools were an institution imposed from above by the government (1978: 653). Further, Corrigan distills the significance of "other 'places' in the social structure [that] confirm and reward the correctness of masculine white manual labouring. Those other places (where it is correct *not* to be) make that moment of 'giving of labour power' the freedom *and* imprisonment which it is. Those negatives declare themselves as ways of speaking about 'other people'—sexism, racism, crawlers, scroungers . . . reinforcing the muscularity and freedom of white, male heavy productive labour" (654).

In his discussion of *Learning to Labour* with respect to the problems and possibilities offered by contemporary ethnography, George Marcus situates the "most devastating flaw" of the study in the "self-fulfilling and circular manner" in which the sample was selected. Willis "draws his boundary of concern around the manifestly cultural form of nonconformist boys without examining the process by which some become conformist and others do not." This leads to a reification of the "larger system" in which the lads live. The absence of "cross-class ethnographic juxtapositions" leaves open the validity of the "unintended consequences" thesis that should arguably also apply to the dominant level but would "make it difficult to sustain the conventional way of representing the dominant class or classes in Marxist theory" (Marcus 1986: 176, 186–87). Willis's achievement remains, however, to draw our attention to the signs of meaningfulness of working-class culture that are not to be simply translated as anything like a simple apathy, insipid reformism, or obstinate passivity.

Gaps in follow-up work to Hoggart's *Uses of Literacy* were consciously filled with *Working-Class Culture: Studies in History and Theory*, edited by John Clarke, Chas Critcher, and Richard Johnson (1979). Its expositions of theory go beyond the empirical material, supplying foundational elements for the intellectual development of the cultural studies project itself. These essays at once engage Marxist theory—particularly the status of history and sociology—and both embrace and critique cultural studies as it had developed from the "culturalist break." In part as a corrective to many sociological accounts, in the central empirical section the authors include material embracing the whole period in which there had been a working class in any identifiable sense. Richard Johnson explores education during a period of working-class activism, 1790–1848 (J. Clarke et al. 1979: 75–102); Paul Willis offers an exemplary ethnographic study of the workplace (185–97); domestic service between the wars is looked at by Pam Taylor (121–39); the relation of football and recreation to capitalist business is examined by Chas Critcher (161–84) and Paul Wild (140–60); and the relationship among organized youth and imperialism and nationalism is plumbed by Michael Blanch (103–20). On the whole, though, these empirical studies tend to privilege the disclosure of class domination over struggle and oppositional practices.

The central section is preceded and followed by more overtly theoretical work, but the editors self-consciously concede that questions of family and the cultural forms of sexuality get short shrift. As Richard Johnson points out (J. Clarke et al. 1979: 41–71), much writing on the British working class had been historical rather than sociological, particularly in the form of histories, especially of popular or working-class movements produced by Labour or left-of-Labour intellectuals and shaped, positively or negatively, by Marxist and communist orthodoxies. These divide into roughly two periods: the founding of the economic and social history tradition between the 1860s and the 1920s, labor history, and the discovery of working-class culture in the post-1945 period, with the emphasis on culture.

The fundamental change occurred during the second period. With the study of culture cast in an elitist mold and labor history essentially cultureless, "historians began to write seriously and with sympathy about the beliefs and behaviour of the mass of historical populations" (J. Clarke et al. 1979: 58). In the 1970s, and in response to the implied homogeneity of working-class culture that grew out of the older Marxist conception of consciousness, Johnson claims that the present arguments will stress "the heterogeneity or complexity of 'working-class culture,' fragmented not only by geographical unevenness and parochialisms, but also by the social and sexual divisions of labour and by a whole series of divisions into spheres or sites of existence" (62). The most recent trend, strongly dependent on continental imports, has been the new priority given to theory and ideology or consciousness. Johnson argues that although culturalist accounts do exhibit vulnerabilities, structuralist critiques most often reduce to the exploration of differences. The opposition is a real one, but "neither of the two traditions which together constitute our field is adequate, taken on its own. *Neither culturalism nor structuralism will do!*" (69).

With the question "Is it possible to pass the practice of writing the history of culture through a 'structuralist' critique and prescribe a more adequate method?" (J. Clarke et al.: 1979: 71), Johnson directs attention to part 3 of *Working-Class Culture*, which he begins by dissecting three approaches: orthodox Marxism, with its central terms of class and consciousness; the work of Williams, Hoggart, Thompson, and others, with culture replacing consciousness; and the structuralist approach, where consciousness/class disappear in favor of ideology and mode of production or ideology and social formation.

Among the Marxists, Gramsci was the first "to take the culture of the popular masses as the direct and privileged object of study and of political practice" (J.

Clarke et al. 1979: 209). As for the second tendency, the "moment of culture can be understood as an attempt to vindicate critical social thought (from Marxism to Left Leavisism) in an exceptionally hostile climate and in circumstances where even 'the people' seemed content" (214). Speaking in the name of experience and materialism, culturalism is a critique of theory-as-dogma; changes in economic relations are to be understood through their experiential or political effects.

Structuralism, however, is fundamentally important as critique in quite another way, and its relation to earlier problematics is not one of supercession. Elements of a theory of working-class culture will cluster around three main arguments: "the nature and rationality of culture-ideology as an abstraction"; "the need to differentiate moments or aspects of cultural-ideological processes"; and "the issue of working-class culture primarily as an example of how the relation, culture to class, may be rethought in the light of earlier discussion" (J. Clarke et al. 1979: 230–31). It is important to keep culture as a category of analysis because "ideologies always work on a *ground:* that ground is *culture.*" However, in the justifiable concern for the (cultural) moment of affirmation, "making," one way of breaking with the "romantic" side of cultural studies is to look for "contradictions, taboos and displacements in a culture," including gender hierarchies (234, 235).

The understanding of the relationship between class and culture lies at the intersection of an analysis of internal relations, "the material conditions of the class itself and the sense that is made of these," and an outside perspective, "the particular relation to capital and capital's need continuously to transform the cultural conditions of labour" (J. Clarke et al. 1979: 236). For capital the stake in labor is its availability and willingness to work and produce surplus. But working-class culture is *the form in which labour is reproduced.* In this respect capitalism is far from being a self-policing system; far from labour continually being reproduced in appropriate forms, these processes require continual management. Moreover, capital's requirements are frequently themselves undergoing transformation. This process of reproduction, then is always a *contested transformation*" (237).

John Clarke (J. Clarke et al. 1979: 238–53) observes that the " 'problem' of working-class culture . . . must be located in the problems of understanding the complex and contradictory forms within which the working class lives its subordination in capitalist societies" (253). This recognition does not, however, overcome the conceptual problem posed by dissolving politics into culture or resolve the issue of the "relationship between different local working class cultures and socialist politics" (Austrin 1981: 367), both of which present difficulties throughout *Working-Class Culture.*

One of those "forms within which the working class lives its subordination" is certainly *style.* The notion that style is of more than passing interest in subcultural analysis was evident in *Resistance through Rituals,* which, however, emphasized class position. *Learning to Labour* adopted this approach and gauged the extent and limitations of the radicalism of working-class boys. Dick Hebdige's *Subculture* (1979) begins with "the idea of style as a form of Refusal" and looks to "recreate the dialectic between action and reaction which renders . . . objects meaningful" to thus expose the "tensions between dominant and subordinate groups . . . reflected in the surfaces of subculture—in the styles made up of mundane objects which have a double meaning." His investigation concentrates on the "process whereby objects are made to mean and mean again as 'style'" in subcultures, whose meanings themselves are always in dispute (2, 3).

Subculture demonstrates the layering of semiotics over Gramscian political theory at cccs. Although there was still the assumption that a literary sensibility was required to "read" society, the two ideas of culture (Arnoldian and ordinary) were reconcilable. Roland Barthes, for example, rather than attaching a value judgment to mass cultural phenomena, was concerned with showing how all such forms are systematically distorted: "The challenge to hegemony which subcultures represent is not issued directly by them. Rather it is expressed obliquely, in style. . . . Our task becomes, like Barthes', to discern the hidden messages inscribed in code on the glossy surfaces of style, to trace them out as 'maps of meaning' which obscurely re-present the very contradictions they are designed to resolve or conceal" (Hebdige 1979: 17–18).

In his seminal article of 1972, Cohen's emphasis had been on class. Hebdige, however, will "re-think the relationship between parent and youth cultures by looking more closely at the whole process of signification in subculture" (1979: 79). This continues, but goes beyond, the research represented in *Resistance through Rituals* (style as coded response); follows Gramsci using the "twin concepts of *conjuncture* and *specificity* (each subculture representing a distinctive 'moment'—a particular response to a particular set of circumstances)" (84); and finally, makes use of two structuralist moments, the early Barthes and *Tel Quel.*

Subcultures demonstrate two ways of dealing with "the Other": conversion into commodities (the commodity form) and labeling and redefinition (the ideological form). Both mod and punk were subverted and diffused when they were taken up by high fashion. Even the success, gauged by upward mobility, of individual punk rockers expressed the ambiguity of a system of exploitation, which the rhetoric of punk had originally contradicted. Punk signified chaos, chaos at every level. But this was possible precisely because punk was so ordered! To explain this paradox, Hebdige draws on Lévi-Strauss's concept of homology (as deployed in Paul Willis's 1978 *Profane Culture*): "the symbolic fit between the values and life-styles of a group, its subjective experience and the musical forms it uses to express or reinforce its focal concerns" (Hebdige 1979: 113).

Remark Hebdige's "reading" of one key sign, the swastika as appropriated by punk in the light of indications that "punk subculture grew up partly as an antithetical response to the reemergence of racism in the mid-70s":

> The signifier (swastika) had been wilfully detached from the concept (Nazism) it conventionally signified, and although it had been re-positioned (as "Berlin") within an alternative subcultural context, its primary value and appeal derived precisely from its lack of meaning: from its potential for deceit. It was exploited as an empty effect. We are forced to the conclusion that the central value "held and reflected" in the swastika was the communicated absence of any such identifiable values. Ultimately, the symbol was as "dumb" as the rage it provoked. The key to punk style remains elusive. Instead of arriving at the point where we can begin to make sense of the style, we have reached the very place where meaning itself evaporates. (1979: 116–17)

But is this a capitulation? Although no final set of meanings can be ascertained, this simply indicates the importance of "*polysemy* whereby each text is seen to generate a potentially infinite range of meanings. . . . Such an approach lays less stress on the primacy of structure and system in language ('langue'), and more upon the *position* of the speaking subject in discourse ('parole')" (117–18). This work, concerned with the process rather than the product, was principally associated with the *Tel Quel* group and the work of Julia Kristeva, who was interested in "the creation of subordinate groups through *positioning* in language . . . and the disruption of the process through which such positioning is habitually achieved." From this perspective, punks "did not so much magically resolve experienced contradictions as *represent* the experience of contradiction itself in the form of visual puns (bondage, the ripped tee-shirt, etc.)" (Hebdige 1979: 120, 121).

Insofar as Hebdige looks for an understanding of subcultures as systems of communication, he focuses on process, "on the fact of transformation rather than on the objects-in-themselves . . . *meaningful* mutations" (1979: 130–31). It is in this sense that the possibility of an equation between black and white working-class youth emerges: both a generational consciousness and a "refusal" of consensus. "It is the unwelcome revelation of difference which draws down upon the members of a subculture hostility, derision, 'white and dumb rages'" (132). The study of subcultural style that seemed "to draw us back towards the real world, to reunite us with 'the people,' ends by merely confirming the distance between the reader and the 'text,' between everyday life and the 'mythologist' whom it surrounds, fascinates and finally excludes" (140). Barthes supplied method, but he condemns us, the reader, to the impossibility of any innocent experience of a society that we are "in" but not "inside." This echoes the criticism of Judith Adler that Hebdige's "interpretation of British youth culture is rhetorical at best. . . . In fact, Hebdige concludes in true Romantic tradition with a dramatization of his own marginality and isolation as critic" (1982: 1459). Marginality . . . Well, this certainly does not pertain to the work: *Subculture* has gone through numerous reprintings, and with its eclectic use of concepts from Gramsci, Althusser, Lacan, Barthes, and Eco it manifests emphatically the range of theoretical modes and practices operative in the field.

Gender and Race

The "single most enduring movement to arise from the late 1960s and early 1970s was the women's liberation movement," Ronald Fraser has asserted (1988: 340). This assessment coincides with those of Nigel Young and David Caute: "It may be significant that the most deeply seated, and least recognized attitude of the [New Left]—its sexism—was the issue that spawned the most important of the movements to survive its demise; Women's Liberation and the other sex-role focused movements" (Young 1977: 367). "The women's movement was both a product and a repudiation of male-dominated radicalism in the late sixties" (Caute 1988: 266).

In England (as in the United States and Germany) the atmosphere of 1968 placed women in positions *within* the movement that led to questions about their place in society at large: they typed, fetched the tea, and slept with the men. This atmosphere was associated with what Julia Swindells and Lisa Jardine argue was the "male Left's attachment to medievalism (or pre-industrialism)" (1990: 59). They characterize E. P. Thompson as "shielded by Williams" (like another one of the oppositional voices of *Culture and Society*) in his account of William Morris as a break from bourgeois liberalism. Thompson's depiction of Morris's wife, Jane Burden, painted "over her class"; "her appearance stands in for Morris's 'oppositional' values and conveniently masks Victorian class relations (erases her class and compensates for his)"; the "cultured narrative . . . mutilated women's experience." In the family, working-class women "either lose [their] class (like Janey) or lose [their] virtue . . . in that case there is no account available to be given (within so-called radical history) of women's class-consciousness" (63–68).

Responding to the undercurrent of bourgeois values on the left, Sheila Rowbotham observed:

> The only way you could be accepted, as a politically active woman, was if you became like a man. I refused to become this sort of asexual political cardboard person. And yet I noticed that it was almost impossible for me to get any of my ideas accepted by men. To begin with, I didn't think it was because they were *men.* And then an American, whose wife was involved in the women's movement, pointed out to me after a meeting in 1968 that it was the men who constantly blocked my proposals. Suddenly the scales fell from my eyes. (quoted in Fraser 1988: 341–42)

In reaction to the machismo of the movement—"'Chicks' was the word" (Caute 1988: 265); "'sexism' is one of the very last additions to the [New Left]'s vocabulary" (Young 1977: 367)—women broke up into small discussion groups, in part in opposition to the mass student meetings where "revolutionary" men were the stars. But at the same time, their discussions of oppression connected conceptually with the goals of the students.[7]

The uneasy tension in the development of the issues of gender and race is enshrined in Stokely Carmichael's injunction that the only position for women in the movement was "prone"; but Black Power certainly did offer a model for action. In Britain, Enoch Powell tapped the prevalant racism and anti-immigrant sentiment of much of the working class and on April 26, 1968, more than four thousand dock workers struck in his support. Indicative of the wedge issue that race represented, and the British New Left's failure to achieve unity with unionized workers, left-wing groups demonstrating against racism clashed with Smithfield Market porters marching in support of immigration control in Whitehall on July 7 (Caute 1988: 92–93). Although cccs was as slow to acknowledge the specific concerns of women, as it was to develop analyses that included issues of race, 1968 was central to both.

Writing from the perspective of the early 1980s, Tricia Davis, Martin Durham, Catherine Hall, Mary Langan, and David Sutton (R. Johnson et al. 1982: 303–24) consider that whereas the earlier feminism of the suffragettes was concerned with formal equality—the vote—contemporary interest had shifted to "a recognition of the inadequacy of the analysis of women's oppression which remained at the institutional level, insisting instead on tackling the personal and informal dimensions of a thoroughly patriarchal society" (304). The question of consciousness, the need to confront racism or sexism personally, was highlighted by the political break represented by 1968, but in both periods the central question of feminism seems to have been how to combine public and private: homemakers and activists or mothers and workers. The application of theoretical leverage to these issues is observable from *Women Take Issue* (Women's Studies Group 1978)—"unquestionably a book of theory" (Webb 1979: 190)—but the shift from ideology and hegemony to identity and subjectivity came later, as did the expansion to sexuality in general, and belied the influences of psychoanalysis and poststructuralism.

The Women's Studies Group at CCCS was started in 1974. One man joined in 1975 and by 1978, when *Women Take Issue: Aspects of Women's Subordination* was published by the group, it consisted of nine women and two men. At the time, it perceived itself as responding to the invisibility of women (only four articles) in the first ten issues of *Working Papers in Cultural Studies,* the official organ of CCCS, which reflected a "continued absence from CCCS of a visible concern with feminist issues." An ongoing political and intellectual difficulty lay in the contradictions in effectively intervening in work at CCCS. In the group's words: "How do we carry out our work without being sucked into the intellectual field as already constituted, i.e. gaining legitimation at the expense of our feminism, losing sight of the informing politics or our work" (Women's Studies Group 1978: 10). It is clear in the group's editorial statement (7–17) that they considered women's studies in a political sense as constituting part of a larger struggle for the transformation of society that would then make women's studies unnecessary. Concomitantly, the group was aware of the ambiguous position of women's studies in academia, where women are both the subject and object of study: the existence of women's studies in an academic context is both the "*result* and the *occasion* of struggles inside and outside that context" (9). Important questions coalesced around the issues of "absences," integrating analyses of social formations structured by both class and sex/gender, the audience to be addressed, and even the meaning of feminism, including whether or not it was possible for men to be feminists.[8] The group as a whole was unable to find consensus on these issues, as the individual pieces attest.

Angela McRobbie (Women's Studies Group 1978: 96–108) suggests the double bind of the articulation of class and gender relations: "The culture of adolescent working class girls can be seen as a response to the material limitations imposed on them as a result of their class position, but also as an index of, and response to their sexual oppression as women. They are both saved by and locked within the culture of femininity" (108). Women spoke directly of their lot, in taped interviews, to Dorothy Hobson (79–95), and women's positions at the economic level were examined by Lucy Bland, Charlotte Brunsdon, Dorothy Hobson, and Janice Winship (35–78). Lucy Bland, Rachel Harrison, Frank Mort, and Cristine Weedon (155–75) used an anthropological approach to tap the physiological or biocentric treatment of dominance and subordination between the sexes that the natural or pregiven sexual division of labor and relations of biological reproduction in *Capital* tend to place outside economically theorized social relations.

The duality expressed in antithetical conceptual frameworks privileging either the anatomical or cultural realm in psychoanalysis is explored by Steve Burniston, Frank Mort, and Christine Weedon (Women's Studies Group 1978: 109–31). They situate their work in a gap defined as an absence in Marxist analysis of a space for questions of sexual oppression. The relationships embedded in the physiological/psychic, instinctual/representational split leading to irreconcilable theoretical positions hold the key to developing a materialist theory of sex/gender relation. The location "of the unconscious within the physiological processes of the organism places psychoanalytic theory once again firmly back in the problematic, in which the individual is defined in *opposition* to the movement of social forces. And the problem of sexuality and sexual liberation thereby appears as the problem of individual liberation, rather than as necessarily involving the transformation of social structures" (113). The law of the Other—for Lacan, it takes the form of the Oedipus complex and the incest taboo, for Lévi-Strauss, the exchange of women between kinship groups—the source of meaning, culture, which Lacan locates in the father, takes as its signifier the phallus. This is in no way neutral, as he (and Lévi-Strauss) would have it. "Lacanian theory necessarily implies a power relation between men and women, in which women are subordinated; yet for Lacan it is not a historically specific privileging, but an eternal law of human culture" (117). It is in this *phallocentrism* that the authors would site a feminist critique of both

Freud and Lacan. Although the positions in feminism are fluid, "the initial recognition that forms of sex gender are cultural, rather than biologically innate, makes a potentially greater control of our own sexuality a viable proposition" (125). This underlines the need to preserve the historical specificity in material practices of the forms of subjectivity as a corrective to biologism and universalism.

According to Janice Winship's reading of *Woman*, this women's magazine characterizes woman, in her perfection, as *man's* woman, in comparison to which the reader, reading the image from the point of view of the man in her, always comes up a failure. Thus, "femininity is not merely a passive acceptance by women of patriarchal domination but represents an *active subordination*" (Women's Studies Group 1978: 134–35). Via Althusser, the ideology of femininity is overdetermined by masculinity and at the same time included "but set apart from the capitalist construction of the 'free' individual." Building on Juliet Mitchell's theme, "masculinity always 'runs through' femininity. Thus in the work/personal life split women are defined/confined by men to be entirely *within* personal life. However, women themselves recognize that collapsed within personal life is the *work* they must perform to establish *men's* personal life" (136–37). Winship finds the organization of the magazine's content to revolve around woman-as-mother in which motherhood's dependency is minimized and women's role as mother is naturalized. The contradictions are managed through a fantasy/reality schema discernable in the contents; "The magazine's schizophrenia, however, is *already rooted in women's lives*" (140). The contradictions that "women recognize, experience and seek advice about cannot be challenged from *within femininity*—which is finally, through contradictions, what the magazine as a whole endorses." Women are encouraged to have confidence in themselves and take initiative, but problems will never be recognized as "*common* oppression . . . the problems will continue to be reproduced and experienced by women as 'individual' problems" (152).

Despite the difficulties with the theoretical language for the uninitiated, the "crossed lines," Rowbotham was nonetheless "sympathetic to the *substance* of the concerns" of *Women Take Issue* (1978: 266). David Webb, too, remained "convinced that the issues raised in this book . . . are essential for understanding the social and economic rôle of women within capitalism" (1979: 191).

A decade later, *Off-Centre: Feminism and Cultural Studies*, edited by Sarah Franklin, Celia Lury, and Jackie Stacey (1991b), continued the tradition of *Women Take Issue* of women working together on feminist concerns. It focuses especially on forms of knowledge, power, and politics and reflects the developments of the 1980s, when analyses of power and oppression (which feminism and cultural studies share with radical politics) and the attendant commitment to collective work, student participation in syllabus construction, and the opening up of spaces for connections to be made between personal and theoretical questions came under conservative attack. From an emphasis on the commonalities of women's oppression, feminist theory has shifted to include differences and indeed a questioning of any possibility of a unified category of "woman," reflecting the significant impact of poststructuralism and postmodernism. Poststructuralism and psychoanalysis manifested their influence through the work of Jacques Lacan and the elaboration of gender difference theory (associated with *m/f* and *Screen*). The stress fell on the production of subjects, and the roles of pleasure, desire, and fantasy in their construction, as complex and heterogeneous rather than stable and unified. Foucault's notion of discourse, "dispersed in a network of micro-relations," as an alternative to the concept of ideology has also been especially relevant. This work "criticized monolithic and totalizing notions of causality and determination and challenged assumptions of a linear, progressive history" (Franklin, Lury, and Stacey 1991b: 5).

Off-Centre points to how the divergences of cultural studies and feminism indicate differing priorities. In addition to the gender-blindness of concepts such as hegemony and ideology in much cultural studies work, there are problems with difference, discourse, and deconstruction, as the absence of any influence of feminist theories of patriarchy attest. The vein of structuralism deriving from social anthropology takes for granted just what feminism is concerned to explain: sexual division of labor and sexual difference. If the linguistic strand and poststructuralism "provided important critiques of some kinds of reductionism and essentialism, and facilitated the analysis of contradictory meanings and identities, their use has often obscured the significance of power relations in the constitution of difference, such as patriarchal forms of domination and subordination" (Franklin, Lury, and Stacey 1991: 9). It is exactly these concerns that are addressed by a poststructuralism derived from psychoanalysis. Methods such as deconstruction bridging the gap between social science and literary analysis have also had advantages for feminists: analyzing cultural processes as texts allowed for the location of the production, criticism, and consumption of literature in patriarchal relations and opened up a "space for more politicized readings of both the literary canon and what had been excluded from it." However, regarding the female body as a "text" "may contribute to the problem of objectification" (10). Reciprocal influences between feminism and cultural studies have also been inhibited by the gender specificity and lack of attention to patriarchal elements in forms of resistance exhibited by work issuing from the "ways of life" understanding of culture and its attendant ethnographic method.

Part 1 of *Off-Centre*, "Representation and Identity," illustrates the overlap of cultural studies and feminist approaches. Angela Partington's analysis (Franklin, Lury, and Stacey 1991b: 49–68) leads to a discussion of the forms of pleasure —social and cultural conditions of viewing melodrama—enjoyed by women in the 1950s as class-specific. Helen Pleasance (69–84) shows how "consumption, unlike romance, does not proffer only one social route for girls, the road to marriage. Rather, it offers the pleasures of continual transformation and change." A contrasting "narrative of cultural processes as open, incomplete and constantly moving" may be constructed on the bases of postmodernism and psychoanalysis against the pessimistic narrative of closure in which the "story is already told, social processes are complete, and meaning is fixed" (77, 78). The author confesses to having constructed the two analyses as irreconcilable, representing the constant tension of the contradiction through which relations of dominance are actually lived. Yvonne Tasker (85–96) looks at feminist evaluations of romance fiction and soap opera. In building on the "gendered genre" opposition of open feminist and closed masculine texts, those texts that seem radical may indeed only give that appearance. A positive step would be to actually "shift from a discourse of textual value, whether of greatness or political correctness" (95). This concern is echoed by Celia Lury (97–108). Her appraisal of the significance of autobiographical writing for feminism concludes that rather than asking how women's writing "could acquire the status of literature, the debate should address the issue of whether, if any notion of the literary is necessarily dependent on the denial of difference, the cost of literariness is worth paying" (108).

Unlike the overlap in part 1, little common ground is evident between the interests and approaches of feminism and cultural studies regarding "Science and Technology," the subject matter of part 2. This has been a fundamental field for feminism but not for cultural studies. When *Women Take Issue* was produced, "the feminist analysis of science was only just beginning to emerge. Since then, it has become one of the most challenging dimensions of feminist theory and politics, raising questions relevant to a wide range of inquiry and research." The cccs Science and Technology Subgroup (formed only in 1986) took a specific interest in "the contested territory of reproductive politics" to address "the power of science, medicine and technology to determine commonsense assumptions concerning reproductive issues" (Franklin, Lury, and Stacey 1991b: 129, 128). The group was convinced that not only should resources be expended in defeating the Alton Bill of 1987 (reducing the time limit for legal abortion to eighteen weeks), but in the struggle to gain popular support, an understanding needed to be developed "about the many ways in which Alton did succeed, particularly in setting new terms of the debate, despite his ultimate failure" (148).

In contrast with part 2, the subject matter of part 3, "Thatcherism and the Enterprise Culture"—ideology and the reproduction of the dominant culture, "British respectability"—has been central to cultural studies but less so to feminism. The themes include Thatcher's image and rhetoric, the politics of work, the "new oppressed," and how feminist discourse has and has not made a difference to gender politics; how many precepts of feminism have been co-opted to the new language of competitive individualism representative of the Thatcher governments; and oppression and resistance in black cultural politics, including how the diversity of black cultures interact with ethnicity, class, gender, and sexuality.

Policing the Crisis (S. Hall et al. 1978) underlined the importance of race in the representations of social problems such as crime, and *The Empire Strikes Back* (CCCS 1982) would criticize the "pathologization of race within race relations and sociology, and the racism of some white feminist analyses." But the "*influence* of debates about, and struggles against, racism on cultural studies continues to be rather uneven" (Franklin, Lury, and Stacy 1991a: 77). Race was taken seriously by Dick Hebdige in his work on subcultures: punk represented the uneasy fusion of the radically different languages—the "essentially antagonistic sources"—of *reggae* and *rock*. Hebdige brings out the deep structural connection between punk and black British subcultures associated with reggae by tracing reggae back to its roots in the West Indies and reinterpreting British youth culture "as a succession of differential responses to the black immigrant presence in Britain from the 1950s" (1979: 27, 29). For the skinheads, "the lost sense of working-class community [was] rediscovered embedded in black West Indian culture." Although audibly opposed to punk, it was reggae (expressive of the "deliberately opaque," "clotted language of Rastafarianism") that "implicitly threatened mainstream British culture from within and as such . . . resonated with punk's adopted values—'anarchy,' 'surrender' and 'decline' " (56–57, 64).

In 1980, Angela McRobbie addressed a major feminist critique of subcultural work primarily to Willis's *Learning to Labour* and Hebdige's *Subculture*. Her position was that the work on youth cultures emphasized "*male* youth cultural forms" (37). For the most part, family and domestic life, women's and girls' leisure, hedonism and fantasy are missing in this literature. In *Learning to Labour*, violence toward and degradation of women is constantly referred to but never directly confronted in the analysis. Even though *Subculture* redresses the neglect of race and racism in subcultural work, Hebdige "seems oblivious to the equal neglect of sexuality and sexism." He does nonetheless offer an advance over *Resistance through Rituals* by making possible an analysis of subcultural meanings "*without* continual recourse to class and so may disrupt (in a positive sense) some of our own commonsense wisdoms about class and class culture" (42, 43). No "politics of youth" emerges automatically from *Subculture;* its hesitancy

> barely disguises the pessimism deeply rooted in all structuralisms, the idea that codes may change but the scaffolding remains the same, apparently immutable. . . . *Subculture* should become a landmark within the politics of culture inside the notoriously traditional Art Colleges because of its emphasis on style and image as *collective* rather than *individual* expression and its investigation of the *social* meaning of style. The problem is just that Hebdige implies you have to choose either style *or* politics and that the two cannot really be reconciled. (47–48)

McRobbie suggests that the further exploration of the relationship between youth culture and politics necessitates the addition of the concepts of populism, leisure, and pleasure to class, sex, and race.

More than a decade after McRobbie, Joyce E. Canaan (Franklin, Lury, and Stacey 1991b: 109–25) took up the subculture question and the absence of gender relations in prior conceptualizations (e.g., Paul Corrigan's "Doing Nothing" [Hall and Jefferson 1976]). Although much work on youth subcultures from within cultural studies had ignored gender in developing class-based analyses, even feminist analyses of male violence against women, which depend on a theorization of a social value system extolling male strength, control, and competition, "do not explore in depth how class and race also shape male violence" (110).

In 1982 a subgroup at CCCS, which began studying race and "race relations" in England in 1978, published a collection responding to the marginalization of racist ideologies and conflicts in left analyses of the "national-popular," *The Empire Strikes Back: Race and Racism in 70s Britain.* However, the group confessed to not having dealt "satisfactorily with the struggles of black women, and [to] have struck an inadequate balance between the two black communities" (i.e., Afro-Caribbean and Asian). The group was "always divided by 'racial' and gender differences, and it was unusual to be able to work together at all. The same political differences which took their toll on group membership, were also part of the creative process of production" (CCCS 1982: 7, 8). John Solomos, Bob Findlay, Simon Jones, and Paul Gilroy (9–46) set out the central theme of the book: "The construction of an authoritarian state in Britain is fundamentally intertwined with the elaboration of popular racism in the 1970s," which ties it closely to *Policing the Crisis*. The aim is to "scrutinize the political practices that developed around the issue of race during the seventies," rather than concentrate on a theory of racist ideologies (9). These authors argue for a historical rather than sociological conception of racism, "conditioned, if not determined, by the historical development of colonial societies which was central to the reproduction of British imperialism." These are racial and ethnic forms of domination emanating from "*endogenous* political economic forces which are dominant in specific societies under study," not "*exogenous* mechanisms" (11, 12).

Three phases are apparent in the periodization of the experience of black workers in Britain after 1948: immediate response to black immigration culminating in the controls of the 1962 Act; policies in education, social services, and employment to deal with "problems" of the black presence; and control and containment from the early 1970s (crisis management) to deal with black resistance to racial domination. However, the state was unsuccessful in harmonizing social and economic processes in a crisis of crisis management and the "problem of how to negotiate a balance between economic needs and legitimacy has become the central issue of neo-conservative thinking." What was new in the 1960s was "that the threat came to be conceptualized as the 'enemy within' rather than a model of subversion from without . . . [through] the categories of crime, sexuality and youth" (CCCS 1982: 19, 23). Thus, a siege mentality developed in the 1970s: authority versus disorder. But the economic crisis and the crisis of race do not strictly correspond. What is needed is contextualization, "how different racial and ethnic groups were inserted historically, and the relations which have tended to erode and transform, or to preserve these distinctions through time . . . as active structuring principles of the present society," in order to explain how "race relations have become the central aspect of attempts to orchestrate politically—and therefore to manage— the effects of organic crisis" (28).

Two approaches to race dominated in the 1970s: placement of racial and nonracial phenomena on equal footing and presentation of the race problem as a part of the black communities themselves. The commonsense solution of repatriation depends on a "kind of historical forgetfulness which reworks the whole meaning of 'Britishness' in powerful images of the purity of nation, family and way of life, now jeopardized by the alien, external wedge"—race as a "specific social problem which has been imposed from the outside" (cccs 1982: 30). In the drift to authoritarian statism, quoting from Stuart Hall, the "police-black front is the front line . . . grow[ing] out of and reflect[ing] back on what is happening to the working class as a whole and to society as the crisis cuts into the latter at all levels" (34). Somehow, Solomos et al. find a note of tempered optimism. However, they do caution that the need to move beyond simple reform must not be articulated within a context of a supposed collapse of capitalist relations of domination, but in that of a state moving beyond its liberal-democratic phase.

Errol Lawrence (cccs 1982: 47–94) examines the ideological premises underpinning the "new racism" as "an organic component of attempts to make sense of the present crisis" that intersects commonsense conceptions of family and the relation of dominance at the interface between ruling bloc and working class (47). It is here that ideologues harness common sense to elite political projects. Lawrence (95–142) sees the crucial question in analyses of the relationship of ethnic minorities to the majority as one of power (obscured by pluralist perspectives), and it is this that severely limits choices for black people. In the area of family relations, sex/gender systems in Afro-Caribbean societies are "*different,*" but this is not a "pathological" difference. As for youths, the fact that they "have brought new understanding and different modes of struggle to bear on their communities' struggles, does not mean that they are not still following in their parents' footsteps or that they don't stand firmly *side by side* their parents in opposition to racism." Not only do race relations and ethnicity studies reflect the "*patriarchal* nature of 'white sociology,' " but sociologists are always there in the background as policy is being formulated (121, 132, 134).

Paul Gilroy (cccs 1982: 143–82) states that "police theorizations of 'alien blackness' as black criminality show where the filaments of racist ideology disappear into the material institutions of the capitalist state." State racism, transformation in the direction of authoritarianism, can be seen in "the methods and aims of policing under crisis conditions," the "extension of social control functions into the agencies and institutions of the welfare state," and the "manipulation of categories and rights of citizenship which has affected black exclusion as a step towards repatriation" (145). Conceptualizations of black culture and the meaning of crime affect whole communities, not just individuals. All the same, the race/crime question has not been easily apprehended by Marxists, as in E. P. Thompson's work, where blacks are not even "acknowledged to be part of the English working class." Although the labeling of black youth as a priori criminals is not necessarily conspiratorial, it is "no less a question of class struggle" (cccs 1982: 147, 174).

The racist "common sense" and the exclusion of blacks via consent "won through the creation of a 'national interest' " also inform Hazel V. Carby's work (cccs 1982: 183–211, 212–35). The "problems" of black students have been met with remedial, compensatory, or coercive practices in a cycle of "pathology," ignoring the wider context of the black community: "students practising forms of resistance as members of the black fraction of the working class." Integration has been replaced by a community relations form of social control. But black youth "determine the terrain on which the next struggle will be fought—the street, the day" (184, 208). Carby remarks on the *historical* construction of black women's sexuality and femininity and notes the similarities of racism and sexism as processes; however, "as soon as historical analysis is made, it becomes obvious that the institutions which have to be analysed are different, as are the forms of analysis needed." Indeed, the concepts of family, patriarchy, and reproduction in feminist theory become problematic when applied to black women. For the women's movement, it is important to ask who "We" are. White feminist researchers need to uncover the gender-specific mechanisms of racism among white women that disrupt "the recognition of common interests of sisterhood" (213, 233, 232). On Asian women, Pratibha Parmar (236–74) takes the baton from Carby and shows how speaking of women categorically perpetuates white female supremacy. Gender, race, and class all contribute to the oppression of Asian women and it is not desirable to separate them.

Even as racist ideologies and black differentiation disorganize—segment— the entire working class, contends Gilroy, autonomous organization by both blacks and women have made it possible for them "to 'leap-frog' over their fellow workers into direct confrontations with the state in the interest of the class as a whole" (cccs 1982: 288, 304). However, the crisis in which this struggle takes place is not yet a crisis of the state form. Fresh organizational forms of politics and strategy are necessary in the contemporary situation in which class consciousness "is not the sole prerogative of male, white, productive labourers" and at odds with Gramsci's " 'totalizing' view of the political party's role" (307, 305).

Thus, in *There Ain't No Black in the Union Jack* (1987), Gilroy's preference is for an analysis in terms of urban social movements. Indicative of racist reasoning is the idea that "blacks comprise a problem"; this is related to the idea that blacks are victims, "objects rather than subjects, beings that feel yet lack the ability to think, and remain incapable of considered behavior in an active mode. This oscillation between black as problem and black as victim has become, today, the principal mechanism through which 'race' is pushed outside of history and into the realm of natural, inevitable events" (11). In exposing this mechanism, Gilroy supplies a powerful corrective to the ethnocentricity of cultural studies.

> I have grown gradually more and more weary of having to deal with the effects of striving to analyse culture within neat, homogeneous national units reflecting the "lived relations" involved; with the invisibility of "race" within the field and, most importantly, with the forms of nationalism endorsed by a discipline which, in spite of itself, tends towards a morbid celebration of England and Englishness from which blacks are systematically excluded. (12)

Gilroy contests the view of race as an "eternal, essential factor of division in society"; racial meanings are not "an autonomous branch of ideology, but . . . a salient feature in a general process whereby culture mediates the world of agents and the structures which are created by their social praxis" (17). He considers class as tying politics to reappropriation of the structures of production but devoid of certainties in a constellation of conflict in which a single "working class" remains to be created. The various meanings attached to the political category of race, their conditions of existence and longevity, are outcomes of struggle and illustrate the openness of the category. Race ceases to be a biological category and becomes a cultural issue in which the exclusivity of Englishness is paramount. Gilroy notes that Raymond Williams combines discussion of race with that of patriotism and nationalism and, *parallel to the discourse of the right,* links the race problem to the arrival of new peoples: immigration. Also from the left, in Thompson and Hobsbawm, it would seem that "the only problem with nationalism is that the Tories have secured a near exclusive monopoly on it" (53).

The crisis of representation, the dislocation between the represented and their representatives, and the question of whether the Labour Party will survive it have been recognized and explored. However, according to Gilroy, the problem runs deeper. He links the right's populist language of nation and the ambiguities that tie it to race to this crisis of representation in which black lawbreaking is taken as proof of British and black incompatibility. New social movements are "struggling not only for the reappropriation of the material structure of production, but also for collective control over socio-economic development as a whole." New conflicts are beginning to form around the defense of identity and questions of personal experience. Distinctive of these movements is their "common struggle for social control of historicity" in which the issue of emancipation is universalized "beyond the particularistic interests of industrial workers employed full time in work that produces surplus value" (Gilroy 1987: 224, 225). And their demands are nonnegotiable. With the state prominent in antiracist activity at the local level, "the language of community has displaced both the language of class and the language of 'race' in the political activity of black Britain." Where the establishment views local control over the neighborhood as "particularly horrible," groups retreat to community action from a world of social relations beyond their control (230, 241).

Just the same, for "an anti-racist to argue for localism is, in a sense, surprising" (Edgar 1987: 44), and to call these struggles class struggles implies a rethinking of class analysis and highlights the emerging concerns for the problematic relationship between identities (and their constructedness) and politics.

From Working-Class Culture to Identity Politics

Work at cccs took off from the inversion of the elite, class-based analyses of culture (high culture of the establishment as opposed to the unculture of the working class) to privilege popular forms and practices. However, the (Arnoldian) art of (humanist, literary) criticism lived on in the early work. But if Williams was right and there was no timeless object, Culture, then new directions had to be sought. With 1968 came the "internationalization of academic culture" and the challenge of theory to cultural studies as practiced theretofore. In Britain these new directions coalesced around the culturalism/structuralism debate and a decided immersion in theory that was not just Marxist. This turn to theory, especially the structuralisms, belied a "preoccupation with founding a *science* of politics and culture, as opposed to the 'art' of criticism" (Aronowitz 1993: 129).

With the prominent exception of work on Thatcherism and the British state undertaken in the context of the Open University, the 1980s signaled a relative diminution of appeals to class in cultural studies work. Difficulties arose from the ambiguities of the social reality of the working class and the difficulties, or failure, associated with identifying such an actor as the working class. As the demise of Eurocommunism signaled the failure of class struggle through the

Party, the investment at CCCS in the contemporary and the local worked in its favor. The inadequacies of the theoretical solutions and the Eurocentrism of Marxist theory, particularly evident to Stuart Hall, who "came from a society where the profound integument of capitalist society, economy, and culture had been imposed by conquest and colonization," facilitated the Gramscian detour. The gains from Gramsci were substantial: "about the nature of culture itself, about the discipline of the conjunctural, about the importance of historical specificity, about the enormously productive metaphor of hegemony, about the way in which one can think questions of class relations only by using the displaced notion of ensemble and blocs" (S. Hall 1992: 279–80, 280).

Two other "interruptions" were fundamental to the development of work at CCCS: feminism and race. In a revealing interview, Hall alludes to a lost, "pre-feminist moment" at the very beginning at Birmingham; later, "Michael Green and myself decided to try and invite some feminists, working outside, to come to the Centre, in order to project the question of feminism into the Centre. So the 'traditional' story that feminism originally erupted from *within* cultural studies is not quite right" (S. Hall 1996a: 499). All the same, feminism "broke in," Hall writes; as "a thief in the night, it broke in; interrupted, made an unseemly noise, seized the time, crapped on the table of cultural studies" (1992: 282). It reorganized the field, beginning with the production of *Women Take Issue,* around questions of the personal as political; radically reorganized questions of power and the issues of gender and sexuality associated with it; and brought subjectivity and psychoanalysis to the center of the theoretical practice of cultural studies.[9] In *Off-Centre,* Franklin, Lury, and Stacey affirm that feminism, along with psychoanalysis and poststructuralism, was a significant influence determining the shift transforming cultural studies in the 1980s from "interest in issues concerning ideology and hegemony to those concerning identity and subjectivity" (1991: 6).

Race was put on the agenda through an internal struggle of which *Policing the Crisis* was a first manifestation. "Hall's analysis underlined the extent which the imaginary working class in which the Centre had invested its ethical project was no longer a tenable source of value" (MacCabe 1992a: 32);[10] however, getting "one of the great seminal books of the Centre," *The Empire Strikes Back,* written involved "a long, and sometimes bitter—certainly bitterly contested—internal struggle against a resounding but unconscious silence" on the part of "Paul Gilroy and the group of people who produced the book" (S. Hall 1992: 283).

Cultural studies at CCCS had come a long way, from popular culture with an at least analytically coherent subject, the working class, to the construction of identities, multiple subjectivities, in hierarchies of knowledge and power. But along the way, Stuart Hall tells us, it was the capacity to hold "theoretical and political questions in an ever irresolvable but permanent tension" inherent in the "displacement," necessitated by the "metaphor of the discursive, of textuality," and "*always* implied in the concept of culture," that defined cultural studies as a project (1992: 284).

CHAPTER 5

A Rose by Any Other Name? The Wide World
and Many Modes of Cultural Studies

I get the feeling that somewhere in some English publisher's vault there is a master-disk from which thousands of versions of the same article about pleasure, resistance, and the politics of consumption are being run off under different names with minor variations. Americans and Australians are recycling this basic pop-theory article, too: with the perhaps major variation that English pop-theory still derives at least nominally from a left populism attempting to salvage a sense of life from the catastrophe of Thatcherism. Once cut free from that context, as commodities always are, and recycled in quite different political cultures, the vestigial *critical* force of that populism tends to disappear or mutate.—MEAGHAN MORRIS, "Banality in Cultural Studies"

Cultural studies is not simply portable as an intellectual "master discourse" that can be plucked from the treasure chest by the globe-trotting theorist to flourish at the suitably amazed natives of foreign shores.—JOHN HARTLEY, "Expatriation: Useful Astonishment as Cultural Studies"

In the wake of the debates of the mid-1950s and their follow-through, intellectuals on the left embarked on a sustained pursuit of new conceptual frameworks. The imported French theory that became so fundamental to the development of cultural studies was rooted in linguistics. Besides providing new tools for the analysis of popular culture, it held an overriding appeal for scholars whose primary subject matter was the text in the classical sense. It contributed to a crisis in English studies just as cultural studies was beginning to expand from its original institutional hub and has continued to fuel ongoing discussions right up to the present. There has been a shift, nonetheless. Earlier concerns were for a theory of politics and social action widely construed; here, of course, alongside the structuralisms, the turn to Gramsci was fundamental as well. Contemporary debates, however, focus on the politics of theory; the Culture Wars and the Science Wars are exemplary.

Beyond Birmingham

After 1968, even mainstream students clamored for more flexibility in the curriculum, and during the mid-1970s, that bastion, Cambridge English, seemed to take on new life. Raymond Williams was promoted and Frank Kermode joined the faculty. But Williams's project raised prickly questions: "If 'culture' was not a permanent resource to be defended or drawn on as the occasion dictated, and 'literature' was not a linguistic thing apart, what exactly became of 'criticism,' the discipline whose own special claims were based on these very convictions?" (Mulhern 1981: 28). As the implications were becoming apparent, George Steiner's lectures made available powerful tools developed by Jakobson and Lévi-Strauss. Even more consequential was Barthes and the idea that the author, rather than the controlling subject, was the unconscious effect of language constituting texts. But even so, the Tripos reform group under Kermode could not budge the conservative wing.

The new wave hit Cambridge in the name of Colin MacCabe, whose appointment in 1975 was controversial enough to prompt the resignation of one member of the Appointments Committee. Structuralism, or, for the less lazy and professionally ignorant, as MacCabe would have it, "the attempt to link questions of signification to questions of subjectivity" (1985: 6), was firmly anchored in the academy by the 1980s. But mainstream institutions could be hostile. At Cambridge, where " 'English' was effectively created in its modern form," MacCabe was denied tenure in 1980 over the issue of structuralism in that university's "worst academic controversy for a generation" (Mulhern 1981: 27).

The construction of English at Cambridge had been an oppositional enterprise. By the 1960s, however, it was moribund. MacCabe contended that if his opponents "had admitted the real terms of the debate—under what terms and with what methods could you continue to teach English language and literature —then they would have already conceded what they were desperate to defend: that there could be no questions about English as a discipline. For them, English had no history. It had been, was, and would continue to be" (1985: 30). In the end, Kermode and Williams were voted off the Appointments Committee in a top-to-bottom house cleaning.

The experiences of both Cambridge and *Screen* suggested to MacCabe that there could be no comfortable divisions between politics and the humanities and social sciences.[1] In Thatcherite Britain, the institution realized that to challenge the authority of literature was to challenge the authority of literary intellectuals as possessing privileged cultural insight and thereby the structure/authority of the institution and, by extension, society itself.

Graeme Turner has charged that "the political basis of cultural studies analyses of the media during the 1970s was significantly and in general overshadowed by the novelty and productiveness of the analytical methods employed. The most notable effect . . . was an explosion of interest in the 'reading' of cultural texts" (1990: 100; see Morley 1992: introduction). One exception outside of CCCS was the Glasgow Media Group's work on the news (1976, 1980, 1982). Another, but from the Birmingham sphere, was Stuart Hall, Ian Connell, and Lidia Curti's examination of the current affairs program *Panorama*.[2] The media do not intervene "to tilt the balance towards one party or another," but they "*are* biased in favour of the Party-system *as such.* . . . the closure towards which this 'sometimes teeth-gritting harmony' tends, overall, is one which, without favouring particular positions in the field of the political class struggle, *favours the way the field of political class struggle is itself structured,*" they wrote (1981: 115–16). By the 1980s, emphasis was passing from the text to the audience. In her study of the soap opera *Crossroads,* Dorothy Hobson (1982) watched with the audience. However, she was more interested in the effectiveness of the encoding end of the chain than the actual outcomes of decoding, indeed arguing for the power of the audience in determining the text in the first place, a text that provides pleasure as well as producing meaning.

Institutionally, the Open University was an early magnet for CCCS personnel as they began to spread out all over Britain and overseas.[3] Between 1982 and 1987 more than five thousand students took the Open University's interdisciplinary course in cultural studies, Popular Culture U203. Members of the course team counted Stuart Hall, Paul Willis, and David Morley. Students aside, the course linked "intellectuals who had been involved in *Screen* reading groups, members of the British Film Institute, academics in polytechnics and universities and film and television practitioners" and performed "a re-education for several hundred teachers besides an uncounted number of the general public." The course deployed Gramsci's concept of hegemony to circumvent the choice between a "culturalist" or "structuralist" perspective. However, according to Antony Easthope, "popular culture, both as text and practice, signifying practice and historical situation, are laid out in a seeming unity . . . this subjectivity the course enforces but does not interrogate" (1988: 73, 80).

Both the limited use of psychoanalysis and the intrusiveness of the poststructuralist conception of pleasure challenged the ease of this solution. Tony Bennett and Janet Woollacott, in *Bond and Beyond*, held that popular cultural works articulate a range of ideologies and to be popular must make concessions to the values and ideologies of subordinate groups. Meaning is to be found in the "social organization of the relationships between texts within specific conditions of reading" (1987: 45). Bennett and Woollacott tried "to clarify and account for the specific pleasures which the Bond novels and films have offered by examining the ways in which the formal and narrative devices they deploy play with and put into suspense the subject positions produced by the ideological discourses—primarily ones of sex and gender, nation and nationhood and, depending on the period, those of Cold War or détente—on which these texts work" (4, 5). Although "Bond films can be experienced as a liberating send-up of redundant ideological categories" (281), Andrew Blake notes that the Bond texts "conceal political realities (in the way predicted by the *Screen*-debate model of 'realism') at least as much as they renegotiate hegemony. Lack of any discussion of this dimension of secret service politics within British political history seriously weakens *Bond and Beyond*, particularly since so much of the book concerns reformulation of the notion of 'Englishness' " (1992: 61).

The accent on the pleasures of the audience was having wide resonance: Ien Ang's 1985 study of *Dallas,* Janice Radway's 1984 work on romance fiction, and David Buckingham's 1987 study of *EastEnders,* among many others. Roland Barthes, as so often, had provided the impetus with *The Pleasure of the Text,* which appeared in English in 1975. By 1987, John Fiske's *Television Culture,* through a sense of the subversiveness of pleasure, could present "a view of popular culture audiences . . . many miles from the manipulated masses of 'effects' studies" (G. Turner 1990: 121).

In England by the 1990s universities had begun to offer specializations such as cultural and media studies (Bristol) and media and cultural studies (Liverpool John Moores).[4] Some gave degrees and combined degrees such as cultural studies, media and cultural studies, information and cultural studies, and contemporary cultural studies. Others opened centers: Centre for Literary and Cultural Studies (Keele), Centre for Cultural Studies (Leeds), Centre for British and Comparative Cultural Studies (Warwick); or established departments and schools: Department of Cultural Studies (East London), Culture and Communication (Hertfordshire), Communications and Image Studies (Kent at Canterbury), Cultural and Education Studies (Leeds), Cultural Studies (Sheffield Hallam), Literary, Cultural and Media Studies (Staffordshire), School of English, Cultural and Communication Studies (Middlesex), History and Cultural Studies (Goldsmiths' College). Names can be misleading, however, as in the case of Goldsmiths' College, where Paul Gilroy taught in the Sociology Department and David Morley and Georgina Born in Media and Communications rather than in the Department of Historical and Cultural Studies. Significantly, however, even at the Open University, where cultural studies was not institutionalized in any significant sense, and where there has been only one real cultural studies course (U203 Popular Culture), the influence has been felt in the more traditional disciplines.

The Settler Colonies

As the 1980s progressed, the cultural studies perspective spread to the Anglo-Saxon, English-speaking settler colonies: Australia, Canada, South Africa, the United States.

Australia enjoyed a "boom" in cultural studies; in fact, the first cultural studies journal, the *Australian Journal of Cultural Studies,* was published there until 1987, when it was moved to England as *Cultural Studies.* However, "Australian accounts of cultural studies which take their bearings from the British tradition" pass under erasure the nonacademic roots of the movement in Australia that "introduces a distortion . . . into current debates" (Frow and Morris 1993: xxvi). As Meaghan Morris said, it was a boom in the sense of "passion and enthusiasm" but also "a pre-emptive prohibition and limitation of activity" (1988: 5). Although a number of the major figures received training in Britain, the historically specific situation of the assimilation of cultural studies in Australia raised some interesting questions and contradictions, grouped loosely around the issues of policy studies and cultural analysis done on the margins versus work done at the metropole.

In the introduction to their anthology, *Australian Cultural Studies: A Reader,* John Frow and Meaghan Morris assert that the really innovative feature of Australian work has been "in developing the *implications* of particular forms of symbolic action, and the *consequences* of particular moments of cultural practice." Although cultural studies in Australia has not necessarily been hostile to theory,

> the doctrinal disputes which have marked and perhaps enabled the emergence of cultural studies elsewhere . . . have not long remained the *focus* of debate in Australia, where they are often resolved in practice by a kind of rigorous *mixing. . . .* Australian cultural studies has not only been a response to the political and social movements of the past three decades . . .

but has also derived many of its themes, its research priorities, its polemics and, in some ways its theoretical emphases and privileged working methods, from an engagement with those movements. (1993: xiv–xv)

Indeed, the policy debate has been very real in Australia and has involved such institutions as the Communication Law Centre at the University of New South Wales and the Centre for International Research in Communication and Information Technologies (CIRCIT) in Melbourne. At Griffith University (Queensland), the pro-policy Institute for Cultural Policy Studies (ICPS) has also been especially active. Tony Bennett, Dean of the School of Cultural and Historical Studies in the Division of Humanities at Griffith, insisted that the attack mounted on the humanities in Australia was on the grounds not of their elitism but of a perceived lack of relevance. To address this challenge the ICPS was established in 1987 for "organizing research, publications, and conference programs capable of playing a positive role within the processes of Australian cultural policy formation." It developed a variety of relationships "with a range of local and national governmental or quasi-governmental agencies operative within the spheres of museum, arts, film, language, and education policies." Writing in 1992, Bennett was convinced that by putting policy questions to cultural studies analysis it might be possible to avoid "banality" and resist "the lure of those debates whose contrived appearance of ineffable complexity makes them a death trap for practical thinking" (33).

Stuart Cunningham described the turn to policy as a "centrist" option. It would be opposed to the cheerful populism and lingering traditional critical stances of the left humanities position and take its distance from the "calling into question [of] the continuing relevance of the neo-Marxist 'motor' of cultural studies" from the right social science position in the wake of the fall of the socialist regimes of the USSR and Eastern Europe. This centrist orientation would "shift its 'command metaphors' away from rhetorics of resistance, oppositionalism and anti-commercialism on the one hand, and populism on the other, toward those of access, equity, empowerment and the divination of opportunities to exercise appropriate cultural leadership" (1991: 423, 434; see also 1992). Such a position would also call for a reconceptualization of general theories and rethinking the politics of culture in a non-British, non–North American situation. Unlike Cunningham's reformism, Tom O'Regan perceived contiguous styles in policy and cultural criticism: "A choice cannot be made *between* policy and cultural criticism—we simply do one or the other depending on the circumstance" (1992: 417).

In *Myths of Oz,* a collection of articles devoted to Australian popular culture, John Fiske argued that "culture does not grow out of the unity of society but out of its divisions. It has to work to *construct* any unity that it has, rather than simply celebrate an achieved harmony" (Fiske, Hodge, and Turner 1987: x). Graeme Turner recognized that Meaghan Morris (1990), who termed it "a book about *blokes,*" and Tony Bennett (1988) both correctly identified a genuine weakness in the "habit of wheeling in British subcultural theory to analyse mainstream Australian popular culture" (1991: 32, 20). The romantic tradition of the subcultures work privileged a discourse of difference as an internal resistance to a hegemonizing national-popular; however, on the periphery the very creation of a national-popular can be considered a project of resistance to the metropole. In Australia, multiculturalism developed as a national project from the 1960s, thus promoting "a constructive, not an organic concept of Australian culture" and accounting for why Australian work "has generally been less concerned to debate the pros and cons of 'essentialism' as a philosophical stance than to examine the *political* conflicts at stake . . . and to articulate the *historical* struggles occurring in the gaps between competing narrative programs (of 'prosperity,' for example), and the complex social experiences that these aspire to organize" (Frow and Morris 1993: ix, xi–xii). In the ex-colony, it is the construction not of a class or subcultural identity but of a national identity that has become the conventional object of cultural critique.[5] The internalized emphases on ideologies of nationalism and the social function of subcultures, as differences within national cultures, act to obscure the importance of differences among cultures on a supranational scale. Here theories of resistance and pleasure unleavened by historical specificity risk homogenizing both "texts and audiences across cultural and political borders," (G. Turner 1992: 642), as Jim Bee (1989) contends in his review of John Fiske's (1987) *Television Culture.*

Australian universities embraced cultural studies in varying ways. Western Sydney–Macarthur and Charles Sturt instituted a so-named specialization. Departments have included Social and Cultural Studies at Victoria University of Technology; Cultural and Policy Studies at Queensland University of Technology; Social, Cultural and Curriculum Studies in Education at New England–Armidale; and the School of Communications and Cultural Studies at Curtin University of Technology. Griffith University has an Australian Key Centre for Cultural and Media Policy; Murdoch founded a Centre for Research in Culture and Communication; and Monash founded a Centre for Comparative Literature and Cultural Studies. The University of Melbourne has offered courses in cultural studies in the Department of English Language and Literature and since 1992 has an interdepartmental Cultural Studies Program. The University of Wollongong instituted an M.A. in cultural studies in 1991 and integrated the Cultural Studies Program into the Communication and Cultural Studies Program in 1996. The University of Queensland (Brisbane) has operated a Women, Ideology and Culture Research Unit; its English Department has offered a subject area in Communication and Cultural Studies heavy with discourse, screen, and textual analysis and in 1995 established the Media and Cultural Studies Centre. John Frow, in his inaugural lecture in 1990 at Queensland, reconfirmed the relationship between cultural studies practice and theoretical urgency by arguing that theory courses should be a required part of the curriculum.

In Canada, cultural studies has remained an Anglophone phenomenon associated with the Birmingham School and, like Australia but with a very different tonality given the linguistic division, concerned with the "national" within, as Laura Mulvey registers:

> The question of Canadian identity is political in the most direct sense of the word, and it brings the political together with the cultural and ideological immediately and inevitably. For the Canada delineated by multinationals, international finance, U.S. economic and political imperialism, national identity is a point of resistance, defining the border fortifications against exterior colonial penetration. Here nationalism can perform the political function familiar in Third World countries. (1986: 10)

However, the tension in the simplification that posits a unitary Canada in a rhetorical simile with the third world is evident. Indeed, "few 'English-Canadian' sociologists and anthropologists are celebrating or even capable of imagining the course of balkanization the country appears embarked on" (Nielsen and Jackson 1991: 289), and there has been little cross-fertilization between Anglophone Canada and Francophone Quebec, where there was already a strong tradition, critical and "nationalist," of cultural sociology and a large research institute, the Institut québécois de recherche sur la culture (Dandurand: 1989).

Greg Nielsen and John Jackson have argued that the deconstruction of the national must form a major project for Canadian cultural studies. The official version of culture in Canadian society on which policy is premised is a simple sum of its parts, with the result that "cultural studies defined as sociological poetics must negate any definition of the one Canadian culture or representations of the one Canadian society." Placing the desirability of Canadian culture in question "assumes an opposite direction to that offered by preceding generations of political economists who have traditionally privileged definitions of cultural unity as a means of combating continental and global imperialism." However, continue Nielsen and Jackson, if cultural studies is to occupy a critical space in the 1990s "as 'the Canada' finally disintegrates then we conclude it can only proceed by exploring the transcultural implications of the social imaginary where autonomy and ultimately sovereignty are being dreamed of; be it between countries, regions or men and women" (1991: 279, 294).

Sampling institutional initiatives, the University of Guelph has a Centre for Cultural Studies and Trent University (Peterborough) has boasted both a Cultural Studies Program and an Institute for the Study of Popular Culture. The Centre at Guelph, founded in 1996, is explicitly concerned with overcoming the "two cultures" divide. The program at Trent was initiated in 1978 and Trent was the first university in Canada to make "the interdisciplinary study of modern culture the basis of an undergraduate degree." According to the departmental brochure (1991–92), the program was initiated "through the cooperative efforts of faculty teaching in the fields of Comparative Literature, Social Theory and the Fine Arts" and has included courses in film, theater, music, mass media, and cultural policy. At Queen's University (Kingston), the Communication, Culture and Society Programme has been offered as a special field concentration in the Departments of Film Studies and Sociology. Carlton University (Ottawa) has had a Textual Analysis, Discourse and Culture research unit, and there has been a cultural studies stream at the doctoral level in sociology. The interdisciplinary research group, the Centre for Research in Communications, Culture and Society, was set up in the mid-1980s and included personnel from the Arts and Social Sciences faculties. In 1988, a new unit, the Centre for Research on Culture and Society, which did not include journalism (and its mass communications program), was born. This split is congruent with Raymond Morrow's (1991: 160) observation that in general in Canada the emergence of communications graduate programs indirectly discouraged cultural research in sociology. Generally, the formation during the 1970s and 1980s of two interdisciplinary fields, political economy and cultural studies, signaled a tentative break with the traditional disciplines. Neither has been without its detractors, and John Harp, in a not surprising rehearsal of a long-standing theme, argued that "incorporating a renewed concept of *community* in analyses of resource exploitation and education can bring about a convergence of political economy and cultural studies which will meet certain criticisms leveled at both" (1991: 207).

In South Africa, cultural studies has remained closely associated with the concerns for working-class culture and identity of its parent formation in the metropole, notwithstanding the context of a foreground of apartheid and race that has determined a specific local trajectory.[6] Pre-1994 cultural analysis was most often associated with political liberation. According to Sarah Nuttall and Cheryl-Ann Michael, "Cultural theorizing in South Africa, with its emphasis on separation and segregation, has been based until recently on the following tendencies: the over-determination of the political, the inflation of resistance, and the fixation on race, or more particularly on racial supremacy and racial victimhood as a determinant of identity. . . . each of these assumptions needs to be overturned" (2000a: 1–2).

The cultural studies approach, with its openness and mobility among the disciplines, or "instability," according to Coplan (1994), has facilitated the asking of questions that were either co-opted, off-limits, or simply hidden in the shadow of the "culturalist" perspective so well manipulated under apartheid. It is in this sense that cultural studies has facilitated the difficult passage, both theoretical and practical, from resistance to inclusiveness and connectedness. This move is characterized by an emphasis on the public function and a shift away from, or at least a reconceptualization of, "identities" and difference and back toward a redeployment of "a revitalized Marxism . . . 'totalizing' not in the sense of claiming a monopoly of explanation, but in the sense of thinking holistically, of relating issues of consciousness and culture to a theory of capitalism and an analysis of the systemic relations between the different levels and institutions of the capitalist state" (Bundy 1996: 37). Indeed, as Michael Green contends, cultural studies "may be of best use, neither as an academic discipline with its own rigours, nor in the revolutions of intellectual/political paradigms (important as these are), but in its consolidation as a public presence. Not an area of new professional 'expertise' with 'answers,' but a space openly available for thought and analysis . . . a continuing activity, responsive to short-term pressures and to the longer-term interests of participants" (quoted in Starfield and Gardiner 2000: 72–73).

Policy orientation recalls one of the characteristics that the appropriation of cultural studies in Australia took, and the strong relationship with the extramural community evokes the context in which Williams, Hoggart, and Thompson were working in the 1950s. A good example in South Africa, and reminiscent of what Laura Chrisman calls "real work"—that is, the way "the knowledge of the complexity and potency of language formations, of the social dynamics embedded and mediated through languages" could be used "to produce textual, theoretical and sociological analyses from which Western academe could learn a huge amount" (1996: 191)—is the Cultural Studies Research Programme at Vista University, implemented through local projects at each of the university's eight campuses. Under apartheid these campuses were located in or near black townships, and now that proximity has made possible the establishment of new relationships between the institutions and their immediate, extramural public (see Starfield and Gardiner 2000).

In a general discussion that highlights the importance of the relationship between state and nation and between local and global, Gary Minkley and Andrew Steyn ask: "Should 'African Cultural Studies' be a 'standpoint knowledge'?" Indeed, the "debate is not only between different theories, or between local conditions of oppression and metropolitan theories, but also between cultural and intellectual practice and politics. Does poststructuralism move intellectual practice beyond politics—or does it extend politics?" (1996: 206)—a point that finds particular resonance in the way cultural studies has developed in the United States.

Cultural studies in the United States, although hugely successful and encompassing, has no group of founding texts such as those of Williams, Hoggart, and Thompson in Britain; neither does it have an original institutional site like that at cccs Birmingham, nor a "grey eminence" like Stuart Hall. And although a number of the leading lights in U.S. cultural studies were trained in Birmingham, development in the United States diverged significantly from the British trajectory. Furthermore, notwithstanding the very different spatiotemporal conjuncture (Britain in the 1950s–60s, United States in the 1980s–90s), it seems that as the term cultural studies began to make inroads during the early 1980s, many found that this was somehow what they had been doing all along!

The 1980s, writes Richard Ohmann, promoted cultural studies in two ways: first, "the teflon presidency made more obvious and urgent the need for cultural exegesis of domination in the U.S."; second, the conservative assault "not only on subaltern groups but on dissident intellectuals stiffened the backs of the latter (now quite numerous in the universities) and made it attractive to them to enlist in an academic project that openly announced itself as oppositional" (1991: 8).

In the United States, the geopolitical events of 1956 had nothing like the consequences that were precipitated in Britain. Politically, an already weak Marxist left was further diminished during the McCarthyist persecutions (1950–54), and within the universities McCarthyism was extended through a covert collaborative relationship with the intelligence community.[7] Intellectually, on top of the ideology of "the end-of-ideology," the very diversity of the New Criticism and the high degree of institutionalization of its formalism precluded the formation of an activist movement along the lines of *Scrutiny* in the humanities with a base such as Leavis had had at Cambridge. A social-critical posture was not to be found in the "value-neutral" social sciences either, taken with behaviorism, structural-functionalism, and quantitative analysis. The United States did, however, have a strong civil rights movement that embarked on an ascending curve of activism from the mid-1950s.

Edward Bacciocco cites five major events, which occurred between January 1959 and November 1960, that set off a student reaction and launched the New Left movement in the United States: "the election of John F. Kennedy as president, the seizure of power by Castro in Cuba, the sit-ins against segregated facilities in the South, the execution of Caryl Chessman at San Quentin, and the furor aroused by the House Un-American Activities Committee (HUAC) hearings in San Francisco" (1974: 21). And there were still some, few, elements of continuity with an indigenous, internationalist Old Left; the New Left in the United States counted a goodly number of "red-diaper babies" and the anti-nuclear weapons movement contributed both personnel and tactics. Marxism and internationalism were powerful themes of communal action but shared the philosophical ground with an existentialism that legitimated countercultural lifestyles (foreshadowed by the Beat Generation—individualism as a license for rebellion, *ecstasis* equated with existence in which even casual sex was considered of value as at least in some way "being-with-the-other"). Agitation for university reform in the desire to favor the flowering of the whole person over a vapid conformism did eventually produce enduring structural changes.

Of course, the movement was international in scope; this was truly an escalating World Revolution. Throughout the 1960s, the United States fought to hold on to geopolitical hegemony in the interstate system in the face of mounting challenges on all fronts. In the aftermath of the Cuban fiasco, the Kennedy administration established the Peace Corps and the Alliance for Progress in 1961. Anti-insurgency warfare and winning "the hearts and minds of the people" matured into the debacle of full-fledged engagement in Vietnam. While the Port Huron Statement issued in 1962 by Students for a Democratic Society was still relatively mild and favored "party realignment," by 1969 the home front revolt had culminated with the Weathermen and in 1970 the diamond sky bled at Altamont, marking the downhill tilt of the San Francisco scene.[8]

The "crisis of the humanities" has been placed squarely on the shoulders of the generation of 1968 ("a collective loss of nerve and faith on the part of both faculty and academic administrators during the late 1960s and early 1970s"). In his 1984 "To Reclaim a Legacy," William Bennett (head of the National Endowment for the Humanities), following Walter Jackson Bate, faults the humanities (history, languages and literature, philosophy) for giving up "the great task of transmitting a culture to its rightful heirs." In Arnoldian terms, he holds that they "can contribute to an informed sense of community by enabling us to learn about and become participants in a common culture, shareholders in our civilization." He and the study group he chaired do not advise a return to the classical curriculum and even maintain that "a respect for diversity" is a "good thing"; however,

> our eagerness to assert the virtues of pluralism should not allow us to sacrifice the principle that formerly lent substance and continuity to the curriculum, namely that each college and university should recognize and accept its vital role as conveyor of the accumulated wisdom of our civiliza-tion . . . the core of the American college curriculum—its heart and soul—should be the civilization of the West, source of the most powerful and pervasive influences on America and all of its people. (19, 16, 17, 21)

The attack was renewed by Lynne Cheney (see Bacon 1990) from the same institutional seat. Patrick Brantlinger is right: "The *Port Huron Statement* lays bare the dilemma of humanistic liberalism in a society that enshrines it in academic institutions, yet systematically thwarts the realization of its ideals. This blockage between theory and practice *is* the crisis Bate and Bennett de-plore" (1990: 5, 6).

The New Left concentrated on a project—savagely repressed by the establish-ment—that balanced (precariously, and not without tensions) civil rights and anti–Vietnam War activity with frontal attacks on the university system, which now "occupied a central position in American society" (e.g., Berkeley 1964, Columbia 1968). The universities, Kirkpatrick Sale explains,

> were indispensable helpmeets of the federal government in the production of weapons, the development of scientific processes, the maintenance of the economy, and the study and manipulation of foreign cultures . . . they were the most important part of an $80-billion "knowledge industry" which accounted for as much as 29 percent of the Gross National Product in 1962 and 40 percent of it in 1970 and which employed some 43 percent of all American workers as the decade opened, more than 50 percent when it closed. Clark Kerr, one of the first to understand the new importance of universities, stated it best: "The university has become a prime instrument of national purpose." (1973: 22)

There is, by its very nature, a certain idealism associated with the academy, and those who manned(!) the barricades in 1968 returned to the university with a double measure. In 1970 Ellen Cantarow asked, "Why teach literature?"[9] Her answer deserves to be quoted in extenso.

> I began to understand that the war in Vietnam was neither accident nor imposition, but simply the most recent in a century and a half of American wars of colonization and imperialism waged in the interests of economic hegemony. . . . For women like myself the most important development around 1967 was the rise of the women's liberation movement. A group of young women had broken away from SDS and SNCC and had begun taking stock of their treatment at the hands of their supposed comrades. . . . If my own life was subject to historical and political influences so was literature. . . . [As alternatives to the models of literature as liberal enrichment and armchair revolution] there are other models . . . Marx, Rosa Luxemburg, Alexander Herzen, for example, and in literary and cultural criticism, Cristopher Caudwell and Raymond Williams. Their work suggests the legitimacy of, the need for, rewriting "literary" criticism as historical and cultural criticism. The process of learning about history, economics, politics, science, that this task involves in turn begins to transform us; for we are forced outside the confines of bureaucratically defined disciplines. . . . That transformation, the need to approach culture, history, economics with the compassion and the sense of real familiarity our new scholarship entails, takes place, my own experience suggests, only as we participate in struggle. (1970: 70, 71, 94–95)

The movement exposed the limiting power of compartmentalized disciplines and issued a plea for the construction of revolutionary ideas of culture in the classroom and, outside the classroom, an active socialist movement and culture.

Ironically, as Cantarow was writing, Paul de Man was setting up headquarters at Yale. In October 1966,[10] the Johns Hopkins Humanities Center had convened an international symposium "to explore the impact of contemporary 'structuralist' thought on critical methods in humanistic and social studies" entitled "Criticism and the Sciences of Man/Les Langages Critiques et les Sciences de l'Homme" (Macksey and Donato 1972: xv). This symposium cast a long shadow over subsequent developments in the humanities and the social sciences in the United States.[11] It planned to identify problems in "common to every field of study": "the status of the subject, the general theory of signs and language systems, the use and abuse of models, homologies and transformations as analytic techniques, synchronic (vs.) diachronic descriptions, the question of 'mediations' between objective and subjective judgements, and the possible relationship between microcosmic and macrocosmic social or symbolic dimensions" (xvi). Not only were a significant number of younger students introduced to the material at hand, but provision was made for them to continue their contacts with the participants in a special program of study abroad.

The publication of the proceedings included Jacques Derrida's work in progress, the essay "Structure, Sign and Play in the Discourse of the Human Sciences." Derrida proposes that in the history of the concept of structure or structurality of structure (the substitution of one "center," or organizing principle or *presence,* such as essence, existence, substance, or subject, after the next, which limited "freeplay," the connotative dimension) a point was reached when an "event," a *rupture* took place. "In the absence of a center or origin, everything became discourse . . . when everything became a system where the central signified, the original or transcendental signified, is never absolutely present outside a system of differences. The absence of the transcendental signified extends the domain and the interplay of signification *ad infinitum*" (Derrida 1972: 249). No facts, only interpretations; no truths, only expedient fictions. And this would extend beyond literature to the human sciences.

Deconstruction, Derrida's brainchild, was embraced by Paul de Man (a discussant at the Johns Hopkins symposium) and taken to its limits by the French and Comparative Literature Departments at Yale (the institutional base of deconstruction from de Man's appointment in 1970). In fact, "America *is* deconstruction," noted Derrida in 1983 (Lehman 1991: 56).[12] Julia Kristeva "observed in 1986 that a hard-line version of deconstruction had 'become a sort of monopoly' in the high echelons of American literary criticism. 'In America, the so-called deconstructionists think that, because ethics and history belong to metaphysics and because metaphysics is criticized by Heidegger or his French followers, ethics and history no longer exist' " (Lehman 1991: 55).

Unlike Britain, where deconstruction never really took hold, the theoretical move in the United States in the humanities and social sciences was through Derrida and "then to the psychoanalytic theories of Jacques Lacan, so managing to by-pass almost altogether the work of the French Marxist theorist, Louis Althusser" (Easthope 1988: xiii).[13] Downgrading experience and intent (the thought behind the act), and thus agency, deconstruction threatened criticism itself. In fact, it has been attacked by both activists on the left as promoting quiescence and traditionalists on the right who detect "the impulse to undermine institutions and ideas by asserting that they undermine themselves" (Lehman 1991: 79). In its North American institutional setting, "cultural studies not only has become almost synonymous with a certain kind of postmodern theorizing but also is now often referred to . . . simply as 'theory' " (Morley 1992: 3). Already by the mid-1980s Stuart Hall could contrast the CCCS experience with the United States, where formal semiotics "became a sort of alternative interpretive methodology."

> When we took on semiotics, we were taking on a methodological requirement: you had to show *why* and *how* you could say that that is what the meaning of any cultural form or practice is. That is the semiotic imperative: to demonstrate that what you were calling "the meaning" is textually constituted. But as a formal or elaborated *methodology,* that was not what semiotics was for us. In America, taking on semiotics seemed to entail taking on the entire ideological baggage of structuralism. (1986: 59)[14]

Nonetheless, the issue of *value* in the United States, as in Britain, was crucial to the directions cultural studies took.

The concern for identities and subjectivities that developed late at CCCS around issues of race and gender were primary in social analysis in the United States (blacks, women, gays and lesbians). Although theory excluded "from cultural study all contemporary cultural forms" in the 1970s and early 1980s, the redeployment of deconstruction to take advantage of its capacity for dismantling hierarchies of power (which made it attractive to the generation of 1968) has been extremely influential in those areas of cultural studies treating themes of race/ethnicity, gender, and the media.[15] As Colin MacCabe argued, cultural studies

> with its commitment to an ethnography of popular cultures and its refusal to privilege literature was an obvious framework for this new work. At the same time the problem of value . . . is more difficult than ever. The belief in the working class as a privileged source of cultural value, either as author or audience, is no longer tenable after decades which have thrown up the claims of women, gays, blacks. At the same time the simple annexation of cultural studies as the academic equivalent of identity politics constantly presupposes that those marginalised identities can themselves produce criteria of value in the same way as the working class within the original model. (1992b: 33)

Cornel West has asserted that there is "something quite positive about deconstruction, having to do with keeping track of the rhetorical operations of power and binary oppositions." It can, however, become too easily linked "to an austere epistemic skepticism. And that . . . makes it very difficult to make the links between rhetorical powers, military powers, political powers, social powers, and other kinds of powers. I see this also in Foucault" (1992: 697).

This last point was stated by Graham Murdock as the need to conceptualize the relationship between both sides of the communications process: "the material and the discursive, the economic and the cultural—without collapsing either one into the other" (1989: 436). Despite the efforts of those like Janet Wolff (1984), who emphasized "social production," this materiality of the cultural process was exactly what tended to get lost as cultural studies migrated from its home shores. Some of the reasons for this slippage are as simple as the American audience's unfamiliarity with British examples and the political-economics of publishing that dictates that the higher the level of abstraction, the wider the market books will find (see Morley 1992: 3–4).

Angela McRobbie reminds us that although intellectually "deconstruction is dazzling" and politically "it is enabling," it does not carry with it the "need to be constrained by materialism (a requirement or obligation which itself would be subject to deconstruction), or held to account by a political agenda" (1992: 720). Thus, although enabling, deconstruction can be profoundly conservative (the more so the more ardently it is practiced) in its skepticism. Denounced right and left, its flourishes are largely confined to the classroom. How could it be otherwise? How could there be a "move beyond" if " 'any "beyond" is already "in place" inside,' and 'repetition replaces revolution,' " wrote Michael Fischer (1985: 139).[16] Granted those potentialities for which McRobbie does vouch, as a *tool,* or radical reflexivity, deconstruction has imposed itself in critical analysis.[17] Unfortunately, altogether too often it simply provides a new twist (into the "abyss") around which to ~~erect~~ construct (can deconstruction *be* a center?) one more in a seemingly endless(!) stream of entertaining but politically impotent(!) pop-cultural cv stuffers.

As the term *cultural studies* gained currency, the United States found it had a "tradition" too. In his *Communication as Culture,* James Carey situates it in the "tradition of social thought on communication . . . a symbolic process whereby reality is produced, maintained, repaired, and transformed . . . [which] comes from those colleagues and descendants of Dewey in the Chicago School: from Mead and Cooley through Robert Park and on to Erving Goffman" (1989: 23).[18] Here communication is associated with the problems of community and common culture. Carey maintains that a "cultural science of communication . . . views human behavior—or, more accurately, human action—as a text" (60). He takes the work of Clifford Geertz as his model, for whom, as for "many students of cultural studies," the starting point is Max Weber. *This* cultural studies

> does not seek to explain human behavior in terms of the laws that govern it or to dissolve it into the structures that underlie it; rather, it seeks to understand it. Cultural studies does not attempt to predict human behavior; rather it attempts to diagnose human meanings. . . . The goals of communications conceived as cultural science are therefore more modest but also more human, at least in the sense of attempting to be truer to human nature and experience as it ordinarily is encountered. (56)

What obviously sets this "American" work apart is its conscious "exceptionalism" (see N. Campbell and Kean 1997). Like its British namesake, the national context is expressly recognized as a privileged field of inquiry. However, the lack of any real attachment to either of the two traditions that came together in the mid-1950s in Britain and out of which a heterogeneous cluster of critical practices became institutionalized, or the tensions that accompanied that initial encounter and continued to shape the trajectory of cultural studies in the decades following the engagement with theory, attest to the very different intellectual tradition.

Carey does overlap the terrain mapped by Fred Inglis in his *Cultural Studies,* which bears the dedication "For Clifford Geertz." Inglis, for his part, recognizes English as "the first parent of Cultural Studies" and explicitly the tradition down through Leavis as formative (1993: 30). However, even here the all-important debates within English Marxism are absent (the Frankfurt School and Wittgenstein, yes, but socialist humanism, no), despite the hagiographic exegeses on Williams, Hoggart, Thompson, and Hall. Differences notwithstanding, like Carey, Inglis makes much of the "local knowledge" and "translation" (as "seeing *as*") of Geertz, who "forcefully noted, and noted it first, that the methical assumptions of social science were breaking up, and that all the apparatus of hard-data-before-theory, fact-value distinction, the objective idiom and taking the view-from-nowhere 'can not prosper when explanation comes to be regarded as a matter of connecting action to its sense rather than behaviour to its determinants' " (163). And Inglis risks a point about the importance of how cultural studies seems to be functioning at a crucial level:

> *This is the way the best and brightest of present-day students in the human sciences want to learn to think and feel.* And having learned to think and feel thus, this is how they want to act and live. There is, as always, a story

behind these assertions. It is the story of how Cultural Studies will make you good. . . . Find a value; give it a history; see what may be done with it in human purposes. Be careful, bring all your sympathies to bear; hate what is hateful; be good. (1993: 229, 240)

Indeed, many seem to have joined the chorus.

Cultural studies "warrened" the disciplines of the humanities and the social sciences from within, dismantled their claims to unique sets of theories, methodologies, and subject matters, and colonized Anglophone universities far and wide in the postimperial zones of geocultural space. In the United States, institutions of higher education as different as the California Institute of the Arts, Claremont Graduate University, Drake University, Duke University, George Mason University, Georgia Institute of Technology, Harvard University, Kansas State University, New York University, University of Arizona at Tucson, University of California-Santa Cruz, University of Illinois-Urbana/Champaign, University of Minnesota, University of North Carolina-Chapel Hill, University of Pittsburgh, University of Rochester, and University of Tennessee vaunt centers, programs, and/or departments identified with the field.

Cultural studies has become ubiquitous. This was nowhere more apparent than at the marathon international conference held at the University of Illinois–Urbana/Champaign in 1990, "Cultural Studies Now and in the Future." The editors of the proceedings, *Cultural Studies* (Grossberg, Nelson, and Treichler 1992), divided the contents into sixteen extensive categories in which any of the forty papers could appear. Richard Dienst, writing for *Screen,* thought it "obvious that the entire conference was organized to summon up a single apparition, Cultural Studies capitalized, as a 'new' discipline fully legitimized in the eyes of the North American University and its various practitioners alike" (1990: 328).[19] To judge from this omnibus presentation at least, cultural policy and lived experience are in retreat (only one paper each), and an analysis of the role of intellectuals is completely absent. Furthermore, according to Angela McRobbie, to return to a prioritization of economic relations and determinations over cultural and political relations is no longer possible. And the place of Gramsci, "who enabled us to understand the force and political effectiveness of the Thatcher years, the success of the New Right and equally the lack of success on the part of the left even to begin to compete with this ideological radicalism," is no longer certain (1992: 720).[20]

Certainly, not everyone has been sanguine about cultural studies. For example, from communications research, in a wide-ranging review, Mike Budd, Robert Entman, and Clay Steinman charge that it is losing its critical edge in the United States: "The problem is exemplified in the work of John Fiske and Lawrence Grossberg," typical of a dominant theme that people habitually use media content against the media itself and to empower themselves. "The crucial aspect of the new discourse of U.S. cultural studies is its optimism and affirmative tone about audiences," which shows a deficiency of institutional and political analysis (1990: 169, 170). As for the future, according to McRobbie, writing in 1992:

> Identity could be seen as dragging cultural studies into the 1990s by acting as a kind of guide to how people see themselves, not as class subjects, not as psychoanalytic subjects, not as subjects of ideology, not as textual subjects, but as active agents whose sense of self is projected onto and expressed in an expansive range of cultural practices, including texts, images, and commodities. If this is the case, then the problem in cultural studies today . . . is the absence of reference to real existing identities in the ethnographic sense. . . . The site of identity formation in cultural studies remains implicitly in and through cultural commodities and texts rather than in and through the cultural practices of everyday life. . . . it is necessary that we somehow move away from the binary opposition which still haunts cultural studies, that is, the distinction between text and lived experience, between media and reality, between culture and society. (730)

Martin Barker and Anne Beezer have argued that cultural studies research has "taken on the status of a 'witness.'" Addressing McRobbie's work, they consider that adopting "a criterion that explanations can only have force if they are found within the discourse of the people whom we are studying" makes it impossible for the theorist to have any independent critical position. Barker and Beezer see a retreat from the concept of class and the replacement of "concern for the power relations between texts and audiences, with concern for the power relations embodied in the research process itself" (1992: 9, 10). In a similar tone but from the "American" tradition, the arguments of those such as Warren and Vavrus (2002b), Czitrom (2002), and McChesney (2002) for a revitalization for the figure of the "public intellectual" and the return of historically informed engagement offer more than convincing invitations to probe the foundations of two of the most outstanding debates of recent years, the Culture Wars and the Science Wars.

The major themes of the contemporary culture wars are not limited to the United States. Instances of debates over history and historical amnesia, language, education and the "canon," including their gendered and racial/ethnic foundations and the power relations ensuring their reproduction, may be observed throughout the world. These "cultural" mechanisms have become centers of controversy due to their common functions, especially as techniques through which *nation* and *nationalism* have taken form as the construction of "otherness" and its attendant struggles have operated to position groups on the hierarchy of the world division of labor. As Gregory Jay notes, "The struggle for representation knows no borders. Many nations are trying to find a way to balance the claims of individuality, ethnic or racial solidarity, democracy, economic development, women's liberation, and nationalism" (1997: 60, 62).

Nonetheless, it has been in the United States where these controversies have been grouped under a single rubric. Heated discussions associated with nationalism, patriotism, the role of religion, and race, ethnic, and gender relations have developed, encrusting the dilemmas over who gets what. The range of conflicts associated with the culture wars in the United States, including the family, art, religion, education, law and politics, abortion, and health care, is such that the culture wars touch "virtually all Americans" (Hunter 1991: xi). All of the parties in these and similar debates seem to believe that the issues have a long-term component involving the reproduction of social norms through education: what should be included in textbooks, how specific narratives of the past legitimate specific hierarchies in the present, what might be possible to imagine for the future. All have understood that differing positions imply value-laden choices and thus are profoundly political in nature and speak to clear but contested power relations in a struggle for control, even though they may take the form of arguments over truth and relativism, tolerance and prejudice.

Indeed, if there is an area where crisis, implicit in the war metaphor, has reached particularly sharp focus, it is in the field of education. As the agendas directing values, morality, and acceptable conduct that are set at the top eventually redirect programs in the elementary and secondary schools, it should be no surprise that debates have tended to implicate the content of higher education and the organizing and legitimating role of the university: as symbolic system (the canon) and as material practice (access or gate-keeping, disciplinary/departmental structures, and pedagogical and research organization).

In one of its most widely recognized manifestations in the United States, the culture wars have been bound up with the struggle over teaching American literature, subjected to new and often disconcerting interpretations, as well as demands for new inclusions and exclusions in the canon, or even its total abolition. These demands to reopen the canon were closely related to issues of race and gender and were often linked explicitly to the movements of the 1960s (Hull, Scott, and Smith 1982; Moraga and Anzaldúa 1983). Indeed, as Jay summarizes, "it is precisely because higher education has done so much (though not enough) to redistribute access to representation that colleges and universities have come under such vitriolic attack" (1997: 57).

Come under attack they certainly did in a whole series of doom-and-gloom writings. Two works stand out: Allan Bloom's *Closing of the American Mind: How Higher Education Has Failed Democracy and Impoverished the Souls of Today's Students* (1987) and E. D. Hirsch's *Cultural Literacy: What Every American Needs to Know* (1988). These books presented an agenda for and outlined the purpose of shaping public schooling and higher education that "abstracted equity from excellence and cultural criticism from the discourse of social responsibility" (Giroux 1992: 123). As many critics immediately realized, Hirsch's "culture" was unproblematic because he had removed it from the dynamics of its construction in struggle and power (see B. Smith 1992: 88–89). It was in this context of the crusade to create "a narrowly specific cultural capital [as] the normative *referent* for everyone, but [to remain] the *property* of a small and powerful caste that is linguistically and ethnically unified" that the Stanford curriculum debate (and many such in universities all over the United States) was played out during the mid-1980s (Pratt 1992: 15).[21]

From the 1960s, colleges and universities, especially public institutions, were pressured to serve greater and greater numbers of students. The culture wars and the parallel movement against "political correctness" (known as PC) took place in a well-defined material context of declining resources due to a worldwide economic downturn and a politically motivated squeeze on public funding of universities: "The democratized university is an inefficient, obsolete notion and not cost-effective, so the PC scare gives a rationale for dismantling it, or at least as it is currently constituted" (J. Williams 1995: 5). Nonetheless, PC attests to the force of the social critiques emanating from the humanities and the social sciences epitomized in cultural studies, and the anti-PC movement shows to what extent challenges have had an effect. Thus, it has been suggested that, by attacking PC, "conservatives have implemented a well-orchestrated and financed campaign to cut budgets, downsize universities, and thus sharply restrict access to higher education." Given the generalized sense of entitlement to education, access can now "*only* be restricted if one can successfully argue that restriction is a function of economic forces beyond our control, and if one can somehow make colleges politically suspect" (Lauter 1995: 73, 81).

The arguments over the politically suspect politicization of the university that pitted those who viewed the realm of knowledge and its institutions as loci of struggle against those who upheld "truth" achieved through value-neutrality as the ideal of scholarship seemed paradoxical in the light of actual practice. As Gerald Graff contends, the "producers of the best objective scholarship [the left] defend partisanship, while the defenders of objectivity [the right] produce mostly partisan political polemics" (1995: 308). The paradox is further compounded when the trajectories of theory and identity politics are considered. Theory, whether loosely characterized as poststructuralism or deconstruction, unmasked the power relations inherent in the Arnoldian high-culture aesthetic, anathema on the right, but also tended to result in formal analyses of "texts," of whatever type, disengaged from concrete political agendas, roundly criticized on the left. According to Joan Scott, "On the right, there are denunciations of the nihilism of theory, which, it is said, will leave us orphans without cultural patrimony. On the left, theory is indicted for its impracticality: it does not connect to 'real life' or 'lived experience' and so cannot lead directly to politics, to revolution, or at least to social reform." Scott goes on to point out that "in the attack on 'theory,' right and left clear the field of all possible critiques of their foundational premises; with those intact, they can fight safely and familiarly among themselves" (1995: 301).

Unlike the antiessentialism of poststructuralism, identity politics presupposes foundations making the point that without presuppositions there can be no action on the part of the marginalized. For Stuart Hall, the poor fit between theory and practice opens up an opportunity for rethinking the terms of the debate. Identity politics, he argues, even in the form of so-called strategic essentialism,

> sees difference as "their traditions versus ours," not in a positional way, but in a mutually exclusive, autonomous and self-sufficient one. And it is therefore unable to grasp the dialogic strategies and hybrid forms essential to the diaspora aesthetic. A movement beyond this essentialism is not an aesthetic or critical strategy without a cultural politics, without a marking of difference. It is not simply re-articulation and re-appropriation for the sake of it. What it evades is the essentializing of difference into two mutually opposed either/ors . . . replac[ing] the "or" with the potentiality or the

possibility of an "and." That is the logic of coupling rather than the logic of a binary opposition. . . . The essentializing moment is weak because it naturalizes and de-historicizes difference, mistaking what is historical and cultural for what is natural, biological, and genetic. (1996b: 472)

Who controls that specific representational form we call "history" and to what end has been a matter of serious controversy over the past decade (e.g., Linenthal and Engelhardt 1996; Windschuttle 1997; E. Wood and Foster 1997), although one must acknowledge again that this is not new, and the university is again at the center of struggles over what, or whose, history is recognized as authoritative and propagated as grounds for legitimate social action. Indeed, the curriculum is a historically specific narrative and pedagogy a particular form of cultural politics.

However, when this historical dimension is taken into consideration, the contemporary culture wars appear as a post-1968 conjunctural moment in a long-term trend. Neither the intellectual arrangements nor the institutional organization of the structures of knowledge were able to successfully negotiate the outcomes of the challenges of the 1960s. And now, once students graduate, it is apparent that the promise of a better life for all who go through the system is not easily kept in a world ultimately ruled by the law of value.

But as Stuart Hall's analysis suggests, the outcome of the contemporary controversies may have profound consequences for the dichotomous thinking, and particularly the divorce of facts from values, that has formed the basis of the epistemology, the "geoculture" of the modern world-system as it has developed over the past five centuries. In this case, what is in question is *civilization* versus *culture*—the first universal, implicit in the term as it was deployed by Lynne Cheney (1988), and the second, particularist.

At first blush, the science wars may seem to be nothing more than a specifically focused instance of the more generalized culture wars. Indeed, the two do share several characteristics. First, the themes of the debates constituting the science wars, like those of the culture wars, have a long history. Second, as the institutions of knowledge formation were opened up to previously excluded groups as a result of the upheavals of the 1960s, entrenched theoretical and methodological perspectives found it more and more difficult to dismiss the critiques and their overtly political agendas that were now mounted from within the institutions themselves. It became clear to many involved that any review of the premises of knowledge formation amounted to an evaluation of the structure of, and structuring of, social relations as well. This dimension of the culture wars was replicated in the science wars. Finally, the disputes in both arenas, if indeed there are two, were polarized and the tone exacerbated by a series of publications feeling the need to defend what had been for a long time, up to the 1960s, largely unchallenged premises and propositions.

What does seem clear is that the "general esteem for this relatively new hybrid—science/technology—seems to have peaked in around 1960." In 1962, when Thomas Kuhn published *The Structure of Scientific Revolutions,* "suggesting the fallacy of viewing scientific knowledge as absolute, objective, and universal . . . [he] opened the door to a new epistemological understanding of science that had the potential to undermine its privileged status" (Trachtman and Perrucci 2000: 8–9).

It is well to remember that it was trained scientists like Kuhn, Paul Feyerabend, and Stephen Toulmin who carried out much of the original work that led to the establishment of the new field of science studies. The dilemma of and challenge to dualism and instrumentality and the insistence on both the collective nature and local contingency of knowledge formation and reproduction figured prominently in science studies from the beginning.[22] It was highlighted in work that characteristically crossed multiple disciplinary boundaries to investigate at the most basic level how scientific knowledge is made (detailed ethnographic studies such as Latour and Woolgar [1979] 1986, Knorr-Cetina 1981, and Lynch 1985) and how their claims are defended and institutionalized, including the structure and historical construction of the rhetoric and politics and power relations legitimating and sustaining public knowledge (Shapin and Schaffer 1985; Shapin 1994). The field has now developed to include analyses that offer alternative visions of what science should or could be and how it might relate to the larger world of social relations.

The chronology of the science wars proper may well be taken to begin in 1992, with the publication of books by physicist Steven Weinberg, *Dreams of a Final Theory: The Search for the Fundamental Laws of Nature,* and by biologist Lewis Wolpert, *The Unnatural Nature of Science: Why Science Does Not Make (Common) Sense.* These two books brought to public attention the work of the group of historians, philosophers, and sociologists who had been involved in reconceptualizing many common views about the nature of science (Wolpert 1993: 110–11, 115–17; Weinberg 1992: 184–90). For Wolpert, the bone of contention is relativism, to which he replies, "Scientists can be very proud to be naive realists" (117). Weinberg agrees, but contends that relativism "is only one aspect of a wider, radical, attack on science itself." He goes on to give examples from Paul Feyerabend, Sandra Harding, and Theodore Roszak and echoes one of the themes of the culture wars in suspecting that "Gerald Holton is close to the truth in seeing the radical attack on science as one symptom of a broader hostility to Western civilization" (189–90). It should be noted that these attacks were directed primarily at the strongest social constructivist and relativist bent of science studies. The fact that these views were controversial even within science studies was, and still is, often overlooked.

In any case, by the early 1990s, it had become "apparent that some scientists felt sufficiently threatened that they were impelled to go public with a defense of the rationality and the benevolence of science and an attack on what they viewed as uninformed, biased, and unwarranted criticism" (Trachtman and Perrucci 2000: 24). The issues came to a head with the anti-antiscience "defense" mounted on a wide front in 1994 by the publication of *Higher Superstition: The Academic Left and Its Quarrels with Science,* by Paul Gross, a biologist at the University of Virginia, and Norman Levitt, a mathematician at Rutgers University. Their scattershot attack posited a unitary science and was directed at a broad "academic left"—feminist theory, postmodern philosophy, deconstruction, deep ecology—that was not only antiscience, but constructed as equally unitary and anti–all science (Martin 1996: 162–63). It "dislikes science," they asserted, in that it dislikes not just the uses to which science is put, but

> the social structures through which science is institutionalized, to the system of education by which professional scientists are produced, and to a mentality that is taken, rightly or wrongly, as characteristic of scientists. Most surprisingly, there is open hostility toward the *actual content* of scientific knowledge and toward the assumption, which one might have supposed universal among educated people, that scientific knowledge is reasonably reliable and rests on a sound methodology. (Gross and Levitt 1994: 6, 2)

The authors touched a chord in the scientific community despite the fact that the book itself stands as a monument to the very type of intellectual dilettantism it attacked. In an analysis of the "reading" of the work of Jacques Derrida by protagonists of the culture wars, Arkady Plotnitsky (who has both scientific and literary credentials) wrote:

> In general, scholarly problems of monumental proportions are, to use the language of topology, found in the immediate vicinity of just about every point of *Higher Superstition*. It is not so much embarrassing errors even as egregious as that of the misreading of "*topique différantielle*" as differential

topology, that are most crucial (we all make mistakes, sometimes absurd mistakes), but the intellectually and scholarly inadmissible practices and attitudes that pervade—and *define*—this sadly irresponsible book. Gross and Levitt's warning concerning "threats to the essential grace and comity of scholarship and the academic life" (ix) becomes, in one of many bizarre ironies of the book, its self-description. . . . The tragedy is that so many scientists, including some among the best scientists, have taken it seriously and accepted its arguments, and even adopted its unacceptable attitudes. (1997: para. 9)

The exchanges that ensued made plain just how fundamental the issues were, and not simply that Snow's "two cultures" of scientists and nonscientists still could not communicate with one another (see Holton 1993; Gieryn 1996; Gross 1996; S. Fuller 2000; Gross, Levitt, and Lewis 1996).[23]

What was missing was a concerted response to Gross and Levitt and their "pro-science" supporters. The editors of *Social Text* took on this project in 1996 with a special issue dedicated to the science wars. They did not know, however, that the physicist Alan Sokal, inspired by his reading of *Higher Superstition,* was involved in an "actively sustained" conspiracy to deceive the journal into publishing his "Transgressing the Boundaries: Toward a Transformative Hermeneutics of Quantum Gravity," in which he "parodied postmodern stylistic conventions and derived politically correct conclusions from an esoteric subfield of science" (Segerstråle 2000a: n.p.).[24] Sokal exposed the hoax in "A Physicist Experiments with Cultural Studies," which appeared almost concurrently in *Lingua Franca,* characterizing the article as combining "nonsense" and "silliness." For those taken in by Sokal and those they represented, it was an extraordinary breach of intellectual ethics and scholarly integrity. For those making common cause with Sokal (and Gross and Levitt et al.), it forcefully demonstrated his point of declining "standards of rigor in the academic community" (Weinberg 1996: 11), specifically the intellectual laxness of those it was designed to attack. This group proved notoriously difficult to define, however, given the diversity of the cultural studies community and the conflation of cultural studies with science studies as the debates played out.

The defenders of traditional science were concerned to protect what they considered to be the "true" idea of science against what they described as "false" representations. For their critics, these defenders seemed not "to recognize the right of other academics to do their own interpretations of science within the particular frameworks of their own disciplines" (Segerstråle 2000b: 21). The problem for the critics of traditional science was that their views permeated far beyond the confines of their specialist disciplines. They had become part both of the undergraduate curricula and of the larger public understanding of science. Ullica Segerstråle relates this to an internal struggle within the political left (recalling the culture wars): the older left of Gross, Levitt, and Sokal "equates science with reliable knowledge, a tool in the struggle for social justice. . . . In contrast, the cultural Left equates science with power that can be used for social oppression of minorities. For them, therefore, science criticism is a way to liberation." The issue, they feel, is whether nonscientists would "have some say in the decision-making process of the professional scientific community" (2000a: n.p.).

The fallout over the Sokal affair has obscured Andrew Ross's own take on the science wars. In his introduction to the *Social Text* collection, he treats the science wars as a "second front" in the "holy Culture Wars" (1996a: 6) and suggests a conjunctural explanation for the controversy, especially near-term decline in governmental support, including funding cuts, for big science (cancellation of the Superconducting Supercollider and closing of the Congressional Office of Technology Assessment) that others have noted. However, this is not just a turf battle over the allocation of scarce research dollars. Ross's analysis also presents a longer-term interpretation of the science wars that situates the only real resolution in a shift in the process privileging formal rationality to one favoring substantive concerns:

> The rise in technoskepticism, then, parallels a crisis in industrialization which is often mistaken for a crisis of the environment. . . . the remoteness of scientific knowledge from the social and physical environments in which it will come to be measured and utilized is as irrational as anything we might imagine, and downright hazardous when it involves materials that can only be properly tested in the open environment. . . . demonstrating the socially constructed nature of the scientist's knowledge . . . may help to demystify, but it must be joined by insistence on methodological reform—to involve the local experience of users in the research process from the outset and to ensure that the process is shaped less by a manufacturer's interests than by the needs of communities affected by the product. This is the way that leads from cultural relativism to social rationality. (2–4)

As for the general public, Trachtman and Perrucci found that the social worth of science had not suffered as a result of the science wars (2000: 166–67).

Indeed, as Brian Martin contends, the likes of Gross and Levitt did not seem to understand that "scientific knowledge can be socially shaped or conditioned and yet be a powerful and effective tool for specific purposes" (1996: 167). The point is brought home by Segerstråle, who argues that most "constructivist sociologists (unlike their postmodern or cultural studies colleagues) are not primarily interested in values and ideology; they see themselves as epistemological radicals" (2000a: n.p.). Sandra Harding insists, "There is plenty of science still to be done once physics is invited and permitted to step down and take its place as one human social activity among many others. What kinds of knowledge about the empirical world do we need in order to live at all, and to live more reasonably with each other on this planet from this moment on? Who should make up the 'we' who answers this question?" (1992: 20).

The science wars, then, are not simply a special case of the culture wars and a plea for more democracy and value consideration in decision making in the context of the innate inequalities that are part of the all-encompassing corporate climate. Rather, they indicate the importance of the questions focusing on the epistemological status of the sciences that have come into play. This becomes clear when we realize that what the science warriors seem not to have adequately considered is that "epistemological radicalism" is now found within the science community itself, especially among those involved in complexity studies.[25] The combination of the conviction that there is a "real" world and that the future is "determined" by the past but that that future is nonetheless unpredictable, and the parallel assaults on dualism (e.g., Barrow 1995; Prigogine 1996) challenge the status of the sciences as discoverers, guardians, and purveyors of authoritative knowledge, that is, truth, by redefining what it means to describe the evolution of natural systems. This amounts to overturning the dominant model shaping our understanding of the human world and the presumed contradiction between determinism and free will; impinges directly on the manner in which scholars make claims for the legitimacy of their interpretations of social reality; and underscores the covert, long-term, structural nature of the debates that have come to be known as the culture wars and the science wars.

Thus, the culture wars and the science wars that have pitted the diverse defenders of truth, objectivity, reason, and Western Civilization against the multifarious protagonists of values, relativism, and multiculturalism over the past two decades are more than a simple, if acrimonious, struggle between the old and the new, the modern and the postmodern or even the traditional. They belong to the long history of debate and outright conflict in the modern world over how valid knowledge may be produced, the grounds and the domain of its authority, who may speak in its voice, and thus what courses of social action may be considered legitimate.

More to the point, at issue today is the epistemological basis of the representational apparatus that has characterized our understanding of the social world over the long term. "What the political correctness debate and related phenomena display, symptomatically, is precisely the connection between representation in the field of knowledge and representation in the fields of society and politics. . . . [It is the impression that] academics are producing *a body of different truths* that threaten certain traditional value systems and institutions" that has engendered the backlash of the culture wars (Jay 1997: 31). Far from the "orthodox" versus "progressive" elements that James Davison Hunter (1991) postulated, the protagonists of the culture wars simply cannot be shoehorned into either/or groups, of whatever stripe. In this sense, Hall's analysis suggests that the conjunctural moment of the culture wars is also a point of structural crisis leading to a restructuring in the field of knowledge—the delegitimation of the principle of the excluded middle and the implicit call for a relational conception of human reality. But the epistemological status of dichotomous thinking is constitutive of and constituted by the role of the natural sciences in the modern world and their location at the privileged pole of the structures of knowledge that have become the objects of contention in the science wars. We will move on, then, to consider the articulation between social change and the structures of knowledge.

PART THREE From Resistance to Transition

CHAPTER 6

Conjunctural Knowledge I: Structures of Order, 1945–1968

"To be," says Quine, "is to be the value of a variable."—A. J. AYER, *Logical Positivism*

Strange and decisive turn: *race* is transmuted into *historicity,* the black Present explodes and is temporalized, negritude—with its Past and its Future—is inserted into Universal History, it is no longer a *state,* nor even an existential attitude, it is a "Becoming."
—JEAN-PAUL SARTRE, "Black Orpheus"

The teleology common to the Novel and to narrated History is the alienation of the facts.
. . . This has to be related to a certain mythology of the universal typifying the bourgeois society of which the Novel is a characteristic product; it involves giving to the imaginary the formal guarantee of the real, but while preserving in the sign the ambiguity of a double object, at once believable and false. . . . It is thanks to an expedient of the same kind that the triumphant bourgeoisie of the last century was able to look upon its values as universal and to carry over to sections of society which were absolutely heterogeneous to it all the Names which were part of its ethos.
—ROLAND BARTHES, *Writing Degree Zero*

A principal characteristic of the modern world-system has been that science has become the summit and the model in the hierarchy of its intellectual disciplines. This "structure of knowledge" attained definitive ascendancy over religious, spiritual, transcendental "belief systems" (which of course did not entirely disappear) as the dominant mode of human understanding only in the nineteenth century. The binary opposition of the sciences and humanities (as parts within and of a whole), manifesting the separation of systematic knowledge from human values over the past five hundred years, has constantly deepened through internal, although not uncontested, transformation in complex articulation with the processes reproducing the material structures of historical capitalism and the social and political struggles of which they were objects. In 1959, C. P. Snow's *Two Cultures* synthesized a widespread perception of the situation: "Literary intellectuals at one pole—at the other scientists, and as the most representative, the physical scientists," in which "the feelings of one pole become the anti-feelings of the other" (1965: 4, 11). In between, some argue, there emerged in the late nineteenth century the human or the social sciences, a "third culture."[1] Cultural studies takes its place within this science/humanities antinomy, but, having challenged the frontiers separating the social sciences and the humanities, continues to labor within an organizational framework privileging the sciences.

Expansion, Hegemony, Consensus

The conjuncture of U.S. hegemony and Kondratieff expansion, 1945–1967/73, coincided with and was marked by a deepened ideological commitment to a universal science, empirical and positivistic, expressing the Enlightenment ideal of endless progress implemented in an ultimately law-like, and therefore at least theoretically predictable, world. This commitment, to an extent as never before, "centered" the structure of knowledge formation during the period.

In 1945, the power of the Bomb sealed U.S. hegemony, albeit momentarily. "Atoms for Peace," or better, the Manhattan Project itself (the prototype of "big science"), soon became the metaphor of material progress through rational (Western) science. In the United States, Vannevar Bush, in his report to the president, *Science, The Endless Frontier* (1945), linked well-being at home and geopolitical dominance abroad to progress in science/technology through government-sponsored basic research in academia and, to a certain extent, industry.[2] U.S. government expenditures for basic science increased a hundred-fold from the pre-1945 to the immediate post-1945 period (D. Greenberg 1967) and the United States has since dominated world knowledge production.[3] Political leaders and institutional policymakers in the core, and eventually throughout the world, presumed a close correlation among science, technological progress, and economic/military security, undergirded by a vast intellectual establishment that reinforced the consensus.

From at least the middle of the nineteenth century, the dominant epistemology of science had been avowedly positivistic: truth associated with observable facts and the laws governing their relations. Logical positivism, in the analytic tradition and heir to empiricism, gained ascendancy during the first half of the twentieth century.[4] Its verification principle, that the meaning of a proposition is the method of its verification, admits as meaningful tautological statements (such as in mathematics and logic) and statements verifiable through observation. All others (such as in metaphysics and theology), being unverifiable, are meaningless, neither true nor false. The corollaries to this principle, that the only valid knowledge is scientific and that science is unitary, deepened the gulf between the (ordered/law-like, factual/expository) sciences and the (chaotic/anarchic, impressionistic/poetic) humanities, with the position of that archipelago of in-between disciplines, the social sciences, a matter of fierce debate.

Even though attacks on the status of the principle of verification, critical review of such precepts as the presumed independence of "facts," and the realization of the importance of context and models have discredited logical positivism, its ghost is still very active. In addition to the ideological infrastructure it offers, this philosophical lineage continues to profit from an enduring association with the very real accomplishments of science and technology (associated with determinism and predictability) in explaining and controlling the material world.

In 1913, J. B. Watson launched behaviorism with the argument that consciousness was the one thing with which psychologists should not be concerned. This was integral to arguments of the logical positivists in assimilating the social sciences to one unified science: sociology is not "in fundamental opposition to some other sciences, called 'natural sciences,' no, *as social behaviorism, sociology is a part of unified science. . . . The fruitfulness of social behaviorism is demonstrated by the establishment of new correlations and by the successful predictions made on the basis of them*" (Neurath [1931–32] 1959: 296, 317). Behaviorism was grounded in empirical studies (often in animal psychology) of actual responses—a controlled, experimental method based on the observation of independent cases—and thus could claim objectivity. By the 1950s, when its moment had waned somewhat in psychology, it became influential in political science, the tendency favoring empirical, quantitative techniques and hypothesis testing.[5]

The post-1945 period was also the moment of ascendancy of functionalism.[6] It putatively examined "the contribution which social items make to the social and cultural life of human collectivities" (P. Cohen 1985: 322). In sociology it de-emphasized social change and conflict. Talcott Parsons's goal of bringing together action and structure, idealism and materialism largely failed. Despite the more than lip service paid to material structures and the contingency of action, the concern for normative control and the socialization of individuality predominated (Alexander 1988: 83). "The basic dynamic categories of social systems are 'psychological,'" wrote Parsons (quoted in Smelser 1988: 110).

In their twentieth-century bid for professional legitimacy, dependent on the "positivist claim that only natural science provided certain knowledge and conferred the power of prediction and control," the social sciences turned away from historical methods to scientism (D. Ross 1991: 390). During the post-1945 period, in collaboration with Robert K. Merton, Paul Lazarsfeld's Bureau of Applied Social Research at Columbia University established a positivist social science based on survey research, statistical methods, and structural-functionalist theory. American social science, empirical and quantitative, became a model for the world.[7] In the words of one sociologist, "As a science, sociology has as its objective the funding of knowledge with the goal of all science of achieving predictability and explanation through research" (Hauser 1981: 63).

Modernization theory represented the effort of Western social science (brought on by the cold war and the hegemonic imperative of decolonization) to come to grips with a world that included the non-Western and nonrich simply by extending (universalizing) first world experiences and analytic viewpoints.[8] It both expressed a real concern for development and harbored a political component as an antidote to the appeal of communism in the third world. Building on Parsons's reconstruction of Weber, modernization "referred to the process of transition from traditional to modern principles of social organization, and this process was what was currently occurring in Asia, Africa, and Latin America" (Leys 1982: 333). According to Peter Evans and John Stephens:

> Just as the modernization perspective adapted easily to social-psychological analyses of the problems of development, it also fit well with neoclassical economic prescriptions. Need achievement and entrepreneurship are easily conflated. Universalism is clearly one of the normative underpinnings of the market. Breaking the traditional bonds that prevent people from participating fully in market exchange is clearly a central component of modernization. Thus the institutional prerequisites of "takeoff" outlined in Rostow's classic *Stages of Economic Growth* (1960) jibe very nicely with those that would be prescribed by someone working in the Parsonian frame. (1988: 741–42)

A Soviet version of modernization, socialist development, mirrored its Western counterpart. Theorists posited contemporary Western/Soviet society as the end point toward which the third world was "developing." In so doing, it would achieve both the same economic successes (industrialization) and similar political organization (democracy/socialism). The comparative perspective that defined societies as countries and cast them as independent "cases" for analysis glossed over conflicts of interest and wider systems of historically constructed relations, including hierarchies of power and values.

Whether in the form of logical positivism or structural-functionalism and modernization, the dominant intellectual currents in Western science and social science carried the humanities along on the same tides and swells. As Terry Eagleton has written of U.S. New Criticism, "The literary text was grasped in what might be called 'functionalist' terms: just like U.S. functionalist sociology, it developed a 'conflict-free' model of society, in which every element 'adapted' to every other." It was a "recipe for political inertia, and thus for submission to the political status quo" (1983: 47, 50). The New Criticism (ranging from the pure aesthetic theory of Wimsatt, Beardsley, and Krieger to the scientific bibliography of Fredson Bowers and the statistical methodology of Caroline Spurgeon) recapitulated Anglo-American empiricism wedded to description, the reality of external relations, and the independence of material objects (subject/object distinction). It would carry through an absolute objectification of the text, but a text, in fact, largely equated with poetry whose very opacity could be manipulated from the inside through an analysis of its "tensions," "paradoxes," "irony," and "ambivalences" to encapsulate it and place it outside history and above social context. Although presented as antiestablishment, New Criticism was in syntony with conservative, or bourgeois-liberal, currents (i.e., the aesthetic of the Old South of Ransom and the politics of T. S. Eliot) and in fact buttressed them in the medium term.[9]

Having flourished from the 1930s through the 1950s, the New Criticism finally succumbed to the onslaughts of structuralism and later poststructuralism, which, however, tended to subtly repeat its denial of history (Lentricchia 1980: xiii). It was, nonetheless, a key element in the academic professionalization of criticism both for its "objectivity" (which, in line with "scientific" thinking, contributed to its legitimation as knowledge) and for its formalist characteristics (which considerably facilitated the instruction of large numbers of undergraduates). Much in the manner of logical positivism, it has continued to be a practical formula, widely practiced if not preached.

It was on this intellectual pegboard that the political struggles of the period were hung. Whenever opinion could not be homogenized, efforts were made to control the expression of dissent in the political domain. A central arena of the campaign was cultural, especially the mass culture propagated from Hollywood. "Far from being an industry representing traditional America, Hollywood was at the center of a contest to determine the future of politics and national identity in the postwar era" (May 1990: 358). It soon became the major purveyor of film and television, and the cultural values that were their baggage, to the whole world, its products no less subject to the trends of the world economy than any other commodities. In the socialist East, dissent was managed through state censorship and individual repression (countered by underground organization, clandestine radio receivers, and samizdat literature)—unless it could be useful, as with the publication of Solzhenitsyn's *One Day in the Life of Ivan Denisovich*, as part of Khrushchev's de-Stalinization program. When protest did erupt, East or West, it was met with an array of force, from job pressures, individual intimidation, incarceration, and torture to proxy violence, covert operations, and direct intervention.

Of course, ideological battles permeated "high culture" as well. During the 1950s the stature of Russian arts in the West was denigrated, as with socialist realism; minimized, as with constructivism; or (innocently?) assimilated into a larger context, as the work of Berdyayev and Dostoevsky was to existentialism (e.g., Friedman 1964). U.S. cultural imperialism was mobilized overtly through USIA and covertly through the CIA and through the Museum of Modern Art (whose board of directors was a revolving door of high U.S. government officials and foreign policy and commercial and banking elites). Asia and Latin America were specifically targeted, along with Europe. The CIA "recognized that dissenting intellectuals who believe themselves to be acting freely could be useful tools in the international propaganda war." Nelson Rockefeller and others at MOMA "consciously used Abstract Expressionism, 'the symbol of political freedom,' for political ends" (Cockcroft [1974] 1992: 83, 90). Abstract expressionism (consecrated with the MOMA exhibit of 1951)—"unequivocal expressions of terror, tragedy, and ultimate harmony in confrontations with Man and His actions, particularly with [the artists'] own inner selves and their activity as artists" (Reise [1968] 1992: 262)—was explicitly contrasted with the "superficial," "state-controlled" Soviet socialist realism. The latter, "the official vulgarity, the certified vulgarity," could be fused with Nazi and fascist "totalitarian" art, as Clement Greenberg hinted (1948: 579, 578). But establishing the superiority of Western (U.S.) culture required dazzling *soubresauts*. Greenberg's rewriting of the history of the debates within the Soviet arts community—constructivism "versus" socialist realism—was necessary for the refusal to incorporate constructivism into the pantheon of the neo-avant-garde (Buchloh 1990).

The European challenge to U.S. hegemony and its guarantor, the binary and hierarchical division of the world, came most notably from France. De Gaulle assuredly did not trust the United States as the tutor of European interests. In 1963 he withdrew French armed forces from NATO command and established an independent *force de frappe*. Here in the core, where the use of military power and economic pressure did not constitute viable, or always adequately effective, options, the United States could employ "cultural diplomacy." The articulation of power, values, and consensus is evidenced in the events surrounding the 1964 Venice Biennial, where France had long dominated. The U.S. presence, under financial strain as was the entire exhibition, found funding through the USIA (the U.S. government would "save" modern art) and overflowed into an annex (unprecedented) where pop art could be presented as a substantial movement. "American critics explained Rauschenberg's victory in terms of aesthetic superiority" and the curator of the U.S. exhibition commented that the " 'whole world recognized that the world art center has moved from Paris to New York.' Yet he admitted privately that 'we might have won it anyway (apart from the question of merit), but we really engineered it' " (Monahan 1990: 369–70). European critics dubbed this "American expansionism."

Great Britain discovered its "new affluence"; Germany experienced the "economic miracle"; and "traditional American families" savored the ideal (if not the reality for many) of an insular and achieved well-being—a status quo to be protected—in suburban Levittowns where everything on the "other side of the tracks" could be ignored. But always the new was contrasted with old forms. Classical music, ballet, and opera were the mainstays of Soviet cultural forays, and the French presence at the 1964 Biennial was decidedly modernist in the person of Roger Bissière.[10] Was it Merce Cunningham's performance that tipped the scales in Rauschenberg's favor for the president of the jury in Venice? The "revolution" of Rauschenberg was presented as "apolitical and affirmative" over against the abstract painters' traditionalism and formalism (Monahan 1990: 387). Pop art could be billed as embodying the ideals of the new Kennedy administration, whereas the (advertised, constructed) essence of abstract expressionism had been perfectly suited to the conservatism of the Eisenhower years. Always, however, the *new* (Hoggart's lantern slides clicking over!). Certainly by 1964, as Monahan suggests, economic power "had already won the battle. The force of the new issuing from American shores had already succeeded in dominating the world with its movies, its magazines, its culture" (407).

This cultural mode of consolidating and defending hegemony in the post-

1945 period rested on a foundation of positive science, universalizing and objectifying, and an experimental/comparative method leading to (putatively disinterested, apolitical) progress associated with predictable, thus manipulable, results. Geoculturally, images of progress were exported in the guise of promises of development. This was a perspective that permeated not only the sciences but the social sciences as well and found strong echoes in the humanities in consistent, if shifting, articulation with U.S. political hegemony and economic expansion. Even when challenged from within a discipline, by an art form, or through political activism, ingrained ideas retained their common-sense quality: Pavlov's dog still wags its behaviorist tail in the popular consciousness and, as with the underclass in the core, the third world is still shouldered with the guilt of its own underdevelopment.

But all the while, this intellectual establishment did not go unchallenged. The hegemonic cultural mosaic legitimating, and masking, relations of power and exploitation is, in fact, the more striking when placed in relation to its anti-systemic, anomaly-projecting underside. The analytic tradition of positive science/social science was contested by phenomenology, existentialism, and structuralism. New Criticism, abstract expressionism, and pop art had to contend with structuralism, surrealism, and the nouveau roman. And then, of course, the Angry Young Men, the Beat Generation, and rock'n'rollers rejected "the system" entirely. Modernization theory was countered by the *dependentistas* and the principles of the human sciences and their institutional structures were challenged by visions of "négritude," Braudelian *Annales* and area studies, and eventually cultural studies.

Countertrends, Resistance, Rejection

On the continent, phenomenology marked a reaction to positivism (as a clear alternative to the analytic tradition) and the perception of a disintegrating civilization in the wake of the 1914–18 war. Edmund Husserl, working in the tradition of the Cartesian project, sought a philosophy of certainty.[11] But if positivism disassociated subject and object, the effect of Husserl's labor to place the human subject at the center of a knowable world did not turn out to be everyone's idea of antiestablishment: "Phenomenology recovered and refurbished the old dream of classical bourgeois ideology . . . pivot[ing] on the belief that 'man' was somehow prior to his history and social conditions" (Eagleton 1983: 58). The existentialists developed Husserl's ideas in directions he sometimes criticized.[12] In breaking with his mentor Husserl, Martin Heidegger attempted to recapture the radically (factical) historical dimension of meaning. Existence can never be completely objectified but remains problematic, a becoming, in which, however, time loses its developmental aspect.

Affirmation of knowledge through participation as against observation (the positive sciences) places the existentialist perspective at a juncture with Dilthey's human studies. The historicism that followed entailed a relativism that repudiated eternal truths or all-encompassing systems of thought. The themes of repetition, destiny, and the tragic manifest an aversion to any easy doctrine of progress. Nonetheless, a reevaluation of metaphysics in the descriptive sense (time, history, and man's place in the world) instead of the speculative sense (the extension of reason beyond the observable to a transcendental reality) may also be attributed to the existentialist perspective.

Since at least the symbolists, artists and writers had organized resistance to establishment models in similar terms. Dada, the immediate progenitor of surrealism, represented the coming together of what was, in practice, already an international movement rejecting a world at war and seemingly at the end of its rope. Originating in Zurich in 1916, Dada "aimed to destroy the reasonable deceptions of man and recover the natural and unreasonable order" (Arp, in Ades 1981: 114). Anarchic, against everything, it demolished itself (logically, as part of that world). But its antibourgeois, anti-art attitude survived in the surrealists' more constructive campaign against realism: "The realist attitude, inspired by positivism . . . has for me an air that is hostile to all intellectual and moral achievement," wrote André Breton ([1924] 1972: 14; my translation). And surrealism recognized the power of the unconscious and the imagination (Freud), for which automatic writing (the manifestation of "psychic automatism") provided a key technique.[13]

Marcel Duchamp and Francis Picabia led the movement in New York, where it strongly influenced Jackson Pollack, the abstract expressionists, and pop art. To avoid diluting the homegrown superiority of his "American-style painters," however, Clement Greenberg effectively expurgated the role of surrealism in their development. Thus, the imposed consensus of the establishment contained a suppressed resistance, a resistance that flowered as insurgent alternatives. Dali's limp watches characterized well a disintegrating consensus about the nature of time, and Magritte's much more perplexing work questioned fundamental "assumptions about the world, about the relationship between a painted and a real object" (Ades 1981: 133).

During the 1950s the nouveau roman confronted many of these same concerns: "a rejection at last of any pre-established order" (Robbe-Grillet [1958]

1963b: 81; my translation).[14] Alain Robbe-Grillet's "new realism" ([1955] 1963d, 1963f), or, as proposed by Michel Butor, "a more highly developed realism" ([1960] 1972b: 11; my translation) took up the baton espousing the creative and transformative potential of the imagination in the context of a debate, especially with Sartre (1947), over the nature of literature. Sartre's position had developed around "*engagement*": "Unlike the poet, the prose writer *uses* language to *communicate* a certain view of the world, and is *responsible* for the moral and political significance of this representation; this constitutes a mode of *action,* which Sartre names 'l'action par dévoilement.' . . . The Nouveau Roman's opposition to this is based on the idea that writing is not a means to an end but an end in itself, an area of free exploration that cannot be constrained by any predetermined meaning" (Britton 1992: 12). Robbe-Grillet lumped Sartre's engagement with socialist realism and attacked both, thus aligning the nouveau roman with the anti-Stalinist left. The world "is neither significant nor absurd; it simply *is,*" wrote Robbe-Grillet ([1956] 1963g: 21; my translation). He dismissed simplistic commitment in favor of "full consciousness of the current problems of [one's] own language, the conviction of their extreme importance, the determination to resolve them from within. That . . . is the only chance of remaining an artist, and undoubtedly besides, by some obscure and far-off consequence, of someday being useful for something—perhaps even for the revolution" ([1957] 1963e: 46–47; my translation). To refuse character construction (associated with the high tide of the individual) and linear narrative (to tell a story had become impossible because it represented an order and "memory is never chronological") does not assume the absence of man or action. Writing for Robbe-Grillet is an intervention—"less a matter of knowing than of conquering" ([1957] 1963e: 33; my translation)—and the reader is invited to participate in the creation and learn to invent his or her own life (1963f: 168–69).

Sartre and Robbe-Grillet, however, are not so far apart as the debate would have it seem; both stressed the active participation of the individual. Indeed, Robbe-Grillet's conception of writing and reading is reminiscent of the existentialist vision itself, which, however, was not without problems. Sartre extolled existentialism as a humanism. As a "style of philosophizing" it generally begins with man rather than with nature (downgrading nonhuman realities) as "thinking subject, initiator of action and a centre of feeling" (Macquarrie 1972: 14–15). Emphasizing action and the themes of freedom, decision, responsibility, and the emotions (within an environment of factical possibility), existentialist discussion tends to center on the individual, although as a unity, including both body and mind in a context: being-in-the-world, being-with-others. This aspect was to be of primary importance to the generation of young people who "seized the moment" in 1968 (and was explicitly linked to the socialist humanism of the first New Left in Britain). However, the individual component may come to predominate over being-in-a-community. There is then an easy slippage from an anticollectivism (as dehumanizing) to an anticommunal bias. Authenticity, radical choice, and self-affirmation unchecked may become an apology for amoralism and totalitarianism, or the simple excuse for a "me generation."[15]

Resistance in the world-system to the constraints of received premises of knowledge formation was certainly not confined to commercial, official, institutional, or high-cultural levels. It could also be constituted by outright rejection and withdrawal. In Britain, the crucial year 1956 was also marked by John Osborne's play, *Look Back in Anger,* which, as Lin Chun says, "expressed a specific political mood of 'rebelling without a cause': vigorous but cynical, idealistic but negative, refusing the status quo but seeing no alternative" (1993: 7). The Angry Young Men "wanted entrance into the very real [world] on the surface where fortunes were made and power wielded"; however, without a "common goal . . . they were not organizing a new revolution" (Feldman and Gartenberg 1958: 15).[16]

In contrast, the Beat Generation sought to create a new world with man at its center, "a utopia based on the intense embrace of experience, often evading logic, bypassing reason, and staying in the presence of sensation."[17] The Beats stressed process, improvisation, and spontaneity (confounding the subject/ object distinction, "cut-ups," found objects, and collages challenged ideas about the art object, and the Happening refused the role of passive consumer to the viewer/audience). The Beats "sought to unname, to undefine" (Phillips 1995: 29, 40). They contested traditional hierarchies of value and the institutions in which they were enshrined. These included universities (Kerouac, Ginsberg, and Burroughs had met at Columbia), museums and concert halls (preferred venues included the streets, clubs, artist co-ops, and coffee houses), and establishment publishing houses (which, fearing obscenity laws, rejected them in turn). Jazz performance presented a model to which Beat art, and life, aspired. "American music is black music; black culture is American culture," Mona Lisa Saloy writes. "The market place knows it; the Beats saw, heard, and dug its eloquence and grandeur." The link between the Beats and the black experience would more fully develop in the struggle for civil rights in the 1960s and prepared the ground for the breakthrough of rock and roll. The "beat goes on," and this "tribute to the African-American cultural legacy" is a "major and inseparable legacy of Beat culture" (1995: 164).

In Britain, too, the Beat-influenced counterculture was felt as a kind of resistance; however, despite the overlap in Britain between the first New Left and the underground, the explicitly political commitment of the former did not favor "dropping out." According to E. P. Thompson, "Natopolitan ideology had engendered within itself its own negation—a new critical temper, the positives of Aldermaston, the negatives of 'hip' and 'beats'" ([1960] 1978a: 31). When Michael Horowitz brought out *New Departures* in 1959, he got material from Burroughs himself in Paris, an example of the connections that were made at the "Beat Hotel" at 9 rue Gît-le-Coeur where Burroughs, Ginsberg, and Corso lived for years and contacts were forged and maintained with a constantly shifting, "on the road," international network. On the publication of Burroughs's *Naked Lunch* in Paris in 1959, James Campbell writes, "Burroughs had probably never heard of the *nouveau roman,* but he used the leftovers of surrealism to more inventive effect than anything by Robbe-Grillet and his colleagues. Nothing was more new in Paris at the end of the 1950s than this American new Novel" (1995: 233). But in Britain, as Peter Jenner remembers, "almost no one actually *went* [to San Francisco]. . . . We took on the PR of it, rather than the reality of it, so it wasn't absolutely imitative, and that was what was so important and that's why it was interesting and that's why it was creative" (quoted in J. Green 1988: 61).

Even the Soviet Union had a 1950s counterculture, which E. P. Thompson paralleled to the Western version: "The rituals and resounding absolutes of orthodox Stalinism have induced a nausea in the younger Soviet generation, giving rise to the critique of the 'revisionists,' the positive rebellion of '56, the negative resistance of the *stilyagi*" ([1960] 1978a: 31). The zoot-suited and tight-skirted stilyagi were hooked on jazz (especially after Wallis Conover began broadcasting on the Voice of America in 1955), and a new group of writers, including Vasily Aksënov (a jazz aficionado himself), "fed into the popular culture by depicting real people of his alienated generation who scorned ideology, possessed no heroes, and sought something like the jazz, sex, and open road of the American beatniks . . . a 'starry ticket' into another world and another future" (Stites 1992: 126–27).

Despite challenges to the establishment launched from humanistic platforms, the scope of critiques of any possibility of a universal humanism widened from the 1950s through the mid-1960s. Léopold Sédar Senghor wrote that negritude "is *a* humanism of the twentieth century" (1970: 180, emphasis added). From the 1930s, this elite counterculture constituted a direct attack on universalizing, Eurocentric culture at the world scale. Such was one of the objectives of the founding of *Présence Africaine* in 1947: "to define African originality." There was, however, a second concern: "to hasten her acceptance into the modern world" (Diop 1947: 7; my translation). The first concern was addressed by the *négritude* poets, writing from the periphery in the language of the center, as the recuperation of a particularistic identity. As they were presented in Sartre's introduction, "Orphée noir" (1948), to Senghor's *Anthologie de la nouvelle poésie nègre et malgache de langue française,* this took the form of an "opposition between Black and White" (Jack 1996: 65). "The Negro will learn to say 'white like snow' to indicate innocence, to speak of the blackness of a look, of a soul, of a deed. As soon as he opens his mouth, he accuses himself, unless he persists in upsetting the hierarchy. And if he upsets it in *French,* he is already poetizing: can you imagine the strange savor that an expression like 'the blackness of innocence' or 'the darkness of virtue' would have for us?" (Sartre [1948] 1988a: 304). The negation of negation (in language), which renders negritude poetry revolutionary, returns when Sartre writes that "the Negro himself . . . creates a kind of antiracist racism" (326). By casting negritude as the weak moment in a dialectic, he remolds the second concern of *Présence Africaine* from one of assimilation to one of historical transformation. In the first instance, it is a question of competing particularities (a plurality of humanisms, for instance, constituting a tactics of resistance); in the second, Sartre implicates that larger system that contains the struggle (the "modern world," the arena of a strategy for the future): "negritude is *for* destroying itself; it is a 'crossing to' and not an 'arrival at,' a means and not an end" (327). Drawing attention to the complex articulation between the universal and the particular implicit in the historicity of negritude, Sartre established a relationship between the political and the cultural and readmitted poetry as a site of committed, *engagée* literature.[18]

Robbe-Grillet (1958) points to the double-edged and paralyzing nature of the existentialist project that placed man at the center of meaning. For him the question is the very hegemony of man, a fundamental ideological pillar of modern thought. His condemnation of "habitual" humanism in which man is everywhere and tragedy is the sublimation of the difference between man and things rests on a profound sense of the way in which being is separated from the world by the construction of an anthropomorphic "nature" (through adjectival metaphor, e.g., "majestic mountain"). Louis Althusser rebuked economism and empiricism, and the humanism and the historicism he found in Sartre (and practically everywhere else), and Michel Foucault announced the possible end of man (1970: 387). In a lecture given in New York in 1968, Jacques Derrida (1972) situated his denunciation of existentialism as a humanism become metaphysic, in his solidarity with the antiwar effort and in the context of the contemporary events in Paris and the assassination of Martin Luther King.

It was nonetheless the constitution by *language,* prior to the subject and in which we all participate, of the existentialist conception of a world of being-in-the-world—a conception central to the nouveau roman: "Language is not contained in consciousness; it contains it" (Robbe-Grillet [1953] 1963a: 117, citing Joë Bousquet)—that meshed so felicitously with the structuralist program. The mediation, picked up by Robbe-Grillet, had been accomplished through Roland Barthes's *Writing Degree Zero* of 1953, itself a reply to Sartre (1947) in the debate over the relationship between politics and literature. The issue was realist representation. Barthes indicts socialist realism for reproducing bourgeois conventions and with this move redefines commitment as an engagement of the form itself; "every Form is also a Value." He locates a literary space, *écriture,* "essentially the morality of form, the choice of that social area within which the writer elects to situate the Nature of his language," between the anarchic, "personal past" of style and the ordered, "familiar History" of language. On this middle ground "the choice of a human attitude, the affirmation of a certain Good" takes place. "A language and a style are blind forces; a mode of writing is an act of historical solidarity. A language and a style are objects; a mode of writing is a function: it is the relationship between creation and society, the literary language transformed by its social finality, form considered as a human intention and thus linked to the great crises of History" (Barthes [1953] 1968: 13, 15, 14). Sartre and Barthes, then, disagreed on the location of commitment in literature, but not on its possibility.

Structuralism bloomed in this intellectual climate. But as François Dosse writes, the "reign of structuralism required a death" and it was the "collapse of the tutelary figure that Sartre incarnated," due in part to "political issues" and in part to "what was beginning to take shape in the intellectual world," that paved the way for the preeminence Claude Lévi-Strauss would assume and with whom structuralism "quickly became identified" (1997a: 3, 5, 4, 10). By the 1950s, structuralism's time had come to be widely influential across the humanities and the social sciences. The work of Ferdinand de Saussure, the Swiss linguist, is fundamental.[19] His *Cours de Linguistique Générale,* a collection of lectures delivered between 1906 and 1911, was published posthumously in 1916 (but, instructively, appeared in English only in 1959). He insisted that language, systems of signs that express meaning, should be studied not just in terms of its individual parts and diachronically, as philologists had done, but also in terms of the relationship between those parts and synchronically, that is, language's current *structural* configuration as well as its *historical* dimensions—a total system, always and ever complete. But signs, the parts, are themselves inseparable wholes constituted by both the concept, the signified (*signifié*), and the sound-image or word, the signifier (*signifiant*). Each unique utterance, *parole,* is referentially arbitrary and finds meaning only within that relational system of differences, *langue,* which itself never appears.

The model was appropriated by anthropologists and applied to nonlinguistic phenomena. Lévi-Strauss, whose major sources, however, were Jakobson and Benveniste (Hénaff 1998: 7), looked for those contrastive relationships analogous to the structure of language that, in a comparative perspective, would yield insights into the fundamental form or essential nature of the mind irrespective of the society in which it might appear.[20] His structuralist method, antiempiricist and challenging the one-to-one correspondence between reality or nature and constructions of meaning, contested former lines of research. The "social" as substantive rather than adjectival was derived from Durkheim and Mauss; the ahistorical, synchronic, "structuralist causality," as against historical determination, from the linguistic model.

This approach (of internal arrangements) is positively present in Althusser and undergirded the new life he brought to the study of ideology. Attractive to Marxists and of great importance in work issuing from CCCS were the "stress on 'determinate conditions,' . . . the recognition by structuralism not only of the necessity of abstraction as the instrument of thought through which 'real relations' are appropriated, but also of the presence, in Marx's work, of a continuous and complex movement *between different levels of abstraction* [and] its conception of 'the whole' " (S. Hall 1980b: 67–68).

The strength of structuralism was to rehabilitate a version of relational thinking—although not the dialectical version. However, for Richard Johnson, the difficulties with "the preferred level of abstraction . . . the tendency . . . to radically simplify the social formation [and] the slide into a functionalist account of ideological social relations" indicated the "need to retain culture-ideology as a couplet, where culture is understood as a ground or result of the work of ideologies. The key problem remains the means by which concrete social individuals, classes and political forces are formed and moved by ideologies, or how an ideology can become a principle of life" (1979: 67, 75). These concerns were addressed through Antonio Gramsci's assertion (1971) of the historical specificity and conjunctural nature of knowledge and the application of his particular concepts of hegemony and common sense (and thus the translation of knowledge back into practice).

An opening to the world had certainly been a central part of Barthes's early program, after which "the various formalist notions of a free and unconstrained self, and of a free, autonomous literary language, are revealed for what they are: the fantasies of the repressed and—in the political extension worked through in *Mythologies*—the prized ideals of bourgeois culture" (Lentricchia 1980: 132). Despite their profound disagreements, Barthes and Sartre share not only the sense of the possibility of commitment in literature, but also that it is manifested through disclosure. Barthes is unabashedly concerned with meaning, the construction of meaning: signification and its *function*. It is indicative that, during this period of anticolonial struggle (Bandung Conference, Suez crisis, Algeria, Vietnam), Barthes, in a major theoretical exegesis of 1957, "Myth Today," took as one of his primary examples the image (the cover of *Paris-Match*) of "a young Negro in a French uniform . . . saluting": "I see very well what it signifies to me: that France is a great Empire, that all her sons, without any colour discrimination, faithfully serve under her flag, and that there is no better answer to the detractors of an alleged colonialism than the zeal shown by this Negro in serving his so-called oppressors" ([1957] 1972: 116). Language can either formulate a concept by expressing it or expunge it by concealing it. Barthes's innovative reading of language as myth accomplishes both.[21] This is how it transforms *history* into *nature*, producing ideology: it is read as a factual system of expression (French imperiality is naturalized in the image of the saluting black soldier), not a semiological system of values (the content—history, blood, and struggle—of all the aspects of the image is expurgated). This explicit concern for the construction of meaning, an opening *of* the world by concentrating on the signifier, and its relation to practice was, however, to remain temporally limited as a dominant program.

If in 1966 Barthes still held out the possibility of a "science of literature," that was soon to fade. Structuralism per se assumes both a "self-sustaining objective structure of the text" and an autonomous subject, "free-standing and transcendental," on which it depends. "Structuralism becomes transformed into poststructuralism when the structures of the text are seen to be always structures in and for a subject. . . . The text of structuralism is intransitive, that of poststructuralism transitive" (Easthope 1988: 32, 33). "Myth Today" suggested a neutral, innocent level of language and a reality outside of ideology. This Althusser rejected: from the earliest age, every subjectivity is situated in language and as "he or she enters the realm of negation, desire, and the family . . . it becomes preposterous to posit any act to listening or speaking which would be free of ideology"; all the same, "there is always a heterogeneity of conflicting ideologies concealed behind the dominant one [and while] it may not be possible to step outside of ideology altogether, it *is* possible to effect a rupture with one, and a rapprochement with another" (Silverman 1983: 30–31).

Structuralism had offered the promise of a new rigor and scientific status, nonreductionist and nonpositivist, for the human sciences. However, just this possibility determined a mandalic turn of structuralism back on itself: the realization of elegant formal analyses that privileged the internal relations of the text. The overly synchronic tendency—the problem of accounting for historical change—along with the scarce significance accorded domains other than language and the historical conditions of the emergence of structuralism itself have also presented abiding difficulties.[22] But "emphasis on the 'constructedness' of human meaning represented a major advance." It spelled the demise of European humanism and positivism alike and the Romanticism of vital essences—material, human, or poetic (Eagleton 1983: 107–8).

The primacy accorded to the analysis of relationships rather than entities is also apparent in the positive resistance to the export of modernization theory. Third world scholars, from Latin America especially, led the way. Reservations about this establishment perspective were advanced early in the 1950s by Raul Prebisch and the Economic Commission for Latin America, or ECLA group, as they observed anti-Ricardian deteriorating terms of trade between "core" and "periphery" (see Baer 1962). The construction of this relation over the long term, "the development of underdevelopment" (Frank 1967, 1969), became the theme of dependency theorists (see Cardoso 1977; Palma 1978). Anomalies suggested that increased contact with the core (metropole, center) impeded development in the periphery (satellite). The logic of modernization was inverted; emphasis on change and material interests and the importance given to political and economic structures over cultural considerations reflected an orthodox Marxist perspective. Such was the strength of modernization as an official doctrine, however, that charges were largely ignored: Andre Gunder Frank's first three books were not even reviewed in establishment journals (Leys 1982: 332, 337) and Fernando Henrique Cardoso and Enzo Faletto's *Dependence and Development in Latin America*, first published in 1969, became available in English only ten years later.

At the level of institutionalized knowledge production, Fernand Braudel and the *Annales* School met head-on the logic of the disciplines, "universalizing, empiricist, sectioning off politics from economics and both from culture, profoundly ethnocentric, arrogant, and oppressive—Gramsci's hegemonic culture at the world level" (Wallerstein 1978: 5).[23] Braudel (1958) found the humanistic framework the great impediment to the "convergence" of the social sciences. Study of the economic and the social (rather than just the political) and the emphasis on the *longue durée* and *conjonctures* (instead of a chronological narrative of "events" or individual biographies) were direct attacks on universalizing nomothetic thought and, even more so, on idiographic history, which had been dominant in France. During the cold war period, *Annales* profited as a non–Anglo-Saxon and non-Soviet pole to which dissidents of any persuasion or nationality, including Marxists, could gravitate (Wallerstein 1991b: 187–201). In this respect it represented another aspect of French, third force nationalism evident from world politics to the fine arts.

In the United States, post-1945 hegemony in the world-system and cold war tensions and decolonization posed problems of global management and called for the rapid development of politically useful "regional knowledge." The result was area studies, institutionalized in university programs (the university serving the national interest), strongly supported by the Social Science Research Council (SSRC) and funded through the federal government and private foundations. In producing "a large supply of skilled specialists available for public service and private business, it was no doubt a great success." That success, however, had entailed a direct challenge to the premises on which existing disciplinary boundaries had been drawn in the social sciences during the second half of the nineteenth century. Three cleavages had defined this differentiation: past–present, "between 'idiographic' history and the 'nomothetic' social sciences (principally three: economics, political science, sociology)"; West–non-West, "the above four disciplines concentrated on the Western world, the non-Western world was studied by two different disciplines: anthropology for the 'tribal' ('primitive') peoples, and Oriental studies for non-Western 'high civilizations' "; state–market–civil society, "which established the boundaries for political science, economics, and sociology" (Wallerstein 1997: 210, 198). Area studies deprived Oriental studies and anthropology of their primary subject matter and ahistorical grounding and, as Immanuel Wallerstein explains, acted like a Trojan horse on the "Western" social sciences: "The initial breach was only geographic. But it was crucial, since it crossed the West–non-West, civilized-barbarian divide. Once the breach was made, everything else could follow; and follow it did, after 1968" (219–20).

Cultural studies found its initial impetus in the specificity of the post-1945

English situation of economic expansion and a relationship of hegemonic subordination to the United States in the cold war structure of bipolar interstate politics. The optimism engendered by the first abetted opposition to the second, in the form of a short-lived internationalism. The constraints of the forces of world capital and geopolitics soon voided the project. Unlike France, Great Britain embraced the junior partnership, and cultural studies, even though remaining oppositional in its commitment to collective work blurring the disciplinary boundaries in the humanities and social sciences, retreated to academia and slipped back into the social-critical space, the one carved out over the preceding century and a half, to deal with the Condition-of-England Question.

The crisis of universal humanism and positivism rumbled through the 1950s to explode in the 1960s. And in the 1970s, cultural studies moved away from its humanist roots in the concern to create a science of culture. But in the same way cultural studies' preoccupation with the popular to the detriment of elite forms recreated a divide that theory negated, the reluctance to question the category science tacitly reproduced the long-term "two cultures" structure of knowledge and undercut challenges to disciplinarity.

CHAPTER 7

Conjunctural Knowledge II: Patterns of Disarray, 1968 and After

Then came the Columbia strike. I was both a student and a teacher as well as a committed feminist, a protestor against the war in Vietnam, and a pacifist. . . . Everything came together—the radical agenda of the youth movement, the New Left and civil rights, the radical new feminist politics we were inventing downtown—all confronting the university's president and trustees, their compromising connections with big money and military research.—KATE MILLETT, introduction to *Sexual Politics*

The study of culture has, over the last few years, been quite dramatically transformed as questions of modernity and postmodernity have replaced the more familiar concepts of ideology and hegemony which, from the mid-1970s until the mid-1980s, anchored cultural analysis firmly within the neo-Marxist field mapped out by Althusser and Gramsci. —ANGELA MCROBBIE, "New Times in Cultural Studies"

Any science that conceives of the world as being governed according to a universal theoretical plan that reduces its various riches to drab applications of general laws thereby becomes an instrument of domination. And man, a stranger to the world, sets himself up as its master.—ILYA PRIGOGINE AND ISABELLE STENGERS, *Order Out of Chaos*

In May 1968 the simmering world revolution exploded. In the United States, the Old Left had succumbed to external pressures of cold war McCarthyism and internal angst in the wake of Soviet de-Stalinization. A (second) New Left coalesced around themes including race relations (not to be disassociated from a global dimension of cold war decolonization), the anti–Vietnam War movement, and university reform. Student movements were everywhere important —United States, Britain, Italy, Japan, Czechoslovakia—but perhaps nowhere more so than in France. De Gaulle's goal of establishing a third force resulted in authoritarian conditions at home, which students experienced in the oppressive practices of both state and Catholic schools. Indeed, the lasting impact of 1968 was on the institutional structures of knowledge formation.

Of course, movements are not at all times, or do not appear in all time frames, equally subversive. For example, existentialism had differing impacts according to the time and place, and the homophobic and phallocentric tendencies of the surrealists fit long-term trends in Western thought. The new women's movements have not been alone in bleaching the credentials of these currents as radical alternatives. Structuralist and poststructuralist strategies, presented as and roundly criticized as profoundly radical, in fact produced new formalisms. *Annales* lost its edge; failing to transcend the disciplines—with only a fig leaf of multidisciplinarity—it moved in both nomothetic and idiographic directions (the so-called *émiettement*). The area studies project, too, imploded, choking on its practical success and retreating in the face of ethical crises and charges of intellectual limitations.

Unable to link up with an activist base, cultural studies moved into the universities. Although the original political project had foundered, the subversive tendencies of its multi(anti)disciplinary, collective practices were deepened with the exploration of issues of identity and subjectivity, but again without seriously calling into question the basic structure of knowledge formation.

Three Challenges

During the post-1968 period of declining U.S. hegemony and world economic contraction, overt challenges to the legitimating premises of *knowledge* intensified around three beliefs: that instrumental science as public knowledge implemented through technology and applied to the real world engenders progress; that there exist universal propositions reflecting timeless truths; and that there are substantial differences constituting a hierarchy of knowledge among the academic disciplines themselves. The first is associated with a crisis of linear chronosophy (see Pomian 1979)—grave, in exposing the identification of progress with endless capitalist accumulation; the second with the crisis of the longue durée structure of knowledge dominated by classical science, which underlay the very idea of progress; and the third with the nineteenth-century crisis of knowledge formation in the sphere of human reality. This crisis resulted in the *conjoncturel*, universalizing and sectorializing, restructuring of academic disciplines, the social sciences, that has sustained the science/humanities antinomy for over a hundred years by resolving medium-term contradictions that came to a head during the second half of the nineteenth century.

In the late 1960s, the ideology of a technological society, based on a value-neutral science providing unlimited growth and progress, reached a turning point. In April 1968, barely two months after the Tet offensive in Vietnam, the Club of Rome convened for the first time to examine major trends, mutually interrelated, from a long-term, global, systems perspective. The study they commissioned reported that growth, far from a blanket panacea, if unchecked, would eventually result in "sudden and uncontrollable decline in both population and industrial capacity" (Meadows et al. 1974: 29).[1]

The development of new technologies based on discoveries in theoretical science, seconded by the managerial/organizational techniques for their large-scale deployment, had accompanied and in part made possible the massive destruction of the war ending in 1945. Of overriding importance, besides electronics (especially radar), was of course atomic research (the Manhattan Project), which was specifically intended for weapons development (Hiroshima and Nagasaki). In the immediate postwar period it was presumed that this technology would undergo metamorphosis into "too cheap to meter" atomic power. But during the next forty years the production of swords far outweighed that of plowshares. Despite a relatively vocal antinuclear weapons movement (associated with an antiwar movement that reached its apogee during the world revolution of 1968), only minor victories were attained. In the post-1968 period these victories were in deployment, as in the case of New Zealand, where ports were closed in the mid-1980s to ships carrying nuclear weapons: proliferation, however, continued. Few credited science with making the world a safer place, although the assertion remained a staple of the political rhetoric of the strong and the legislative pitch of the military industrial complex.

Nuclear power was not as obviously pernicious as nuclear weapons; hence the movement contesting it got a slower start. Only after 1968 did it become a real force, gaining support with each well-publicized incident of radiation release or catastrophic "meltdown" (Three Mile Island 1979, Chernobyl 1986) and most recently with concern over radioactive waste. Because objection has been based heavily on technical concerns—accidents, waste disposal, and damage compensation—the drawbacks of fossil fuels (greenhouse effect) and growth of demand for electricity could reverse the antinuclear consensus. As of the late 1980s, the establishment did not envision the development of new, cleaner technologies; it perceived the problem as one of public relations (Nuclear Energy Agency 1989: 9, 10). Public outcry notwithstanding, the long-term commitment to nuclear power, buttressed by official public relations campaigns, is massive in the core and increasing in the periphery. All the same, in both the third world (the mixed blessings were clear in the Philippines and Zaire, where the exploitative nature of the projects in favor of core capital was apparent) and the core, progress through technology represented by nuclear power has seemed a chimera.[2]

Vastly expanded chemical industries, many producing the pesticides and fertilizers necessary for the new high-yield strains of food grains of the "green revolution," were also typical of the postwar period. But then Rachel Carson published *Silent Spring* in 1962, exposing pesticide pollution. This marked the opening salvo in the contemporary ecology crusade, as distinct from the long-established (and establishment) reformist conservation movement, and effectively launched it as a popular concern in the core. Even such mainstream, relatively conservative conservation organizations as the Sierra Club and the National Audubon Society, although shunning any hint of radicalism, became more activist (e.g., Mitchell and Stallings 1970). The movement has exploded to include diverse philosophies, methods, and goals, for instance, radical, confrontational direct action, Greenpeace and Earth First!; revolutionary rejection of any human-centered attitude toward nature, the Deep Ecology movement (Devall and Sessions 1985; Wexler 1990); grave concerns for the economics of growth (L. Brown 1978; Meadows et al. 1974; Schumacher 1973); electoral politics (Ryle 1988; Gorz 1980); and the politics of the relationship between green knowledge and cultural transformation (Jamison 2001).[3]

In Europe and North America, some trade-offs have been negotiated between capital and the environment. However, in the former COMECON countries of Eastern Europe, the hazards of unbridled development through rapid industrialization may now be readily observed in the calamitous pollution of land, water, and air. By the early 1970s, the unexpected consequences of the green revolution, one of the standard-bearers of modernization (and Western science) had become painfully clear in the periphery. Not surprisingly, many of the same concerns—long-term degradation of the life support capacity of the biosphere (Sahel, tropical rain forests, ozone layer) and near-term catastrophe (Bhopal 1984)—are shared, within the more restricted ambit of their activity, by the antinuclear power movement.

In fact, support for social change remained broad but covert. As David Dellinger wrote, "The antinuclear movement has a hidden agenda: that is, fighting for a society based on equality and democracy rather than dependence on energy monopolies and the nuclear industry" (1982: 233). But is this so, and if so, to what extent? Lester Milbrath, focusing on the core (United States, Great

Britain, and Germany), attempted to document quantitatively (both in terms of belief and behavior) the efforts and relative success of a "newly developing environmentally-oriented ethic" at odds with the "Dominant Social Paradigm," which posits humans as set apart from other creatures and masters of their destiny living in an unlimited world of ceaseless progress (Milbrath 1984: 7–8). Significantly, those who "perceive a large environmental problem . . . [and] want basic social change to solve it and . . . perceive that there are limits to growth . . . [reached] 18–19% in the United States, 24% in England and 29% in Germany." This suggests the possibility of a transition to a "New Environmental Paradigm," even that such a transition may already be in progress (59, 14, 43–65). Indeed, as German Greens are wont to say, "We are neither left nor right; we are in front." More than a yuppie bubble, what has united these tendencies with movements in the periphery, often including those with other agendas and very different modes of engagement (e.g., diverse fundamentalisms), is their disenchantment with old forms expressing the Enlightenment project (see Borgmann 1992).[4]

The case of the debate over global warming is instructive in that it has recently taken a turn: even the administration of the younger Bush seems to now agree with the academic community that asserts "there can no longer be any reasonable doubt of global warming itself and its generally malign consequences for the environment and human economy" (Wilson 2002: 67). However, on the one hand, it remains a matter of debate how different will be the effects experienced in particular high-density population locales, at least if they are noncoastal. Will a particular area be hotter or colder, suffocated in dust storms or washed away in floods? On the other hand, policymakers, for their part, are either reticent on the causes or extol a voluntary approach to their solution. Nonetheless, although many put their faith in the ethical agency of individuals and nongovernmental agencies in the belief that humanity will "choose wisely . . . [and] find the way to save the integrity of this planet and the magnificent life it harbors" (189), the solutions Edward O. Wilson enumerates still depend on "cooperation among the three secular stanchions of civilized existence: government, the private sector, and science and technology" (164).

Few contemporary voices, in either core or periphery, have questioned more stridently the progressive nature of modern society by denouncing its scientific/technological fundaments than elements of the women's movement.[5] Women have been in the vanguard of the antinuclear movement and highly visible calling for strong regulation of pollution and toxic waste (Milbrath 1984: 75). Taking another tack, they have singled out the female body itself as an exemplary locus of scientific confrontation (Gallagher and Laqueur 1987). Despite the "unprecedented cultural authority, and massive material investments guarantee[ing] its truths," the demystification of "the scientific discourse focused on the female body" proceeds apace. By the late 1960s, with roots in the reproductive issues of contraception, abortion, and child care, feminist thinking began to take on a new aspect, challenging "patriarchal privilege" (long justified on "scientific" principles) and the previously unquestioned premises of liberal society itself: "rejecting the linearity, the mechanistic thinking of technological society, replacing it with a sense of organic wholeness, roundness, interconnectedness" (Rothman 1989: 252–53).

For our Europe-centered system since 1500, progress has meant expansion. However, in the late twentieth century this movement seems to many to have reached its global ecological limit of incorporating land (resources) and people (labor power). The withdrawal from colonial empires and the rise of anti-Western movements in the periphery may already represent fluctuations near the asymptotic limit to expansion. Prior "skeptical reassessments" of the idea of progress have been primarily core phenomena occurring in the wake of Kondratieff B-phases, but the structural reversal of expansion and geopolitical change of the present conjuncture make "doubts about progress . . . stronger today than previously" (Wallerstein 1991a: 232). The argument that living standards, *measured on a world scale,* have exhibited a long-term polarization (Wallerstein 1983: 98–105) has given the lie to the ideology of constructing a better world through universal science and technology and fits tightly with the argument exposing the exhaustion of (endless) progress conceived as (endless) expansion in linear time.

Complex Science

Notwithstanding the naturalization, as commonsense, of classical science, its premises are under attack today by its very practitioners.[6] The unity offered by Newtonian science has reached its limit, undermined by the internal development of science itself. Built on the model of celestial mechanics, it started to show cracks during the last quarter of the nineteenth century, when mathematicians began to investigate continuous but nondifferentiable functions and transfinite arithmetic and proved the three-body problem insoluble. Until recently, these developments were largely overshadowed by the successes at the level of the very large of relativity and the very small of quantum mechanics. Since the late 1960s, research has led to a reconceptualization of the world as one of complexity, deterministic but unpredictable. The new conceptual scheme includes order-within-chaos (strange attractors), order-out-of-chaos (dissipative structures), and visual representation of pathological functions and natural forms exhibiting non-integer dimensions (fractal geometry). An examination of publication data shows a veritable explosion of the relevant literature.[7]

Paul Davies (1989) characterizes contemporary scientific research as falling into three categories: at the frontiers of the very large, the very small, and the very complex. The new appreciation of complexity (e.g., Aida et al. 1985; Atlan et al. 1985), dealing with the universal features of complex systems, irrespective of the peculiar aspects of the different systems (Peliti and Vulpiani 1988), was foreseen by Warren Weaver in 1948.[8] Grégoire Nicolis and Ilya Prigogine (1989), for instance, concentrate on natural complexity seen as part of everyday experience; limitations in predictability and self-organization of real systems are presented as intimately related to the inseparable notions of time and irreversibility. This rethinking—a synthetic approach as opposed to a reductionist one, strong cross-disciplinarity, and the inclusion of "intractable" problems (Pagels 1988; Stein 1989)—marks a transition away from the Newtonian worldview. Newtonian mechanics, which became the model of classical science and, in a larger context, a cornerstone of Enlightenment thought, was the result of the quest for a theory of harmony in the universe "expressed by simple, but hidden, means" (Ekeland 1988: 6). Hand-in-hand with classical dynamics went the idea of progress (from a "dis-ordered" to a "well-ordered" society). Not so long ago, Sir James Lighthill apologized on behalf of the "broad global fraternity of practitioners of mechanics . . . for having misled the general educated public by spreading ideas about the determinism of systems satisfying Newton's laws of motion [their complete predictability] that, after 1960, were to be proved incorrect" (1986: 38).

Evidence of order underlying the surprisingly chaotic evolution of certain dynamical systems (especially those with few degrees of freedom) became apparent with the discovery of the "strange attractors" associated with these systems, beginning with Edward Lorenz's weather models (1963a, 1963b, 1964) in the mid-1960s. With Mitchell Feigenbaum's (1983) discovery of universal behavior in cascading bifurcations of nonlinear systems, the mesoscale of humanly perceivable phenomena gained a universal constant. Robert Shaw has argued that chaotic behavior is *completely ubiquitous* in the physical world." Borrowing from information theory, he characterized the onset of turbulence as the passage of a system from an information sink to an information source. Strange attractors transmit perturbations from the microscale to the macroscale. The implications are that the nineteenth-century view of the world as a machine is wrong not only in the small but also in the large: "Constant injection of new information into the macroscales may place severe limits on our predictive ability, but it as well insures the constant variety and richness of our experience" (1981: 107, 108).[9]

Ilya Prigogine and Isabelle Stengers (1984) deal explicitly with the conceptual transformation of science challenging Newtonian mechanics as related to contemporary research in thermodynamics, focusing on nonlinearity (instability, fluctuations, order-out-of-chaos). The irreversibility of the evolution of far-from-equilibrium systems, characterized by self-organizing processes and dissipative structures, determines an arrow of time. The authors explore the interconnectedness of chance and necessity and the reconciliation of being and becoming. Chaos is presented not as the opposite but as the source and confederate of order. Prigogine finds science and mankind in an age of transition. That the universe has a history including complexity supposes a new dialogue of man with man and of man with nature. Nature is to be treated as active rather than passive, and science must go "beyond a purely conservative approach to global problems, as is usually the case in the 'ecological' point of view" (1986: 506). All of these studies, contrasted with time-reversible classical science, call for a reconceptualization of time itself.[10]

The paleontologist Stephen Jay Gould (1989) denounces the idea of evolution as either the march of progress or a cone of increasing diversity, substituting an image of diversification and decimation, history as unrepeatable and therefore unpredictable, in an exposition of the theme of contingency in the historical sciences. He also proposes a reconceptualization of the arrow of time: life's arrow, based on a statistical property, bottom-heavy asymmetry, of groups of clades to replace "vague, untestable, and culturally laden notions of 'progress'" (Gould, Gilinsky, and German 1987: 1437).

Compared to the ordered mathematical world of Newton and Descartes, the world of Cantor's sets and Peano's space-filling curves seemed esoteric indeed. However, Benoit Mandelbrot (1983) has shown how the structures these (and other) late nineteenth-century mathematicians conceptualized are inherent in the everyday world around us. His fractal geometry of shapes that do not fit into the Euclidean categories of points, lines, planes, and solids describes naturally occurring phenomena such as coastlines and snowflakes; branching systems such as trees and vascular and pulmonary systems; and oscillating systems such as sleep cycles and heart fibrillations.[11]

Parallels to this view of reality emphasizing "creativity over adaptation and survival, openness over determinism, and self-transcendence over security"

(Jantsch 1981: v) can be found throughout the disciplines.[12] The new developments in the sciences are serving as active models or analogies (although all too
often applied indiscriminately) beyond the sciences. The thought that " 'unpredictable' does not necessarily mean 'unintelligible' " leading to a rehabilitation
of the idea of freedom (F. Turner 1997: xiv–xv) animates the collection com-
piled by Eve, Horsfall, and Lee (1997). David Byrne recognizes the methodological problems inherent in applying complexity theory to the human world. He
adheres to a "critical realism" as a "philosophical ontology to correspond to the
scientific ontology of chaos/complexity" (1998: 64). The studies collected in
Kiel and Elliott (1996) illustrate the great possibilities offered, and the enormous difficulties encountered, in developing research strategies that take into
consideration deterministic chaos. In the final chapter, Harvey and Reed (1996)
call on the modified naturalistic epistemology of Roy Bhaskar to begin to
outline what studies of "dissipative social systems" might look like. These and
other studies emanating from the social sciences continue the strong direct
opposition long expressed and indeed growing in the humanities to a hierarchy
of academic disciplines presumed to reflect a hierarchy in the domains of
knowledge.

Collapsing Disciplines

In the 1960s, various new forms—the "new journalism" (Wolfe 1973); creative
nonfiction (fiction in form, factual in content); Truman Capote's "nonfiction
novel"; Norman Mailer's "history 'in the form of a novel' " (Hollowell 1977: x)—
questioned objectivity and discrimination of fact and fiction. When journalists
such as Tom Wolfe, Gay Talese, and Jimmy Breslin wanted to "convey the
immediacy of experience and give it coherence and significance, [they] turned
to the *novelist*. . . . Novelists . . . set out to gather the facts, not as an end in
themselves, but as raw material for their art. The name for writers who set out
to gather facts about people and events is *journalist*" (Agar 1990: 76).

As "blending of narrative form" muddled fact and fiction (Hollowell 1977:
15), in 1965 Arthur C. Danto staked out a relationship between narrative and the
human sciences: "Narratives . . . are used to explain changes, and, most characteristically, large-scale changes taking place, sometimes, over periods of time
vast in relationship to single human lives. It is the job of history to reveal to us
these changes, to organize the past into temporal wholes, and to explain these
changes at the same time as they tell what happened" (255). And now, scientific
research as social practice has been linked to narrative: "We must understand
narrative not as a literary form in which knowledge is written, but as the

temporal organization of the understanding of practical activity" (Rouse 1990: 179).

This view of the relationship of science and narrative may seem at odds with the science/humanities opposition depicted in the work of historian Hayden White (1973, 1978), but his imagery resembles more a juxtaposition of the historical disciplines with a pristine positive science unaffected by the observer.[13] By redefining a "scientific fact as a discursive event . . . one eliminates the hierarchy science-literature that isolates the observer from what he is observing" (W. Anderson 1983: 276–77). White's conception of history could not be further from Ranke's "*wie es eigentlich gewesen ist*": more poesis than mimesis, a history that can change the world (M. Ermarth 1975: 962–63); "a new form of narrative, which would effect the undisciplining of the discipline of history, . . . an exit from history, as we understand it, and a sublimation of politics" (De Bolla 1986: 50). This does not mean, however, "that there is no such thing as a historical 'event,' that there is no possibility of distinguishing between 'fact' and 'fiction,' or that everything is 'ideology.' . . . What it does mean is that what counts as an event, as a fact, and as an adequate representation or explanation of historical phenomenon must be adjudged to be 'relative' to the time, place and cultural conditions of its formulation" (White 1995: 244). History, like science, is being transformed from within (Gearhart 1987; for the "new historicism," see Veeser 1989).

Despite the rebirth of historical analysis in new forms, contemporary mainstream social science continues to treat states and nation-states as cases and to analyze their variation to uncover and explain distinct paths of development (P. Evans and Stephens 1988) or to pursue an infatuation with idiographic "social history." At the same time, however, proliferating subdisciplines evidence overlap in scholarly work: for example, historical sociology, political sociology, economic history. Anthropology, which actively deploys literary methods, has invaded the turf of sociology (with whom it has shared ethnographic method) in the study of small groups and large-scale cultural practice in the developed world as its traditional subject matter has disappeared.

As an alternative to the established social science disciplines, area studies lost ground as a "top-down enterprise," but not before laying the foundation for the emergence of new areas with "bottom-up origins": women's studies and ethnic studies. Theirs were the "forgotten voices" that would be heard not just as describing the experience of marginality but as "revisers of the central theoretical premises of social science" (Wallerstein 1997: 227–28). As the *Annales* approach fragmented, world-systems analysis carried forward the repudiation of the premises of nineteenth-century social science and reaffirmed the reality of phenomenological time without falling back on an essentialist notion of history as a single, neutral chronology, that is, without reinventing "total history." By positing a unique, temporally bounded, and spatially delimited (but expanding) social system defined by an axial division of labor as the coherent unit of analysis, it rejects both idiographic (additive) and nomothetic (law-bound) universalisms, thus achieving parsimony without reductionism. Reintegrating the social science disciplines in composite studies of long-term, large-scale social change, it comes to terms with the sectorializing resolution of the nineteenth-century structural crisis of knowledge formation, just as scientists open up the middle ground between chaos and order.

Cultural studies, from its inception, sparred with history, sociology, anthropology, and literary studies. Challenges to disciplinary boundaries from within cultural studies were not, however, extended to the natural sciences, due, first, to the Althusserian framework prevalent in the 1970s and early 1980s (including *Women Take Issue* and challenged by Edward Thompson) that established "the aspiration to scientificity as a goal of much Marxist social theory" (Franklin, Lury, and Stacey 1991b: 131). Second, "the pathologization of forms of popular culture," which was a hallmark of the Frankfurt School, "was at odds with [cultural studies'] more positive evaluation of popular cultural forms" (131). The subgroup for science and technology was not formed at CCCS until 1986. During the 1980s, interest in science flowed from other, shifting theoretical influences (Foucault, deconstruction, and postmodernism) that undermined the "presumptions of a liberationist Marxist science . . . the roles of disciplines and of intellectuals . . . [and] questioned presumptions of progress, the role of grand theory and empiricist notions of representation" (133). Altered constituencies, the "new social movements" (ecology, antinuclear), and struggles against racism, sexism, and homophobia, and the biological arguments on which they are often based, also entailed reexaminations of the cultural studies agenda. The very ubiquity of technology in popular culture has rendered its absence as a field a striking omission in cultural studies.

Certainly, some of these issues were assessed in *Off-Centre* in 1991. It cited the 1973 anthology *Our Bodies, Ourselves* by the Boston Women's Health Collective, the women's movement that "identified scientific and medical power-knowledges as key sources of patriarchal control over women" (Franklin, Lury, and Stacey 1991b: 134). Sandra Harding's *The Science Question in Feminism* (1986) reviewed the entire field and "pronounced that 'feminist analytical categories *should* be unstable at this point in history' " (Franklin, Lury, and Stacey 1991b:

135). Significant in Harding's work was her identification of the source of progressive developments in social and political movements rather than individual agents. Unfortunately, her analysis remained at the level of theory (although she is opposed to "totalizing theory") and, to an extent, of method. The fact that "there is very little sign that institutional science is being deconstructed in light" of Harding's work or the body of feminist scholarship it examines— "Positivism has not lost its credibility because it is epistemologically inconsistent"—signals the "need to move away from the assessment of science as an epistemological system, and towards an assessment of it as a cultural belief system, as indeed a faith." This supplies the link with cultural studies, where "science as a 'whole way of life' becomes a viable subject of inquiry" (137, 138).

Emily Martin's "ethnography of women's body images," *The Woman in the Body: A Cultural Analysis of Reproduction* (1987), "ultimately returns us to the foundationalist premises of Marxism." Donna Haraway "takes these as her satiric foil in a thorough overturning of the assumptions that have underpinned much leftist and feminist cultural analysis of the past decade" (Franklin, Lury, and Stacey 1991b: 142). Denying that women simply as women have any unified oppositional status and that there are any easy resolutions to postmodern dilemmas, her *Primate Visions: Gender, Race and Nature in the World of Modern Science* (1989) "is a multi-layered text—its postmodern plot concerned with questions of power, knowledge and pleasure in late twentieth-century Western capitalist society" (Franklin, Lury, and Stacey 1991b: 143). If identity politics mediated the cultural studies engagement with science, the tools are those of poststructuralism and postmodernism.

In sum, the symptoms of the epistemological crisis of the current conjuncture are apparent. It is no longer possible unabashedly and uncritically to associate science with progress; the internal development of science is undermining its own position of supreme authority. Disciplinary boundaries reflecting a hierarchy of knowledge, with the sciences at the privileged pole, are already effectively blurred, and the trend, of which cultural studies has constituted a moving force, is increasing "fuzziness."

Crisis of the "Two Cultures"

From the time it emerged in the late 1950s and 1960s, cultural studies had "to undertake a work of demystification to bring into the open the regulative nature and role the humanities were playing in relation to the national culture" (S. Hall 1990: 15). The critical attitude toward the assumption that the arts and humanities produce disinterested knowledge put cultural studies in syntony with a rising intellectual tide. Braudel suggested the themes of "*mathématisation, réduction à l'espace, longue durée*" for the orientation of collective research and a "convergence" among the social sciences, which he esteemed had become a necessity due to the very progress of the "sciences of man . . . at odds with a retrograde and insidious humanism which can no longer offer them a proper framework" (1958: 753, 725; my translation). Robbe-Grillet directly attacked the naturalistic error that persisted even in Saussurian linguistics (Lentricchia 1980: 119). He saw noncontingent, nonprovisional "nature" as paralyzing, "the source of every kind of humanism, in the traditional meaning of the term." He did not wish, however, to negate man, but "to refuse the idea of 'pananthropism'" (Robbe-Grillet [1958] 1963b: 63–64; my translation). Althusser emphasized a slippage by which "the relations of production, political and ideological social relations, have been reduced to historicized '*human relations,*' i.e., to inter-human, intersubjective relations. This is the favourite terrain of historicist humanism" (Althusser and Balibar 1970: 139–40). That social construct, the rugged, independent, self-interested but responsible individual of liberalism, that "subject," has lost his/her ideological underpinnings and now declares overlapping allegiances. The unique object—and the individual creator, the hero of modernism —has also been toppled. Even as the relationship between science and ideology is being unveiled in such practical fields as curriculum studies (Apple 1990), a traditional concern of cultural studies, the cultural surrogate of science, modernity, appears more and more to be a source of subjugation, oppression, and repression than of liberation (Rosenau 1992: 6).

To be sure, those who consider themselves postmodernists may question "any possibility of rigid . . . boundaries . . . in nearly every field of human endeavor" (Rosenau 1992: 6). However, postmodern double-coding (Jencks), ahistorical fragmentation and skepticism (Lyotard), decentering and free play, the lapse of the signified, *différance* (Derrida), archaeologies and genealogies of knowledge/power (Foucault) do not have to lead to an infinite deconstructive regress, to a self-contradictory, subjective and irrational, void. Yet, this was exactly what happened as structuralists began to concentrate solely on the sign. Formal deconstruction "of the most elegant, mannered kind" was the result, divorced from any politically active referent. "Their contribution to the resolution of the cultural crisis . . . is nonexistent" (S. Hall 1990: 22). Despite the wailings of conservative intellectuals, poststructuralist/deconstructionist practices have entered (in fact, constitute in some areas) the academic mainstream, but only in direct proportion to their political devitalization.

Science now is forging beyond the world of independent, hard-bodied units for one of open systems and relationships, just as, congruently, the humanities tilt with humanism. It is becoming apparent that, as Prigogine and Stengers write, the "dichotomy between the 'two cultures' is to a large extent due to the conflict between the atemporal view of classical science and the time-oriented view that prevails in a large part of the social sciences and humanities" (1984: xxviii). Science is rediscovering time and the humanities are reconsidering the subject/object distinction. This has the consequence of throwing the structural separation of the sciences (the realm of "truth") and the humanities (the sphere of "values") into crisis and raises the question of whether or not this is part of a secular crisis of the long-term processes by which the modern world-system has remained recognizable (been reproduced) over the preceding five centuries and will remain recognizable (continue to be reproduced) into the future.

CHAPTER 8

The Near Future of the Long Term: A Bricoleur's World

Addressing the long-term crisis of the structures of knowledge, *Open the Social Sciences: Report of the Gulbenkian Commission on the Restructuring of the Social Sciences* advanced C. P. Snow's "two cultures" division as a relational pattern recognizable over the long term. The study of natural things was privileged over what came to be characterized as the arts or humanities, the two domains grounded in the Cartesian dualism of "nature and humans," of "matter and mind," of "the physical world and the social/spiritual world" (Gulbenkian Commission 1996: 2).

In 1637, addressing a process already underway for two centuries (Lee 2003), René Descartes published his *Discourse on Method*. Proceeding from the solid existential foundation in the knowing subject ("Je pense, donc je suis"), he established a set of rules of right reason and a reductive and deductive method that would lead to useful knowledge in the form of laws to "make ourselves, as it were, masters and possessors of nature" (1980: 33). Arguing against the Scholastics, it was the search for Truth, not a consideration for values, that drove Descartes's thought. Half a century later, Isaac Newton synthesized Francis Bacon's new "Organon," an empirical, experimental, and inductive approach, with Descartes's highly individualistic project. Pierre Simon de Laplace "took the final and crucial step towards an ideology of total determinism" (Hahn 1967: 18). By the turn of the nineteenth century, when Napoleon queried him about the place of God in his system, Laplace could respond that he had no need of that hypothesis (Koyré 1957: 276).

Built on the model of celestial mechanics, classical science posited that observable effects were physically determined and the discovery of universal laws governing such determination would lead to accurate prediction, both future and past. Reversibility (an artifact of the sign-independence of the time expression in the equations of the laws of motion whose "integration" describes the trajectories particles follow) was endogenous to the mathematics involved. Furthermore, when gravity was designated the motor of motion and located in matter itself, that quintessential attribute of the supreme being, creativity, was bestowed on man. Thus, the humanities, concerned not with the certitude of regularities but with the finitude of the unique and unpredictable, could also account for change, particularly for emergence, but through recourse to individual agency—imagination bridging the "gap between mind and the external world" (Wasserman 1975: 346). This "secularization," the contested divorce of systematic knowledge from human values, deepened with the encroachment of positivism on the domain of social inquiry. The intellectual hierarchy was sealed with John Stuart Mill's arguments for the application of the principles of the "exact sciences" to "the backward state of the moral sciences" and Auguste Comte's move to establish positivism as the methodological ground of historical and social knowledge formation.

From the 1880s through the 1920s, this secular trend, moving "far from equilibrium," underwent a major structural shift, restoring medium-term stability: the *Methodenstreit*. It was in the Germanies, rather than in England or France, where the great movement of reform and rejuvenation of the university, both as a teaching and a research structure, had been taking place during the nineteenth century. As the German historical school developed the criteria of objectivity and critical use of archival documents into a science of history, *Geschichtswissenschaft*, the universality of Ranke's vision grounded in the timeless " 'holy hieroglyphe'—God with his plan and his will" (Breisach 1983: 233), balanced the picture of uniqueness and ceaseless change historians painted. However, with the rise of the Prussian state and its expansionist agenda, theological underpinnings gave way to the construction of a *Volksgeist* as a foundation for an inclusive German nationalism underwriting unification. The decline of the transcendent element left historicism, as science, open to positivist challenge and charges of relativism. In the first instance, it could preserve its objectivity only at the loss of its ethical orientation; in the second, it would cease to qualify as a producer of systematic knowledge.

The Methodenstreit, or controversy over the purpose, properties, method, and domain of sociocultural knowledge (Oakes 1975: 19–20), which ensued in reaction to positivism, had as a central theme the construction of a philosophical defense of a connection between meaning or values, *Wert*, and systematic knowledge, *Wissen*. Wilhelm Dilthey considered the methods of German philosophy of history fundamentally flawed. The original immersion in the "factuality of the historical" and reliance on "original intuition" deteriorated into "Hegel's 'Spirit,' which comes to consciousness of its freedom in history, or Schleiermacher's 'Reason,' which permeates and shapes nature . . . an abstract substance which condenses the historical world process in a colorless abstraction, a subject outside space and time." Sociology, on the other hand, whether in the form practiced by Comte or Mill, announced the end of the "epoch of metaphysics" by "subordinating the historical world to the system of knowledge of nature." What was really created, according to Dilthey, was "a naturalistic metaphysics of history, which as such was much less suited to facts of the historical process than Hegel's or Schleiermacher's was" (1988: 139).

In 1883, Dilthey began to make his case for an interpretative or hermeneutic approach to historically oriented human studies, the *Geisteswissenschaften,* roughly all of the humanities and the social sciences including history taken as a group, as distinguished from the *Naturwissenschaften,* the natural sciences: "We must meet the challenge to establish human sciences through epistemology, to justify and support their independent formation, and to do away definitively with subordinating their principles and their methods to those of natural sciences" (1988: 142). Dilthey considered it philosophy's task to demonstrate that the Geisteswissenschaften were "no less fundamental, comprehensive, and objective" than the Naturwissenschaften (Makkreel 1992: 38). The original experiential foundation in descriptive psychology Dilthey proposed denied Ranke's claim that objectivity entailed the effacement of the self, and Dilthey purposefully rejected the impersonal and abstract *Kulturwissenschaften,* with its occlusion of conflict and the unstated postulate of progress, in an ongoing debate with the Baden neo-Kantians Wilhelm Windelband and his student Heinrich Rickert.

Dilthey aspired to overcome the extremes of both idealism (he was empirical) and positivism (he posited no general laws: because human choice can make changes, life is not totally predetermined). For Dilthey, the original connectedness of life is directly available through lived experience (*Erlebnis*) and historical reason is replaced with reflective understanding (*Verstehen*), which articulates potential human significance provided by Erlebnis into "definite and exclusive possibilities" to "find meaning in history without positing a final goal" (Makkreel 1992: 257, 243). "A dynamic system (*Wirkungszusammenhang*)," the subject matter of human studies, Dilthey writes, "differs from the causal system (*Kausalzusammenhang*) of nature in that it produces values and realizes ends according to the structure of psychic life. . . . Historical life is creative. It is constantly active in the productions of goods and values" (quoted in Makkreel 1992: 315). Any appeal to logic as transcendental subject (Windelband) or to an idealized concept of value (Rickert) denied the historicity of values and the value of historicity itself, including the historicity of knowledge or truth.

To maintain the scientific status of human studies and respond to charges of relativism while maintaining the roots of inquiry in actual historical existence, Dilthey advanced a hermeneutic approach based on the study of "typical" individuals as a consideration of the possibilities and limits of an individual's existence in a specific historical-cultural context. He tried to fuse subject and object, arguing that both consciousness and the world shared the same temporality and historicity. But in the end, his effort to secure rigorous certitude without sacrificing human finitude was undermined by the project itself, partaking as it did of the same fundamental commitment to the Cartesian *Fragestellung* in which truth was grounded in the "scientific objectivity" of the "self-knowing subject" (Bambach 1995: 181–82).

In the same year as the appearance of Dilthey's *Einleitung in die Geisteswissenschaften,* 1883, the Methodenstreit erupted in economics. The "historical school" challenged the universality of deductive theory in the classical approach in favor of inductive history. The historical approach of Schmoller emphasized the concrete, price history, actual past behavior, and description, whereas Menger's neoclassical, "pure" theory stressed the abstract, price theory, typical economic behavior, and universal theoretical models. The marginal revolution soon overcame the historicists' position and established economics as a value-free discipline displacing political economy, and Dilthey's project was finally put to rest by Max Weber. Weber argued against both the positivists and their opponents. He held fast to the axiological dimension and identified interpretation or understanding as the goal of human studies while emphasizing the verifiability of knowledge in the sense of "*sufficient* ground": "A historical 'interpretative' inquiry into motives is *causal* explanation in absolutely the same *logical* sense as the causal interpretation of any concrete natural process," he wrote ([1903–6] 1975: 194). Operationally, however, he lifted his "ideal type" out of time and context; "historians [were] separated completely from the world of values they investigated. They [became] totally detached observers who objectively created islands of explained actions in a landscape of total obscurity" (Breisach 1983: 284).

The outcome of the Methodenstreit resulted in a universalizing and sectorializing restructuring of the disciplines of the social sciences and secured the obfuscations of the world-liberal compact. Although it did not go unchallenged, this disciplinary structure was firmly in place and largely taken for granted during the 1945–68 period. It opposed universal science, the empirical and positivistic sphere of "truth," expressing the Enlightenment ideal of endless progress implemented in an ultimately law-like, thus predictable, world, to the particularistic humanities, the impressionistic and chaotic realm of "values." The social sciences were to a certain extent torn between the scientism (quantification), in the quest for legitimacy, of economics, sociology, and political science and the more humanistic (narrative) bent of history and anthropology.

As for cultural studies, Fred Inglis (1993) insists that from the beginning it was concerned with the study of values, from the inside. The geopolitical crises that spawned the first New Left in Britain convinced the early protagonists of the necessity of basing social analysis on the lived experience and individual agency of real historical human beings. This was associated with an inversion of the high/low cultural divide that redefined working-class culture as intrinsically valuable and worthy of study. Hoggart questioned the impressionistic social commentary of the novel just as he contested the quantitative models of social science. These latter fractured the whole-way-of-life concept of culture he shared with Williams and sapped it of meaning. Both quantitative methods and the orthodox Marxist base-superstructure model robbed Thompson's whole-way-of-struggle of its history as experience and agency. Furthermore, cultural studies employed a variety of methods over a range of subject matter, which spanned all of the humanistic and social scientific disciplines. By the end of the 1960s, as cultural studies moved out from the original consideration for working-class culture, the concerns for values, agency, and historical time— humanism left and right—came into conflict with the antihumanist and atemporal ("scientific") tendencies of the structuralisms. Just as surely, however, antiessentialism and the demise of the subject seriously undermined the Cartesian dualities on which Dilthey's project collapsed.

Since the late 1960s, complexity studies, emphasizing irreversibility and self-organization in a deterministic but unpredictable world, have effectively abdicated the role of guarantor of truth in knowledge and reintroduced the arrow-of-time into the natural sciences. The recognition that the "universals" of science are historical suggests to a growing number of scientists that the human world might better be taken as a model for the natural world than vice versa.

Together, cultural studies and complexity studies constitute an inclusive and comprehensive challenge to the organization of knowledge over the past five hundred years into a unitary "whole," constituted as a hierarchical structure composed of opposing "parts," the value-neutral sciences (the sphere of regularities) and the value-laden humanities (the realm of differences) and, by extension, the social relations with which they are articulated. These discussions are especially relevant today in the context of the perceived "crisis of the university" (itself a manifestation of the transformative, systemic crisis of the modern world-system), the Culture Wars and the Science Wars. The "crisis in education only reflects the larger crisis of American and European world-hegemony," Patrick Brantlinger has written (1990: 7). The interlocking pressures can be summed up as a triple conjuncture since 1968: one is economic or material, that of declining resources meeting expanding demand (world-scale crisis of accumulation); another is political or ideological, that of rising expectations based on the rhetoric of success through education encountering the reality of limitations on both rewards and access (world-scale crisis of liberalism); and a third is intellectual or theoretical, that of an objective, value-neutral ideal at the heart of the institutional apparatus of the university challenged by "alternative knowledges" and epistemologies of skepticism and complexity (world-scale crisis of the structure of knowledge).

No longer can phenomena in the natural world be perceived as falling into exhaustive, mutually exclusive categories. Likewise, with the realization that knowledge is social and fundamentally interrelated, the historical boundaries distinguishing university departments are increasingly abraded by the cross-disciplinary inquiry scholars practice. But because universities, departments, professional associations, and individual professors have institutional interests in preserving their domains, only limited observable movement, beyond so-called interdisciplinary studies programs and the phenomenon of the electronic university (important as a network model), is as yet evident. Multi-culturalism and cultural studies with programs explicitly aimed at "bridging the gap between the social sciences and the humanities" may signal advances, but pluralist elisions of questions of power can be debilitating. On analogy, the easy co-optation of the 1970s Marxism is not encouraging on the organizational front. Fresh organizational strategies, however, are being experimented with outside of traditional settings. For instance, the Think Tank model has become common, particularly in policy areas; the Santa Fe Institute (founded in 1984), devoted to the study of complex systems, does both experimental and theoretical work through networks of overlapping, multi(non)disciplinary groups (Pines 1988).

Beginning in the mid–nineteenth century, the differences among the three great ideologies produced by the modern world-system paled to such an extent that socialism and conservatism could be seen to converge to a left and right liberalism. The real story of the post–cold war world is not the "victory of the West" but the disintegration of this liberal compact that began in 1968 and was completed in 1989 (Wallerstein 1995). Liberalism, unlike its siblings, legitimated a politics of the conjuncture: medium-term increments of reformist change adding up to endless (long-term), linear progress suggest a golden, extrapolatable "now" with no allusion to either a future transformation (socialism) or an idyllic past (conservatism). The parallel to Newtonian dynamics is clear, and self-fulfilling. Science itself offered the linear development model, based empirically and epistemologically on independent units. But in the post–cold war world of politics and knowledge formation, it has become increasingly difficult to convince those at the bottom to buy into this "order" in the expectation of a better future. As liberalism has proved unable to deliver on its universalist message of progress (on a world scale), science now provides us with alternative models of physical reality, relationally constituted self-organizing systems and fractal geometry, and of change and transition, complexity theory and chaos theory—all in defiance of the law of the excluded middle so fundamental to classical science, classical logic, and everyday common sense. At the same time, the recognition of the indeterminacy of meaning in the humanities and the arrival on the scene of "alternative knowledges" informing the social sciences, a product of the expansion of faculty and student body after 1968 to include those speaking from marginalized subject positions (both products of the historical development of the university as an institution), have cast into sharp focus the political dimension of knowledge formation and undermined the idea of scholarship as a perfectly disinterested activity amenable to objective evaluation.

As the complex disciplinary whole (sciences/social sciences/humanities) self-deconstructs, the postmodern view—"relative absolutism, or fragmented holism . . . the developing and jumping nature of scientific growth, and the fact that all propositions of truth are time- and context-sensitive" (Jencks 1989: 59)—gains currency. All the same, language (like time) does not necessarily lose its symbolic, syntactical, representational dimension with the restoration of the digressive, rhythmic, semiotic disposition. Postmodernism, says Elizabeth Deeds Ermarth, does not rule out reuniting the two: meaning that is both "the power to sustain linear arguments, transfer information, communicate conclusions" and play, which may be "discredited . . . [but belongs to a] realm of qualitative values like proportion, complexity, flexibility, pleasure, and eroticism taken in its most expanded sense" (1992: 146, 143). We trust bridges even though chaotic systems are ubiquitous in the physical world; at the same time, the play of the sign may, but need not be, foreclosed at any given juncture. This is just the point of imagination, pleasure, and creativity, and it relies as much on randomness in choice among microfluctuations (in the brain) as the phase changes of macrosystems (e.g., social systems) do: small fluctuations at critical parameter values, rapidly magnified, determining transition scenarios.

In this context, the history of cultural studies conceived as multiple trajectories—in the short term, the refusal of the logic and practice of U.S. hegemony and the cold war; in the medium term, a revolt against the nineteenth-century universalizing and sectorializing structure of the disciplines and the liberal compact it underwrote; and in the long term, when viewed with complexity studies, part of the subversion of the opposition between science and the humanities, that is, the crisis of the two cultures—revitalizes the political project. Complexity studies describe the world of nature, like the human world, as bringing order out of chaos; it too is creative. However, moments of transition, "where the system can 'choose' between or among more than one possible future," are historically rare and arise only when dynamical systems, including social systems, become unstable as they are driven far from equilibrium by their own internal development (Prigogine and Stengers 1984: 169–70). If it is true that the contemporary crisis is systemic, that is, of the material structures and social relations of the Europe-centered world as it has developed since the sixteenth century, and there is every reason to believe it is (Hopkins et al. 1996), then we are living one of those unstable moments of transition (comparable to the transition from feudalism) when the future becomes an open future, rather than a law-bound Newtonian one, determined only by creative choices and contingent circumstances.

Although the postmodern problematizes any nineteenth-century idea of the social, we have not reached the end of responsibility and social agendas. To the contrary. Heidegger conceptualized the unity of past, present, and future, and now science too defines events in terms of fundamental, transformational choice among future possibilities out of a present past (contingencies)—in the language of responsible social action, *kairos*: the decisive time, the propitious time. Such a moment is one of "real change, fundamental change, structural change" in the social world; it is a time of crisis, of the demise of the system and therefore a time of "moral choice . . . human choice . . . the rare moment when free will is possible" (Wallerstein 1991b: 146–47).

And the epistemological status of history, argues Elizabeth Ermarth, may also be taken as "an inflection of culture since around 1400. . . . 'History' as a category, like 'time' and 'space,' as we have come to conceive of it over many centuries, is an instance of representation that we have almost completely naturalized." The postmodern novel and the new history are just instances of practices that, as enactment, open up the possibility of redefining time "as a function of position, as a dimension of particular events. . . . Postmodern time belongs to a figure, an arrangement in which 'the other world surrounds us always and is not at all the end of some pilgrimage' " (1992: 4, 54, 10–11, 16).

Destabilizing pressures are forcing change; this is an occasion for optimism, not resignation, for the future abounds with possibilities. But it is also an occasion for committed, purposeful action, as no final outcomes are predictable. The transition, lasting for the next fifty years perhaps, will be rich in fluctuations, that is, social instability—a lack of order already constitutes the "new world order." Unstable systems, in fact, impose fewer constraints, fewer limits. The exercise of free will is thus less restricted and, being capable of massive amplification, could constitute an irreversible and determining moral choice for a qualitatively different social world.

With the structural sequestration of the spheres of knowledge no longer an unquestioned given, interpretations of relationships among constituent parts of concrete wholes could offer a mode of freeing knowledge production from the aporia of uncovering infinite disconnected particulars in search of impossible universals. Constructing new visions of intersubjectivity, such as action based on "strategic essentialisms" (functionally reminiscent of negritude's "antiracist racism" as presented by Sartre a half-century ago) redeployed in attempts to reclaim agency for those groups for whom antiessentialist arguments problematize the very existence, addresses, on the one hand, the enormous implications of what Martin Barker and Anne Beezer see as the "growing reluctance to imagine possible futures" (1992: 15). On the other hand, rearticulating those structures of difference, historically produced in struggle, in which social values reside could lead to the shift from what Stuart Hall called a "logic of binary opposition" to a "logic of coupling."

The fact that choice really matters, that it can have a transformative effect, realizes the cultural studies project in the widest sense: the ethical imperative of scholarly participation in the transformation of the social world and its constituting and constitutive intellectual structures. It is at this point where passively dreaming utopia turns into the active, purposeful bricolage, the social event, of creating a more substantively rational world by imagining a future with *values*, the rallying cry of cultural studies, reunited with *knowledge*, the watchword of science.

Notes

Introduction

1   E.g., Brantlinger (1990), I. Davies (1995), Inglis (1993), Morley and Chen (1996), G. Turner (1990). During (1993) casts a wide net, as do Gelder and Thornton (1997) ("subcultures," from the Chicago School to the virtual world online). The Grossberg, Nelson, and Treichler (1992) collection presented an encompassing, but not uncontroversial, vision of the field as of the early 1990s. Andrew Tudor (1999), in addition to the "culture and civilization" tradition, draws attention to the antecedents of cultural studies in the theorizing and empirical research focused on "mass society and media effects," and Tom Steele (1997) devotes a detailed study to cultural studies and adult education. The collection edited by David Morley and Kevin Robins (2001) aims at applying cultural studies perspectives to British culture and society rather than addressing the intellectual formation itself. The omnibus volume edited by Toby Miller (2001a), "designed to show where cultural studies exists and what it does there" (2001b: 12), includes a separate chapter, "Bibliographic Resources for Cultural Studies."

2   By way of introduction to the world-systems perspective, see Hopkins and Wallerstein (1980), Hopkins et al. (1982), Hopkins et al. (1996), and Wallerstein (1974, 1983, 2000).

3   Fred Inglis has stated that a "biography is . . . the readiest way we have of getting some purchase on our history and understanding who has been responsible for it" (1991: 3); even in a purposefully nonhagiographic study, the barest of notes on some of the principals is nonetheless useful. Raymond Henry Williams (1921–1988) was born on the Welsh border, physically and culturally. His roots were in the working class and the countryside and he was educated as a scholarship student in an "alien" middle-class, British culture. At once common man and intellectual, theater critic and novelist, social critic and activist, Williams was as much attached to the past as his socialist ideals wedded him to a responsible construction of a better future. Edward Palmer Thompson (1924–1993) rubbed shoulders with some of the most interesting men of the preceding generation; visitors to his childhood home—from Robert Graves to Tagore, Gandhi, and Nehru—nourished the liberal sentiments he inherited from his father, a scholar and Methodist missionary who had worked in India. Richard Hoggart was born in 1918 in a district of Leeds and scholarships permitted him to receive his B.A. (in English) and M.A. at the University of Leeds. Stuart McPhail Hall was born in Jamaica (1932) and educated at Jamaica College and Oxford (Rhodes Scholar, 1951) and "at different

times . . . 'hailed' or interpellated as 'coloured,' 'West-Indian,' 'Negro,' 'black,' 'immigrant'" (1985b: 108). On Williams, see especially Higgins, who states, "Any real assessment of the force of Williams's work needs to be historical as well as theoretical. It needs to attend to the terms of the conceptual vocabularies available to him, a sense of their limits, as well as a sense of what use and difference he made of and to them, before seeking to describe the limitations of Williams's thinking" (1999: 172); Gorak (1988); and Inglis (1995), who offers a forum for a multitude of those who knew Williams. On Thompson, see Bess (1993) and Kaye and McClelland (1990). On Hoggart, see his autobiography, *Life and Times* (1992). On Hall, see Grossberg (1985).

4 The categories *Britishness* and *Englishness* themselves present thorny problems; these become particularly relevant for what is often presented as British cultural studies and the trajectory of the absences it inscribes (Scotland, Wales, and Ireland and the relationship between ethnicity and empire in the construction of national identity). The constellation of "indigenous nations" has been examined by Peter J. Taylor in an exploration of the question of whether the conception of Englishness constructed between 1880 and 1920 "is ripe for revision under contemporary conditions" (2001: 129).

5 In 1997, well after the present manuscript had taken form, Dennis Dworkin published his *Cultural Marxism in Postwar Britain: History, the New Left, and the Origins of Cultural Studies.* This fine study treats some of the issues covered in this chapter, and in the third and fourth as well, albeit with a very different focus and contrasting methodological approach.

6 On hegemony in the modern world-system, see Bousquet (1979, 1980), Hopkins and Wallerstein (1979), Wallerstein (1984), Arrighi (1990), and Taylor (1997). On the British role during the period of U.S. hegemony, see Taylor (1990). For an overview of the debates, see Goldstein (1988).

7 The late nineteenth-century realignment of British politics was addressed directly as a "crisis of liberalism" in the cccs volume edited by Mary Langan and Bill Schwarz (1985), *The Crisis in the British State.*

8 Suggestive of an interesting juxtaposition between an English and a non-English context, Ien Ang explains that in the Netherlands and other countries of northwest Europe, "where social-democratic visions of culture are rife," there is "very little space for any critical intellectual engagement in cultural politics except within the constraining mould of 'relevance for policy,' be it government policy or industry policy. The result has been a *de facto* hegemony of complacent, top-down, rationalist, and instrumentalist discourses of culture, an emphasis on 'cultural planning' which tends to treat as nuisance—or as downright superfluous—an inquiry into some of the 'irrationalities' . . . of the system" (1992: 315). This parallels antiregulationist, free-market-for-culture arguments in the debates over state support in Australia. See G. Turner (1992) for a discussion of John Docker's *Popular Culture versus the State: An Argument against Australian Content Regulations for Television.* Of late, there has been a proliferation of collections linking a cultural studies approach with particular, generally national contexts: e.g., Spain—Graham and Labanyi (1995), *Spanish Cultural Studies, An Introduction,* subtitled *The Struggle for Modernity,* and Jordan and Morgan-Tamosunas (2000); Russia—Kelly and Shepherd (1998); France—Le Hir and Strand (2000) and Forbes and Kelly (1995); Germany—Burns (1995); "Inter-Asia"—Chen (1998) and the journal *Inter-Asia Cultural Studies.* It should be noted that many of these studies are authored by scholars

writing from the "outside," and often the interpretive perspective either draws not at all on the British tradition or substantially widens it.

1 The Politics of Culture I, 1945–1968

1 Kenneth Morgan writes that in 1941 George Orwell "hailed the effect of the war in demolishing the old class-ridden society and in demonstrating practical socialism at work." Morgan concludes that Labour's victory was related to the Party's unique identification "with a sweeping change of mood during the war years, and with the new social agenda that emerged" (1984: 18, 44). In a later venue the author states that "a determining factor of British history after 1945 was that these images and slogans conflicted in crucial respects with the social reality," and he cites the "myth" of the dissolution of the British class system (1990: 17). See also Addison (1975) and, for a social history of the Labour years, Addison (1985).

2 Britain received the most Marshall Plan aid, "about 23 per cent of all dollars made available" (Saville 1993: xxvi), and a substantial loan from Canada. An embarrassment to Churchill and other conservatives when it appeared, the Beveridge report, *Social Insurance and Allied Services*, continues to elicit scholarly interest (e.g., Hills, Ditch, and Glennerster 1994).

3 "Today we are more likely to remember the whole period as an age of illusion. . . . Uncritical transference of Galbraith's [*The Affluent Society*, 1958] thesis into the British context helped obscure the fact that Britain had not, in fact, solved its economic problems" (Bogdanor and Skidelsky 1970: 7, 8).

4 Although the Atlantic Pact was to a large extent orchestrated by Foreign Secretary Ernest Bevin (E. Barker 1983: 103–44).

5 Arthur Calder-Marshall put Raymond Williams in this same position, characterizing *The Long Revolution* as "the rationalization of the case history of a signalman's son, translated through the educational process into the perplexity of adult education" (1961: 217).

6 Ioan Davies counts "socialist Zionism" as the "third illusion," along with "international Bolshevism" and the "British civilizing mission (symbolized by the left's relationship with India)," shattered in 1956 (1995: 10).

7 According to Stuart Hall, the term New Left was borrowed from the French *nouvelle gauche*, associated with the independent tendencies of Claude Bourdet and *France-Observateur* (1989: 14). E. P. Thompson linked the emergence of the New Left to the generation of youth who grew up with both the "nuclear promise and nuclear threat" and entered into political activity "because they think it necessary to watch the politicians." For Thompson it was definitely an international phenomenon: "not that of the triumph of one camp over the other, but the dissolution of the camps and the triumph of the common people." The trend, both East and West, was characterized by renewed interest in the "young Marx," "humanist propositions," "moral agency," and "individual responsibility" (1959b: 1, 7, 10). Raymond Williams cites *Conviction*, edited by Norman Mackenzie (1958), with *The Uses of Literacy* and *Culture and Society*, which signaled that a "new Left existed or was on the edge of forming" (1960: 345). David Widgery (1976) documents the story of the British left from the Communist Party split in 1956 through the early 1970s and the Vietnam Solidarity Movement. *The Socialist Register: 1976* (Miliband and Saville 1976) collects a number of useful essays on the impact of the events of 1956 and after, including Ken Coates's (1976) review of Widgery

(1976), pointing out numerous inaccuracies and confusions. Participants of the first New Left reminisce thirty years later in Archer et al. (1989). See also R. Williams (1970) and, for a detailed overview, Chun (1993).

8   "Energies that had been locked up in the [CPGB] apparatus soon invigorated the traditional non-Communist Labour Left" (R. Williams 1960: 343). Mervyn Jones puts the number of members who left the Party at 7,000 out of 33,000 (1976: 85), as does John Saville (1976: 16), and Margot Heinemann counts "about a fifth of the total" of 33,960 in 1956 (1976: 50). Lin Chun quotes Heinemann's defense of those who, like Heinemann, stayed in the Party and felt that the "fight for a cleaner analysis of what had gone wrong and a more critical line could have been won through the democratic processes of the party if the critics had stayed rather than resigned. . . . the fall of Khrushchev and the coming of the Brezhnev era indicated that our EC's [CPGB Executive Committee] earlier analysis has been too optimistic" (1993: 20–21). See also Birchall (1972), MacEwen (1976), and N. Wood (1959).

9   The question entertained in Kingsley Amis's pamphlet *Socialism and the Intellectuals* (1957) needed to be rephrased from "What attraction has the political world to offer the intellectual?" to "What has the intellectual to offer the political world, and why is it beginning to feel the need of him?" as Mervyn Jones (1957: 15) did in one of the five symposium articles in the second issue of *Universities and Left Review*. Harold Silver concurred with the stress Thompson placed on the centrality of ideas and the importance of breaking down "Left anti-intellectualism," but put responsibility on the working-class militant as well as the socialist intellectual (1957: 17–18).

10 Founded by John Saville, Dorothy Thompson, and Edward Thompson, the genesis of the printed *New Reasoner* stemmed from the positions taken in the de-Stalinization debates internal to the CPGB. Its forerunner, *The Reasoner* (under Marx's dictum, "To leave error irrefuted is to encourage immorality"), was created as an organ of opposition within the Party in reaction to the silence of the official CPGB press on Khrushchev's speech. Just before the third number appeared, Budapest was attacked, and in a last-minute editorial, readers were urged "to dissociate themselves from the leadership of the British Communist Party in their support—which was unequivocal—of Soviet intervention in Hungary." Contrary to their intentions before the Hungarian intervention, Thompson and Saville both resigned from the Party (Saville 1976: 6, 15). "Wooly and unselfconciously middle-class," *Universities and Left Review* was formed around Raphael Samuel and *Oxford Left* (Widgery 1976: 510), with Stuart Hall, Gabriel Pearson, and Charles Taylor, and combined economic description with cultural analysis.

11 Protest against the use of nuclear weapons was first heard publicly in 1943 in an Independent Labour Party meeting, but the real story of Hiroshima and Nagasaki did not begin to come out until well after the war due to U.S. censorship and the McMahon Atomic Energy Act of 1946. During the Korean War, the establishment of a Non-Violence Commission by the Peace Pledge Union to "study and discuss the possibility of direct action to seek withdrawal of American forces, stoppage of the manufacture of atomic weapons in Britain, withdrawal of Britain from NATO, and disbandment of the British Armed Forces" went unnoticed by the then Labour government (Driver 1964: 20). The Commission had contacts with two U.S. groups, Peacemakers and the Congress for Racial Equality, and launched "Operation Gandhi" with a sit-down at the War Office in 1952. The first Aldermaston (seat of the Atomic Weapons Research

Establishment) demonstration also took place in April 1952, but Aldermaston received wide attention only with the mass Easter marches that began in 1958. Following Britain's first A-bomb test in October 1952, debates proliferated on the H-bomb, conscription, and military spending. Local groups organized and discovered a base in the National Committee for the Abolition of Nuclear Weapons Tests (originally founded in 1955). Campaign for Nuclear Disarmament (CND) was formed in January 1958 and almost immediately came out for unilateral nuclear disarmament. See Duff (1971), Farley (1960), S. Hall (1963), Minnion and Bolsover (1983), Parkin (1968), Peers (1963), and Walters (1962); for later developments, see P. Byrne (1988).

12 Peter Searby, John Rule, and Robert Malcolmson (1993) have caught the flavor of and demonstrated the importance of Edward Thompson's teaching, especially during this early period. In 1956 John Saville wrote to Thompson that it was "significant that of all the intellectual groups in the Communist Party, the historians have come out best in the discussions of the past nine months" (Saville 1976: 7). The "social history of *ideas* was always . . . one of the main preoccupations" of the Communist Party Historians' Group (Hobsbawm 1978: 44). A number of strands can be traced back to it: the History Workshop movement and labor history as well as cultural studies; also, studies dealing with "ruling classes, power and the States" connect to the "tradition" whose "paramount contributions . . . as a 'collective,' " Harvey Kaye notes, have been "the development of 'class-struggle analysis' . . . 'history from the bottom up' . . . the recovery and assemblage of a 'radical democratic tradition' " and an undermining of the " 'Grand Narratives' of both the right and the left" (1990: 253–55). See also Kaye (1984), Poirier (1983), Samuel (1980), and Schwarz (1982).

13 In another venue, Raymond Williams (1960) explicitly identified the Labour Party with the establishment that most young socialists and radicals were against. He warned that if it did not change it would continue to decline—this in 1960!

14 From its inception *Universities and Left Review* called for a "regeneration of the whole tradition of free, open, critical debate"; "Stalinism bred a fear whose consequence has been that whole areas of contemporary life have fallen beyond the reach of our 'political' commitment. Literature, art, are our feeling for the quality of life and the community in an industrial society—these have all been consigned to some a-political limbo. And yet, the paradox is that when socialist values lose their relevance for the total scale of man's activities, they lose their 'political' point as well" (Editorial 1957: ii). Two articles on commitment appeared in the first issue of *Universities and Left Review* and one in the second. The fourth issue featured a whole section on commitment, with seven articles. In the introduction to this set, Stuart Hall affirmed, "The question of the 'neutrality' of literature and the 'politics of culture' is not a form of political reversion. . . . [Socialist realism cannot be used] to blackmail [the Left] into the position that literature and art stand neutral between all possible values" (1958a: 14). On the one hand, the cultural sphere represented by creative works of art and literature grouped under this slogan of commitment was soon exhausted; on the other hand, cultural analysis concerned with mass media and social consciousness maintained its appeal. The latter was connected with a notion of commitment that could "be placed in a historical setting along with all its attendant terminology—the language of 'class,' 'art,' of labels like 'romantic' and 'realist' " and that demanded a "critical study of values" (Briggs 1958: 453).

15 "If the Natopolitan detached the 'ought' of morality from the 'is' of circumstance, in Stalin-

ism the 'is' towered above the 'ought.' Morality, East and West, gave rise to two opposing absolutes: the Absolute of Working-Class Power and the Absolute of Personal Integrity. And yet each absolute, within its own system, served the *status quo*" (E. Thompson 1960b: 28).

16 In 1958, Hall had acknowledged the real increase in workers' wage packets and asserted that the "worker *knows himself* much more as consumer than as producer. . . . Capitalism as a social system is now based upon consumption. . . . the 'whole way of life' is breaking down into several *styles of living* . . . 'exquisitely' differentiated one from another. The very fact that it is sometimes difficult to disentangle one 'style' from another . . . adds to the general sense of class-confusion. . . . a working class can develop a false sense of 'classlessness' " (1958b: 28–29, 30). Raymond Williams referred to classlessness as "simply a failure of consciousness" (1961: 325). Ralph Samuel complained of the "increasingly pervasive influence upon socialist discussion" that the "idea that our society is classless, or is tending to become classless," was having and rebutted the argument that he asserted set up "a *status* model of contemporary society in which description of 'competing styles of life' and 'Keeping up with the Joneses' largely displaces structural analysis of the society" (1959: 44).

17 For E. P. Thompson it was but a slippery slope from structure to structuralism. In his polemical critique of Althusserian structuralism, he would submit that in the question of the critical problem between agency and process proposed by Engels, "for William Morris the accent falls even more sharply upon agency" (1978: 280). For Morris, substitute Thompson.

18 However, by 1976 in the postscript to the second edition of *Morris,* Thompson is in substantial agreement with the emphasis Williams placed on Morris's political works over his prose and verse romances.

19 E. P. Thompson puts the fragmentation "after 1963" (1978: ii): "We failed to implement our original purposes, or even to sustain what cultural apparatus we had" (quoted in Sedgwick 1964: 131). This date is consonant with the failure of direct action, especially the collapse of CND.

20 With its meticulous empiricism, *The Making of the English Working Class* achieved instant respectability and became vastly influential both in England and in the United States, where most American leftist historians lined up with Thompson "in his continuing debate with supporters of French structuralist Marxism; endorsing his effort to develop a distinctively Marxist historiography which allowed for contingency, stressed human agency, [and] was expressed in an 'empirical idiom' " (Novick 1988: 461).

2   The Politics of Culture II, 1790–1968

1 Williams's "tradition" is an analytical construct, one "history" among many. At least E. P. Thompson, in his review of *The Long Revolution,* was "very doubtful as to whether The Tradition is a helpful notion at all" (1961: 25), and he has not been alone. However, slighting the first New Left, Simon During, in his introduction to the *Cultural Studies Reader,* cites this as *the* ground from which cultural studies emerged: "Cultural studies appears as a field of study in Great Britain in the 1950s out of Leavisism" (1993: 2).

2 The sales of *Reflections* and Parts 1 and 2 of *The Rights of Man* may be conservatively estimated at over 30,000 and 100,000 copies, respectively, in the two years following their publication. Burke was quickly translated and his impact on French and German literature was imme-

diately felt. Paine's book was particularly adapted to reading aloud and it aroused the political consciousness of many a working man who heard it in radical and reform group meetings.

3 The "war of the unstamped . . . the movement for the repeal of the taxes on knowledge during 1830–1836 was led primarily by working-class reformers. . . . It involved an overt attempt to violate the press laws, by means of the publication and dissemination of hundreds of illegal tracts and ephemeral newspapers." Middle-class reformers favored a cheap press in the hands of propertied moderates instead of either the monopoly stamped or the "demagogic" unstamped press. For working-class reformers the function of a working man's press "as the only valid 'mirror of the opinions of the people,' was to record 'the movements of the mass towards that point in the education of the mind when the many will be emancipated from the rascality of the few' " (Wiener 1969: xiv, 23, 116).

4 The two (and their journals) were merged in 1871 as the Anthropological Institute of Great Britain and Ireland. The ethnologicals won out intellectually, but it was clear that what was at stake was "man's place in nature," more adequately expressed etymologically as "anthropology."

5 During the 1840s railway mileage more than tripled and made it feasible for large numbers of students to attend boarding schools. Dr. Arnold was appointed headmaster of Rugby in 1828 with a clear mandate that resulted in the form system and the prefect system as a method of administrating discipline. The educational structures he fostered survived until the upheavals of the 1960s. See Honey (1977), Bamford (1970), and Sanders (1942).

6 Robert Lowe, "the champion of inequality," was responsible for this "rationalization," that is, reduction of grants to schools. This was the same Lowe who would oppose the extension of the franchise, believing that democracy impeded the progress of the state. To "cultural critics like Matthew Arnold," it was "the utilitarian nightmare that Dickens had pilloried in *Hard Times,* the fetishism of 'facts, facts, facts' " (Gay 1993: 281). The provision also had the effect of changing the function of Her Majesty's Inspectors (like Arnold) from that of supervisors who studied teachers' problems with the goal of improving the level of instruction to that of simple monitors testing achievement (Connell 1950: 235)—a qualitative to a quantitative function. Arnold was substantially in agreement with Sir James Phillips Kay-Shuttleworth, secretary to the Committee of the Privy Council on Education, who complained that the "school's enslavement to the three RS . . . would debilitate it as a civilizing agency" (D. Jones 1977: 44).

7 In effect, he said farewell to poetry in 1853: "If we must be *dilettanti:* if it is impossible for us, under the circumstances amidst which we live, to think clearly, to feel nobly, and to delineate firmly: if we cannot attain to the mastery of the great artists;—let us, at least, have so much respect for our art as to prefer it to ourselves" (Arnold 1853: 15). This declaration is generally recognized as the major turning point in Arnold's life, announcing his shift from poetry to prose and criticism. Basil Willey (1949: 251) ranked Arnold as the most important critic of his time, as well as one of the better poets. Joseph Carroll (1982: xi) agrees, and John Henry Raleigh argues that "no other foreign critic, and perhaps few native ones, have acquired such a reputation and exercised such a palpable influence on American culture" (1961: 1). William E. Buckler, echoing Stephen Spender and Park Honan, wrote, "He was, quite simply, the founder of the main line of modern criticism in English. During the 1860s and 1870s, he gave criticism an identity, a broad-based cultural complexity and intellectual respectability, and a social mission that was both modern and indispensable" (quoted in Thesing 1988: 199).

8   Arnold borrowed the term from Sainte-Beuve, whom he admired enormously and with whom he shared a revulsion for extremism. They also shared an interest in establishing and maintaining continuity between literary order and political order. See Super (1963) and Whitridge (1938).

9   See also Doyle (1982), Palmer (1965), and Court (1992).

10 Tripos refers to the final honors examination for the B.A. degree at Cambridge. The new course, "English Literature, Life, and Thought," a "permissive, text-centered course" to be "modern and literary in orientation," was entrusted to Mansfield Forbes, a historian, E. M. W. Tillyard, a classicist, and I. A. Richards, trained in mental and moral sciences (Mulhern 1979: 20–22).

11 On *Scrutiny*, see also Filmer (1977), Musgrave (1973), and Leavis's own retrospect (1963).

12 The edition published in the United States in 1957 bore the subtitle *Changing Patterns in English Mass Culture.*

13 This was also the title of the conference proceedings (National Union of Teachers 1961).

14 Passed in 1815, the Corn Law protected home-grown grain from foreign imports until the price reached the famine level of 80 shillings per quarter. The repeal of 1846 was influenced by the Irish potato famine of 1845. At this same time the Customs Bill abolished or reduced duties on many other foodstuffs and manufactured goods. Repeal of the Corn Laws was exemplary of the complex relationships between conditions at home—a loss for the landed gentry; cheaper food and therefore more purchasing power for consumer (manufactured) goods from the worker's perspective; the possibility of lower wage bills from the employer's viewpoint—and worldwide free trade that relied on the control of the seas established by the end of the Napoleonic period.

15 Reform was driven almost wholly by internal Parliamentary considerations rather than external pressures. Even the "so-called Hyde Park riots were small beer indeed in the context of nineteenth-century agitation, and the evidence is slender to connect this event with Disraeli's advocacy of a Tory reform bill" (E. Evans 2001: 436). On the making of the 1867 reform, see Cowling (1967) and F. Smith (1966).

16 By the 1880s Arnold had become quite conservative on the Irish question: "After Gladstone's Home Rule bill was defeated, and Lord Salisbury's Conservatives took office, Arnold next demanded greater British firmness with the restive Irish public. In 'The Zenith of Conservatism,' for example, he asks that freedom of speech, freedom of assembly, and freedom of the press be reduced in Ireland" (Honan 1981: 414).

17 The influence of Spencer's brand of ultraliberal sociology faded with British political and economic decline. What did develop was the "intensely empirical" work of Booth, Rountree, and the Webbs that "eschewed social theory in favor of the immediate problems of state policy" (Mulhern 1979: 13).

3   Centre for Contemporary Cultural Studies I

1   Of the "Penguins," Hoggart commented: "They struck . . . at the status quo . . . [with] a certain disposition towards knowledge and towards people. That disposition is, again to be quite basic, 'democratic' " (1970: 119–20). Skeptics wondered if the money from Penguin was not a covert pay-off for Hoggart's crucial testimony in the *Lady Chatterley* trial. Hoggart

rejected this charge, citing not only his acquaintance with Lane but the comment of Lane's advisor W. E. Williams at the time: "Oh, give him what he asks, Allen. You've made a fortune by riding cultural change without understanding it" (Hoggart 1992: 90).

2   Hoggart regarded the hiring of Stuart Hall as one of the best ideas he had ever had and considered that they were always very good friends. Teaching and committee duties at all levels of the university absorbed much of Hoggart's time, while Hall ran the Centre day-to-day and "progressively shaped the pattern of intellectual work" (Hoggart 1992: 98).

3   The research was funded by the Rowntree Trust and conducted over a period of three years at CCCS. The original report was published by CCCS in 1970.

4   E. P. Thompson defended the very corporatism—a result of tremendous investment in human struggle—of the labor movement and the "tradition of *dissent*" that Anderson (and Tom Nairn) derided or ignored. He generally dismantles this work, but he is no more sanguine about the immediate possibilities. If the British working class had refused "to take up an offensive posture over so many decades, this is not just because of some 'corporate' conservatism but also because of an active rejection of what appeared as the only alternative ideology and strategy—Communism" (1965: 74).

5   Fred Halliday maps the international extent and depth of the movement and lists specific obstacles in Britain: "short periods of study, a general ignorance of Marxism and aversion to theory in general, proliferation of antagonistic factions on the campus, and the continuing pretence of apolitical debate between the parties" (1969: 316). The articles in *Student Power,* edited by Julian Nagel, are concerned with the "student crisis [as] a world wide phenomenon" (1969: n.p.). The specificity of the movement in Britain is treated in *Student Power: Problems, Diagnosis, Action,* edited by Alexander Cockburn and Robin Blackburn: the "main student movements are quite aware that their struggle is against the social system as a whole; they refuse to participate in it on its own terms" (1969: 8). Widgery (1976) assembles many documents from the period. Caute (1988) and Fraser (1988) both treat the events in Britain in the context of a world movement; such a movement is theorized by Immanuel Wallerstein (1991a: 65–83).

6   "Only half the marchers were students . . . while 12 per cent were non-student manual workers under twenty-five. Nearly 70 per cent of the demonstrators had turned out to protest not only about Vietnam but about capitalism and the structure of British society" (Fraser 1988: 281).

7   First published as *Working Papers in Cultural Studies,* no. 10 (1977).

8   On this perspective, see Coward and Ellis (1977).

4   Centre for Contemporary Cultural Studies II

1   Slack (1996) also points out the degree of influence the work of Ernesto Laclau had, apparent in Stuart Hall (1980c). On articulation, see Hall (1980b, 1980c, 1985b, 1986).

2   See, for instance, Judith Williamson's *Decoding Advertisements: Ideology and Meaning in Advertising* (1978).

3   First published as "Encoding and Decoding in the TV Discourse," CCCS Stencilled Paper No. 7, 1973.

4   In 1973, *Screen* (vol. 14, nos. 1–2 and 3) introduced the work of Christian Metz to its English

audience, followed in 1975 with Metz's influential "The Imaginary Signifier" (vol. 16, no. 2). This, and other articles in the same issue, opened up questions of the text and the author and the constitution of the subject as exemplified in the work of Lacan and Kristeva. "As far as I am concerned," writes Metz, "the film-maker is only an effect of the text, the effect of the textual system of the films he has made" (1973: 209–10). Not all members of the editorial board were convinced, and in the fourth number of volume 16 four members of the board presented their criticisms. By the summer of 1976, the internal debate had escalated and these four had resigned (see Buscombe et al. 1976). As *Screen* became increasingly Lacanian in perspective, it came into conflict with much of the work in cultural studies done in the 1970s; the positions are clarified in the documents of the *Days of Hope* controversy (see T. Bennett et al. 1981). Colin MacCabe, for *Screen*, argued that far from being progressive and a genuine political critique, the realism of these programs, "based round the experience of an English working-class family during the period from the imposition of conscription in 1916 until the General Strike in 1926," with great stress laid on the accuracy of presentation, precoded the reality presented, making it impossible for it to criticize society (quoted in T. Bennett et al. 1981: 302). Morley argued that "screen theory" isolated the positioning of the subject from everything outside the specific encounter of the text and reader (cccs 1980: 163–73).

5   A selection of articles, culled from the first nine issues of *Working Papers in Cultural Studies,* Stencilled Occasional Papers, and recent work. The emphasis is on texts and cultural forms rather than practices and institutions.

6   *Resistance through Rituals* was published in 1975 as *Working Papers in Cultural Studies,* no. 7/8 and reflected three years of work of the Sub-Cultures Group at cccs.

7   In 1970, the first Women's Liberation Conference in Britain was held at Oxford. It formulated four demands: free twenty-four-hour nurseries, immediate equalization of wages, equal opportunity for education and employment, and free contraception and abortion on demand.

8   The Women's Forum (1976–77) was closed to men. Its existence alongside the Women's Studies Group reproduced the always problematic political/intellectual split.

9   Besides the fatigue of yearly crises and the tensions of an emerging generational separation, feminism played a prominent role in Hall's departure from cccs. Hall was for feminism. "So being targeted as 'the enemy,' as the senior patriarchal figure, placed me in [an] impossibly contradictory position. . . . I was checkmated by feminists. . . . It was a structural thing. I couldn't any longer do any useful work, from that position. It was time to go" (S. Hall 1996a: 500).

10 *The Politics of Thatcherism,* edited by Stuart Hall and Martin Jacques (1983), had its roots in the concerns of *Policing the Crisis* (the lead article, Hall's "The Great Moving Right Show," had appeared in *Marxism Today* in 1979). It gave rise to a debate over "authoritarian populism" in which Hall disputed the interpretation of his analysis that suggested that "Thatcherism was successful because it had greater ideological coherence than its enemies" (M. Barker 1992: 93). Hall argued that he had long ago dissociated himself "from the discourse theoretical approach to the analysis of whole social formations"; far from an "uncontradictory monolith," he had "tried to show how Thatcherism has managed to stitch up or 'unify' the contradictory strands in its discourse" (1985a: 122). See also Jessop et al. (1984, 1985).

1   Late in the decade, *Screen,* along with the academic left, reached a political impasse with roots in the student movements of the late 1960s and early 1970s. MacCabe, a prominent figure in the development of *Screen* as a theoretical journal in the 1970s, writes: "If one granted that the political and the ideological were autonomous and specific then it was quite possible to struggle within various institutions, particularly . . . education, without necessarily taking up positions automatically designated as left by some outside political agency . . . secure in the knowledge that these struggles would finally come into convergence with the most funda- mental economic and political struggles. . . . In retrospect it is easy to mock the position as one of fundamental bad faith in which the strenuous aims of the revolution could always be left to other sectors while one battled away for small-scale reforms. . . . Althusser certainly takes his importance within the Eurocommunist movement of the seventies as western Communist parties tried to combine ever more serious commitment to the democratic institutions of capitalism together with a commitment to transform basic economic rela- tions. Any European-wide chances for such a movement foundered in the autumn of 1977 when the French Communist Party broke the Union of the Left fearing that victory for that Union would find the Party's power reduced" (1985: 16–17).

2   First published in *Working Papers in Cultural Studies,* no. 9, 1976.

3   The basic characteristics of the Open University were no campus; studies basically by corre- spondence for mostly adult students; no entrance qualifications; wide use of broadcasting and other media; instruction dispensed through "course teams" and distributed nationally, on a nontraditional timetable. See Tunstall (1974), Ferguson (1976), and Perry (1977).

4   Institutional data in this chapter are gleaned from the 1994 edition of the *Commonwealth Universities Yearbook,* Striphas (1998), and direct queries.

5   In 1992, Meaghan Morris might well have included Australian cultural studies in this project; what "is really eloquent . . . [is] the absolute invisibility of twenty years of feminist criticism of media, film theory, art, and Australian culture and its more recent intersection with a whole range of debates around Aboriginal studies, Pacific studies and so on" (1992: 651).

6   Brenda Cooper and Andrew Steyn have written that "neither African studies nor cultural studies exist in South Africa, either as concepts with a shared definition nor in clearly identifiable and similar institutions across the country"; however, their objective was to alert the reader to the way these studies were spread out over disciplines and situated among diverse approaches rather than constituting a "unified subject" (1996a: 7). Institutionalization is not totally absent: for example, the Cultural Studies Research Programme at Vista University and the Contemporary Cultural Studies Unit at the University of Natal (now Centre for Cultural and Media Studies) was set up in 1985 but resulted "from a staff/student initiative dating back to 1976" to study strategies of cultural resistance in the wake of the Soweto uprising (Tomaselli 1988a: 7). Certainly, the literature has grown rapidly in the past few years, ranging from a culturalist perspective (Wits History Workshop and work such as that of Charles van Onselen) to a structuralist—Althusser/Gramsci—approach (Tomaselli). Examples of subject matter include the relationship between the black labor force and popular music (Coplan 1994); representation and identity formation (Thornton 1996; Hamilton 1998); citizenship issues and

colonialism, along with their articulation to cultural questions and power relations (Thornton 1995; Mamdani 1996); and tensions and connections between races (van Onselen 1996). Essays in *Senses of Culture* (Nuttall and Michael 2000b) treat a range of topics, from citizenship to the arts and popular culture. *Transgressing Boundaries* (Cooper and Steyn 1996b) mixes theoretical essays with case studies on arrow toxins (Bunn), the Lydenburg heads (Hall), and the representation of slavery in contemporary West African literature (Maduakor). For discussions of the cultural studies perspective and examples of work in the 1980s, see *Rethinking Culture,* edited by Keyan G. Tomaselli (1988b), especially the preface by Ntongela Masilela, where the argument for the "Africanization" of cultural studies based on "the great cultural texts of the African Revolution" (1988: 3) is made (with a list of important works), and Keyan G. Tomaselli's introduction, with its brief chronology, and then the essays by Muller et al., Tomaselli, Muller, Frederikse et al., Steadman, and Basckin.

7 "The government took a sledgehammer to squash a gnat." By 1950 membership in the CPUSA was around 43,000 and by 1957 it had fallen to only about 10,000; circulation of the *Daily Worker* went from 23,000 between 1945 and 1950 to 10,433 in 1953. "By June 1953 over one hundred university professors had taken the Fifth, fifty-four of whom had been dismissed or suspended, and the others put on probation or under censure" (Caute 1988: 187, 185–86, 414). On the collaboration between the CIA and the FBI and the academic community, see Diamond (1992).

8 "[Students for a Democractic Society] was the force, beginning in the spring of 1960 . . . which had shaped the politics of a generation and rekindled the fires of American radicalism for the first time in thirty years, the largest student organization ever known in this country and the major expression of the American left in the sixties" (Sale: 1973, 5). On the New Left in the United States, see also Teodori (1969). On 1968, including the international dimensions, see Caute (1988) and Fraser (1988); as a revolution in the world-system, see Arrighi, Hopkins, and Wallerstein (1989) and Wallerstein (1991a, 65–83); on the Old and New Left, see Isserman (1987) and Widgery (1976); for personal recollections of Weathermen, see Stern (1975) and Grathwohl (1976); and on the San Francisco scene, Hoskyns (1997).

9 The book containing her essay was put out by Pantheon in a series titled "Antitextbooks."

10 François Dosse (1997a) has called 1966 the "annum mirabile" of structuralism. Barthes, Greimas, Machery, and Lacan, among so many others, published key texts and Foucault's *The Order of Things* sold fifteen thousand copies over the summer; journals were created by the legion; and finally Bernard Pingaud was able to write, in his introduction to a special issue of *L'Arc* devoted to Sartre and the past fifteen years in which "philosophy had been supplanted by the social sciences," that "We are no longer existentialists, but structuralists" (quoted in Dosse 1997a: 326–27).

11 Representatives from anthropology, classical studies, comparative literature, linguistics, literary criticism, history, philosophy, psychoanalysis, semiology, and sociology all attended the Johns Hopkins symposium. The program "also reflected the active participation at all stages in the planning of colleagues from the Sixième Section of the École Pratique des Hautes Études. In addition to those colleagues present at the sessions, the organizers also owe a debt of gratitude to MM Fernand Braudel and Claude Lévi-Strauss for counsel and encouragement" (Macksey and Donato 1972: xvii).

12 De Man's rise, his postmortem fall, and the acrimonious debate that ensued after his death

and the discovery of his past is chronicled by David Lehman (1991). De Man was able to keep secret both his collaboration with the Nazi occupation of Belgium and his less than honorable relationship with his first wife and children. Gerald Graff (1979) gives an account of the mesh between deconstruction and contemporary life in the United States.

13 In matters of oppositional theory, the emphases on psychology and cultural criticism at the expense of the dimensions of history, class, and economic crisis gave critical theory (Frankfurt School, some of whose members had found a home in the United States during the war) more impact in the United States than in countries with substantial Marxist movements (see Bottomore 1984; Arato and Gebhardt 1978); the antipositivism of critical theory also made it problematic for structural Marxists.

14 See Hénaff on Lévi-Strauss: "The structural approach can be considered a *moment* . . . as one method among others. . . . This method, within its limits and in its specificity, merits simply the attention and respect due to any good tool" (1998: 5–6).

15 French theory of the 1960s missed any "encounter with mass culture" (excepting the early Barthes of *Mythologies*). "*Tel Quel* simply ignored popular culture as mere consumerist repetition in favour of the revolutionary potential of the great texts of literary modernism. In that sense de Man was pushing at an open door. Once he disengaged this primacy of literature both from its political context and its crucial engagement with science, he was able to fashion a practice of reading which could ignore politics (along with all contemporary culture) in favour of a powerful skepticism which would re-read the canon but leave it completely intact. It is then no accident that all criticism can do, at its best, is to reproduce the paradoxes of literature because to suggest anything else would allow an extra literary set of concerns to intrude" (MacCabe 1992a: 31–32). The review *Tel Quel*, founded in 1960 and functioning as a "vehicle of a theory and practice of the text" (Ffrench and Lack 1998: 2), was a key actor in the "transition from Sartre's hegemony to that of the human sciences" (Kauppi 1994: xv; see also Ffrench 1995).

16 Fischer concluded that deconstruction does indeed make a difference by reinforcing established political and educational arrangements! "Instead of challenging . . . the 'solemn conventions of Anglo-American academic discourse' . . . deconstruction allows us to live with them" (1985: 125). According to Norman Denzin, cultural studies threatens existing disciplinary formations both by challenging their control in such areas as "mass communications, social problems, the family, and the cultural text" and "at the same time, new areas of study— for example, the popular film, popular music, pornography, and pulp literature—have emerged, which appear, on the surface, to have no place in a scholarly curriculum" (1992: 75), resulting in resistance or attempts at co-optation (see Becker and McCall 1990).

17 Stephan Fuchs and Steven Ward place deconstruction in the framework of Kuhn's paradigmatic and normal science as "one of the most influential intellectual and social movements in the humanities and social sciences during the 1970s and 1980s" (1994: 481). As Ben Agger writes, they argue that "moderate" deconstruction "takes over when a field organizes itself around certain assumptions which are exempt from deconstruction so that practical work can go forward . . . [and] becomes merely a form of intellectual contest . . . not a groundless critique of 'everything' conducted in nonrepresentational playful writing." This, however, is not deconstruction "because it embodies 'foundationalism' (the posit of first principles or assumptions), which Derrida criticizes" (Agger 1994: 501). Derrida the sociologist would say

that "what is somewhat hastily called deconstruction is not, if it is of any consequence, a specialized set of discursive procedures, even less the rules of a new hermeneutic method, working on texts or utterances in the shelter of a given and stable institution. It is, at the very least, a way of taking a position, in its work of analysis, concerning the political and institutional structures that make possible and govern our practice, our competences, our performances. Precisely because it is never concerned only with signified content, deconstruction should not be separable from this politico-institutional problematic and should seek a new investigation of responsibility, an investigation which questions the codes inherited from ethics and politics. This means that too political for some, it will seem paralyzing to those who only recognize politics by the most familiar road signs" (quoted in Agger 1994: 501). Deconstruction becomes sociology with the move from literary texts to all social texts. Derridean sociology (e.g., Agger 1989a, 1989c; R. Brown 1987; Denzin 1991; Game 1991; Seidman 1991) "rejects the 'logocentric' assumptions and practices of positivism, which in the case of quantitative empiricism, try to solve intellectual problems with sheer technique, thus falsely achieving what Derrida calls foundation. Deconstructive sociology (e.g., Agger 1989b; Gilbert and Mulkay 1984; Knorr-Cetina 1981) reads method as a rhetorical text—a way of making an argument. Deconstructive sociology does not abolish methods but 'narrates' their hidden metaphysics, thus starting arguments conducted explicitly in terms of values and other ontological assumptions" (Agger 1994: 503).

18 Work on symbolic interactionism has further solidified this link of the Chicago School with cultural studies: a weak connection in Becker and McCall (1990) and more comprehensively in Denzin (1992). The centrality of pragmatism, symbolic interactionism, and especially the work of John Dewey in the historical development of this "American" tradition has most recently been stressed by Warren and Vavrus (2002b) and a number of the authors represented in their edited collection (2002a).

19 With the book in mind, a major challenge from the floor called into question the way speakers were recognized: "Access to the microphones entailed nothing less than who would or would not participate in 'the future' of Cultural Studies" (Dienst 1990: 328). See especially the interventions of Alexandra Chasin and bell hooks with not only specific objections but suggestions for solutions (Grossberg, Nelson, and Treichler 1992: 293–94).

20 "The notion that Marxism and cultural studies slipped into place, recognized an immediate affinity, joined hands in some teleological or Hegelian moment of synthesis, and there was the founding moment of cultural studies, is entirely mistaken.... At a certain point, the questions I still wanted to address in short were inaccessible to me except via a detour through Gramsci. ... while Gramsci belonged and belongs to the problematic of Marxism, his importance for this moment of British cultural studies is precisely the degree to which he radically *displaced* some of the inheritances of Marxism in cultural studies. The radical character of Gramsci's 'displacement' of Marxism has not yet been understood and probably won't ever be reckoned with, now we are entering the era of post-Marxism" (S. Hall 1992: 280–81).

21 Stanford had had a Western civilization course from 1935 to 1970 and by 1980 had reinstituted such a course. It eventually included the Eurocentric and monumentalist reading list evincing the "structure of otherness" that, "depending on your perspective," constitutes either "the main *obstacle to* or the main *bulwark against* relational approaches to culture that sparked the debate" (Pratt 1992: 20).

22 Underlining the problematic role of the "social"—not to be conceived as "a 'dimension,' an 'influence,' or a 'factor' to be juxtaposed with the 'factors' of evidence and rationality"— Latour and Woolgar removed the term from the subtitle of the second edition (1986) of their *Laboratory Life: The Social Construction of Scientific Facts* (1979). As Shapin further observes, the claim "was that 'the social dimension' of knowledge needed to be attended to in order to understand what counts as a fact of discovery, what inferences are made from facts, what is regarded as rational or proper conduct, how objectivity is recognized, and how the credibility of claims is assessed. The target here was not at all the legitimacy of scientific knowledge but the legitimacy of individualist frameworks for interpreting scientific knowledge" (1995: 300). The "strong program" in the sociology of scientific knowledge was set out by David Bloor. It would be causal ("concerned with the conditions which bring about belief or states of knowledge"), impartial ("with respect to truth and falsity, rationality or irrationality, success or failure"), symmetrical (with the "same types of cause explain[ing], say, true and false beliefs"), and reflexive ("its patterns of explanation would have to be applicable to sociology itself"; 1991: 7). On social constructivism and its critiques, see Sismondo (1993a, 1993b), Knorr-Cetina (1993), Fuchs (1992), Hagendijk (1990), Laudan (1981).

23 A recent collection (Labinger and Collins 2001) suggests that communication across the superdisciplines, although requiring heroic efforts, is possible, which is the point of the title, *The One Culture? A Conversation about Science.*

24 The original article, the *Lingua Franca* revelation, responses, reactions in the press (domestic and foreign), and longer essays and colloquies on the "affair" are conveniently collected in Editors of Lingua Franca (2000); A. Ross (1996b) has edited an expanded version of the special issue of *Social Text* without the Sokal piece.

25 Ilya Prigogine has argued that the "sciences are not the reflection of a static rationality to be resisted or submitted to; they are furthering understanding in the same way as are human activities taken as a whole" (1988: 3). He goes so far as to state, "I believe that what we do today depends on our image of the future, rather than the future depending on what we do today" (quoted in Snell and Yevtushenko 1992: 28).

6 Conjunctural Knowledge I

Portions of chapter 6 appeared previously in another form in Lee (1996).

1 F. R. Leavis (1962) responded to Snow in a replay of the exchange between Huxley and Arnold in the 1880s. See Lepenies (1988) for the establishment of a "third culture" (especially sociology) between science and literature. On the historical construction of the disciplines and emergence of the social sciences, see Gulbenkian Commission (1996).

2 Bush's 1945 report, along with the recommendations of the President's Scientific Research Board and the Hoover Commission, among others, eventually resulted in the creation of the National Science Foundation in 1950. Government concern on the heels of the *Sputnik* launching in 1957 resulted in the passage of the National Defense Education Act in 1958. See Schaffter (1969) and Clowse (1981).

3 E.g., as gauged by Nobel prizes awarded in science (Broad 1991), or by "major social sciences advances" (Deutsch, Markovits, and Platt 1986: 407).

4 See Ayer (1959), Hanfling (1981), Giere and Richardson (1996), and Weitz (1966).

5　The Vienna Circle "rejected the view . . . that there is a radical distinction between the natural and the social sciences" (Ayer 1959: 21), and in 1942, C. G. Hempel renewed the idiographic/nomothetic debate by "repudiat[ing the] rejection of law in historiography" (Weitz 1966: 254). On behaviorism, see J. Watson (1925) and Skinner (1971); for political science, Dahl (1963) and Meehan (1971); for origins, O'Donnell (1985); and for an overview of the conceptual framework, Zuriff (1985).

6　Exponents of functionalism in anthropology included Alfred Radcliffe-Brown and Bronislaw Malinowski (whose work influenced Talcott Parsons). Functional psychology emphasized function over the facts of mental phenomena; it purported to be active rather than static and descriptive. Functionalism in architecture (a founding tenet, with Le Corbusier's "house as a machine for living," of the International Modern Movement) may be traced to Viollet-le-Duc and Louis Sullivan ("form follows function"). Problems with functionalism in the built environment became clear early in the century: conflicts of interests and larger social issues evaporated and the definition of function itself was fraught with contradictions and hidden moral assumptions (F. Scott 1982: 607–8). In 1935 the American Sociological Society severed its links to the powerful (but not very quantitative) Chicago Department of Sociology and founded the *American Sociological Review*. In 1937, Parsons's *The Structure of Social Action* laid the foundation for the post-1945 hegemony of structural-functionalism. His work was continued by a group of Harvard graduates, particularly Robert K. Merton, Kingsley Davis, and Marion Levy. Ernest Nagel (1956) delivered a devastating critique of Merton's 1949 work, *Social Theory and Social Structure*.

7　See Lazarsfeld (1982). Sociologists "of different persuasions joined hands in attempting, unsuccessfully, to have sociology included in the original legislation establishing the National Science Foundation" (Volkart 1981: 65–66). In 1968 the social sciences were added to a list of fields the Foundation was directed to support and a separate directorate for social science was finally created in 1991. However, Klausner and Lidz reckon that "it is hard to imagine that the current achievements [and failings, (Richard E. Lee)] of the social sciences would seem measurably different had NSF included a Division of Social Sciences from the outset" (1986: 193). On U.S. leadership, Paul Lamy has argued that "as the influence of American sociology increased, other national sociological communities found themselves in a relationship of dependence" that to a degree reflected the relative wealth and power of the state (1976: 104, 107–8). From C. Wright Mills (1959) came a notable attack; the value-neutrality link between positive science and U.S./world social science was further challenged in the 1960s (e.g., Gouldner 1961; Gray 1968) and the humanism versus positivism debate has been ongoing among sociologists (e.g., Tibbetts 1982; Lemke, Shevach, and Wells 1984).

8　See presentations in Eisenstadt (1966, 1973), Huntington (1968), and Rostow (1960). For critical reviews of Rostow, see Baran and Hobsbawm (1961), who situate the importance of his work in its value as a cold war document rather than in its intellectual content; for Huntington, see Leys (1982). Donal Cruise O'Brien documented the "shift in teleological emphasis through which democracy as a goal for developing polities has been gradually displaced by another ideal, that of institutional order" (1972: 351).

9　Robert Gorham Davis's remark that the "New Criticism implies a 'reactionary position in politics and a dogmatic position in theology' . . . won't hold up." The New Critics, "in sharp contrast to [the] political manifestos and asides, are square in the middle of the bourgeois liberal tradition. The explicit politics of these men is a pseudo-politics. It constitutes an enabling mythology that ties their criticism to social yearnings and nostalgia, but not to any possibility of action or affiliation." Their main political effect "was to help embed literary criticism, along with its producers, tightly and securely within the network of bourgeois institutions" (Ohmann 1972: 149–50). See Ransom (1941), Brooks (1947), Krieger (1956), Wimsatt and Brooks (1957), Kermode (1964), and Graff (1970). For a bracing corrective to many criticisms, see Jancovich (1993).

10 From the 1950s through the early 1960s New York saw the Bolshoi, yes, but also the English Royal Ballet and the French Madeleine Renaud and Jean-Louis Barrault companies. Later, the opening to the People's Republic of China brought its "classical" companies to the United States in similar bids for cultural legitimacy. The United States first seized the avant-garde but, once captured, even U.S. ballet companies toured Europe, the Far East, *and* the U.S.S.R.

11 Husserl asserted that the heart of philosophical investigation was description that should begin with deep introspection jettisoning any "natural attitude" (of independently existing objects) in favor of the contents of consciousness alone. The aim was to return philosophy to the realm of the concrete, but a concrete that was internal and dependent on intuition for access. See Kolakowski (1974) and Spiegelberg (1965). Aron Gurwitsch (1966, 1974) pioneered the application of phenomenological principles to social research, especially psychology. Alfred Schütz extended Husserl's method to the social world (an "interpreted world") in a Weberian context in reaction to the prevalent positivism and behaviorism. Eventually arguing against the a priori individual, his work maintained an allegiance to description and commonsense knowledge (Wagner 1983). Phenomenology was the philosophical foundation for ethnomethodology and its study of everyday activities (Garfinkel 1967; Sharrock and Anderson 1986) and has also influenced literary criticism (Lentricchia 1980).

12 Rather than the transcendental subject, Heidegger's hermeneutical phenomenology (based on interpretation instead of consciousness) begins with the "givenness" of existence itself—hence "existentialist." Maurice Friedman (1964) finds precursors to existentialism in Heraclitus and the Old Testament; Walter Kaufmann (1975), with Friedman, included Dostoevsky, and like most scholars counted Søren Kierkegaard as the progenitor of the movement. Existentialism casts a wide net. Kierkegaard's philosophy developed in relation to Protestantism. Sartre and Camus were avowed atheists, but not Jaspers. Religion provided the springboard for Heidegger's philosophy, and Dostoyevsky and Berdyayev are inseparable from Russian Orthodoxy. Buber's philosophy reflects the Hasidic tradition; his work along with that of Gabriel Marcel offers a strongly intersubjective corrective to individualistic interpretations of Heidegger and Sartre and, with that of Karl Jaspers, counters nihilistic readings of Nietzsche, Sartre, and Camus. Existentialism has been widely influential in the organization and operation of institutions and popularized with the public at large. From a renewed emphasis on humanism in education, existentialist perspectives have found a significant place in psychology and psychotherapy (e.g., R. D. Laing). Literature and the visual arts have also been inspired by existentialism, functioning as both sites of speculation and conduits of dissemination. Even theology has not been immune (e.g., Paul Tillich). However, the language is often phallocentric and, in practice, existentialism certainly has had a masculinist predisposition; a woman could only "be really alive" on male terms and in competition with males (the career of Simone de Beauvoir is archetypal).

13 Balzac was Marx's favorite author and "realism" was the battle cry of 1848. On the eve of the Revolution, Jules Michelet contended that "literature, emerging from the shadow of fantasy, will come alive and be real, will be a *form of action;* it will no longer be the entertainment of some individual, or of idlers, but the voice of the people to the people." Although the Revolution "failed," the artists who had been on the barricades carried forward the movement in the spirit of De Sanctis ("Art can be nothing other than the objective representation of reality, an undeformed expression of it"), or, according to Courbet, "Art consists 'in knowing how to find the fullest expression of things that exist.' ... *Man* ... became the center of the new esthetic" (quoted in De Micheli 1959: 11, 14–15, 17; my translation). However, realism soon became identified with the bourgeois liberal establishment and exhausted much of its emancipatory appeal with the fall of the Paris Commune in 1871. The avant-garde of the late nineteenth century and twentieth century contested the premises of realism by figuring an internal world and was antipositivist and strongly influenced by non-Western cultural expressions.

14 Theorized in France by its practitioners Alain Robbe-Grillet, Nathalie Sarraute, Michel Butor, Claude Simon, and Jean Ricardou, the nouveau roman found resonance in the work of Susan Sontag in the United States, Rayner Heppenstall in England, and Uwe Johnson in Germany. In the line (in defiance of the bourgeois novel, epitomized by Balzac) passing through Flaubert, Dostoevsky, Proust, Kafka, Joyce, Faulkner, and Beckett, the nouveau roman self-consciously announced the future (Robbe-Grillet 1955; 1961: 146; 1963: 11). Opposing realism (Robbe-Grillet, because it imposed "a falsely transparent and reassuring order on social and personal experience"; Sarraute, for the " 'trust' which the reader is obliged to place in the realist character, and . . . no longer viable in this 'age of suspicion' "), these authors believed writing (practice) to be conscious and closely linked to theory (Britton 1992: 8, 3). Butor is generally positive in his assessment of surrealism, especially the (shared) postulate concerning the exploratory and transformative power (over the "real") of the imagination (1964: 182). See also Ricardou (1967, 1971, 1975), Ricardou and Rossum-Guyon (1972), and Sturrock (1969).

15 Victor Farias (1989) has made the case that Heidegger embraced Nazism out of commitment and not as a simple career move. This was not a flirtation; he remained a dues-paying member of the Party until the end of the war.

16 Of the Angry Young Men: "John Osborne resembled, most of all, the militant Socialist of the thirties, but Osborne was not advancing any programs of action. Kingsley Amis declared himself also to be a Labor Party man, but his radicalism was so riddled with skepticism as to be untenable. George Scott, despairing for the Socialists, formed a temporary alliance with the Tories. Thomas Hinde, viewing Socialists and Tories as two sides of a bad coin, eschewed politics altogether. Colin Wilson, whose Outsider philosophy begins with the rejection of humanism and rationalism, tried to develop a deeply subjective religious existentialism" (Feldman and Gartenberg 1958: 14).

17 Recent years have seen a revival of interest in the Beats and the appearance of biographies and popular accounts as well as previously unpublished material and the reissue of much of the literary production of the protagonists of the movement. On the Beats, Ann Charters's two-volume *The Beats: Literary Bohemians in Postwar America* (1983) is still the best single source; Charters (1992) and S. Watson (1995) usefully introduce the material and the personal

relationships. Some effects of the Beat Generation artistic movement, according to Ginsberg: "Spiritual liberation, sexual 'revolution' or 'liberation,' i.e., gay liberation, somewhat catalyzing women's liberation, black liberation, Gray Panther activism. Liberation of the word from censorship. Demystification and/or decriminalization of some laws against marijuana and other drugs. The evolution of rhythm and blues into rock and roll as a high art form . . . The spread of ecological consciousness . . . Opposition to the military-industrial machine civilization . . . Attention to what Kerouac called (after Spengler) a 'second religiousness' developing within an advanced civilization. Return to an appreciation of idiosyncrasy as against state regimentation. Respect for land and indigenous peoples and creatures. . . . The essence of the phrase 'beat generation' may be found in *On the Road* with the celebrated phrase: 'Everything belongs to me because I am poor' " (1995: 19).

18   Frantz Fanon was bitterly critical of "Orphée noir" in *Black Skin, White Masks.* "For Fanon," writes John Noyes, "the dialectic becomes unsustainable where it fantasizes the present within a universal historical knowledge that is nonetheless situated in Europe and incorporated in whiteness. . . . For Fanon, the critique of the dialectic is the key to understanding how the politics of perspective is veiled by a discourse of method" (2000: 59).

19   Nothing better validates Fredric Jameson's dictum "The history of thought is the history of its models" (1972: v) than the genealogy of structuralism. The American tradition is generally termed "descriptive linguistics," for the most part documenting and preserving native American languages. Thus the work of C. S. Peirce, which in many ways paralleled that of Saussure and is only now being revived, was for long marginalized.

20   Lévi-Strauss predicted a transformative role for structural linguistics in the social sciences. He credits Nicholas Troubetzkoy with formulating the four basic operations of the structural method: "First, structural linguistics shifts from the study of *conscious* linguistic phenomena to study of their *unconscious* infrastructure; second, it does not treat *terms* as independent entities, taking instead as its basis of analysis the *relations* between terms; third, it introduces the concept of *system*—'Modern phonemics does not merely proclaim that phonemes are always part of a system; it *shows* concrete phonemic systems and elucidates their structure'—; finally, structural linguistics aims at discovering *general laws,* either by induction 'or . . . by logical deduction, which would give them an absolute character' " (1963: 33). For an account of Lévi-Strauss and his work, see Hénaff (1998).

21   Barthes takes Saussure's first-order system and with a lateral shift employs the sign in an extended role as signifier in a second-order system, myth, which produces signification. In the process, the original sign or collection of signs is drained of content, reduced to pure form, rendered arbitrary to serve as signifier in the new system. At the level of myth, the image of the black soldier hails French imperialism as it establishes it, but with the loss of some knowledge, for the image is emptied of the history it had at the level of linguistic sign. "*Myth hides nothing:* its function is to distort, not to make disappear. . . . the ubiquity of the signifier in myth exactly reproduces the physique of the *alibi.* . . . Myth is a *value,* truth is no guarantee for it; nothing prevents it from being a perpetual alibi: it is enough that its signifier has two sides for it always to have an 'elsewhere' at its disposal" (Barthes 1957: 121, 123).

22   Although Lévi-Strauss did his utmost to do justice to both the synchronic and the diachronic, Braudel characterized the anthropologist's conception of time as "very long" and "too long," indeed as eternal; if it existed, it would be "the time of the sages" (1958: 748).

23 On the *Annales* School, see Stoianovich (1976), Kinser (1981), Clark (1985), Hunt (1986), Dosse (1987), and the special issue of *Review* (vol. 1, nos. 3/4, winter–spring, 1978) devoted to the subject.

7 Conjunctural Knowledge II

Portions of chapter 7 appeared previously in another form in Lee (1996).

1 The methods and conclusions of the "Project on the Predicament of Mankind" were summarized in *Limits to Growth* (Meadows et al. 1974), which lent its name to the debate. Roszak (1969) and R. B. Fuller (1969) presented utopian and utopia-or-else alternatives. Slusser and Slusser show clear intent both in title, *Technology: The God That Failed,* and in content: "Man has learned to *believe* that experimentation is good; it leads to knowledge and to technology which will improve life . . . [but] man's arrogant disregard for the finite cyclical nature of the planet he inhabits threatens to make that planet hostile to all forms of life" (1971: 11–12). King and Schneider (for the Club of Rome) dub 1968 "the Great Divide." It marked the high point and the end of postwar economic growth. Accompanying the social unrest and student uprisings, "general and vocal public awareness of the problems of the environment began to emerge. . . . The topic of recent Club of Rome meetings has been 'The Great Transition.' We are convinced that we are in the early stages of the formation of a new type of world society." Sustainability is a goal for the future, but only solidarity, not equality, would be achieved (1991: ix, xix, 49, 96–97). Meadows, Meadows, and Randers return to the themes of *Limits to Growth* and contend that some of the limits have already been "overshot." The types of "soft" tools they recommend for working toward sustainability are "visioning, networking, truth-telling, learning and loving" (1992: 224).

2 Opposition to construction of new reactors has been successful (Price 1990), and these are not the only ventures in trouble; very large-scale hydroelectric projects (e.g., Brazil, Canada, the Danube) have also faced reappraisal. China, however, is proceeding with the Three Gorges Dam on the Yangtze.

3 Carson's work resulted in the cancellation of the registration of DDT in the United States in 1971. Her book is perhaps the best known of an annunciatory group (e.g., Leopold 1949; Ehrlich 1968). In the United States the popular optimism launched with the first Earth Day in 1970 gave way to official negligence during the Reagan administration and the outright antienvironmentalism of the (Republican) U.S. 104th Congress. However, alarm has grown around the world, and during the Earth Summit of 1992 (see S. Johnson 1993) the U.S. position was a minority one. Some of the more important organizations were founded around the turning point 1967–73: Friends of the Earth, 1969, as a lobbying group; the National Resources Defense Council, 1970, to draft bills and undertake educational programs; Greenpeace, 1971, for nonviolent direct action. Despite heightened public awareness, in both Eastern and Western Europe Greens—the German Green Party declared itself the "alternative to the traditional parties" (*Programme* 1983: 6)—have been effectively weakened by splits over participation in government and "paying the bills."

4 Seeking legitimacy, Christian fundamentalism, strong in the United States and in contrast to religious fundamentalisms of noncore zones, cloaked itself in the language of ("creation") science (see Kitcher 1982).

5   Brydon and Chant argue that top-down views of development "have little or no place for women" (1989: 6–7). Women's issues and the movements they spawn may be vastly different in both content and policy orientations in the periphery and in conflict from region to region or among social groups. Evelyn Fox Keller, however, expressed a basic dilemma for feminism: "By rejecting objectivity as a masculine ideal, it simultaneously lends its voice to an enemy chorus and dooms women to residing outside of the realpolitik modern culture; it exacerbates the very problem it wishes to solve" (1982: 593).

6   From "inside" the sciences, Ilya Prigogine and Isabelle Stengers state that "a radical change in the outlook of modern science, the transition toward the temporal, the multiple, may be viewed as the reversal of the movement that brought Aristotle's heaven to earth. Now we are bringing earth to heaven. We are discovering the primacy of time and change, from the level of elementary particles to cosmological models. Both at the macroscopic and microscopic levels, the natural sciences have thus rid themselves of a conception of objective reality that implied that novelty and diversity had to be denied in the name of immutable universal laws. They have rid themselves of a fascination with a rationality taken as closed and a knowledge seen as nearly achieved. They are now open to the unexpected, which they no longer define as the result of imperfect knowledge or insufficient control" (1984: 306).

7   See Lee (1992) for the literature; for introductions to far-from-equilibrium systems and self-organization, see Nicolis (1989); for chaos, see Ford (1989); on fractal geometry, see Mandelbrot (1983). The total number of entries in the Permuterm Index of the *Science Citation Index* has shown flat, linear growth since the 1960s, whereas entries under the rubric "chaos" and its cognates have multiplied exponentially.

8   Weaver (1948) distinguished among the *simple problems* of classical physics with few variables, *disorganized complexity* with many variables amenable to description by statistical methods, and a middle region of *organized complexity* in which problem solving must depend on analyzing systems as organic wholes. He predicted that during the late twentieth century this latter activity—to be based on computers and interdisciplinary, "mixed team" research—would constitute the third great advance of science. Doyne Farmer and Norman Packard speak of questions in the "new wave science" that "cry out for *synthesis* rather than reduction" (Farmer et al. 1986: viii), where research on systems involving at least two time scales is based on simulation and cuts across disciplinary lines.

9   Ruelle and Takens (1971) employed the term " 'strange' attractor" to describe the phase-space portrait of the stable but nonperiodic behavior of a dynamical system whose evolution reached neither a steady state represented by a fixed point in phase space nor continuous repetition shown as a limit cycle. Li and Yorke (1975) first defined "chaotic" as describing a nonperiodic $\{F^n(x)\}$ sequence. Feigenbaum's "δ" is the fixed value to which the rate of onset of complex behavior converges as a limit in one common route to chaos.

10   "The integration of the laws of motion leads to the trajectories that the particles follow. . . . The basic characteristics of trajectories are *lawfulness, determinism,* and *reversibility*. . . . The remarkable feature is that once the forces are known, any single state is sufficient to define the system completely, not only its future but also its past" (Prigogine and Stengers 1984: 60).

11   "For all of Euclid, $D=D_T$. . . . *A fractal is by definition a set for which the Hausdorff Besicovitch dimension strictly exceeds the topological dimension* [$D>D_T$]. Every set with a noninteger D is a fractal. . . . But D may be an integer. . . . I call D a *fractal dimension*" (Mandelbrot 1983: 15).

"Twentieth-century mathematics flowered in the belief that it had transcended completely the limitations imposed by its natural origins . . . [but] the same pathological structures that the mathematicians invented to break loose from 19th-century naturalism turn out to be inherent in familiar objects all around us," Freeman Dyson writes (quoted in Mandelbrot 1983: 3–4). Mandelbrot himself savors the word he invented: "I coined *fractal* from the Latin adjective *fractus*. The corresponding Latin verb *frangere* means 'to break': to create irregular fragments. It is therefore sensible—and how appropriate for our needs!—that, in addition to 'fragmented' (as in *fraction* or *refraction*), *fractus* should also mean 'irregular,' both meanings being preserved in *fragment*" (1983: 4).

12 The physicist Richard Kitchener proposes five main features of a new approach involving "a 'paradigm switch' from (1) part to whole, (2) structure to process, (3) 'objective' to epistemic science, (4) a 'foundations' metaphor to a network model of knowledge, and (5) truth to 'approximate truth' " (1988: 15).

13 Note his discussion of the *Annales* School: "Historical theorists such as the *Annalists,* who were interested in transforming historiography into a science, could legitimately point out that the natural sciences had little interest in storytelling as an aim of their enterprise. . . . The transformation of a field of study into a genuine science has always been attended by an abandonment of anything like an interest in inventing a story to tell about its object of study in favor of the task of discovering the laws that governed its structures and functions. . . . Getting the 'story' out of 'history' was therefore a first step in the transformation of historical studies into a science" (White 1987: 169).

Works Cited

Addison, Paul. 1975. *The Road to 1945: British Politics and the Second World War.* London: Cape.

——. 1985. *Now the War Is Over: A Social History of Britain 1956–51.* London: BBC/Cape.

Ades, Dawn. 1981. "Dada and Surrealism." In *Concepts of Modern Art,* revised and enlarged ed. Edited by Nikos Stangos. London: Thames and Hudson.

Adler, Judith. 1982. Review of *Subculture: The Meaning of Style,* by Dick Hebdige. *American Journal of Sociology* 87, no. 6 (May): 1458–59.

Agar, Michael. 1990. "Text and Fieldwork: Exploring the Excluded Middle." *Journal of Contemporary Ethnography* 19, no. 1 (April): 73–88.

Agger, Ben. 1989a. *Fast Capitalism: A Critical Theory of Significance.* Urbana: University of Illinois Press.

——. 1989b. *Reading Science: A Literary, Political and Sociological Analysis.* Dix Hills, NY: General Hall.

——. 1989c. *Socioontology: A Disciplinary Reading.* Urbana: University of Illinois Press.

——. 1994. "Derrida for Sociology? A Comment on Fuchs and Ward." *American Sociological Review* 59, no. 4 (August): 501–5.

Aida, S., et al. 1985. *The Science and Praxis of Complexity: Contributions to the Symposium Held at Montpellier, France, 9–11 May 1984.* Tokyo: United Nations University.

Alexander, Jeffrey C. 1988. "The New Theoretical Movement." In *Handbook of Sociology.* Edited by Neil J. Smelser. Beverly Hills: Sage.

Althusser, Louis, with Etienne Balibar. 1970. *Reading Capital.* London: New Left Books.

Amis, Kingsley. 1957. *Socialism and the Intellectuals.* London: Fabian Society.

Anderson, Perry. 1964. "Origins of the Present Crisis." *New Left Review* 23 (January–February): 26–53.

——. 1968. "Components of the National Culture." *New Left Review* 50 (July–August): 3–57.

Anderson, Wilda C. 1983. "Dispensing with the Fixed Point: Scientific Law as Historical Event." *History and Theory* 22, no. 3: 264–77.

Ang, Ien. 1992. "Dismantling 'Cultural Studies'? By Way of Introduction." *Cultural Studies* 6, no. 3 (October): 311–21.

Apple, Michael W. 1990. *Ideology and Curriculum,* 2d ed. New York: Routledge.

Arato, Andrew, and Eike Gebhardt, eds. [1977] 1990. *The Essential Frankfurt School Reader.* New York: Continuum.

Archer, Robin, Diemut Bubeck, Hanjo Glock, Lesley Jacobs, Seth Moglen, Adam Steinhouse, and Daniel Weinstock, eds. 1989. *Out of Apathy: Voices of the New Left Thirty Years On.* New York: Verso.

Arnold, Matthew. [1882] 1953. "A Liverpool Address." In *Five Uncollected Essays of Matthew Arnold.* Edited by Kenneth Allott. Liverpool: University Press of Liverpool, 79–93.

———. [1853] 1960. "Preface to First Edition of *Poems.*" In *On the Classical Tradition.* Vol. 1 of *The Complete Prose Works of Matthew Arnold.* Edited by R. H. Super. Ann Arbor: University of Michigan Press, 1–15.

———. [1864] 1962a. "The Function of Criticism at the Present Time." In *Lectures and Essays in Criticism.* Vol. 3 of *The Complete Prose Works of Matthew Arnold.* Edited by R. H. Super. Ann Arbor: University of Michigan Press, 258–85.

———. [1866] 1962b. "On the Study of Celtic Literature." In *Lectures and Essays in Criticism.* Vol. 3 of *The Complete Prose Works of Matthew Arnold.* Edited by R. H. Super. Ann Arbor: University of Michigan Press, 291–386.

———. [1862] 1962c. "The Twice Revised Code." In *Democratic Education.* Vol 2. of *The Complete Prose Works of Matthew Arnold.* Edited by R. H. Super. Ann Arbor: University of Michigan Press, 212–43.

———. [1867] 1965. *Culture and Anarchy.* In *Culture and Anarchy with Friendship's Garland and Some Literary Essays.* Vol. 5 of *The Complete Prose Works of Matthew Arnold.* Edited by R. H. Super. Ann Arbor: University of Michigan Press, 85–229.

———. [1880] 1973. "The Future of Liberalism." In *English Literature and Irish Politics.* Vol. 9 of *The Complete Prose Works of Matthew Arnold.* Edited by R. H. Super. Ann Arbor: University of Michigan Press, 136–60.

———. [1882] 1974. "Literature and Science." In *Philistinism in England and America.* Vol. 10 of *The Complete Prose Works of Matthew Arnold.* Edited by R. H. Super. Ann Arbor: University of Michigan Press, 53–73.

Aronowitz, Stanley. 1993. *Roll Over Beethoven: The Return of Cultural Strife.* Hanover, NH: Wesleyan University Press.

Arrighi, Giovanni. 1990. "The Three Hegemonies of Historical Capitalism." *Review* 13, no. 3 (summer): 365–408.

Arrighi, Giovanni, Terence K. Hopkins, and Immanuel Wallerstein. 1989. *Antisystemic Movements.* London: Verso.

Atlan, Henri, et al. 1985. *La sfida della complessità.* A cura di Gianluca Bocchi e Mauro Ceruti. Milano: Feltrinelli.

Austrin, Terry. 1981. Review of *Working Class Culture: Studies in History and Theory.* Edited by John Clarke, Chas Critcher, and Richard Johnson. *Sociological Review* 29, no. 2 (May): 365–67.

Ayer, A. J., ed. 1959. *Logical Positivism.* New York: Free Press.

Bacciocco, Edward J. Jr. 1974. *The New Left in America: Reform to Revolution 1956 to 1970.* Stanford: Hoover Institution Press.

Bacon, Kenneth H. 1990. "NEH Head Lynne Cheney Sheds Her Low Profile to Champion Educational Focus on 'Great Books.' " *Wall Street Journal,* November 14, A18.

Baer, W. 1962. "The Economics of Prebisch and ECLA." *Economic Development and Cultural Change* 10 (January): 169–82.

Baldick, Chris. 1983. *The Social Misson of English Criticism, 1848–1932*. Oxford: Clarendon Press, 1987.

Bambach, Charles R. 1995. *Heidegger, Dilthey, and the Crisis of Historicism*. Ithaca: Cornell University Press.

Bamford, T. W. 1970. *Thomas Arnold on Education: A Selection from His Writings with Introductory Material*. Cambridge, England: Cambridge University Press.

Baran, Paul A., and E. J. Hobsbawm. 1961. "The Stages of Economic Growth." *Kyklos* 14, no. 2: 234–42.

Barker, Elizabeth. 1983. *The British Between the Superpowers, 1945–50*. London: Macmillan.

Barker, Martin. 1992. "Stuart Hall, *Policing the Crisis*." In *Reading into Cultural Studies*. Edited by Martin Barker and Anne Beezer. New York: Routledge, 81–100.

Barker, Martin, and Anne Beezer. 1992. "Introduction: What's in a Text." In *Reading into Cultural Studies*. Edited by Martin Barker and Anne Beezer. New York: Routledge, 1–20.

Barrow, John D. 1995. *The Artful Universe: The Cosmic Source of Human Creativity*. Boston: Back Bay.

Barry, Peter. 1995. *Beginning Theory: An Introduction to Literary and Cultural Theory*. New York: Manchester University Press.

Barthes, Roland. [1953] 1968. *Writing Degree Zero*. Translated by Annette Lavers and Colin Smith. New York: Noonday Press.

——. [1957] 1972. *Mythologies*. Translated by Annette Lavers. New York: Noonday Press.

Becker, Howard S., and Michal M. McCall, eds. 1990. *Symbolic Interaction and Cultural Studies*. Chicago: University of Chicago Press.

Bee, Jim. 1989. "First Citizen of the Semiotic Democracy." *Cultural Studies* 3, no. 3: 353–59.

Bennett, Tony. 1988. "Ozmosis: Looking at Pop Culture." *Australian Left Review* (April/May): 33–35.

——. 1992. "Putting Policy into Cultural Studies." In *Cultural Studies*. Edited by Lawrence Grossberg, Cary Nelson, and Paula Treichler. New York: Routledge, 23–37.

Bennett, Tony, Susan Boyd-Bowman, Colin Mercer, and Janet Woollacott, eds. 1981. *Popular Television and Film: A Reader*. London: British Film Institute.

Bennett, Tony, and Janet Woollacott. 1987. *Bond and Beyond: The Political Career of a Popular Hero*. London: Macmillan Education.

Bennett, William J. 1984. " 'To Reclaim a Legacy': Text of Report on Humanities in Education." *Chronicle of Higher Education* 29, no. 14 (November 28): 16–21.

Benton, Ted. 1984. *The Rise and Fall of Structural Marxism: Althusser and His Influence*. London: Macmillan.

Bess, Michael D. 1993. "E. P. Thompson: The Historian as Activist." *American Historical Review* 98, no. 1 (February): 18–38.

Birchall, Ian. 1972. "The British Communist Party 1945–64." *International Socialism* 50: 24–34.

Birnbaum, Norman. 1960. Foreword to *Out of Apathy*. Edited by E. P. Thompson. London: NLB/Stephens and Sons, ix–xii.

Blake, Andrew. 1992. "Tony Bennett and Janet Woollacott, *Bond and Beyond*." In *Reading into Cultural Studies*. Edited by Martin Barker and Anne Beezer. New York: Routledge, 49–64.

Blakemore, Steven. 1988. *Burke and the Fall of Language: The French Revolution as Linguistic Event*. Hanover, NH: University Press of New England.

Bloor, David. 1991/1976. *Knowledge and Social Imagery.* 2d ed. Chicago: University of Chicago Press.

Bogdanor, Vernon, and Robert Skidelsky. 1970. *The Age of Affluence 1951–1964.* London: Macmillan.

Borgmann, Albert. 1992. *Crossing the Postmodern Divide.* Chicago: University of Chicago Press.

Bottomore, Tom. 1984. *The Frankfurt School.* New York: Tavistock/Horwood.

Bousquet, Nicole. 1979. "Esquisse d'une théorie de l'alternance de périodes de concurrence et d'hégémonie au center de l'économie-monde capitaliste." *Review* 2, no. 4 (spring): 501–18.

———. 1980. "From Hegemony to Competition: Cycles of the Core." In *Processes of the World-System.* Edited by T. K. Hopkins and Immanuel Wallerstein. Beverly Hills: Sage, 46–83.

Bradley, Ian. 1985. *The Strange Rebirth of Liberal Britain.* London: Chatto and Windus.

Brantlinger, Patrick. 1990. *Crusoe's Footprints: Cultural Studies in Britain and America.* New York: Routledge.

Braudel, Fernand. 1958. "Histoire et Sciences sociales: La longue durée." *Annales* 13, no. 4 (October–December): 725–53.

Breisach, Ernst. 1983. *Historiography: Ancient, Medieval, and Modern.* Chicago: University of Chicago Press.

Breton, André. [1924] 1972. "Manifeste du surréalisme." In *Manifestes du surréalisme.* Paris: Gallimard.

Briggs, Asa. 1958. "The Context of Commitment." *New Statesman* 56, no. 1438 (October 4): 453–54.

Britton, Celia. 1992. *The Nouveau Roman: Fiction, Theory and Politics.* New York: St. Martin's Press.

Broad, William J. 1991. "For U.S., No Nobels May Mean a Fluke." *New York Times,* October 29, C5.

Brooks, Cleanth, 1947. *The Well Wrought Urn: Studies in the Structure of Poetry.* New York: Reynal and Hitchcock.

Brown, Lester R. 1978. *The Twenty-Ninth Day: Accommodating Human Needs and Numbers to the Earth's Resources.* New York: Norton.

Brown, Richard Harvey. 1987. *Society as Text: Essays on Rhetoric, Reason, and Reality.* Chicago: University of Chicago Press.

Brunsdon, Charlotte, and David Morley. 1978. *Everyday Television: "Nationwide."* London: British Film Institute.

Brydon, Lynne, and Sylvia Chant. 1989. *Women in the Third World: Gender Issues in Rural and Urban Areas.* New Brunswick, NJ: Rutgers University Press.

Buchloh, Benjamin H. D. 1990. "Cold War Constructivism." In *Reconstructing Modernism: Art in New York, Paris, and Montreal 1945–1964.* Edited by Serge Guibaut. Cambridge, MA: MIT Press.

Budd, Mike, Robert M. Entman, and Clay Steinman. 1990. "The Affirmative Character of U.S. Cultural Studies." *Critical Studies in Mass Communications* 7, no. 2 (June): 169–84.

Bundy, Colin. 1996. "Sharing the Burden? A Response to Terry Lovell." In *Transgressing the Boundaries: New Directions in the Study of Culture in Africa.* Edited by Brenda Cooper and Andrew Steyn. Athens: Ohio University Press, 31–38.

Burke, Edmund. [1790] 1968. *Reflections on the Revolution in France.* Edited with an introduction by Conor Cruise O'Brien. London: Penguin.

Burns, Rob, ed. 1995. *German Cultural Studies: An Introduction.* New York: Oxford University Press.

Buscombe, Edward, Christine Gledhill, Alan Lovell, and Christopher Williams. 1976. "Why We Have Resigned from the Board of *Screen.*" *Screen* 17, no. 2 (summer): 106–9.

Bush, Vannevar. 1945. *Science, the Endless Frontier: A Report to the President.* Washington, DC: U.S. Government Printing Office.

Butler, Marilyn, ed. 1984. *Burke, Paine, Godwin, and the Revolution Controversy.* Cambridge English Prose Texts. New York: Cambridge University Press.

Butor, Michel. [1964] 1972a. "Réponses à 'Tel Quel.'" In *Essais sur le roman.* Paris: Gallimard, 173–84.

——. [1960] 1972b. "Le roman comme recherche." In *Essais sur le roman.* Paris: Gallimard, 7–14.

Byrne, David. 1998. *Complexity Theory and the Social Sciences: An Introduction.* New York: Routledge.

Byrne, Paul. 1988. *The Campaign for Nuclear Disarmament.* London: Routledge.

Calder-Marshall, Arthur. 1961. "Letters to the Editor: 'The Long Revolution.'" *Times Literary Supplement* (April 7): 217.

Campbell, James. 1995. *Exiled in Paris: Richard Wright, James Baldwin, Samuel Beckett, and Others on the Left Bank.* New York: Scribner's.

Campbell, Neil, and Alasdair Kean. 1997. *American Cultural Studies: An Introduction to American Culture.* New York: Routledge.

Cantarow, Ellen. 1970. "Why Teach Literature? An Account of How I Came to Ask That Question." In *The Politics of Literature: Dissenting Essays on the Teaching of English.* Edited by Louis Kampf and Paul Lauter. New York: Pantheon Books, 57–100.

Cardoso, Fernando Henrique. 1977. "The Consumption of Dependency Theory in the United States." *Latin American Research Review* 12, no. 3: 7–24.

Cardoso, Fernando Henrique, and Enzo Faletto. 1979. *Dependency and Development in Latin America.* Berkeley: University of California Press.

Carey, James W. 1989. *Communication as Culture: Essays on Media and Society.* Boston: Unwin Hyman.

Carlyle, Thomas. [1839] 1904a. "Chartism." In *Critical and Miscellaneous Essays.* Volume 4 of *The Works of Thomas Carlyle in Thirty Volumes.* New York: Scribner's, 118–204.

——. [1849] 1904b. "The Nigger Question." In *Critical and Miscellaneous Essays.* Volume 4 of *The Works of Thomas Carlyle in Thirty Volumes.* New York: Scribner's, 348–83.

——. [1867] 1904c. "Shooting Niagara: And After?" In *Critical and Miscellaneous Essays.* Volume 5 of *The Works of Thomas Carlyle in Thirty Volumes.* New York: Scribner's, 1–48.

Carroll, Joseph. 1982. *The Cultural Theory of Matthew Arnold.* Berkeley: University of California Press.

Carson, Rachel. 1962. *Silent Spring.* New York: Fawcett Crest.

Caute, David. 1988. *The Year of the Barricades: A Journey Through 1968.* New York: Harper and Row.

Centre for Contemporary Cultural Studies [CCCS]. 1978. *On Ideology.* London: Hutchinson.

——. 1980. *Culture, Media, Language: Working Papers in Cultural Studies, 1972–79.* London: Hutchinson/CCCS.

——. 1982. *The Empire Strikes Back: Race and Racism in 70s Britain.* London: Hutchinson/CCCS.

Charters, Ann, ed. 1983. *The Beats: Literary Bohemians in Postwar America,* 2 vols. Volume 16 of *Dictionary of Literary Biography.* Detroit: Gale Research.

——, ed. 1992. *The Portable Beat Reader.* New York: Penguin.

Chen, Kuan-Hsing, ed. 1998. *Trajectories: Inter-Asia Cultural Studies.* New York: Routledge.

Cheney, Lynne. 1988. *Humanities in America: A Report to the President, the Congress, and the American People*. Washington, DC: National Endowment for the Humanities.

Cheyette, Bryan. 1993. *Constructions of "The Jew" in English Literature and Society: Racial Representations, 1875–1945*. Cambridge, England: Cambridge University Press.

Chrisman, Laura. 1996. "Appropriate Appropriations? Developing Cultural Studies in South Africa." In *Transgressing Boundaries: New Directions in the Study of Culture in Africa*. Edited by Brenda Cooper and Andrew Steyn. Athens: Ohio University Press, 184–95.

Chun, Lin. 1993. *The British New Left*. Edinburgh: University of Edinburgh Press.

Clark, Stuart. 1985. "The *Annales* Historians." In *The Return of Grand Theory in the Human Sciences*. Edited by Quentin Skinner. Cambridge, England: Cambridge University Press.

Clarke, John, Chas Critcher, and Richard Johnson, eds. 1979. *Working-Class Culture: Studies in History and Theory*. London: Hutchinson/CCCS.

Clarke, Simon. 1980. "Althusserian Marxism." In *One-Dimensional Marxism: Althusser and the Politics of Culture*. By Simon Clarke et al. New York: Allison and Busby, 7–102.

Cline, Catherine Ann. 1976. Review of *Paper Voices*, by A. C. H. Smith et al. *American Historical Review* 81, no. 4 (October): 865.

Clowse, Barbara Barksdale. 1981. *Brainpower for the Cold War: The Sputnik Crisis and National Defense Education Act of 1958*. Westport, CT: Greenwood Press.

Coates, Ken. 1976. "How Not to Reappraise the New Left." In *The Socialist Register: 1976*. Edited by Ralph Miliband and John Saville. London: Merlin Press, 111–27.

Cockburn, Alexander, and Robin Blackburn, eds. 1969. *Student Power: Problems, Diagnosis, Action*. Baltimore: Penguin.

Cockcroft, Eva. [1974] 1992. "Abstract Expressionism, Weapon of the Cold War." In *Art in Modern Culture: An Anthology of Critical Texts*. Edited by Francis Frascina and Jonathan Harris. New York: HarperCollins.

Cohen, Percy S. 1985. "Functional Analysis." In *The Social Science Encyclopedia*. Edited by Adam Kuper and Jessica Kuper. New York: Routledge.

Cohen, Phil. [1972] 1980. "Subcultural Conflict and Working-Class Community." In *Culture, Media, Language: Working Papers in Cultural Studies*. Collected by CCCS. London: Huchinson/CCCS, 78–87.

Cohen, Stanley, and Jock Young, eds. 1973. *The Manufacture of News: A Reader*. Beverly Hills: Sage.

——, eds. 1981. *The Manufacture of News: Social Problems, Deviance and the Mass Media*. Revised ed. Beverly Hills: Sage.

Commonwealth Universities Yearbook 1994: A Directory of the Universities of the Commonwealth and the Handbook of Their Association. London: Association of Commonwealth Universities.

Connell, W. F. [1950] 1971. *The Educational Thought and Influence of Matthew Arnold*. Introduction by Fred Clark. Westport, CT: Greenwood Press.

Cooper, Brenda, and Andrew Steyn. 1996a. Introduction to *Transgressing the Boundaries: New Directions in the Study of Culture in South Africa*. Edited by Brenda Cooper and Andrew Steyn. Athens: Ohio University Press, 7–12.

——, eds. 1996b. *Transgressing the Boundaries: New Directions in the Study of Culture in South Africa*. Athens: Ohio University Press.

Coplan, David. 1994. *In the Time of Cannibals: The Word Music of the Basotho People of South Africa*. Chicago: University of Chicago Press.

Corner, John. 1991. "Studying Culture: Reflections and Assessments. An interview with Richard Hoggart." *Media, Culture and Society* 13, no. 2 (April): 137–52.

Corrigan, Philip. 1978. Review of *Learning to Labour: How Working Class Kids Get Working Class Jobs*, by Paul E. Willis. *Sociological Review* 26, no. 3 (August): 653–55.

Court, Franklin E. 1992. *Institutionalizing English Literature: The Culture and Politics of Literary Study, 1750–1900*. Stanford: Stanford University Press.

Coward, Rosalind, and John Ellis. 1977. *Language and Materialism: Developments in Semiology and the Theory of the Subject*. New York: Routledge and Kegan Paul.

Cowling, Maurice. 1967. *1867: Disraeli, Gladstone and Revolution: The Passing of the Second Reform Bill*. London: Cambridge University Press.

Cranston, Maurice. 1959. Review of *Culture and Society*, by Raymond Williams. *London Magazine* 6, no. 5 (May): 60–62.

Craton, Michael. 1982. *Testing the Chains: Resistance to Slavery in the British West Indies*. Ithaca: Cornell University Press.

Cruise O'Brien, Donal. 1972. "Modernization, Order, and the Erosion of a Democratic Ideal: American Political Science 1960–70." *Journal of Development Studies* 8, no. 4 (July): 351–78.

Cunningham, Stuart. 1991. "Cultural Studies from the Viewpoint of Cultural Policy." *Meanjin* 50, nos. 2–3 (winter–spring): 423–36.

——. 1992. "TV Violence: The Challenge of Public Policy for Cultural Studies." *Cultural Studies* 6, no. 1 (January): 97–115.

Curran, Charles. 1956. "The Passing of the Tribunes." *Encounter* 6, no. 6 (June): 17–21.

Czitrom, Daniel. 2002. "Does Cultural Studies Have a Past?" In *American Cultural Studies*. Edited by Catherine A. Warren and Mary Douglas Vavrus. Urbana: University of Illinois Press, 13–22.

Dahl, Robert A. 1963. *Modern Political Analysis*. Englewood Cliffs, NJ: Prentice-Hall.

Dandurand, Renée. 1989. "Fortunes and Misfortunes of Culture: Sociology and Anthropology of Culture in Francophone Quebec, 1965–1985." *Canadian Review of Sociology and Anthropology/ La Revue canadienne de Sociologie et d'Anthropologie* 26, no. 3 (May): 485–532.

Danto, Arthur C. 1965. *Analytical Philosophy of History*. London: Cambridge University Press.

Davies, Ioan. 1995. *Cultural Studies and Beyond: Fragments of Empire*. New York: Routledge.

Davies, Paul, ed. 1989. *The New Physics*. Cambridge, England: Cambridge University Press.

De Bolla, Peter. 1986. "Disfiguring History." *Diacritics* 16, no. 4 (winter): 49–58.

Dellinger, David. 1982. "The Antinuclear Movement." In *Nuclear Power: Both Sides. The Best Arguments for and against the Most Controversial Technology*. Edited by Michio Kaku and Jennifer Trainer. New York: Norton.

De Micheli, Mario. [1959] 1966. *Le avanguardie artistiche del Novecento*. Milano: Feltrinelli.

Denzin, Norman K. 1991. *Images of Postmodern Society*. London: Sage.

——. 1992. *Symbolic Interactionism and Cultural Studies: The Politics of Interpretation*. Cambridge, MA: Blackwell.

Derrida, Jacques. 1972. "Structure, Sign, and Play in the Discourse of the Human Sciences." In *The Structuralist Controversy: The Languages of Criticism and the Sciences of Man*. Edited by Richard Macksey and Eugenio Donato. Baltimore: Johns Hopkins University Press.

——. [1972] 1982. "The Ends of Man." In *Margins of Philosophy*. Translated, with additional notes, by Alan Bass. Chicago: University of Chicago Press.

Descartes, René. [1637] 1980. *Discourse on Method and Meditations on First Philosophy.* Translated by Donald A. Cress. Indianapolis: Hackett.

Deutsch, Karl W., Andrei S. Markovits, and John Platt, eds. 1986. *Advances in the Social Sciences, 1900–1980.* Lanham, MD: University Press of America.

Devall, Bill, and George Sessions. 1985. *Deep Ecology: Living As If Nature Mattered.* Salt Lake City: Gibbs Smith.

Diamond, Sigmund. 1992. *Compromised Campus: The Collaboration of Universities with the Intelligence Community, 1945–1955.* New York: Oxford University Press.

Dienst, Richard. 1990. "Cultural Studies—Now and in the Future: University of Illinois Champaign-Urbana 5 April–9 April 1990." *Screen* 31, no. 3 (autumn): 328–31.

Dilthey, Wilhelm. [1883] 1988. *Introduction to the Human Sciences: An Attempt to Lay a Foundation for the Study of Society and History.* Translated and with an introductory essay by Ramon J. Betanzos. Detroit: Wayne State University Press.

Diop, Alioune. 1947. "Niam n'goura ou les raisons d'etre de *Présence Africaine.*" *Présence Africaine* 1 (November–December): 7–14.

Dosse, François. 1987. *L'histoire en miettes: Des "Annales" à la "nouvelle histoire."* Paris: Éditions La Découverte.

——. 1997. *History of Structuralism: The Rising Sign, 1945–1966.* Translated by Deborah Glassman. Minneapolis: University of Minnesota Press.

Doyle, Brian. 1982. "The Hidden History of English Studies." In *Re-Reading English.* Edited by Peter Widdowson. London: Methuen, 17–31.

Driver, Christopher. 1964. *The Disarmers: A Study in Protest.* London: Hodder and Stoughton.

Duff, Peggy. 1971. *Left, Left, Left: A Personal Account of Six Protest Campaigns 1945–65.* London: Allison and Busby.

During, Simon, ed. 1993. *The Cultural Studies Reader.* New York: Routledge.

Dworkin, Dennis. 1997. *Cultural Marxism in Postwar Britain: History, the New Left, and the Origins of Cultural Studies.* Durham, NC: Duke University Press.

Eagleton, Terry. 1983. *Literary Theory: An Introduction.* Minneapolis: University of Minnesota Press.

Easthope, Antony. 1988. *British Post-Structuralism: Since 1968.* London: Routledge.

Edgar, David. 1987. "Racism and Patriotism: Should the Left Be Trying to Recapture the Idea of 'One Nation'?" Review of *There Ain't No Black in the Union Jack,* by Paul Gilroy. *The Listener* 117, no. 4 (June): 44–45.

Editorial. 1957. *Universities and Left Review* 1, no. 1 (spring): i–ii.

——. 1960. *New Left Review* 1: 1–3.

——. 1978. *History Workshop* 6 (autumn): 1–6.

"Editorial: ULR to New Left Review." 1959. *Universities and Left Review* 7 (autumn): 1–2.

Editors of *Lingua Franca.* 2000. *The Sokal Hoax: The Sham That Shook the Academy.* Lincoln: University of Nebraska Press.

Education Group, CCCS. 1981. *Unpopular Education: Schooling and Social Democracy in England Since 1944.* London: Hutchinson/CCCS.

Education Group II. 1991. *Education Limited: Schooling, Training and the New Right in England Since 1979.* London: Unwin Hyman.

Ehrlich, Paul R. 1968. *The Population Bomb.* New York: Sierra Club/Ballantine Books.

Eisenstadt, S. N. 1966. *Modernization: Protest and Change.* Englewood Cliffs, NJ: Prentice-Hall.

——. 1973. *Tradition, Change, and Modernity.* New York: Wiley.

Ekeland, Ivar. 1988. *Mathematics and the Unexpected.* Chicago: University of Chicago Press.

Ermarth, Elizabeth Deeds. 1992. *Sequel to History: Postmodernism and the Crisis of Representational Time.* Princeton: Princeton University Press.

Ermarth, Michael. 1975. "Hayden White: *Metahistory.*" Book review. *American Historical Review* 80, no. 4 (October): 961–63.

Evans, Eric J. 2001. *The Forging of the Modern State: Early Industrial Britain, 1783–1870.* 3d ed. Edinburgh Gate, U.K.: Pearson Education.

Evans, Peter B., and John D. Stephens. 1988. "Development and the World Economy." In *Handbook of Sociology.* Edited by Neil J. Smelser. Beverly Hills: Sage.

Eve, Raymond A., Sara Horsfall, and Mary E. Lee, eds. 1997. *Chaos, Complexity, and Sociology: Myths, Models, and Theories.* Thousand Oaks, CA: Sage.

Farias, Victor. 1989. *Heidegger and Nazism.* Philadelphia: Temple University Press.

Farley, Christopher. 1960. "C.N.D. after the Election II." *New Left Review* 1: 18–19.

Farmer, Doyne, Alan Lapedes, Norman Packard, and Burton Wendroff, eds. 1986. *Evolution, Games and Learning: Models for Adaptation in Machines and Nature. Proceedings of the Fifth Annual International Conference of the Center for Nonlinear Studies, May 20–24, 1985. Physica D: Nonlinear Phenomena,* 22D.

Fawthrop, Tom. 1968. "Hull." *New Left Review* 50 (July–August): 59–64.

Feigenbaum, Mitchell J. 1983. "Universal Behavior in Nonlinear Systems." *Physica D: Nonlinear Phenomena,* 7D: 16–39.

Fekete, John. 1977. *The Critical Twilight: Explorations in the Ideology of Anglo-American Literary Theory from Eliot to McLuhan.* Boston: Routledge and Kegan Paul.

Feldman, Gene, and Max Gartenberg, eds. 1958. *The Beat Generation and the Angry Young Men.* New York: Citadel Press.

Ferguson, John. 1976. *The Open University from Within.* New York: New York University Press.

Ffrench, Patrick. 1995. *The Time of Theory: A History of Tel Quel (1960–1983).* New York: Oxford University Press.

Ffrench, Patrick, and Roland-François Lack. 1998. Introduction to *The Tel Quel Reader.* Edited by Patrick Ffrench and Roland-François Lack. New York: Routledge.

Filmer, Paul. 1977. "Literary Study as Liberal Education and as Sociology in the Work of F. R. Leavis." In *Rationality, Education and the Social Organization of Knowledge: Papers for a Reflexive Sociology of Education.* Edited by Cris Jenks. Boston: Routledge and Kegan Paul, 55–85.

Fischer, Michael. 1985. *Does Deconstruction Make Any Difference? Poststructuralism and the Defense of Poetry in Modern Criticism.* Bloomington: Indiana University Press.

Fiske, John. 1987. *Television Culture.* New York: Routledge.

Fiske, John, Bob Hodge, and Graeme Turner. 1987. *Myths of Oz: Reading Australian Popular Culture.* Boston: Allen and Unwin.

Forbes, Jill, and Michael Kelly, eds. 1995. *French Cultural Studies: An Introduction.* New York: Oxford University Press.

Ford, Joseph. 1989. "What Is Chaos, That We Should Be Mindful of It?" In *The New Physics.* Edited by Paul Davies. New York: Cambridge University Press, 348–72.

Foucault, Michel. 1970. *The Order of Things: An Archaeology of the Human Sciences.* New York: Vintage, 1973.

Frank, Andre Gunder. 1967. "The Sociology of Underdevelopment or the Underdevelopment of Sociology." *Catalyst* 3 (summer): 20–73.

——. 1969. *Latin America: Underdevelopment or Revolution.* New York: Monthly Review Press.

Franklin, Sarah, Celia Lury, and Jackie Stacey. 1991a. "Feminism and Cultural Studies: Pasts, Presents, Futures." *Media, Culture and Society* 13, no. 2 (April): 171–92.

——, eds. 1991b. *Off-Centre: Feminism and Cultural Studies.* London: Harper Collins Academic.

Fraser, Ronald, ed. 1988. *1968: A Student Generation in Revolt.* New York: Pantheon.

Freidson, Eliot. 1958. Review of *The Uses of Literacy,* by Richard Hoggart. *American Journal of Sociology* 64, no. 1 (July): 97–98.

Friedman, Maurice, ed. [1964] 1991. *The Worlds of Existentialism: A Critical Reader.* Atlantic Highlands, NJ: Humanities Press.

Fromm, Erich, ed. [1965] 1966. *Socialist Humanism: An International Symposium.* Garden City, NY: Anchor Books.

Frow, John. 1990. *The Social Production of Knowledge and the Discipline of English.* St. Lucia, Australia: University of Queensland Press.

Frow, John, and Meaghan Morris, eds. 1993. *Australian Cultural Studies: A Reader.* Urbana: University of Illinois Press.

Fryer, Peter. 1984. *Staying Power: Black People in Britain Since 1504.* Atlantic Highlands, NJ: Humanities Press.

——. 1988. *Black People in the British Empire: An Introduction.* London: Pluto Press.

Fuchs, S. 1992. *The Professional Quest for Truth: A Social Theory of Scientific Knowledge.* Albany: State University of New York Press.

Fuchs, Stephan, and Steven Ward. 1994. "What Is Deconstruction, and Where and When Does It Take Place? Making Facts in Science, Building Cases in Law." *American Sociological Review* 59, no. 4 (August): 481–500.

Fuller, R. Buckminster. 1969. *Utopia or Oblivion: The Prospects for Humanity.* New York: Bantam.

Fuller, Steve. 2000. "Science Studies Through the Looking Glass: An Intellectual Itinerary." In *Beyond the Science Wars: The Missing Discourse about Science and Society.* Edited by Ullica Segerstråle. Albany: State University of New York Press, 185–217.

Gallagher, Catherine, and Thomas Laqueur, eds. 1987. *The Making of the Modern Body: Sexuality and Society in the Nineteenth Century.* Berkeley: University of California Press.

Game, Ann. 1991. *Undoing the Social: Towards a Deconstructive Sociology.* Toronto: University of Toronto Press.

Garfinkel, Harold. 1967. *Studies in Ethnomethodology.* Englewood Cliffs, NJ: Prentice-Hall.

Gay, Peter. 1993. *The Cultivation of Hatred.* Vol. 3 of *The Bourgeois Experience: Victoria to Freud.* New York: Norton.

Gearhart, Suzanne. 1987. "History as Criticism: The Dialogue of History and Literature." *Diacritics* 17, no. 3 (fall): 56–65.

Gelder, Ken, and Sarah Thornton, eds. 1997. *The Subcultures Reader.* New York: Routledge.

Geras, Norman. 1972. "Althusser's Marxism." *New Left Review* 71 (January–February): 57–88.

Giere, Ronald N., and Alan W. Richardson, eds. 1996. *Origins of Logical Empiricism.* Minneapolis: University of Minnesota Press.

Gieryn, Tom. 1996. "Policing STS: A Boundary-Work Souvenir from the Smithsonian Exhibition on 'Science in American Life.' " *Science, Technology and Human Values* 21, no. 1 (winter): 100–115.

Gilbert, G. Nigel, and Michael Mulkay. 1984. *Opening Pandora's Box: A Sociological Analysis of Scientists' Discourse*. Cambridge, England: Cambridge University Press.

Gilroy, Paul. 1987. *There Ain't No Black in the Union Jack*. London: Hutchinson.

Ginsberg, Allen. 1995. Prologue to *Beat Culture and the New America: 1950–1965*. New York: Whitney Museum of American Art, 17–19.

Giroux, Henry A. 1992. "Liberal Arts Education and the Struggle for Public Life: Dreaming about Democracy." In *The Politics of Liberal Education*. Edited by Darryl J. Gless and Barbara Herrnstein Smith. Durham, NC: Duke University Press, 119–44.

Glasgow Media Group. 1976. *Bad News*. London: Routledge and Kegan Paul.

——. 1980. *More Bad News*. London: Routledge and Kegan Paul.

——. 1982. *Really Bad News*. London: Writers and Readers.

Glucksmann, André. 1972. "A Ventriloquist Structuralism." *New Left Review* 72 (March–April): 68–92.

Goldstein, Joshua S. 1988. *Long Cycles: Prosperity and War in the Modern Age*. New Haven: Yale University Press.

Gorak, Jan. 1988. *The Alien Mind of Raymond Williams*. Columbia: University of Missouri Press.

Gorz, André. 1980. *Ecology as Politics*. Boston: South End Press.

Gould, Stephen Jay. 1989. *Wonderful Life: The Burgess Shale and the Nature of History*. New York: Norton.

Gould, Stephen J., Norman L. Gilinsky, and Rebecca Z. German. 1987. "Asymmetry of Lineages and the Direction of Evolutionary Time." *Science* 236, no. 4807 (June 12): 1437–41.

Gouldner, Alvin W. 1961. "Anti-Minotaur: The Myth of a Value-free Sociology." *Social Problems* 9, no. 2 (fall): 199–212.

Graff, Gerald. 1970. *Poetic Statement and Critical Dogma*. Evanston, IL: Northwestern University Press.

——. 1979. *Literature against Itself*. Chicago: University of Chicago Press.

——. 1995. "A Paradox of the Culture War." In *PC Wars: Politics and Theory in the Academy*. Edited by Jeffrey Williams. New York: Routledge, 308–12.

Graham, Helen, and Jo Labanyi, eds. 1995. *Spanish Cultural Studies: An Introduction. The Struggle for Modernity*. New York: Oxford University Press.

Gramsci, Antonio. 1971. *Selections from the Prison Notebooks*. Edited and translated by Quintin Hoare and Goeffrey Nowell-Smith. New York: International Publishers.

Grathwohl, Larry. 1976. *Bringing Down America: An FBI Informer with the Weathermen*. New Rochelle, NY: Arlington House.

Gray, David J. 1968. "Value-free Sociology: A Doctrine of Hypocrisy and Irresponsibility." *Sociological Quarterly* 9, no. 1 (winter): 176–85.

Green, Jonathon. 1988. *Days in the Life: Voices from the English Underground, 1961–1971*. London: Heinemann.

Green, T. H. [1881] 1964. "Liberal Legislation and Freedom of Contract." In *The Political Theory of T. H. Green: Selected Writings*. Edited by John R. Rodman. New York: Appleton-Century-Crofts, 43–73.

Greenberg, Clement. 1948. "Irrelevance versus Irresponsibility." *Partisan Review* 15, no. 5 (May): 573–79.

Greenberg, D. S. 1967. *The Politics of Pure Science*. New York: New American Library.

Gross, Paul R. 1996. "Reply to Tom Gieryn." *Science, Technology and Human Values* 21, no. 1 (winter): 116–20.

Gross, Paul R., and Norman Levitt. 1994. *Higher Superstition: The Academic Left and Its Quarrels with Science.* Baltimore: Johns Hopkins University Press.

Gross, Paul R., Norman Levitt, and Martin W. Lewis, eds. 1996. *The Flight from Science and Reason.* New York: New York Academy of Sciences.

Grossberg, Lawrence. 1985. "Stuart Hall." In *The Biographical Dictionary of Neo-Marxism.* Edited by Robert Gorman. Westport, CT: Greenwood, 197–200.

Grossberg, Lawrence, Cary Nelson, and Paula Treichler. 1992. *Cultural Studies.* New York: Routledge.

Grossberg, Lawrence, and Janice Radway. 1992. "Editorial Comment." *Cultural Studies* 6, no. 2 (May): ii–iii.

Gulbenkian Commission on the Restructuring of the Social Sciences. 1996. *Open the Social Sciences: Report of the Gulbenkian Commission on the Restructuring of the Social Sciences.* Stanford: Stanford University Press.

Gurwitsch, Aron. 1966. *Studies in Phenomenology and Psychology.* Evanston, IL: Northwestern University Press.

——. 1974. *Phenomenology and the Theory of Science.* Evanston, IL: Northwestern University Press.

Hagendijk, R. 1990. "Structuration Theory, Constructivism, and Scientific Change." In *Theories of Science in Society.* Edited by S. E. Cozzens and T. F. Gieryn. Bloomington: Indiana University Press, 43–66.

Hahn, Roger. 1967. *Laplace as a Newtonian Scientist.* Los Angeles: Clark Memorial Library, UCLA.

Hall, Catherine. 1989. "The Economy of Intellectual Prestige: Thomas Carlyle, John Stuart Mill, and the Case of Governor Eyre." *Cultural Critique* 12 (spring): 167–96.

Hall, Stuart. 1958a. "Inside the Whale Again?" *Universities and Left Review* 4 (summer): 14–15.

——. 1958b. "A Sense of Classlessness." *Universities and Left Review* 5 (autumn): 26–32.

——. 1963. "The Cuban Crisis: Trial Run or Steps towards Peace." *War and Peace* 1, no. 1 (January): 2–16.

——. 1971. Introduction. *Working Papers in Cultural Studies* 1 (spring): 5–7.

——. 1979. "The Great Moving Right Show." *Marxism Today* (January): 14–20.

——. 1980a. "Cultural Studies and the Centre: Some Problematics and Problems." In *Culture, Media, Language: Working Papers in Cultural Studies, 1972–79.* Edited by Stuart Hall, Dorothy Hobson, Andrew Lowe, and Paul Willis. London: Hutchinson.

——. 1980b. "Cultural Studies: Two Paradigms." *Media, Culture and Society* 2: 57–72.

——. 1980c. "Race, Articulation and Societies Structured in Dominance." In *Sociological Theories: Race and Colonialism.* Paris: UNESCO, 305–45.

——. 1980d. "Theory and Experience 1." *New Statesman* 99, no. 2567 (May 30): 818–19.

——. 1982. "The Rediscovery of Ideology." In *Culture, Society and the Media.* Edited by M. Gurevitch et al. London: Methuen.

——. 1985a. "Authoritarian Populism: A Reply to Jessop et al." *New Left Review* 151 (May–June): 115–24.

——. 1985b. "Signification, Representation, Ideology: Althusser and the Post-Structuralist Debates." *Critical Studies in Mass Communication* 2, no. 2 (June): 91–114.

——. 1986. "On Postmodernism and Articulation: An Interview with Stuart Hall." Edited by Lawrence Grossberg. *Journal of Communication Inquiry* 10, no. 2: 45–60.

——. 1989. "The 'First' New Left: Life and Times." In *Out of Apathy: Voices of the New Left Thirty Years On*. Edited by Robin Archer, Diemut Bubeck, Hanjo Glock, Lesley Jacobs, Seth Moglen, Adam Steinhouse, and Daniel Weinstock. New York: Verso, 11–38.

——. 1990. "The Emergence of Cultural Studies and the Crisis of the Humanities." *October* 53 (summer): 11–23.

——. 1992. "Cultural Studies and Its Theoretical Legacies." In *Cultural Studies*. Edited by Lawrence Grossberg, Cary Nelson, and Paula Treichler. New York: Routledge, 277–94.

——. 1996a. "The Formation of a Diasporic Intellectual: An Interview with Stuart Hall by Kuan-Hsing Chen." In *Stuart Hall: Critical Dialogues in Cultural Studies*. Edited by David Morley and Kuan-Hsing Chen. London: Routledge, 484–503.

——. 1996b. "What Is This 'Black' in Black Popular Culture?" In *Stuart Hall: Critical Dialogues in Cultural Studies*. Edited by David Morley and Kuan-Hsing Chen. New York: Routledge, 465–75.

Hall, Stuart, Ian Connell, and Lidia Curti. 1981. "The 'Unity' of Current Affairs Television." In *Popular Television and Film: A Reader*. Edited by Tony Bennett, Susan Boyd-Bowman, Colin Mercer, and Janet Woollacott. London: British Film Institute.

Hall, Stuart, Chas Critcher, Tony Jefferson, John Clarke, and Brian Roberts. 1978. *Policing the Crisis: Mugging, the State, and Law and Order*. New York: Holmes and Meier.

Hall, Stuart, and Martin Jacques, eds. 1983. *The Politics of Thatcherism*. London: Lawrence and Wishart.

Hall, Stuart, and Tony Jefferson, eds. 1976. *Resistance through Rituals: Youth Subcultures in Post-War Britain*. London: Hutchinson/cccs.

Hall, Stuart, and Paddy Whannel. 1964. *The Popular Arts*. London: Hutchinson, 1965.

Halliday, Fred. 1969. "Students of the World Unite." In *Student Power*. Edited by Alexander Cockburn and Robin Blackburn. Baltimore: Penguin, 287–326.

Hamilton, Carolyn. 1998. *Terrific Majesty: The Powers of Shaka Zulu and the Limits of Historical Invention*. Cambridge, MA: Harvard University Press.

Hanfling, Oswald. 1981. *Logical Positivism*. New York: Columbia University Press.

Harding, Sandra. 1992. "Why Physics Is a Bad Model for Physics." In *The End of Science: Attack and Defense*. Edited by Richard Q. Elvee. Lanham, MD: University Press of America, 1–21.

Harp, John. 1991. "Political Economy/Cultural Studies: Exploring Points of Convergence." *Canadian Review of Sociology and Anthropology/La Revue canadienne de Sociologie et d'Anthropologie* 28, no. 2 (May): 206–24.

Hartley, John. 1992. "Expatriation: Useful Astonishment as Cultural Studies." *Cultural Studies* 6, no. 3 (October): 449–67.

Harvey, David L., and Michael Reed. 1996. "Social Science as the Study of Complex Systems." In *Chaos Theory in the Social Sciences: Foundations and Applications*. Edited by L. Douglas Kiel and Euel Elliott. Ann Arbor: University of Michigan Press, 295–323.

Harvie, Christopher. 1988. "Revolution and the Rule of Law." In *The Oxford History of Britain*. Edited by Kenneth O. Morgan. New York: Oxford University Press, 470–517.

Hauser, Philip M. 1981. "Sociology's Progress toward Science." *American Sociologist* 16 (February): 62–64.

Hebdige, Dick. 1979. *Subculture: The Meaning of Style.* London: Methuen.

Heffer, Simon. 1995. *Moral Desperado: A Life of Thomas Carlyle.* London: Weidenfeld and Nicolson.

Heinemann, Margot. 1976. "1956 and the Communist Party." In *The Socialist Register: 1976.* Edited by Ralph Miliband and John Saville. London: Merlin Press, 43–57.

Hénaff, Marcel. 1998. *Claude Lévi-Strauss and the Making of Structural Anthropology.* Translated by Mary Baker. Minneapolis: University of Minnesota Press.

Heuman, Gad. 1994. *"The Killing Time": The Morant Bay Rebellion in Jamaica.* Knoxville: University of Tennessee Press.

Higgins, John. 1999. *Raymond Williams: Literature, Marxism and Culural Materialism.* New York: Routledge.

Hills, John, John Ditch, and Howard Glennerster, eds. 1994. *Beveridge and Social Security: An International Retrospective.* Oxford: Clarendon Press.

Hobsbawm, E. J. [1968] 1969. *Industry and Empire: From 1750 to the Present Day. The Pelican Economic History of Britain, Volume 3.* New York: Penguin.

——. 1978. "The Historians' Group of the Communist Party." In *Rebels and Their Causes: Essays in Honour of A. L. Morton.* Edited by Maurice Cornforth. London: Lawrence and Wishart, 21–47.

Hobson, Dorothy. 1982. *Crossroads: The Drama of a Soap Opera.* London: Methuen.

Hoggart, Richard. 1958. "A Sense of Occasion." In *Conviction.* Edited by N. Mackenzie. London: MacGibbon and Kee.

——. 1961. *The Uses of Literacy: Changing Patterns in English Mass Culture.* Boston: Essential Books.

——. 1966. "Literature and Society." In *A Guide to the Social Sciences.* Edited by Norman MacKenzie. New York: New American Library.

——. [1957] 1967. *The Uses of Literacy: Aspects of Working-class Life, with Special References to Publications and Entertainments.* London: Chatto and Windus.

——. [1969] 1970a. "Contemporary Cultural Studies: An Approach to the Study of Literature and Society." In *Contemporary Criticism.* Stratford-upon-Avon Studies 12. London: Edward Arnold. First published as CCCS Occasional Paper No. 6.

——. [1963] 1970b. "Schools of English and Contemporary Society." In *About Literature.* Vol 2 of *Speaking to Each Other: Essays by Richard Hoggart.* New York: Oxford University Press.

——. [1970] 1982. "Allen Lane and Penguins." In *An English Temper: Essays on Education, Culture and Communications.* London: Chatto and Windus.

——. 1992. *An Imagined Life.* Vol. 3: 1959–91, of *Life and Times.* London: Chatto and Windus.

Hollowell, John. 1977. *Fact and Fiction: The New Journalism and the Nonfiction Novel.* Chapel Hill: University of North Carolina Press.

Holt, Thomas C. 1992. *The Problem of Freedom: Race, Labor, and Politics in Jamaica and Britain, 1832–1938.* Baltimore: Johns Hopkins University Press.

Holton, Gerald. 1993. *Science and Anti-Science.* Cambridge, MA: Harvard University Press.

Honan, Park. 1981. *Matthew Arnold: A Life.* Cambridge, MA: Harvard University Press.

Honey, J. R. de S. 1977. *Tom Brown's Universe: The Development of the English Public School in the Nineteenth Century.* New York: Quadrangle/New York Times Book Co.

Hopkins, Terence K. 1990. "Note on the Concept of Hegemony." *Review* 13, no. 3 (summer): 409–11.

Hopkins, Terence K., and Immanuel Wallerstein, eds. 1980. *Processes of the World-System.* Beverly Hills: Sage.

Hopkins, Terence K., and Immanuel Wallerstein, with the Research Working Group on Cyclical

Rhythms and Secular Trends. 1979. "Cyclical Rhythms and Secular Trends of the Capitalist World-Economy: Some Premises, Hypotheses and Questions." *Review* 2, no. 4 (spring): 483–500.

Hopkins, Terence K., et al. 1982. *World-Systems Analysis: Theory and Methodology.* Beverly Hills: Sage.

———. 1996. *Age of Transition: Trajectory of the World-System, 1945–2025.* London: Zed Press.

Hoskyns, Barney. 1997. *Beneath the Diamond Sky: Haight-Ashbury, 1965–1970.* New York: Simon and Schuster.

Howell, George. 1972. *A History of the Working Men's Association from 1836–1850.* Newcastle-upon-Tyne, England: Graham.

Hoyles, John. 1982. "Radical Critical Theory and English." In *Re-Reading English.* Edited by Peter Widdowson. New York: Methuen, 44–60.

Hull, Gloria T., Patricia Bell Scott, and Barbara Smith. 1982. *All the Women Are White, All the Blacks Are Men, But Some of Us Are Brave: Black Women's Studies.* Old Westbury, NY: Feminist Press.

Hunt, Lynn. 1986. "French History in the Last Twenty Years: The Rise and Fall of the *Annales* Paradigm." *Journal of Contemporary History* 21 (April): 209–24.

Hunter, James Davison. 1991. *Culture Wars: The Struggle to Define America.* New York: Basic Books.

Huntington, Samuel P. 1968. *Political Order in Changing Societies.* New Haven: Yale University Press.

Huxley, Thomas H. [1881] 1968. "Science and Culture." In *Science and Education.* Vol. 3 of *Collected Essays.* New York: Greenwood Press, 134–59.

Inglis, Fred. 1991. *The Cruel Peace: Everyday Life and the Cold War.* New York: Basic Books.

———. 1993. *Cultural Studies.* Cambridge, MA: Blackwell.

———. 1995. *Raymond Williams.* New York: Routledge.

Isserman, Maurice. 1987. *If I Had a Hammer . . . The Death of the Old Left and the Birth of the New Left.* New York: Basic Books.

Jack, Belinda Elizabeth. 1996. *Negritude and Literary Criticism: The History and Theory of "Negro-African" Literature in French.* Westport, CT: Greenwood Press.

Jameson, Fredric. 1972. *The Prison-House of Language: A Critical Account of Structuralism and Russian Formalism.* Princeton: Princeton University Press.

Jamison, Andrew. 2001. *The Making of Green Knowledge: Environmental Politics and Cultural Transformation.* New York: Cambridge University Press.

Jancovich, Mark. 1993. *The Cultural Politics of the New Criticism.* New York: Cambridge University Press.

Jantsch, Eric, ed. 1981. *The Evolutionary Vision: Toward a Unifying Paradigm of Physical, Biological, and Sociocultural Evolution.* Boulder, CO: Westview Press.

Jay, Gregory S. 1997. *American Literature and the Culture Wars.* Ithaca: Cornell University Press.

Jencks, Charles. 1989. *What Is Post-Modernism?* 3d revised and enlarged ed. New York: St. Martin's Press.

Jessop, Bob, Kevin Bonnett, Simon Bromley, and Tom Ling. 1984. "Authoritarian Populism, Two Nations, and Thatcherism." *New Left Review* 147 (September–October): 32–60.

———. 1985. "Thatcherism and the Politics of Hegemony: A Reply to Stuart Hall." *New Left Review* 153 (September–October): 87–101.

Johnson, Richard. 1978. "Thompson, Genovese, and Socialist-Humanist History." *History Workshop* 6 (autumn): 79–100.

——. 1979. "Histories of Culture/Theories of Ideology: Notes on an Impasse." In *Ideology and Cultural Production*. Edited by Michèle Barrett, Philip Corrigan, Annette Kuhn, and Janet Wolff. New York: St. Martin's Press, 49–77.

Johnson, Richard, Gregor McLennan, Bill Schwarz, and David Sutton, eds. 1982. *Making Histories: Studies in History-Writing and Politics*. London: Hutchinson/cccs.

Johnson, Stanley P., ed. 1993. *The Earth Summit: The United Nations Conference on Environment and Development* UNCED. Boston: Graham and Trotman/Martinus Nijhoff.

Jones, Donald K. 1977. *The Making of the Education System 1851–81*. Students Library of Education. Boston: Routledge and Kegan Paul.

Jones, Mervyn. 1957. "Discussion: Socialism and the Intellectuals—One." *Universities and Left Review* 1, no. 2 (summer): 15–17.

——. 1976. "Days of Tragedy and Farce." In *The Socialist Register: 1976*. Edited by Ralph Miliband and John Saville. London: Merlin Press, 67–88.

Jordan, Barry, and Rikki Morgan-Tamosunas, eds. 2000. *Contemporary Spanish Cultural Studies*. London: Arnold.

Kaufmann, Walter, ed. 1975. *Existentialism: From Dostoevsky to Sartre*. Revised and expanded ed. New York: Meridian.

Kauppi, Niilo. 1994. *The Making of an Avant-Garde: Tel Quel*. New York: Mouton de Gruyter.

Kaye, Harvey J. 1984. *The British Marxist Historians*. Oxford: Polity Press.

——. 1990. "E. P. Thompson, the British Marxist Historical Tradition and the Contemporary Crisis." In *E. P. Thompson: Critical Perspectives*. Edited by Harvey J. Kaye and Keith McClelland. Philadelphia: Temple University Press, 252–75.

Kaye, Harvey J., and Keith McClelland, eds. 1990. *E. P. Thompson: Critical Perspectives*. Philadelphia: Temple University Press.

Keller, Evelyn Fox. 1982. "Feminism and Science." *Signs* 7: 589–602.

Kelly, Catriona, and David Shepherd, eds. 1998. *Russian Cultural Studies: An Introduction*. New York: Oxford University Press.

Kermode, Frank. 1964. *Romantic Image*. New York: Random House.

Kiel, L. Douglas, and Euel Elliott, eds. 1996. *Chaos Theory in the Social Sciences: Foundations and Applications*. Ann Arbor: University of Michigan Press.

King, Alexander, and Bertrand Schneider. 1991. *The First Global Revolution: A Report by the Council of the Club of Rome*. New York: Pantheon.

Kinser, Samuel. 1981. "*Annaliste* Paradigm? The Geohistorical Structuralism of Fernand Braudel." *American Historical Review* 86, no. 1 (February): 63–105.

Kitchener, Richard F. 1988. "Introduction: The World View of Contemporary Physics: Does It Need a New Metaphysics?" In *The World View of Contemporary Physics*. Edited by Richard F. Kitchener. Albany: State University of New York Press.

Kitcher, Philip. 1982. *Abusing Science: The Case against Creationism*. Cambridge, MA: MIT Press.

Klausner, Samuel Z., and Victor M. Lidz. 1986. *The Nationalization of the Social Sciences*. Philadelphia: University of Pennsylvania Press.

Knorr-Cetina, Karin. 1981. *The Manufacture of Knowledge: An Essay on the Constructivist and Contextual Nature of Science*. New York: Pergamon.

——. 1993. "Strong Constructivism—from a Sociologist's Point of View: A Personal Addendum to Sismondo's Paper." *Social Studies of Science* 23: 555–63.

Kolakowski, Lesek. 1974. *Husserl and the Search for Certitude*. New Haven: Yale University Press.

Koyré, Alexander. 1957. *From the Closed World to the Infinite Universe*. Baltimore: Johns Hopkins University Press.

Krieger, Murray. 1956. *The New Apologists for Poetry*. Minneapolis: University of Minnesota Press.

Labinger, Jay A., and Harry Collins, eds. 2001. *The One Culture? A Conversation about Science*. Chicago: University of Chicago Press.

Laing, Stuart. 1986. *Representations of Working-Class Life: 1957–1964*. London: Macmillan.

Lamy, Paul. 1976. "The Globalization of American Sociology: Excellence or Imperialism." *American Sociologist* 11, no. 2 (May): 104–14.

Langan, Mary, and Bill Schwarz, eds. 1985. *Crisis in the British State, 1880–1930*. London: Hutchinson/CCCS.

Latour, Bruno, and Steve Woolgar. 1986/1979. *Laboratory Life: The Construction of Scientific Facts*. 2d ed. Princeton: Princeton University Press.

Laudan, L. 1981. "The Pseudo-Science of Science." *Philosophy of the Social Sciences* 11: 173–98.

Lauter, Paul. 1995. " 'Political Correctness' and the Attack on American Colleges." In *Higher Education Under Fire: Politics, Economics, and the Crisis of the Humanities*. Edited by Michael Bérubé and Cary Nelson. New York: Routledge, 73–90.

Lazarsfeld, Paul F. 1982. *The Varied Sociology of Paul F. Lazarsfeld*. Edited by Patricia L. Kendall. New York: Columbia University Press.

Leavis, F. R. 1962. *Two Cultures? The Significance of C. P. Snow*. New York: Pantheon.

——. [1963] 1986. "*Scrutiny*: A Retrospect." In *Valuation in Criticism and Other Essays*, by F. R. Leavis. Edited by G. Singh. New York: Cambridge University Press.

Leavis, F. R., and Denys Thompson. 1933. *Culture and Environment*. London: Chatto and Windus.

Lee, Richard. 1992. "Readings in the 'New Science' ": A Selective Annotated Bibliography." *Review* 15, no. 1 (winter): 113–71.

——. 1996. "Structures of Knowledge." In *The Age of Transition: Trajectory of the World-System, 1945–2025*. By Terence K. Hopkins et al. London: Zed Press, 178–206.

Lee, Richard E. 2003. "The 'Third' Arena: Trends and Logistics in the Geoculture of the Modern World-System." *Emerging Issues in the 21st Century World-System*. Edited by Wilma A. Dunaway. Westport, CT: Greenwood, 120–27.

Le Hir, Marie-Pierre, and Dana Strand, eds. 2000. *French Cultural Studies: Criticism at the Crossroads*. Albany: State University of New York Press.

Lehman, David. 1991. *Signs of the Times: Deconstruction and the Fall of Paul de Man*. New York: Poseidon Press.

Lemke, James, David Shevach, and Richard H. Wells. 1984. "The Humanism-Positivism Debate in Sociology: A Comment on Tibbetts's Reconsideration." *Sociological Inquiry* 54, no. 1 (winter): 89–97.

Lentricchia, Frank. 1980. *After the New Criticism*. Chicago: University of Chicago Press.

Leopold, Aldo. [1949] 1970. *Sand County Almanac*. New York: Sierra Club/Ballantine.

Lepenies, Wolf. 1988. *Between Literature and Science: The Rise of Sociology*. Translated by R. J. Hollingdale. New York: Cambridge University Press.

"Letter to Our Readers." 1959. *The New Reasoner* 10 (fall): 128–35.

Lévi-Strauss, Claude. 1963. *Structural Anthropology*. Translated by Claire Jacobson and Brooke Grundfest Schoepf. New York: Basic Books.

Lewis, Gordon K. 1978. *Slavery, Imperialism, and Freedom: Studies in English Radical Thought.* New York: Monthly Review Press.

Leys, Colin. 1982. "Samuel Huntington and the End of Classical Modernization Theory." In *Introduction to the Sociology of "Developing Societies."* Edited by Hamza Alavi and Teodor Shanin. New York: Monthly Review Press.

Li, Tien-Yien, and James A. Yorke. 1975. "Period Three Implies Chaos." *American Mathematical Monthly* 82, no. 10 (December): 985–92.

Lighthill, Sir James. 1986. "The Recently Recognized Failure of Predictability in Newtonian Dynamics." *Proceedings of the Royal Society of London* 407, no. 1832 (September 8): 35–48.

Linebaugh, Peter. 1992. *London Hanged: Crime and Civil Society in the Eighteenth Century.* Cambridge, England: Cambridge University Press.

Linebaugh, Peter, and Marcus Rediker. 1990. "The Many-Headed Hydra: Sailors, Slaves, and the Atlantic Working Class in the Eighteenth Century." *Journal of Historical Sociology* 3, no. 3 (September): 225–52.

Linenthal, Edward T., and Tom Engelhardt. 1996. *History Wars: The Enola Gay and Other Battles for the American Past.* New York: Metropolitan Books.

Lombardo, Patrizia. 1992. "Cultural Studies and Interdisciplinarity." *Critical Quarterly* 34, no. 3 (autumn): 3–10.

Lorenz, Edward N. 1963a. "Deterministic Nonperiodic Flow." *Journal of the Atmospheric Sciences* 20, no. 2 (March): 130–41.

——. 1963b. "The Mechanics of Vacillation." *Journal of the Atmospheric Sciences* 20, no. 5 (September): 448–64.

——. 1964. "The Problem of Deducing the Climate from the Governing Equations." *Tellus* 16, no. 1 (February): 1–11.

Lynch, Michael. 1985. *Art and Artifact in Laboratory Science.* London: Routledge.

MacCabe, Colin. 1985. *Theoretical Essays: Film, Linguistics, Literature.* Manchester, England: Manchester University Press.

——. 1992a. "Cultural Studies and English." *Critical Quarterly* 34, no. 3 (autumn): 1–2.

——. 1992b. Editorial. *Critical Quarterly* 34, no. 3 (autumn): 1–2.

MacEwen, Malcolm. 1976. "The Day the Party Had to Stop." In *The Socialist Register: 1976.* Edited by Ralph Miliband and John Saville. London: Merlin Press, 24–42.

Mackenzie, Norman, ed. 1958. *Conviction.* London: MacGibbon and Kee.

Macksey, Richard, and Eugenio Donato, eds. 1972. *The Structuralist Controversy: The Languages of Criticism and the Sciences of Man.* Baltimore: Johns Hopkins University Press.

Macquarrie, John. [1972] 1973. *Existentialism.* New York: Penguin.

Makkreel, Rudolf A. 1992. *Dilthey: Philosopher of the Human Studies.* Princeton: Princeton University Press.

Mamdani, Mahmood. 1996. *Citizen and Subject: Contemporary Africa and the Legacy of Late Colonialism.* Princeton: Princeton University Press.

"Man in the News: A Fountain of New Socialist Ideas." 1961. *Times* (London), March 25.

Mandelbrot, Benoit B. 1983. *The Fractal Geometry of Nature.* New York: W. H. Freeman.

Marcus, George E. 1986. "Contemporary Problems of Ethnography in the Modern World-System." In *Writing Culture: The Poetics and Politics of Ethnography.* Edited by James Clifford and George E. Marcus. Berkeley: University of California Press, 164–93.

Martin, Brian. 1996. "Social Construction of an 'Attack on Science.'" *Social Studies of Science* 26: 161–73.

Masilela, Ntongela. 1988. "Preface: Establishing an Intellectual Bridgehead." In *Rethinking Culture*. Edited by Keyan G. Tomaselli. Bellville, South Africa: Anthropos, 1–4.

Matthew, H. C. G. 1988. "The Liberal Age (1851–1914)." In *The Oxford History of Britain*. Edited by Kenneth O. Morgan. New York: Oxford University Press, 518–81.

May, Lary. 1990. "The Politics of Consumption: The Screen Actor's Guild, Ronald Reagan, and the Hollywood Red Scare." In *Reconstructing Modernism: Art in New York, Paris, and Montreal 1945–1964*. Edited by Serge Guibaut. Cambridge, MA: MIT Press.

McCalman, Iain. 1988. *Radical Underworld: Prophets, Revolutionaries and Pornographers in London, 1795–1840*. Cambridge, England: Cambridge University Press.

McCarthy, Patrick J. 1964. *Matthew Arnold and the Three Classes*. New York: Columbia University Press.

McChesney, Robert W. 2002. "Whatever Happened to Cultural Studies?" In *American Cultural Studies*. Edited by Catherine A. Warren and Mary Douglas Vavrus. Urbana: University of Illinois Press, 76–93.

McDonnell, Kevin, and Kevin Robins. 1980. "Marxist Cultural Theory: The Althusserian Smoke-screen." In *One-Dimensional Marxism: Althusser and the Politics of Culture*. Edited by Simon Clarke et al. New York: Allison and Busby, 157–231.

McRobbie, Angela. 1980. "Settling Accounts with Subcultures: A Feminist Critique." *Screen Education* 34 (spring): 37–49.

——. 1991. "New Times in Cultural Studies." *New Formations* 13 (spring): 1–17.

——. 1992. "Post-Marxism and Cultural Studies: A Post-Script." In *Cultural Studies*. Edited by Lawrence Grossberg, Cary Nelson, and Paula Treichler. New York: Routledge, 719–30.

Meadows, Donella H., Dennis L. Meadows, and Jørgen Randers. 1992. *Beyond the Limits: Confronting Global Collapse, Envisioning a Sustainable Future*. Post Mills, VT: Chelsea Green.

Meadows, Donella H., Dennis L. Meadows, Jørgen Randers, and William W. Behrens III. 1974. *The Limits to Growth*. 2d ed. New York: Signet.

Meehan, E. J. 1971. *The Foundations of Political Analysis*. Homewood, IL: Dorsey Press.

Merton, Robert K. 1949. *Social Theory and Social Structure: Toward the Codification of Theory and Research*. Glencoe, IL: Free Press.

Metz, Christian. 1973. "Answers from Christian Metz." *Screen* 14, nos. 1–2 (spring–summer): 208–10.

——. 1975 "The Imaginary Signifier." *Screen* 16, no. 2 (summer): 14–76.

Milbrath, Lester W., with the advice and assistance of Barbara V. Fisher. 1984. *Environmentalists: Vanguard for a New Society*. Albany: State University of New York Press.

Miliband, Ralph, and John Saville, eds. 1976. *The Socialist Register: 1976*. London: Merlin Press.

Mill, John Stuart. [1843] 1988. *The Logic of the Moral Sciences*. La Salle, IL: Open Court.

Miller, Toby, ed. 2001a. *A Companion to Cultural Studies*. Malden, MA: Blackwell.

——. 2001b. "What It Is and What It Isn't . . . Cultural Studies." In *A Companion to Cultural Studies*. Edited by Toby Miller. Malden, MA: Blackwell.

Millet, Kate. [1969] 1990. Introduction to *Sexual Politics*. In *Sexual Politics*. New York: Simon and Schuster.

Mills, C. Wright. 1959. *The Sociological Imagination*. New York: Oxford University Press.

Millum, Trevor. 1975. *Images of Women: Advertising in Women's Magazines*. London: Chatto and Windus.

Minkley, Gary, and Andrew Steyn. 1996. "South African Cultural Studies in the Moment of the 1990s: 'Dominant Voices' and Trends in Theory." In *Transgressing Boundaries: New Directions in the Study of Culture in Africa*. Edited by Brenda Cooper and Andrew Steyn. Athens: Ohio University Press, 196–207.

Minnion, John, and Philip Bolsover, eds. 1983. *The CND Story: The First 25 Years of CND in the Words of the People Involved*. London: Allison and Busby.

Mitchell, John G., with Constance L. Stallings. 1970. *Ecotactics: The Sierra Club Handbook for Environmental Activists*. New York: Pocket Books.

Monahan, Laurie J. 1990. "Cultural Cartography: American Designs at the 1964 Venice Biennale." In *Reconstructing Modernism: Art in New York, Paris, and Montreal 1945–1964*. Edited by Serge Guilbaut. Cambridge, MA: MIT Press.

Moraga, Cherríe, and Gloria Anzaldúa. 1983. *This Bridge Called My Back: Writings by Radical Women of Color*. New York: Kitchen Table Press.

Morgan, Kenneth O. 1984. *Labour in Power 1945–1951*. Oxford: Clarendon Press.

——. 1990. *The People's Peace: British History 1945–1989*. Oxford: Oxford University Press.

Moritz, Charles. 1963/1964. "Hoggart, (Herbert) Richard." In *Current Biography Yearbook, 1963*. New York: H. W. Wilson.

Morley, David. 1980. *The "Nationwide" Audience: Structure and Decoding*. London: British Film Institute.

——. 1981. "'The Nationwide Audience': A Critical Postscript." *Screen Education* 39 (summer): 3–14.

——. 1986. *Family Television: Cultural Power and Domestic Leisure*. London: Comedia.

——. 1992. *Television, Audiences and Cultural Studies*. New York: Routledge.

Morley, David, and Kuan-Hsing Chen, eds. 1996. *Stuart Hall: Critical Dialogues in Cultural Studies*. New York: Routledge.

Morley, David, and Kevin Robins, eds. 2001. *British Cultural Studies: Geography, Nationality, and Identity*. New York: Oxford University Press.

Morris, Meaghan. 1988. "Banality in Cultural Studies." *Discourse* 10, no. 2 (spring–summer): 3–21.

——. 1990. "A Small Serve of Spaghetti: The Future of Australian Studies." *Meanjin* 49, no. 3: 470–80.

——. 1992. "Discussion: Graeme Turner." In *Cultural Studies*. Edited by Lawrence Grossberg, Cary Nelson, and Paula Treichler. New York: Routledge.

Morrow, Raymond A. 1991. "Introduction: The Challenge of Cultural Studies to Canadian Sociology and Anthropology." *Canadian Review of Sociology and Anthropology/La Revue canadienne de Sociologie et d'Anthropologie* 28, no. 2 (May): 153–72.

Mulhern, Francis. 1979. *The Moment of "Scrutiny."* London: New Left Books.

——. 1981. "The Cambridge Affair." *Marxism Today* (March): 27–28.

Mulvey, Laura. 1986. "Magnificent Obsession." *Parachute* 42: 6–12.

Murdock, Graham. 1989. "Cultural Studies: Missing Links." *Critical Studies in Mass Communications* 6, no. 4: 436–40.

Musgrave, P. W. 1973. "Scrutiny and Education." *British Journal of Educational Studies* 21: 253–76.

Nagel, Ernest. 1956. "A Formalization of Functionalism." In *Logic without Metaphysics*. Glencoe, IL: Free Press.

Nagel, Julian. 1969. *Student Power*. London: Merlin Press.

National Union of Teachers. 1961. *Popular Culture and Personal Responsibility.* London: National Union of Teachers.

Neurath, Otto. [1931–32] 1959. "Sociology and Physicalism." In *Logical Positivism.* Edited by A. J. Ayer. New York: Free Press.

Newsinger, John. 1994. *Fenianism in Mid-Victorian Britain.* Boulder, CO: Pluto Press.

Nicolis, Grégoire. 1989. "Physics of Far-from-Equilibrium Systems and Self-Organization." In *The New Physics.* Edited by Paul Davies. New York: Cambridge University Press, 316–47.

Nicolis, Grégoire, and Ilya Prigogine. 1989. *Exploring Complexity: An Introduction.* New York: W. H. Freeman.

Nielsen, Greg M., and John D. Jackson. 1991. "Cultural Studies, a Sociological Poetics: Institutions of the Canadian Imaginary." *Canadian Review of Sociology and Anthropology/La Revue canadienne de Sociologie et d'Anthropologie* 28, no. 2 (May): 279–98.

Novick, Peter. 1988. *That Noble Dream: The "Objectivity Question" and the American Historical Profession.* New York: Cambridge University Press.

Noyes, John. 2000. "The Place of the Human." In *Senses of Culture: South African Culture Studies.* Edited by Sarah Nuttall and Cheryl-Ann Michael. New York: Oxford University Press, 49–60.

Nuclear Energy Agency. 1989. *Nuclear Energy in Perspective.* Paris: Organization for Economic Co-operation and Development.

Nuttall, Sarah, and Cheryl-Ann Michael. 2000a. "Introduction: Imagining the Present." In *Senses of Culture: South African Culture Studies.* Edited by Sarah Nuttall and Cheryl-Ann Michael. New York: Oxford University Press, 1–23.

——, eds. 2000b. *Senses of Culture: South African Culture Studies.* New York: Oxford University Press.

Oakes, Guy. 1975. Introductory essay in *Roscher and Knies: The Logical Problems of Historical Economics,* by Max Weber. New York: Free Press.

O'Connor, Alan. 1989. *Raymond Williams: Writing, Culture, Politics.* New York: Blackwell.

O'Donnell, John M. 1985. *The Origins of Behaviorism: American Psychology, 1870–1920.* New York: New York University Press.

Ogden, C. K., and I. A. Richards. [1923] 1989. *The Meaning of Meaning: A Study of the Influence of Language upon Thought and of the Science of Symbolism.* San Diego: Harcourt Brace Jovanovich.

Ohmann, Richard. 1972. "Teaching and Studying Literature at the End of Ideology." In *The Politics of Literature: Dissenting Essays on the Teaching of English.* Edited by Louis Kampf and Paul Lauter. New York: Pantheon Books, 130–59.

——. 1991. "Thoughts on Cultural Studies in the United States." *Critical Studies* 3, no. 1: 5–15.

O'Regan, Tom. 1992. "MisTaking Policy: Notes on the Cultural Policy Debate." *Cultural Studies* 6, no. 3 (October): 409–23.

Orwell, George. [1940] 1968. "Inside the Whale." In *The Collected Essays, Journalism and Letters of George Orwell. Volume I. An Age Like This, 1920–1940.* Edited by Sonia Orwell and Ian Angus. New York: Harcourt, Brace and World, 493–527.

Pagels, Heinz R. 1988. *The Dreams of Reason: The Computer and the Rise of the Sciences of Complexity.* New York: Simon and Schuster.

Paine, Thomas. [1791–92] 1984. *Rights of Man.* Introduction by Eric Foner. Notes by Henry Collins. London: Penguin.

Palma, Gabriel. 1978. "Dependency: A Formal Theory of Underdevelopment or a Methodology for the Analysis of Concrete Situations of Underdevelopment." *World Development* 6: 881–924.

Palmer, D. J. 1965. *The Rise of English Studies: An Account of the Study of English Language and Literature from Its Origins to the Making of the Oxford English School.* New York: Oxford University Press.

Parkin, Frank. 1968. *Middle Class Radicalism: The Social Bases of the British Campaign for Nuclear Disarmament.* New York: Praeger.

Parsons, Talcott. [1937] 1980. *The Structure of Social Action.* New York: McGraw-Hill.

Pater, Walter. [1873] 1980. *The Renaissance: Studies in Art and Poetry: The 1893 Text.* Edited and with textual and explanatory notes by Donald L. Hill. Berkeley: University of California Press.

Peers, Dave. 1963. "The Impasse of CND." *International Socialism* 12 (spring): 6–10.

Peliti, L., and A. Vulpiani, eds. 1988. *Measures of Complexity: Proceedings of the Conference, Held in Rome September 30–October 2, 1987.* Berlin: Springer-Verlag.

Perry, Walter. 1977. *The Open University.* San Francisco: Jossey-Bass.

Phillips, Lisa. 1995. "Beat Culture: America Revisioned." In *Beat Culture and the New America: 1950–1965.* By Lisa Phillips et al. New York: Whitney Museum of American Art, 23–40.

Pines, David. 1988. *Emerging Synthesis in Science: Proceedings of the Founding Workshops of the Santa Fe Institute, Santa Fe, New Mexico.* Redwood City, CA: Addison-Wesley.

Plotnitsky, Arkady. 1997. " 'But It Is Above All Not True': Derrida, Relativity, and the 'Science Wars.' " *Postmodern Culture* 7, no. 2: n.p.

Poirier, F. 1983. "L'école historique anglaise: Développement capitaliste et mouvement ouvrier." In *Les aventures du marxisme.* Edited by René Gallisot. Paris: Syros, 59–79.

Pomian, Krzysztof. 1979. "The Secular Evolution of the Concept of Cycles." *Review* 2, no. 4 (spring): 563–646.

Pratt, Mary Louise. 1992. "Humanities for the Future: Reflections on the Western Culture Debate at Stanford." In *The Politics of Liberal Education.* Edited by Darryl J. Gless and Barbara Herrnstein Smith. Durham, NC: Duke University Press, 13–31.

Price, Terence. 1990. *Political Electricity: What Future for Nuclear Energy?* Oxford: Oxford University Press.

Prigogine, Ilya. 1986. "Science, Civilization and Democracy: Values, Systems, Structures and Affinities." *Futures* 18, no. 4: 493–507.

——. 1988. "The New Convergence of Science and Culture." *UNESCO Courier* (May): 9–13.

——. 1996. *The End of Certainty: Time, Chaos, and the New Laws of Nature.* New York: Free Press.

Prigogine, Ilya, and Isabelle Stengers. 1984. *Order out of Chaos: Man's New Dialogue with Nature.* Foreword by Alvin Toffler. New York: Bantam Books.

Programme of the German Green Party. 1983. Preface by Jonathon Porritt. London: Heretic Books.

Raleigh, John Henry. 1961. *Matthew Arnold and American Culture.* Berkeley: University of California Press.

Rancière, Jacques. 1974. *La Leçon d'Althusser.* Paris: Seuil.

Ransom, John Crowe. 1941. *The New Criticism.* Norfolk, CT: New Directions.

Reise, Barbara M. [1968] 1992. "Greenberg and The Group: A Retrospective View." In *Art in Modern Culture: An Anthology of Critical Texts.* Edited by Francis Frascina and Jonathan Harris. New York: HarperCollins.

Ricardou, Jean. 1967. *Problèmes du nouveau roman.* Paris: Éditions du Seuil.

——. 1971. *Pour une théorie du nouveau roman.* Paris: Éditions du Seuil.

——, ed. 1975. *Claude Simon: Analyse, théorie.* Colloque, Centre Cultural International de Cerisy-la-Salle. Paris: Union Générale d'Éditions.

Ricardou, Jean, and Françoise van Rossum-Guyon, eds. 1972. *Nouveav roman: Hier, aujourd'hui.* Colloque, Centre Cultural International de Cerisy-la-Salle. Paris: Union Générale d'Éditions.

Richards, I. A. [1924] 1925. *Principles of Literary Criticism.* San Diego: Harcourt Brace Jovanovich.

——. [1926] 1974. *Science and Poetry.* London: Haskell House.

Robbe-Grillet, Alain. [1953] 1963a. "Joë Bousquet le rêveur." In *Pour un nouveau roman.* Paris: Gallimard.

——. [1958] 1963b. "Nature, humanisme, tragédie." In *Pour un nouveau roman.* Paris: Gallimard.

——. [1961] 1963c. "Nouveau roman, homme nouveau." In *Pour un nouveau roman.* Paris: Gallimard.

——. [1955] 1963d. "A quoi servent les théories." In *Pour un nouveau roman.* Paris: Gallimard.

——. [1957] 1963e. "Sur quelques notions périmées." In *Pour un nouveau roman.* Paris: Gallimard.

——. 1963f. "Temps et description dans le récit d'aujourd'hui." In *Pour un nouveau roman.* Paris: Gallimard.

——. [1956] 1963g. "Une voie pour le roman futur." In *Pour un nouveau roman.* Paris: Gallimard.

Rodman, John R. 1964. Introduction to *The Political Theory of T. H. Green.* Edited by John R. Rodman. New York: Appleton-Century-Crofts, 1–40.

Rosenau, Pauline Marie. 1992. *Post-Modernism and the Social Sciences: Insights, Inroads, and Intrusions.* Princeton: Princeton University Press.

Ross, Andrew. 1996a. "Introduction." *Social Text* 46/47, 14, nos. 1–2 (spring–summer): 1–13.

——, ed. 1996b. *Science Wars.* Durham, NC: Duke University Press.

Ross, Dorothy. 1991. *The Origins of American Social Science.* Cambridge, England: Cambridge University Press.

Rostow, W. W. 1960. *The Stages of Economic Growth: A Non-Communist Manifesto.* Cambridge, England: Cambridge University Press.

Roszak, Theodore. 1969. *The Making of a Counter Culture: Reflections on the Technocratic Society and Its Youthful Opposition.* New York: Anchor Books.

Rothman, Barbara Katz. 1989. *Recreating Motherhood: Ideology and Technology in a Patriarchal Society.* New York: Norton.

Rouse, Joseph. 1990. "The Narrative Reconstruction of Science." *Inquiry* 33: 179–96.

——. 1993. "What Are Cultural Studies of Scientific Knowledge?" *Configurations* 1, no. 1 (winter): 1–22.

Rowbotham, Sheila. 1978. "Crossed Lines." Review of *Women Take Issue: Aspects of Women's Subordination,* by Women's Studies Group. *New Society* 44 (May 4): 266–67.

Ruelle, David, and F. Takens. 1971. "On the Nature of Turbulence." *Communications in Mathematical Physics* 20: 167–92.

Rustin, Michael. 1989. "The New Left as a Social Movement." In *Out of Apathy: Voices of the New Left Thirty Years On.* Edited by Robin Archer, Diemut Bubeck, Hanjo Glock, Lesley Jacobs, Seth Moglen, Adam Steinhouse, and Daniel Weinstock. New York: Verso, 117–28.

Ryle, Martin. 1988. *Ecology and Socialism.* London: Radius.

Sale, Kirkpatrick. 1973. *SDS.* New York: Random House.

Saloy, Mona Lisa. 1995. "Black Beats and Black Issues." In *Beat Culture and the New America: 1950–1965.* By Lisa Phillips et al. New York: Whitney Museum of American Art, 153–65.

Samuel, Ralph. 1959. "Class and Classlessness." *Universities and Left Review* 6 (spring): 44–50.

———. 1980. "British Marxist Historians, 1880–1980: Part One." *New Left Review* 120 (March–April): 21–96.

———. 1989. "Born-again Socialism." In *Out of Apathy: Voices of the New Left Thirty Years On*. Edited by Robin Archer, Diemut Bubeck, Hanjo Glock, Lesley Jacobs, Seth Moglen, Adam Steinhouse, and Daniel Weinstock. New York: Verso, 39–57.

Sanders, Charles Richard. [1942] 1972. *Coleridge and the Broad Church Movement: Studies in S. T. Coleridge, Dr. Arnold of Rugby, J. C. Hare, Thomas Carlyle and F. D. Maurice*. New York: Russell and Russell.

Sartre, Jean-Paul. [1948] 1988a. "Black Orpheus." Translated by John MacCombie. In *"What Is Literature?" and Other Essays*. Cambridge, MA: Harvard University Press, 289–330.

———. [1947] 1988b. "What Is Literature?" Translated by Bernard Frechtman. In *"What Is Literature?" and Other Essays*. Cambridge, MA: Harvard University Press, 21–245.

Saville, John. 1976. "The XXth Congress and the British Communist Party." In *The Socialist Register: 1976*. Edited by Ralph Miliband and John Saville. London: Merlin, 1–23.

———. 1993. Introduction to *Labour's High Noon: The Government and the Economy 1945–51*. Edited by Jim Fyrth. London: Lawrence and Wishart, xv–xxxviii.

Schaffter, Dorothy. 1969. *The National Science Foundation*. New York: Praeger.

Schumacher, E. F. 1973. *Small Is Beautiful: Economics As If People Mattered*. New York: Harper and Row.

Schwartz, Gary. 1978. Review of *Resistance through Rituals: Youth Subcultures in Post-War Britain*. Edited by Stuart Hall and Tony Jefferson. *American Journal of Sociology* 84, no. 3 (November): 789–91.

Schwarz, Bill. 1982. " 'The People' in History: The Communist Party Historians' Group, 1946–56." In *Making Histories: Studies in History-Writing and Politics*. Edited by Richard Johnson, Gregor McLennan, Bill Schwarz, and David Sutton. London: Hutchinson/CCCS, 44–95.

Scott, Frederick. 1982. "Sullivan, Louis Henry 1856–1924: U.S. Architect." In *Makers of Nineteenth Century Culture 1800–1914*. Edited by Justin Wintle. Boston: Routledge and Kegan Paul.

Scott, Joan W. 1995. "The Rhetoric of Crisis in Higher Education." In *Higher Education Under Fire: Politics, Economics, and the Crisis of the Humanities*. Edited by Michael Bérubé and Cary Nelson. New York: Routledge, 293–304.

Searby, Peter, John Rule, and Robert Malcolmson. 1993. "Edward Thompson as a Teacher: Yorkshire and Warwick." In *Protest and Survival: Essays for E. P. Thompson*. Edited by John Rule and Robert Malcolmson. New York: New Press, 1–23.

Sedgwick, Peter. 1964/1976. "The Two New Lefts." In *The Left in Britain, 1956–68*. Edited by David Widgery. Baltimore: Penguin, 131–53.

Segerstråle, Ullica. 2000a. "History of Science: Stirred, Not Shaken." h-nexa@h-net.msu.edu.

———. 2000b. "Science and Science Studies: Enemies or Allies?" In *Beyond the Science Wars: The Missing Discourse about Science and Society*. Edited by Ullica Segerstråle. Albany: State University of New York Press.

Seidman, Steven. 1991. "The End of Sociological Theory: The Postmodern Hope." *Sociological Theory* 9: 131–46.

Senghor, Léopold Sédar. 1970. "Negritude: A Humanism of the Twentieth Century." In *The Africa*

Reader: Independent Africa. Edited by Wilfred Cartey and Martin Kilson. New York: Random House, 179–92.

Shapin, Steven. 1994. *A Social History of Truth: Civility and Science in Seventeenth-Century England.* Chicago: University of Chicago Press.

———. 1995. "Here and Everywhere: Sociology of Scientific Knowledge." *Annual Review of Sociology* 21: 289–321.

Shapin, Steven, and Simon Schaffer. 1985. *Leviathan and the Air Pump: Hobbes, Boyle and the Experimental Life.* Princeton: Princeton University Press.

Sharrock, Wes, and Bob Anderson. 1986. *The Ethnomethodologists.* New York: Tavistock/Horwood.

Shaw, Robert. 1981. "Strange Attractors, Chaotic Behavior, and Information Flow." *Zeitschrift für Naturforschung* 36a, 1: 80–112.

Silver, Harold. 1957. "Discussion: Socialism and the Intellectuals—Two." *University and Left Review* 1, no. 2 (summer): 17–18.

Silverman, Kaja. 1983. *The Subject of Semiotics.* New York: Oxford University Press.

Sismondo, Sergio. 1993a. "Response to Knorr Cetina." *Social Studies of Science* 23: 563–69.

———. 1993b. "Some Social Constructions." *Social Studies of Science* 23: 515–53.

Skinner, B. F. 1971. *Beyond Freedom and Dignity.* New York: Knopf.

Slack, Jennifer Daryl. 1996. "The Theory and Method of Articulation in Cultural Studies." In *Stuart Hall: Critical Dialogues in Cultural Studies.* Edited by David Morley and Kuan-Hsing Chen. London: Routledge, 112–27.

Slusser, Dorothy M., and Gerald H. Slusser. 1971. *Technology—The God That Failed: The Environmental Catastrophe.* Philadelphia: Westminster Press.

Smelser, Neil J. 1988. "Social Structure." In *Handbook of Sociology.* Edited by Neil J. Smelser. Beverly Hills: Sage.

Smith, A. C. H., with Elizabeth Immirzi and Trevor Blackwell. 1975. *Paper Voices: The Popular Press and Social Change, 1935–1965.* Introduction by Stuart Hall. Totowa, NJ: Rowman and Littlefield.

Smith, Barbara Herrnstein. 1992. "Cult-Lit: Hirsch, Literacy, and the 'National Culture.'" In *The Politics of Liberal Education.* Edited by Darryl J. Gless and Barbara Herrnstein Smith. Durham, NC: Duke University Press, 75–94.

Smith, Francis Barrymore. 1966. *The Making of the Second Reform Bill.* Cambridge, England: Cambridge University Press.

Snell, Marilyn Berlin, and Yevgeny Yevtushenko. 1992. "Beyond Being and Becoming." *New Perspectives Quarterly* 9, no. 2 (spring): 22–28.

Snow, C. P. 1965. *The Two Cultures and A Second Look.* New York: Cambridge University Press.

Sparks, Colin. 1977. "The Evolution of Cultural Studies." *Screen Education* 22 (spring): 16–30.

Spiegelberg, H. 1965. *The Phenomenological Movement.* 2d ed. The Hague: Nijhoff.

Starfield, Jane, and Michael Gardiner. 2000. "Citizenship and Modernity in Soweto." In *Senses of Culture: South African Cultural Studies.* Edited by Sarah Nuttall and Cheryl-Ann Michael. New York: Oxford University Press, 61–84.

Steele, Tom. 1997. *The Emergence of Cultural Studies: Adult Education, Cultural Politics and the "English" Question.* London: Lawrence and Wishart.

Stein, Daniel L., ed. 1989. *Lectures in the Sciences of Complexity: The Proceedings of the 1988 Complex*

Systems Summer School Held June–July 1988 in Santa Fe, New Mexico. Redwood City, CA: Addison-Wesley.

Stern, Susan. 1975. *With the Weathermen: The Personal Journal of a Revolutionary Woman.* Garden City, NY: Doubleday.

Stites, Richard. 1992. *Russian Popular Culture: Entertainment and Society since 1900.* New York: Cambridge University Press.

Stocking, George W., Jr. 1971. "What's in a Name? The Origins of the Royal Anthropological Institute (1837–71)." *Man* 6, no. 3 (September): 369–90.

Stoianovich, Traian. 1976. *French Historical Method: The Annales Paradigm.* Ithaca: Cornell University Press.

Striphas, Ted. 1998. "Cultural Studies' Institutional Presence: A Resource and Guide." *Cultural Studies* 12, no. 4 (October): 571–94.

Sturrock, John. 1969. *The French New Novel: Claude Simon, Michel Butor, Alain Robbe-Grillet.* New York: Oxford University Press.

Super, R. H. 1963. "Documents in the Matthew Arnold—Sainte-Beuve Relationship." *Modern Philology* 60, no. 3 (February): 206–10.

Swindells, Julia, and Lisa Jardine. 1990. *What's Left? Women in Culture and the Labour Movement.* New York: Routledge.

Taylor, Peter J. 1990. "Britain's Changing Role in the World-Economy." *Review* 13, no. 1 (winter): 33–48.

———. 1997. "Modernities and Movements: Antisystemic Reactions to World Hegemony." *Review* 20, no. 1 (winter): 1–17.

———. 2001. "Which Britain? Which England? Which North?" In *British Cultural Studies: Geography, Nationality, and Identity.* Edited by David Morley and Kevin Robins. New York: Oxford University Press.

Teodori, Massimo, ed. 1969. *The New Left: A Documentary History.* New York: Bobbs-Merrill.

"Themes." 1968. *New Left Review* 47 (January–February): 1.

Therborn, Göran. 1968. "From Petrograd to Saigon." *New Left Review* 48 (March–April): 3–11.

Thesing, William B. 1988. Afterword to *Matthew Arnold in His Time and Ours: Centenary Essays.* Edited by Clinton Machann and Forrest D. Burt. Charlottesville: University Press of Virginia, 197–206.

Thompson, Denys, ed. 1964. *Discrimination and Popular Culture.* Baltimore: Penguin.

Thompson, E. P. 1955. *William Morris: Romantic to Revolutionary.* London: Lawrence and Wishart.

———. 1957. "Socialist Humanism." *New Reasoner* 1, no. 1 (summer): 105–43.

———. 1958. "N.A.T.O., Neutralism and Survival." *Universities and Left Review* 4 (summer): 49–51.

———. 1959a. "Commitment in Politics." *Universities and Left Review* 6 (spring): 50–55.

———. 1959b. "The New Left." *The New Reasoner* 9 (summer): 1–17.

———. 1960. "At the Point of Decay." In *Out of Apathy.* Edited by E. P. Thompson. London: NLB/Stephens and Sons, 3–15.

———. 1961. Review of *The Long Revolution,* by Raymond Williams. *New Left Review* 9, 10, 11 (May–June, July–August, September–October): 24–33, 34–39, corrigendum.

———. [1963] 1966. *The Making of the English Working Class.* New York: Vintage.

———. 1976. "Romanticism, Moralism and Utopianism: The Case of William Morris." *New Left Review* 99 (September–October): 83–111.

——. 1977. *William Morris: Romantic to Revolutionary.* Revised ed. New York: Pantheon.

——. [1960] 1978a. "Outside the Whale." In *The Poverty of Theory and Other Essays.* London: Merlin, 1–33.

——. [1965] 1978b. "The Peculiarities of the English." In *The Poverty of Theory and Other Essays.* London: Merlin, 35–91.

——. 1978c. "The Poverty of Theory: Or an Orrery of Errors." In *The Poverty of Theory and Other Essays.* London: Merlin, 193–397.

——. 1981. "The Politics of Theory." In *People's History and Socialist Theory.* Edited by Raphael Samuel. Boston: Routledge and Kegan Paul, 396–408.

——. [1976] 1984. "E. P. Thompson." In *Visions of History.* Edited by MARHO. New York: Pantheon, 5–25.

Thornton, Robert. 1995. "The Colonial, the Imperial, and the Creation of 'the European' in Southern Africa." In *Occidentalism: Images of the West.* Edited by James G. Carrier. Oxford: Clarendon Press, 192–217.

——. 1996. "The Potential of Boundaries: Steps towards a Theory of the Social Edge." In *Postcolonial Identities in Africa.* Edited by Richard P. Werbner and Terence Ranger. London: Zed Press.

Tibbetts, Paul. 1982. "The Positivism-Humanism Debate in Sociology: A Reconsideration." *Sociological Inquiry* 52, no. 3 (summer): 184–99.

Todd, Olivier. 1968. "Interview: The Americans Are Not Invincible." *New Left Review* 47 (January–February): 2–19.

Tomaselli, Keyan G. 1988a. Introduction to *Rethinking Culture.* Edited by Keyan Tomaselli. Bellville, South Africa: Anthropos, 6–10.

——, ed. 1988b. *Rethinking Culture.* Bellville, South Africa: Anthropos.

Trachtman, Leon E., and Robert Perrucci. 2000. *Science Under Siege? Interest Groups and the Science Wars.* Lantham, MD: Rowman and Littlefield.

Triesman, David. 1968. "Essex." *New Left Review* 50 (July–August): 70–71.

Tropp, Asher. 1958. Review of *The Uses of Literacy,* by Richard Hoggart. *American Sociological Review* 23, no. 2 (April): 221.

Tudor, Andres. 1999. *Decoding Culture: Theory and Method in Cultural Studies.* Thousand Oaks, CA: Sage.

Tunstall, Jeremy, ed. 1974. *The Open University Opens.* Amherst: University of Massachusetts Press.

Turner, Frank M. 1975. "Victorian Scientific Naturalism and Thomas Carlyle." *Victorian Studies* 18, no. 3 (March): 325–43.

Turner, Frederick. 1997. Foreword to *Chaos, Complexity, and Sociology: Myths, Models, and Theories.* Edited by Raymond A. Eve, Sara Horsfall, and Mary E. Lee. Thousand Oaks, CA: Sage.

Turner, Graeme. 1990. *British Cultural Studies: An Introduction.* Media and Popular Culture 7. Boston: Unwin Hyman.

——. 1991. "Return to Oz: Populism, the Academy and the Future of Australian Studies." *Meanjin* 50, no. 1 (autumn): 19–31.

——. 1992. " 'It Works for Me': British Cultural Studies, Australian Cultural Studies, Australian Film." In *Cultural Studies.* Edited by Lawrence Grossberg, Cary Nelson, and Paula Treichler. New York: Routledge.

van Onselen, Charles. 1996. *The Seed Is Mine: The Life of Kas Maine, a South African Share-cropper 1894–1985.* Cape Town, South Africa: David Philip.

Veeser, H. Aram., ed. 1989. *The New Historicism.* New York: Routledge.

Volkart, Edmund H. 1981. "Seventy-five Years of It." *American Sociologist* 16 (February): 64–67.

Wagner, Helmut. 1983. *Alfred Schütz: An Intellectual Biography.* Chicago: University of Chicago Press.

Wallerstein, Immanuel. 1974. *The Modern World-System I: Capitalist Agriculture and the Origins of the European World-Economy in the Sixteenth Century.* New York: Academic Press.

——. 1978. "*Annales* as Resistance." *Review* 1, nos. 3/4 (winter–spring): 5–7.

——. 1983. *Historical Capitalism.* New York: Verso.

——. 1984. "The Three Instances of Hegemony in the History of the Capitalist World-Economy." *International Journal of Comparative Sociology* 24, nos. 1/2 (January–April): 100–108.

——. 1988. "The Inventions of TimeSpace Realities: Towards an Understanding of our Historical Systems." *Geography* 73, no. 4 (October): 289–97.

——. 1991a. *Geopolitics and Geoculture: Essays on the Changing World-System.* Cambridge, England: Cambridge University Press.

——. 1991b. *Unthinking Social Science: The Limits of Nineteenth-Century Paradigms.* Cambridge, England: Polity Press.

——. 1993. "The TimeSpace of World-Systems Analysis: A Philosophical Essay." *Historical Geography* 23, nos. 1–2: 5–22.

——. 1995. *After Liberalism.* New York: New Press.

——. 1997. "The Unintended Consequences of Cold War Area Studies." In *The Cold War and the University: Toward an Intellectual History of the Postwar Years.* New York: New Press, 195–230.

——. 2000. *The Essential Wallerstein.* New York: New Press.

Walters, Nicolas. 1962. "Damned Fools in Utopia." *New Left Review* 13–14 (January–April): 119–28.

Warren, Catherine A., and Mary Douglas Vavrus, eds. 2002a. *American Cultural Studies.* Urbana: University of Illinois Press.

——. 2002b. Introduction to *American Cultural Studies.* Edited by Catherine A. Warren and Mary Douglas Vavrus. Urbana: University of Illinois Press, 1–11.

Wasserman, Earl R. 1975. "The English Romantics: The Grounds of Knowledge." In *Romanticism: Points of View.* 2d ed. Edited by Robert F. Gleckner and Gerald E. Enscoe. Detroit: Wayne State University Press.

Watson, J. B. 1925. *Behaviorism.* New York: Norton.

Watson, Steven. 1995. *The Birth of the Beat Generation: Visionaries, Rebels, and Hipsters, 1944–1960.* New York: Pantheon.

Weaver, Warren. 1948. "Science and Complexity." *American Scientist* 36, no. 4: 536–44.

Webb, David. 1979. Review of *Women Take Issue: Aspects of Women's Subordination,* by Women's Studies Group. *Sociological Review* 27, no. 1 (February): 190–91.

Weber, Max. [1903–6] 1975. *Roscher and Knies: The Logical Problems of Historical Economics.* Translated and with an introduction by Guy Oakes. New York: Free Press.

Weinberg, Steven. 1992. *Dreams of a Final Theory.* New York: Pantheon.

——. 1996. "Sokal's Hoax." *New York Review of Books* (August 8).

Weitz, Morris, ed. 1966. *20th Century Philosophy: The Analytic Tradition.* New York: Free Press.

West, Cornel. 1992. "Discussion: Paul Gilroy, bell hooks, Cornel West." In *Cultural Studies.* Edited by Lawrence Grossberg, Cary Nelson, and Paula Treichler. New York: Routledge, 696–705.

Wexler, Mark N. 1990. "Deep Ecology: An Emerging Critique of Conventional Wisdom." *Quarterly Journal of Ideology* 14, no. 1: 15–38.

White, Hayden. 1973. *Metahistory: The Historical Imagination in Nineteenth-Century Europe.* Baltimore: Johns Hopkins University Press.

———. 1978. *Tropics of Discourse: Essays in Culture and Criticism.* Baltimore: Johns Hopkins University Press.

———. 1987. *The Content of the Form: Narrative Discourse and Historical Representation.* Baltimore: Johns Hopkins University Press.

———. 1995. "Response to Arthur Marwick." *Journal of Contemporary History* 30, no. 2 (April): 233–46.

Whitehead, Phillip. 1975. "The Images We Deserve." Review of *Paper Voices*, by A. C. H. Smith, and *Images of Women*, by Trevor Millum. *The Listener* 93, no. 2407 (May 22): 683.

Whitridge, Arnold. 1938. "Matthew Arnold and Sainte-Beuve." *Publications of the Modern Language Association of America* 53, no. 1 (March): 303–13.

Widgery, David. 1976. *The Left in Britain, 1956–68.* Baltimore: Penguin.

Wiener, Joel H. 1969. *The War of the Unstamped: The Movement to Repeal the British Newspaper Tax, 1830–1836.* Ithaca: Cornell University Press.

Willey, Basil. 1949. *Nineteenth Century Studies: Coleridge to Matthew Arnold.* New York: Columbia University Press.

Williams, Jeffrey, ed. 1995. *PC Wars: Politics and Theory in the Academy.* New York: Routledge.

Williams, Raymond. 1960. "The New British Left." *Partisan Review* 27, no. 2 (spring): 341–47.

———. 1961. *The Long Revolution: An Analysis of the Democratic, Industrial, and Cultural Changes Transforming Our Society.* New York: Columbia University Press.

———. 1966. *Communications.* London: Chatto and Windus.

———. 1970. "An Experimental Tendency." *The Listener* 84, no. 2175 (December 3): 785–86.

———. [1979] 1981. *Politics and Letters: Interviews with New Left Review.* London: New Left Books/Verso.

———. [1958] 1983. *Culture and Society: 1780–1950.* New York: Columbia University Press.

———. 1989. "The Future of Cultural Studies." In *The Politics of Modernism: Against the New Conformists.* New York: Verso, 151–62.

Williamson, Judith. 1978. *Decoding Advertisements: Ideology and Meaning in Advertising.* London: Marion Boyars.

Willis, Paul. 1978. *Profane Culture.* London: Routledge and Kegan Paul.

———. [1977] 1981. *Learning to Labour: How Working Class Kids Get Working Class Jobs.* New York: Columbia University Press.

Wilson, Edward O. 2002. *The Future of Life.* New York: Knopf.

Wimsatt, W. K., and Cleanth Brooks. 1957. *Literary Criticism: A Short History.* New York: Knopf.

Windschuttle, Keith. 1997. *The Killing of History: How Literary Critics and Social Theorists Are Murdering Our Past.* New York: Free Press.

Wolfe, Tom. 1973. *The New Journalism.* New York: Harper and Row.

Wolff, Janet. 1984. *The Social Production of Art.* New York: New York University Press.

Wolpert, Lewis. 1993. *The Unnatural Nature of Science.* Cambridge, MA: Harvard University Press.

Women's Studies Group, CCCS. 1978. *Women Take Issue: Aspects of Women's Subordination.* London: Hutchinson/CCCS.

Wood, Ellen Meiksins, and John Bellamy Foster. 1997. *In Defense of History: Marxism and the Postmodern Agenda*. New York: Monthly Review Press.

Wood, Neal. 1959. *Communism and British Intellectuals*. New York: Columbia University Press.

Young, Nigel. 1977. *An Infantile Disorder? The Crisis and Decline of the New Left*. London: Routledge and Kegan Paul.

Zuriff, G. E. 1985. *Behaviorism: A Conceptual Reconstruction*. New York: Columbia University Press.

Index

base superstructure model, 4, 28–29, 210

Beat Generation, 151, 180, 183–84; Ginsberg's assessment of, 232–33 n.17

behaviorism, 175, 180; phenomenology and, 231 n.11

Beveridge Report, 12, 217 n.2

Bond and Beyond (Bennett and Woollacott, 1987), 143

Bourdieu, Pierre. See *On Ideology*

Braudel, Fernand, 189–90, 204; Lévi-Strauss and, 233 n.22

British elections: 1945, 12; 1951, 13; 1955, 13; 1959, 13, 17

Britishness, 216 n.4. See also *Education Limited*

Bureau of Applied Social Research (Merton and Lazarsfeld at Columbia University), 176

Burke, Edmund: *Reflections on the Revolution in France* (1790) and, 39, 220–21 n.2. See also *Culture and Society*

Campaign for Nuclear Disarmament, 16–17, 28, 219 n.11, 220 n.19

Canada: cultural studies and, 147–148; Canadian identity and, 147; communications research and, 148. *See also* universities and cultural studies

canon, 160–61

Carlyle, Thomas: *Chartism* (1839) and, 41–42, 44; "The Negro Question" (1849) and, 43–44; and philanthropists, 43; Condition-of-England Question and, 43; Ireland and Jamaica and, 44; laissez-faire and, 44; education and universal suffrage and, 44; "Shooting Niagara, and After?" (1867) and, 49. See also *Culture and Society*

Carson, Rachel, 195, 234 n.3

Cartesian dualities, 210

Cato Street conspiracy, 40

causation (causal system, causal explanation), 208–9

Central Intelligence Agency (CIA), 178, 226 n.7

Centre for Contemporary Cultural Studies (CCCS), 5–6, 12, 34, 73, 137–39; Marxism, structuralism, and semiotics and, 74, 187;

history and history writing and, 74; interdisciplinarity and, 74; founding by Hoggart, University of Birmingham, 75; funding of, 75; Stuart Hall and, 75, 80, 224 n.9; early directions, 75–76; 1968 and, 80; external review and, 80; Richard Johnson and, 80; interdisciplinarity and, 106–7; turn to theory and, 137; Gramsci and, 138; feminism and, 138; race and, 138; intellectual trajectory, 137–39

chaos, 198–200, 202, 210, 213, 235 nn.7, 9 *See also* complexity studies

chaos theory, 212, 235 n.9. *See also* complexity studies

Chartism: London Working Men's Association (1836) and, 41; People's Charter and, 41; Cuffay and, 42; education and, 44–45

chemical industry, 195

civil rights, 183

class, 68, 98, 100, 110, 122; and classlessness, 31, 220 n.16

Club of Rome: limits to growth and the great transition, 194, 234 n.1

cold war, 14–15, 26, 28–29, 190, 192, 213

collective research, 129, 204; CCCS and Marx and, 107

commitment, 219 n.14

Committee of 100, 17

Communications (Raymond Williams, 1966), 77

Communist Party Historians' Group (CPHG), 219 n.12; Thompson and, 18, 19. See also *Making Histories*

Communist Party of Great Britain, 15, 52, 218 nn.8, 10

Communist Party of the United States of America, 226 n.7

complexity studies, 197–99, 210, 212–13, 235–36 nn.6–11; and social science(s), 200

Comte, Auguste, 207

Condition-of-England Question, 36, 74, 98–106, 191

Congress for Racial Equality, 218 n.11

conservation movement. *See* ecology

conservatism, 62, 211–12

Conservative politics, 63, 66

Culture Wars and Science Wars, 6, 141, 160–69, 211. *See also* culture wars; science wars

Dada, 181
decolonization, 176, 190, 192
deconstruction, 154–56, 202, 204, 227 n.12, 227–28 n.17; as sociology, 228 n.17
Deep Ecology, 195
de Gaulle, Charles, 179, 192
de Man, Paul, 153, 226–27 n.12
democracy, 168, 177, 221 n.6, 222 n.1
dependentistas and dependency theory, 180, 189
Derrida, Jacques, 154, 165–66; existentialism and, 186. *See also* deconstruction
Descartes, René, 206; Cartesian *Fragestellung* and, 209
determinism (determination), 168, 187, 199, 206, 208, 210, 214
development and development studies, 176–77, 180; feminism and, 235 n.5
Dilthey, Wilhelm, 181; and *Methodenstreit*, 207–9
discipline(s), 153, 158, 160, 166–67, 210, 229 n.1; hierarchy of, 173, 193, 212; boundaries of, 190–91; universalizing and sectorializing, 190, 193, 202, 209, 213; complexity studies and, 200; subdisciplines and, 201
dissipative structures, 198; social systems and, 200. *See also* complexity studies

Earth Day, 234 n.3
Earth First!, 195
Earth Summit, 234 n.3
Eco, Umberto, 110
ecology, 195–96, 199, 202, 234 n.3; and environmental ethic, 196
Economic Commission for Latin America (ECLA), 189
economic expansion or contraction, 191, 193. *See also* Kondratieff phase
economics, 209–10. *See also* idiographic and nomothetic distinction
écriture, 186
education (English), 45, 102; Revised Code

(1862) and, 45–46; Elementary Education Act (1870) and, 63. *See also* adult education; Arnold, Matthew; *Education Limited*; *Unpopular Education*
education (U.S.), 160, 161
Education Limited (Education Group II, 1991), 104–6; New Right in, 104; class in, 104–5; *Unpopular Education* in, 104–5; New Right in, 105; neoliberal privatization in, 105; 1988 Act in, 105; curriculum divisions in, 105; Britishness in, 106
The Empire Strikes Back (CCCS, 1982), 99, 131–35; authoritarian state in Britain and, 133, 134; *Policing the Crisis* and, 133; new racism in, 134; power in, 134; sociologists in, 134; black criminality in, 134; Marxist analysis (Thompson) in, 135; racist common sense in, 135; racism and sexism as process in, 135; class consciousness in, 135; Gramsci in, 135; CCCS and, 138
Engels, Frederick, 220 n.17
Englishness, 36, 216 n.4; in *Bond and Beyond*, 143
English radicalism, 38
English studies, 36, 51–54; India Civil Service and, 51; Newcastle Commission (1861) and, 51; mechanics institutes, working-men's colleges, extension lectures and, 51; women and, 51; at Oxford and Cambridge, 51–52; Tripos (1917) and, 52; Newbold Report (*The Teaching of English in England*, 1921) and, 52; crisis in, 60, 140; at Cambridge, 141
Enlightenment, 198, 210
environmentalism. *See* ecology
epistemology, 163, 168–69, 174, 212; crisis of, 203; and *Methodenstreit*, 208
essentialism, 129, 146, 162, 202, 210; strategic, 214
ethnic studies, 201
Ethnological Society of London, 42
ethnology. *See* anthropology
ethnomethodology: phenomenology and, 231 n.11
Eurocommunism, 225 n.1

event: historical, 201

Everyday Television: "Nationwide" (Brundson and Morley, 1978), 111

excluded middle, 169, 212

existentialism, 178, 180–81, 186, 231 n.12; as a humanism, 182, 186; socialist humanism and first New Left and, 183

experience, 30, 32, 210; as *Erlebnis*, 208

fact(s), 163, 175; and fiction, 200–201

Family Television (Morley, 1986), 114

Fanon, Franz: critique of "Orphée Noir" (Sartre), 233 n.18

Federal Bureau of Investigation (FBI), 226 n.7

feminism, 124–31; collective work and, 129; development and, 235 n.5. See also *Off-Centre; Women Take Issue*

film, 178

first New Left, 4, 28, 33, 73, 183–84, 210; *active* neutrality and, 15; *nouvelle gauche,* 217 n.7; according to Thompson and Williams, 217 n.7; Leavisism and, 220 n.1

Foucault, Michel, 186, 202

fractal geometry, 198, 199, 212, 235 n.7, 235–36 n.11. *See also* complexity studies

freedom: Atlantic working class and, 38–39; redefinition of liberty as, 63; complexity studies and, 200

free trade, 62; Anti–Corn Law League (1838) and, 62; liberalism, laissez-faire, J. S. Mill's *Principles of Political Economy* and, 62

free will, 168, 214

French Revolution, 5, 31, 36, 61–62; progress and popular sovereignty and, 62

Friends of the Earth, 234 n.3

functionalism, 175–76, 230 n.6

fundamentalism, 234 n.4

Geisteswissenschaften, 208

gender: race (in Arnold, Carlyle, and J. S. Mill) and, 63–64

Germany: economic miracle, 179

Glasgow Media Group, 141

global warming, 196

Gould, Stephen Jay, 199

Gramsci, Antonio, 140, 187; cultural studies and, 138, 158. See also *Crisis in the British State; Culture, Media, Language;* hegemony (Gramsci); *Making Histories; On Ideology; Resistance through Rituals; Subculture: Meaning of Style; Unpopular Education; Working-Class Culture*

Grand National Consolidated Trades Union, 41

Great Apathy (Thompson), 15

Great Britain: new affluence, 179. *See also* affluence

Great Exhibition (1851), 45

Green, T. H.: new liberalism and, 65–66

Greenpeace, 195, 234 n.3

green revolution, 195

Greens (German), 196; Green Party, 234 n.3

Hall, Stuart, 16, 33–34, 74, 215–16 n.3; assumes direction of CCCS, 80; to chair at Open University, 80; Hoggart and CCCS and, 223 n.2; feminism at CCCS and, 224 n.9

Harding, Sandra, 202–3

hegemony (geopolitical), 3–4, 216 n.6; United States and, 11, 174, 176, 179–80, 190–91, 193, 213

hegemony (Gramsci), 129, 142; CCCS and, 138. *See also* Gramsci, Antonio; *Learning to Labour, Making Histories; On Ideology; Resistance through Rituals; Unpopular Education*

Heidegger, Martin, 180, 213, 231 n.12; Nazism and, 232 n.15

historical capitalism, 173–74

historical system, 2

historicism, 181, 185; historical school and, 207, 209. See also *Methodenstreit*

history, 200–202, 210; philosophy of and *Methodenstreit,* 207–9; inductive, 209; epistemological status of, 213. *See also* idiographic and nomothetic distinction; *Making Histories*

History Workshop, 219 n.12

Hobbes, Thomas, 61–62

Hoggart, Richard, 34, 37, 58, 84, 106, 179, 210, 215–16 n.3; F. R. Leavis and, 54, 106; Q. D. Leavis and, 54, 106; UNESCO and, 80; Lévi-Strauss and structuralism at CCCS and, 81; Penguins and, 222 n.1; Hall and CCCS and, 223 n.2

Hollywood, 178

homophobia, 202

humanism, 184–85, 191, 204–5, 210, 217 n.7. *See also* socialist humanism

humanities, 177, 180, 203–5, 207, 210–12; science(s) and/or social science(s) and, 173–75, 186, 191, 213

Hungary, 4, 11, 15–16, 218 n.10

Husserl, Edmund, 180, 231 n.11

Huxley, T. H.: on (value-neutral) progress through science, 66–67; debate with Arnold and, 67, 229 n.1

idealism, 208

ideal type, 209

identity, 193; at CCCS, 139; politics, 162, 203

ideology, 74, 77, 108, 129, 187–89, 201, 211; *Long Revolution* (Thompson's review) and, 27; science and, 204. *See also Crisis in the British State*; culturalism vs. structuralism; *Culture, Media, Language; The Empire Strikes Back; Family Television; The Manufacture of News; The "Nationwide" Audience; Off-Centre; On Ideology; Paper Voices; Resistance through Rituals; There Ain't No Black in the Union Jack; Unpopular Education; Women Take Issue; Working-Class Culture*

idiographic and nomothetic distinction, 190, 193

Images of Women (Millum, 1975), 110

imagination, 213

imperialism, 33, 37, 66

Independent Labour Party, 66, 218 n.11

individuals, 209. *See also Making Histories*

industrialization, 177

information theory, 198

interdisciplinarity, 106–7

intersubjectivity, 214

Ireland: potato famine and, 48, 222 n.14; revolt (1867) and, 48, 68; home rule and Liberal split and, 66; Arnold and, 222 n.16

jazz, 183, 184. *See also The Popular Arts*

Johnson, Richard: assumes direction of CCCS, 80

kairos, 213

Khrushchev's secret speech, 4, 11, 15, 218 n.10

knowledge, 53, 57, 207, 209, 210–11, 214. *See also On Ideology*

Kondratieff phase, 174, 197

Korean War, 218 n.11

Kristeva, Julia, 154, 224 n.4. *See also Culture, Media, Language; On Ideology; Subculture*

Kulturwissenschaften, 208

Labour Party, 219 n.13

Lacan, Jacques, 154, 224. *See also Culture, Media, Language; Off-Centre; On Ideology; Screen* and screen theory; *Women Take Issue*

Lane, Alan: *Lady Chatterley,* Hoggart, and the Penguins, 222–23 n.1

language, 212

Language and Ideology Group (CCCS), 89

langue, 187

Laplace, Pierre Simon de, 206

law (general, universal, scientific, natural), 206–7, 208, 210, 213, 235 n.10

Learning to Labour (Willis, 1977), 117–19, 122; *Resistance through Rituals* and, 117; hegemony (Gramsci) and, 117; labor power in, 118; style in, 118; methods in, 117–19

Leavis, F. R.: and Leavisism, 37, 68; *Scrutiny* and, 53. *See also Culture and Society*

Leavis, Q. D., 53, 68, 229 n.1; *Scrutiny* and, 53

Let us Face the Future (Labour Party manifesto), 12

Lévi-Strauss, Claude, 81, 187; and structuralism, 186, 227 n.14; and structural linguistics, 223 n.20. *See also On Ideology; Subculture: Meaning of Style; Women Take Issue* liberal consensus, 5, 61, 66, 69, 209, 212–13

liberalism, 36, 211–12; Green and transformation of, 65–66; Welfare State and, 66; individual and, 204; crisis of, 216 n.7

Liberal politics, 63, 66

literary studies, 202

literature, 141; American, 161

living standards (world-scale), 197

logic, 209, 212

logical positivism, 174–75, 177; behaviorism and, 175, 230 n.5; verification principle and, 175; Vienna Circle and, 230 n.5

The Long Revolution (Raymond Williams, 1961), 23–29, 59, 77, 99, 217 n.5; creation in, 24; communication in, 24; culture in, 24; individual and society in, 24–25; contemporary Britain in, 25; political movements in, 25; community in, 25; Thompson's review of, 26–28, 220 n.1

Lowe, Robert, 63, 221 n.6

MacCabe, Colin, 141, 224 n.4, 225 n.1

Making Histories (Johnson, McLennan, Schwarz, and Sutton, eds., 1982), 95–98; structuralist Marxism in, 95; Britishness in, 95; CPHG in, 95–96, 98; Gramsci in, 96, 98; problems of inquiry in, 97; Marx in, 97, 98; Popular Memory Group in, 97–98

The Making of the English Working Class (E. P. Thompson, 1963), 31, 99, 220 n.20; class in, 31–32, 34

Mandelbrot, Benois, 236 n.11

Manhattan Project, 174, 194

The Manufacture of News (Cohen and Young, 1973), 110

marginal revolution, 209

Marshall Plan, 12, 217 n.2

Marxism (Marx and Marxist), 32, 37, 58, 187, 189–90, 210, 217 n.7, 223 n.5; English, 33; theory and, 84–85, 119, 138, 202; foundationalist premises of, 203; realism and, 232 n.13. *See also* cultural studies

McCarthyism, 226 n.7

McMahon Atomic Energy Act, 218 n.11

meaning, 207; indeterminiacy of, 212. *See also* signification

media studies, 109–14; "Encoding/Decoding" (Hall, 1973) in, 110–11

Media Studies Group, 111

Menger, Karl, 209

method(s), 210; reductive and deductive, 206

Methodenstreit, 207–9

Metz, Christian. See *Screen* and screen theory

Mill, John Stuart, 62, 64, 66, 207

modernity (modernism), 204

modernization theory, 176–77, 180, 195, 230 n.8; dependency and critique of, 189

modern world-system, 211; crisis of, 205, 211; 1968 and, 226 n.8

Morant Bay rebellion, 47–48, 67; Jamaica Committee and, 47; Eyre Defence Committee and, 47–48

Morris, William: Thompson and Williams on, 220 nn.17–18. See also *William Morris*

multiculturalism, 168, 211

Museum of Modern Art (MOMA), 178

myth: as semiological system of values (Barthes), 188

Nagel, Ernest: critique of *Social Theory and Social Structure* (Merton, 1949), 230 n.6

nation (nationalism, national identity), 100, 160, 178; German, 207

National Audubon Society, 195

National Committee for the Abolition of Nuclear Weapons Tests, 219 n.11

National Defense Education Act, 229 n.2

National Resources Defense Council, 234 n.3

National Science Foundation, 229 n.2, 230 n.7

National Union of Teachers Conference (1960), 59; *Discrimination and Popular Culture* (Denys Thompson, 1964) and, 59

The "Nationwide" Audience (Morley, 1980), 111–12; beyond screen theory, 113

Natopolitanism, 29, 184, 219–20 n.15

Naturwissenschaften, 208

narrative, 200–201

négritude, 180, 184–85, 214; and Sartre, 185, 214

subject/object distinction, 177, 183, 205; Dilthey's project to fuse, 209

Suez, 4, 11, 15, 16

surrealism, 180–81, 193, 232 n.14

survey research, 176

symbolic interactionism, 228 n.18

technology, 194–95, 197

television, 110–14, 178

Tel Quel, 95, 227 n.15. See also *Culture, Media, Language; Subculture: Meaning of Style*

text(s), 113, 140, 162, 177; subject and, 188. *See also* culturalism vs. structuralism

Thatcherism. See *Politics of Thatcherism*

theory, 140, 162, 223 n.5; deductive, 209

There Ain't No Black in the Union Jack (Gilroy, 1987), 99–100, 135–37; black as victim in, 136; ethnocentricity of cultural studies in, 136; class in, 136, 137; race and exclusivity of Englishness (Williams, Thompson, Hobsbawm) in, 136; right populist language of nation and crisis of representation in, 136; new social movements in, 136–37

Think Tank (model), 211

Thompson, Edward Palmer, 4, 18–19, 31–33, 37, 58, 202, 215–16 n.3; teaching and, 219 n.12; on break-up of first New Left, 220 n.19; structuralist Marxism and, 220 n.20; on working class and Anderson, 223 n.4. See also *Making of the English Working Class; The New Reasoner; The Reasoner*

time, 181, 199, 202, 210, 212, 214; two cultures and, 205; as *kairos*, 213. *See also* complexity studies

TimeSpace (geopolitical, cyclico-ideological, structural, transformative), 3–6

transformation, 214. See also *TimeSpace*

transition, 213, 214; from Feudalism to Capitalism, 213

Tripos, 141, 222 n.10

truth(s), 160, 162, 168–69, 181, 193, 206, 209–10

two cultures, 7, 148, 174, 191; crisis of, 203–5, 213; Cartesian dualism and, 206

understanding (*Verstehen*): Dilthey and, 208; Weber (interpretation) and, 209

United States: and cultural studies, 150–59; British counterpart and, 150–51; communication in, 156–57; Geertz and, 157; criticism of, 158–59. *See also* universities and cultural studies

United States Information Agency (USIA), 178–79

unit of analysis, 98, 99, 157, 202

universalism: idiographic and nomothetic, 202

universities, 160–63, 207, 212; and New Left (U.S.), 152–53; crisis of, 211. *See also* 1968

universities and cultural studies, 193; English, 143–44; Australian, 146–47; Canadian, 148; South African, 149–50, 225 n.6; in the United States, 158

Universities and Left Review, 16, 28, 218 nn.9–10, 219 n.14

university reform, 151, 192

Unpopular Education (Education Group, 1981), 102–4; Gramsci and hegemony in, 103; Labour Party in, 103; capitalist and sexual division of labor in, 103. See also *Education Limited*

The Uses of Literacy (Richard Hoggart, 1957), 59, 73, 75, 98, 217 n.7; scholarship boys in, 14, 54–58; *Scrutiny* and, 55, 56; methods and 55; class in, 56; Thompson's critique of, 57; in *Universities and Left Review*, 58; meaningless change and, 68

value(s), 30, 73, 163, 173, 178, 206–10, 212, 214; in cultural studies, 155, 158, 160, 179

Venice Biennial (1964), 179

verification principle, 175

Vienna Circle, 210 n.5. *See also* logical positivism

Vietnam Solidarity Committee, 78, 80

Vietnam War, 79–80, 151, 192, 193

Voice of America, 184

Vološinov, V. N. See *Culture, Media, Language*

Wallerstein, Immanuel, 3, 190, 223 n.5

Weathermen, 151, 226 n.8

Weaver, Warren: complexity and, 198, 235 n.8
Weber, Max, 209
William Morris (E. P. Thompson, 1955), 18–19
Williams, Raymond Henry, 19, 32–34, 37, 58, 106, 210, 215–16 n.3, 217 n.5; text-based histories of cultural studies and, 4; adult education and, 18; F. R. Leavis and, 54; Cambridge English and, 141; classlessness and, 220 n.16
Windelband, Wilhelm, 208–9
Women's Forum, 224 n.8
Women's Liberation (women's movement), 124, 153, 193; Thompson (and the male Left) and, 124–25; critique of scientific/technological society and, 196–97; antinuclear movement and, 196
Women's Liberation Conference, 224 n.7
women's studies, 201
Women's Studies Group, 126
Women Take Issue (Women's Studies Group,

1978), 126–28, 130, 202; social transformation in, 126; academia in, 126; class and gender in, 127; psychanalysis in, 127; Marxist analysis in, 127; law of the Other (Lévi-Strauss and Lacan) in, 127; *Woman* in, 128; Althusser (overdetermination) in, 128; cccs in, 138
working class, 48, 57, 119; at cccs, 139. See also *Working-Class Culture*
working-class culture, 74, 119, 210. See also *Working-Class Culture*
Working-Class Culture (Clarke, Critcher, and Johnson, eds., 1979), 119–22; empirical studies in, 119; theory and ideology in, 120; culturalism and structuralism in, 120–21; Marxism in, 120–21; Gramsci in, 120; class and culture in, 121
Working Papers in Cultural Studies, 107, 126
world-systems analysis, 201, 215 n.2

Richard E. Lee is an Assistant Professor of Sociology and Deputy
Director of the Fernand Braudel Center at SUNY-Binghamton.

Library of Congress Cataloging-in-Publication Data
Lee, Richard E.
Life and times of cultural studies : the politics and transformation
of the structures of knowledge / Richard E. Lee.
p. cm. — (Philosophy and postcoloniality)
Includes bibliographical references and index.
ISBN 0-8223-3160-8 (cloth : alk. paper)
ISBN 0-8223-3173-x (pbk. : alk. paper)
1. Culture—Study and teaching—History—20th century.
2. Intellectual life—History—20th century. 3. World politics—1945— .
4. University of Birmingham. Centre for Contemporary Cultural Studies.
I. Title. II. Series.
HM623.L44 2003   306'.071—dc21   2003010578